ADVANCES IN DISTRIBUTED MULTIMEDIA SYSTEMS

SERIES ON SOFTWARE ENGINEERING AND KNOWLEDGE ENGINEERING

Series Editor-in-Chief
S K CHANG (*University of Pittsburgh, USA*)

Vol. 1 Knowledge-Based Software Development for Real-Time Distributed Systems
Jeffrey J.-P. Tsai and Thomas J. Weigert (Univ. Illinois at Chicago)

Vol. 2 Advances in Software Engineering and Knowledge Engineering
edited by Vincenzo Ambriola (Univ. Pisa) *and Genoveffa Tortora* (Univ. Salerno)

Vol. 3 The Impact of CASE Technology on Software Processes
edited by Daniel E. Cooke (Univ. Texas)

Vol. 4 Software Engineering and Knowledge Engineering: Trends for the Next Decade
edited by W. D. Hurley (Univ. Pittsburgh)

Vol. 5 Intelligent Image Database Systems
edited by S. K. Chang (Univ. Pittsburgh), *E. Jungert* (Swedish Defence Res. Establishment) *and G. Tortora* (Univ. Salerno)

Vol. 6 Object-Oriented Software: Design and Maintenance
edited by Luiz F. Capretz and Miriam A. M. Capretz (Univ. Aizu, Japan)

Vol. 7 Software Visualisation
edited by P. Eades (Univ. Newcastle) *and K. Zhang* (Macquarie Univ.)

Vol. 8 Image Databases and Multi-Media Search
edited by Arnold W. M. Smeulders (Univ. Amsterdam) *and Ramesh Jain* (Univ. California)

Vol. 9 Advances in Distributed Multimedia Systems
edited by S. K. Chang, T. F. Znati (Univ. Pittsburgh) *and S. T. Vuong* (Univ. British Columbia)

Forthcoming titles:

Acquisition of Software Engineering Knowledge
edited by Robert G. Reynolds (Wayne State Univ.)

Monitoring, Debugging, and Analysis of Distributed Real-Time Systems
Jeffrey J.-P. Tsai, Steve J. H. Yong, R. Smith and Y. D. Bi (Univ. Illinois at Chicago)

Series on Software Engineering and Knowledge Engineering

Vol. 9

Series Editor

S K Chang

ADVANCES IN DISTRIBUTED MULTIMEDIA SYSTEMS

editors

S K Chang

T F Znati

University of Pittsburg

S T Vuong

University of British Columbia

World Scientific

Singapore • New Jersey • London • Hong Kong

Published by

World Scientific Publishing Co. Pte. Ltd.

P O Box 128, Farrer Road, Singapore 912805

USA office: Suite 1B, 1060 Main Street, River Edge, NJ 07661

UK office: 57 Shelton Street, Covent Garden, London WC2H 9HE

British Library Cataloguing-in-Publication Data
A catalogue record for this book is available from the British Library.

ADVANCES IN DISTRIBUTED MULTIMEDIA SYSTEMS

ISBN 981-02-3560-7

Printed in Singapore by Uto-Print

PREFACE

The steady advances in computing and communication technologies over the last decade have greatly increased the capabilities of current computer systems and revolutionized the way we use these computers in our everyday life. Advances in VLSI technology has significantly increased processor speed and reduced the size and cost of memory chips, while advances in secondary and tertiary storage have made gigabit magnet disks and optical disks systems affordable. Disk costs have decreased sufficiently so that bundling multiple disks together to form a Redundant Array of Inexpensive Disks (RAID) provides a cost effective, flexible, efficient, and reliable access mechanism to large amounts of data.

Telecommunication advances in the development of high speed communication technologies, on the other hand, have led to a low bit error rate, high bandwidth communication devices. At the same time, the phenomenal growth rate of the Internet and the World Wide Web continues to demonstrate the intense desire to connect geographically separated users and systems via high speed communication networks. The continuous evolution of communication networks is bringing about a vision of a world where information is exchanged reliably and securely among computer based systems, not constrained by bandwidth limitations or proprietary considerations. It is the vision of a universal network that accommodates heterogeneity and multiple networking sub-architectures, and where extension and convergence take place simultaneously.

The revolutionary changes in chip size to performance ratio brought about by the VLSI design techniques and the resulting improvement in processing storage and transmission link capacities saw the merger of the fields of data communication and computer technologies. The successful integration of data, voice and video is driving the technology and the technical standards organization to a unified treatment of the information, making virtually all data and information sources easily accessible.

More importantly, the convergence of computer and communication technologies has spawned the development of **distributed multimedia systems** which promise an even greater change in the personal usage of computers.

Multimedia is rapidly revolutionizing the way people live, work, and interact with each other. It is impacting the way businesses, government services, education, entertainment, and health care are operating, and increasingly finding its way into our homes, our places of work and our means of entertainment. In response, major industries are rethinking their market strategy and forming a web of new alliances connecting telecommunication, computing, publishing, entertainment and other global enterprises.

A distributed multimedia system (**DMS**) involves the integrated production, manipulation, presentation, storage and communication of multimedia information encoded through continuous and discrete means. More formally, the term media refers to the collection of means by which communication is achieved among communicating entities. **Multimedia applications** are, therefore, characterized by their simultaneous use of continuous, time dependent media, such as audio and video, and discrete, time independent media which often consists of text, graphics, or drawings. Examples of multimedia applications include distance learning, remote video conferencing, video-on-demand services, on-line shopping and computer-based, interactive game play.

The common attributes of these applications include distributed user access, exchange of time-dependent and time-independent media, real-time audio or video capture, playback, off-line browsing as well as editing of stored multimedia data. Support of these attributes require the integration of continuous and discrete data. This integration can occur at different levels, including storage and retrieval, processing, and communication. At the lowest level, time dependent media data consists of a sequence of samples, each with an associated relative timing position. The exchange of this time dependent information often requires that the data be processed, stored, retrieved and transported by the communication network in a predictable and timely fashion. Furthermore, both time dependent and time independent information are usually communicated in the form of **media streams** which must be **synchronized**.

The purpose of synchronization is to maintain spatial and temporal relationships defined within and between media streams in order to ensure that related media streams are presented concurrently at the appropriate times. Spatial relations define the layout or placement of media objects on output devices at a particular instance in time. Temporal relationships, on the other hand, are used to describe the temporal dependencies that exist between media objects. A computer-based access to a **multimedia book**, for instance, may require that the display of still and animated images be synchronized with the display of the text and audio playback related to these images.

Eliminating the undesirable effects, such as lip sync and delay jitter, facilitates improved comprehension during multimedia presentations.

In addition to their timing constraints, multimedia applications typically consume large amounts of storage, processing, and communication resources.

Large-scale, on-demand multimedia servers must be capable of providing independent and interactive access to a vast amount of multimedia information to a large number of concurrent clients and support a full spectrum of interactive stream play-out control operations, such as *random access*, *fast forward*, *pause*, *rewind*, *slow rewind*, and *frame advance*. To meet these requirements, the servers must provide a large amount of storage in one or more forms, such as large high-performance magnetic disks, large disk arrays or a high capacity fast optical storage. In many cases, the collective storage of the system can exceed a few tens of terabytes. Furthermore, the server must also support resource managements functions, such as media processing, file system support, scheduling support, and admission control. The server must determine how to distribute the data over the storage devices and manage associated metadata information to facilitate the stream play-out control operations. The data layout scheme must support maximum parallelism in the use of the storage devices, and scale to the number of concurrent clients accessing the same storage device, facilitate interactive control and random access operation, allow simple scheduling schemes that ensure on-time retrieval and transmission of data often from unsynchronized storage devices.

In addition to their storage requirements, a multimedia application may demand stringent, real-time processing of its continuous and discrete media data. In this context, the system must seek to optimize the value it delivers to the user by talking full advantage of the applications-specified timeliness and importance of the information.

Process models for multimedia computing must allow applications to adapt their pattern of execution to optimize resource utilization without necessarily sacrificing their ability to execute predictably in time. The deterministic aspect of the computation model ensures that applications execute in a predictable manner and guarantees bounded response time to events such as interruptions, message arrivals, and access to input and output devices. Furthermore, mechanisms for allocating resources to processes must allow applications to dynamically alter their desired level of service in order to adapt to the current perceived state of the system. Tradeoffs must, therefore, be made and appropriate execution techniques must be selected. Such a task is further complicated by the need to integrate the often compute-intensive multimedia applications with the interactive and batch activities found in conventional applications.

The performance goals for designing traditional distributed systems are to optimize for minimal interactive response time under conditions of light load and to ensure a degree of fairness and acceptable average response time under heavy load. They do not support the timing requirements on a per task basis.

To deal effectively with the difficulty of scheduling real-time continuous media activities with conventional interactive and batch activities new multi-level schedulers and resource managers may be required.

Another critical resource to be managed effectively in order to meet the requirements of multimedia applications, is network bandwidth. Multimedia applications are characterized by a wide range of *bandwidth specifications* and *real-time performance requirements.* The bandwidth specifications reflect the quantitative and qualitative characteristics of the application's traffic. The quantitative bandwidth specifications define the application's average or maximum bandwidth requirements, while the qualitative characteristics specify the traffic's burstiness or traffic generation pattern. The real-time performance requirements specify an association between a set of time dependent parameters and their corresponding values. The *minimum* required association between these parameters and their respective values expresses the application's end-to-end performance requirements or *Qualities of Service* (*QoS*).

QoS can be thought of as a measure of the collective effect of service performances which determine the degree of satisfaction of the user. It manifests itself in a number of parameters, all of which have either subjective or objective values. These parameters include *maximum packet delay, average packet delay, packet delay-jitter, packet loss probability*, and *on-time reliability.*

Multimedia applications which require steady and continuous access to network bandwidth are referred to as **continuous bit rate** (**CBR**) applications. Examples of **CBR** applications include many telephony applications and video conferencing using uncompressed video streams. These applications use fixed amounts of bandwidth at fixed points in time. Other applications whose bandwidth demands vary over time are categorized as **variable bit rate** (**VBR**) applications. A **VBR** applications bandwidth demands can vary for a multitude of reasons ranging from changing compression ratios to dynamic input streams. Addressing and efficiently supporting the sensitivities of different media in an integrated environment represent a major challenge faced by network infrastructure components supporting multimedia systems and applications.

With the advent of multimedia applications, the focus of the communication network has shifted from initial emphasis on reliable delivery of text to include support for QoS requirements of continuous media data.

Complex control algorithms and sophisticated routing, scheduling, and resource allocation mechanisms are needed to support the bandwidth and QoS requirements in a context where the network transmission speeds are increasing at a rate faster than the processing speed. Thus, the network control algorithms and protocols must be sufficiently simple to operate at or near link bandwidth speeds, but be flexible enough to support applications with different QoS requirements.

As stated above, multimedia support encompasses different requirements at different levels ranging from the storage, retrieval and processing of multimedia information to its transmission and display. The temporal and loss sensitivities of many types of media along with their bandwidth and synchronization requirements often dictate that the multimedia applications obtain service guarantees from their supporting infrastructure components.

Such guarantees form the basis of a contract between the application and the supporting system.

The contract stipulates that, for a given application profile, the system meets its specified **QoS** requirements, as long as the multimedia applications generates and processes data within the terms of the agreed upon profile. The multimedia applications accept the fact that the multimedia system can refuse to service, without penalty, all data traffic deemed in excess of the contracted profile.

Depending upon the application and media type, the **QoS** requirements may involve the maintenance of very stringent temporal constraints. Further, different multimedia applications can be sensitive to many different factors and possess a variety of service constraints. Therefore, multimedia applications are often categorized based upon the type of guarantees they require with respect to these factors and service constraints.

Two types of guarantees are usually specified: *deterministic* and *statistical.* A *deterministic* guarantee is defined with respect to an upper limit on the *QoS* parameters, in terms of delay, loss or jitter. A *statistical* guarantee is determined by some average numbers of the *QoS* parameters observed over a period of time which usually extends over the duration of the multimedia session.

Due to the distributed nature of multimedia systems and the temporal sensitivity of the composite media, supporting the end-to-end performance requirements of multimedia applications and adequately addressing the ill-effects of latency is of critical importance. The successful operation of a multimedia system, and indeed its very existence, depends upon how well various system components manage and cope with the effects of latency. It is widely accepted that without some form of resource reservation, it is extremely difficult, if not impossible, to provide performance guarantees. Consequently, the multimedia system should embed the proper mechanisms to monitor and control resource usage for each application.

This approach requires that an application specifies its performance requirements *a priori*, and unless these requirements can be met, the application is either blocked or rejected. The system must then monitor the activity of each application and ensure that resources are used in a way such that all applications' performance guarantees are met.

A great deal of research, related to the many significant technical issues involved in the development of large-scale multimedia computing and communication systems, is currently underway. The research activities in multimedia will undoubtedly continue to evolve over the next several years, leading hopefully to a better understanding of the design and technical issues related to distributed multimedia systems.

The purpose of this volume is to bring together many of the detailed discussion of the technical issues, principle, current results, and likely directions, drawing upon the research literature and activity in academia, industry and standards communities.

It is our hope that the research ideas and proposed solutions presented in this book provide an organized framework to highlight current activities and important topics in the field of distributed multimedia systems and technology.

The first part of this book presents an overview and describes recent advances in content-based access to multimedia information, digital communication networks and tele-learning research.

The key to content-based access of multimedia information is to discover, encode and maintain the associations among media objects. The first paper by Chang discusses how to access multimedia information by content, through combining various query mechanisms and enabling visual relevance feedback, user-guided navigation and user-controlled discovery of new associations. To illustrate content-based multimedia information retrieval, application examples are drawn from digital libraries, computer-assisted medical diagnosis and intelligent web searchers.

To support distributed multimedia applications, advanced networking infrastructure and technologies such as ATM and next generation Internet are needed. The second paper by Jang provides an overview of and Service Providers' perspectives on business strategy and network architecture for the delivery of value added services across an ATM infrastructure. Distributed learning environments are now a reality. Based on the Internet and the open architecture worldwide web, learners have easy access to courses offered by institutions throughout the world. One example of what is possible is a course offered on Virtual-U from Simon Fraser University in 1997 and again in 1998.

This third paper by Calvert and Pantel discusses the principles involved in creating an effective distributed learning environment and then illustrate this with a description of the web-based Virtual-U system developed at Simon Fraser University. The distributed learning environments of tomorrow promise to provide advanced pedagogical tools and extensive access. The impact on learning can be substantial. This paper provides a good overview and insight to this rapidly expanded field.

The second part of this book focuses on modeling and specification. The first paper, by Lin *et al.* argue that *QoS* requirements must be specified from a user perspective and propose a framework to facilitate the transformation of the application's *QoS* requirements into a set of *QoS*-messages which can be used to interact with the multimedia system and negotiate different levels of *QoS* guarantees. The second paper, by Anisimov *et al.*, addresses the problems of specifying synchronization requirements for real-world size multimedia presentations. The authors propose a compositional Petri Net model which enables compact and readable specification of complex, large-scale system specifications, while preserving fine granularity and user interactions. The model can be applied to verify the correctness of specifications of multimedia synchronization. The third paper, by Rikli, presents a fluid model which can be used to assess the performance of an Asynchronous Transfer Mode (ATM) statistical multiplexer fed with traffic sources that can operate in various modes with variable rate and intensities duration. The author considers both calm and violent scenes with either impulsive or persistent states.

The third of this book deals with network architectures to support multimedia applications. It is expected that multimedia systems will provide integrated access to a wide range of computing and communication facilities. It is therefore imperative that communication architectures be designed to meet the *QoS* requirements of multimedia applications and allow these applications to evolve as new technological advances are made.

In the first paper, Boykin *et al.* argue that in order to meet these goals, the network architecture must manage efficiently the network resources, and provide sufficient flexibility to account for both tolerant real-time and best-effort applications. The proposed framework incorporates the necessary functionalities to provide elastic and predictive service guarantees. These guarantees are achieved using traffic *isolation*, to prevent connections from interfering with each other, *policing*, to ensure that connections do not violate their contract specifications, and *scheduling* to ensure that the bandwidth is allocated in a manner such that each connection meets its *QoS* requirements.

In the second paper, Hashimoto *et al.* introduce a client-agent-server architecture to support end-to-end *QoS* management functions and end-to-end *QoS* negotiation protocols. The architecture supports two different dynamic rate control methods, namely packet rate control method and frame rate control method.

The packet rate control method controls the packet interval at the sender side to reduce the packet loss rate under the admissible packet loss rate. The frame rate control method uses the feedback message sent from the receiver side to control the transmitted frame rate at the sender side and ensure that the rate at which video frames are displayed remains constant under various load conditions.

In the third paper, Shih *et al.* argue that there is a need for a good presentation development methodology to facilitate the analysis of the presentation script, the collection of multimedia resources, and the realization of a presentation layout and navigation control flow. The authors propose a new authoring system which is based on data and flow control with multiple enhanced notations and additional diagram components, especially useful for multimedia presentation design.

The fourth part of this book focuses on issues related to the design and implementation of multimedia servers. One of the most important problems in multimedia technologies is accessing large distributed databases and objects. The size of these databases, coupled with the the distributed nature of multimedia systems, is making it imperative to develop methodologies that allow efficient access and retrieval of different types of multimedia objects and information. The three papers presented in this part of the book address these issues and describe frameworks for accessing and managing objects in an efficient manner.

In the first paper, Hong discusses a flexible and reliable CORBA-based distributed multimedia system called MAESTRO, which can be used to facilitate the process of development, operation and management of various distributed multimedia applications. MAESTRO's architecture, multimedia collaborative service API and distributed multimedia services are presented together with a prototype implementation of a number of multimedia collaborative applications, such as video conferencing, white board, electronic notebook, chat, and application sharing. In the second paper, Kanezuka *et al.* discuss quality of service (QoS) as the major attribute of a (multimedia) object, which together with its state can be changed by an applied method. From this notion, they introduce novel QoS-based equivalence and compatibility relations for object methods and demonstrate that using these relations and QoS-based compensation, recovery time for distributed objects can be reduced. The formal framework of QoS-based relations promises a flexible way of treating distributed multimedia object systems.

The third paper by Lee and Cheng proposes an elastic reservation model for rescheduling requests for VOD services so as to improve the service access ratio. Using the time adaptation approach, releasable resources are presented as a multi-stage graph that allows optimal adaptation to be found — as the shortest path of the graph. Simulation results confirm significant reduction of the reject ratio and improvement of the acceptance ratio for VOD service requests.

The fifth part of this book discusses the performance of MPEG-2 encoding, and describes algorithms for routing with *QoS* constraints. In the first paper, Liu first presents an experimental study of the MPEG-2 encoding scheme performance. The author indicates that the specifications of MPEG compression scheme leave an unanswered optimization problem on the determination of the various parameters for compression, such as the typical setting of a group of pattern (GOP), in terms of I, P and B frames, in order to achieve the best compression ratio. To address these issues, the author developed an integrated MPEG-2 system which includes the preprocessing methods needed to detect the shot boundaries, and to measure the degrees of motion activity and image complexity. Using a slightly augmented MPEG-2 compression scheme, the author investigates performance tradeoffs on the visual quality and achieved compression ratio. The author shows that the augmented MPEG-2 system is able to reduce disk storage without increasing image distortion.

The second paper, by Nour *et al.*, presents a routing procedure which considers different *QoS* classes, in terms of sensitivity to delay and reliability. The authors formulate the problem of routing with QoS constraints as a set of objective functions which optimize a given set of constraints which reflect the current states of the network nodes and links, and the requested *QoS* support.

The authors then propose a dynamic routing algorithm which derives a set of paths that are likely to satisfy the user requirements in terms of throughput, delay and loss rate, and selects the best path which satisfies the delay and loss rate requirements.

The final part of this book focuses on the implementation of interactive multimedia systems. In the first paper, Fushikada *et al.* discuss an interesting research topic in multimedia concerning the development of algorithms and associated technology to retrieve information based on its content. The authors describe a system which uses visualized sound index to retrieve video information based on its content. The second paper describes a multimedia conferencing system. A key feature of this system is its efficient support of multi-casting for group communication.

The impact of multimedia computing will continue to extend its reach into more and more facets of our daily lives. It is our hope that this book, which reflects the significant efforts put forth by researchers and implementers in the field of multimedia computing and technologies, will be helpful in understanding the principles and issues and providing a comprehensive survey of the research focus in multimedia applications and the underlying computer and networking technologies.

Most of the papers in the volume are expanded versions of technical papers or invited lectures presented by the authors at the 1997 Pacific Workshop on Distributed Multimedia Systems that was held in Vancouver, Canada from July 24 to July 25, and a few papers are invited contributions. We thank the authors for their efforts and cooperation to bring this book to its timely completion. The support of the University of British Columbia, the University of Pittsburgh and Knowledge Systems Institute is also gratefully acknowledged.

S. K. Chang
Son T. Vuong
Taieb Znati
April 4, 1999

CONTENTS

Overview

Advances in Multimedia Information Access

S.K. Chang
Department of Computer Science
University of Pittsburgh
Pittsburgh, PA 15260, USA
Phone +1-412-624-8423
E-mail chang@cs.pitt.edu

Abstract

The key to content-based access of multimedia information is to discover, encode and maintain the associations among media objects. Media enhanced interaction metaphors employ multiple paradigms to facilitate the discovery, encoding and maintenance of these associations. Although the metaphors themselves may be conceptual, their effective incorporation into the user interface for multimedia information access often requires the use of visual querying mechanisms. To access multimedia information by content, various query mechanisms need to be combined, and the user interface should be visual as much as possible and also enable visual relevance feedback, user-guided navigation and user-controlled discovery of new associations. In this paper we first review the technology issues in the visual representation of the information space and strategies for visual reasoning. We then describe applications in digital library, medical information fusion and intelligent web searcher to illustrate different scenarios of multiparadigmatic interaction for accessing multimedia information. For integrated technology comparison, we give a taxonomy of visual querying paradigms and compare various interaction techniques. Several research challenges are then discussed, with emphasis on the modeling, integration and evaluation of the *Hypermapped Virtual World* interaction metaphor.

Keywords

Content-based information retrieval, multimedia information systems, visual querying systems

1.1 Introduction

Recent advances in storage technologies have made the creation of multimedia databases both feasible and cost-effective. Wideband communications also greatly facilitate the distribution of multimedia information across communication networks. Parallel computers lead to faster voice, image and video processing systems. High resolution graphics and dedicated co-processors enable the presentation of visual information with superior image quality. Multimedia information systems have found their way into many application areas, including geographical information systems (GIS) [44], office automation (OA) [56], distance learning [47], health care [57], computer-aided design (CAD) [2], computer-aided engineering (CAE) [41], and scientific databases (SDB) applications [1].

Wider applications also lead to both more numerous and more sophisticated end users. Multimedia information systems, like other types of information systems, have increasingly become knowledge-based systems, with capabilities to perform many sophisticated tasks by accessing and manipulating domain knowledge. The above mentioned technological advances dictate a better methodology to design knowledge-based, user-specific multimedia information systems. The design methodology, taking into consideration the diversified application requirements and users' needs, should provide a unified framework for multimedia representation, querying, indexing and spatial/temporal reasoning.

Multimedia databases, when compared to traditional databases, have the following special requirements [31], [32]:

(1) The size of the data items may be very large. The management of multimedia information therefore requires the accessing and ma-

nipulation of very large data items.

(2) Storage and delivery of video data requires guaranteed and synchronized delivery of data.

(3) Various query mechanisms need to be combined, and the user interface should be highly visual and should also enable visual relevance feedback and user-guided navigation.

(4) The on-line, real-time processing of large volumes of data may be required for some types of multimedia databases.

The focus of this paper is on the third requirement mentioned above. For multimedia databases, there are not only different media types, but also different ways to query the databases. The query mechanisms may include free text search, SQL-like querying, icon-based techniques, querying based upon the entity-relationship (ER) diagram, content-based querying, sound-based querying, as well as virtual-reality (VR) techniques. Some of these query mechanisms are based upon traditional approaches, such as free text search ("retrieve all books authored by Einstein") and SQL query language ("SELECT title FROM books WHERE author = Einstein"). Some are developed in response to the special needs of multimedia databases such as content-based querying for image/video databases ("find all books containing the picture of Einstein") [30], and sound-based queries that are spoken rather than written or drawn [65]. Some are dictated by new software/hardware technologies, such as icon-based queries that use icons to denote query targets ("a book") and objects ("a sketch of Einstein"), and virtual reality queries where the query targets and objects can be directly manipulated in a virtual reality environment (the book shelves in a Virtual Library). Except for the traditional approaches and those relying on sound, the other techniques share the common characteristic of being highly visual. Therefore, we will concern ourselves mainly with multiparadigmatic visual interface to accessing multimedia documents.

A visual interface to multimedia databases, in general, must support some type of visual querying language. Visual query languages (VQLs) are query languages based on the use of visual representations to depict the domain of interest and express the related requests. Systems implementing a visual query language are called Visual Query Systems (VQSs) [5], [9]. They include both a language to express the queries in a pictorial form and a variety of functionalities to facilitate human-computer interaction. As such, they are oriented to a wide spectrum of users, ranging from people with limited technical skills to highly sophisticated specialists. In recent years, many VQSs have been proposed, adopting a range of different visual representations and interaction strategies. These interaction paradigms will be discussed in Section 1.5.1, but most existing VQSs restrict human-computer interaction to only one kind of interaction paradigm. However, the presence of several paradigms, each one with different characteristics and advantages, will help both naive and experienced users in interacting with the system. For instance, icons may well evoke the objects present in the database, while relationships among them may be better expressed through the edges of a graph, and collections of instances may be easily clustered into a form. Moreover, the user is not required to adapt his perception of the reality of interest to the different views presented by the various data models and interfaces.

The way in which the query is expressed depends on the visual representations as well. In fact, in the existing VQSs, icons are typically combined following a spatial syntax [18], while queries on diagrammatic representations are mainly expressed by following links and forms are often filled with prototypical values. Moreover, the same interface can offer to the user different interaction mechanisms for expressing a query, depending on both the experience of the user and the kind of the query itself [10].

To effectively and efficiently access information from multimedia databases, we can identify the following design criteria for the user interface: (1) various query mechanisms need to be combined seamlessly, (2) the user interface should be visual as much as possible, (3) the user interface should enable visual relevance feedback, (4) the user interface should support user-guided navigation, and (5) the user interface should facilitate the user-controlled discovery of new associations among media objects.

Addressing these issues, this paper explores the design of multiparadigmatic visual interfaces to multimedia databases. In Section 1.2, we discuss the visual representation of the information space. Strategies for visual reasoning are surveyed in Section 1.3 . In Section 1.4 we describe three application examples to illustrate the concept of multiparadigmatic visual interface for multimedia databases. Section 1.5.1 gives a taxonomy of visual querying paradigms, and Section 1.5.2 deals with multimedia database interaction techniques. Research challenges and some concluding remarks are given in Section 1.6.

1.2 Representation of the Information Space

In a visual interface for multimedia databases, the information stored in the multimedia database needs to be visualized in an information space. This visualization can either be carried out by the user in the user's mind, in which case it is essentially the user's conceptualization of the database; or the visualization could be accomplished by the system, in which case the visualization is generated on the display screen. In this Section, we describe the different representations of the information space.

Database objects, in general, are abstracted from real-life objects in the real world. Therefore, we can distinguish the *logical information space* and the *physical information space.* In the logical space, the abstract database objects are represented. In the physical space, the abstract database objects are materialized and represented as physical objects such as images, animation, video, voice, etc. The physical objects either *mimic* real-life objects such as objects in a virtual reality, or *reflect* real-life objects such as diagrams, icons and sketches.

The real world, from which the database objects are abstracted, is the environment that the database objects must relate to. The real world also is often abstracted in the information space. Only in the virtual reality information space, will the real world be represented in a direct way (see later).

The *logical information space* is a multi-dimensional space, where each point represents an object (a record, a tuple, etc.) from the database. A database object, e_j, or an *example*, is a point in this space. Conceptually, the entire information space then corresponds to all the database objects in a database. The logical information space is thus a unified view of the database, i.e. a universal relation.

Each attribute of a database object represents one dimension in this multi-dimensional space. Therefore, in the logical information space, different dimensions actually have different characteristics: continuous, numerical, discrete, or logical.

A *query* q_i is an arbitrary region in this information space. A *clue* x_k is also an arbitrary region in the logical information space, but it may contain additional directional information to indicate *visual momentum*, such as the direction of browsing. Therefore, an example e_j is a clue, and so is a visual query q_i. A hypermap (Section 1.6) when used as a metaphor is also a clue.

The information retrieval problem is to construct the "most desirable" query q_i with respect to the examples e_j and the clues x_k presented by the user. The "most desirable" query is one which will retrieve the largest number of relevant database objects and whose "size" in the information space is relatively small. The process of visual reasoning, which will be discussed in Section 1.3, may help the user find the most desirable query from examples and clues.

The logical information space may be further structured into a *logical information hyperspace*, where the *clue* becomes hyperlinks that provides directional information, and the information space can be navigated the user by following the directional clues. Information is "chunked", and each chunk is illustrated by an example (the hypernode).

The *physical information space* consists of the materialized database objects. The simplest example is as follows. Each object is materialized as an icon, and the physical information space consists of a collection of icons. These icons can be arranged spatially, so that the spatial locations approximately reflect the relations among database objects. More recently, *intelligent visualization systems* are being developed, for task-specific visualization assistance [39]. Such systems can offer assistance in deriving perceptually effective materialization of database objects.

In the physical information space, the objects reflect real-world objects, but the world is still an abstraction of the real world. One further step is to present information in a *virtual reality information space*. Virtual Reality allows the users to be placed in a 3D environment they can directly manipulate. What the users see on the screen will be the same as what can be experienced in the real world. 3D features can be used to present the results in a virtual reality (VR) setting. For example, the physical location of medical records can be indicated in a (simplified) 3D presentation of a Virtual Medical Laboratory by blinking icons. If the database refers to the books of a library, we can represent a Virtual Library in which the physical locations of books are indicated by blinking icons in a 3D presentation of the book stacks of the library. What the user sees on the screen will be the same (after simplifications) as what can be experienced in the real world. VR such as the Virtual Library or the Virtual Medical Laboratory can become a new query paradigm. For example, the user can select a book by picking it from the shelf, like in the real world.

It is worth noting that we are talking about "nonimmersive" VR [60] i.e. the user is placed in a 3D environment he or she can directly manipulate without wearing head-mounted stereo displays or special gloves, but acting only with mouse, keyboard, and monitor of a conventional graphics workstation. This is an alternative form of VR that is being explored in several research laboratories. The use of 3D modeling and rendering is the same as in immersive VR, because the scene is displayed with the same depth cues: perspective view, hidden-surface elimination, color, texture, lighting, shading. Researchers working in nonimmersive VR report that the user is drawn into the 3D world, since mental and emotional immersion takes place, in spite of the lack of visual or perceptual immersion. Moreover, mouse/keyboard controlled interaction techniques are easy to learn and use and are often faster than Dataglove interaction techniques. Therefore, significant advantages come from using such familiar and inexpensive tools, that lower startup costs. Indeed, immersive VR technology has still many limits and problems (producing and synchronizing stereo images, handling of immersive input devices, etc.), so that researchers spend much more time focusing on the devices rather than on applications and interaction techniques. As a further advantage, nonimmersive VR does not force office workers to wear special equipment that isolate them from their usual environment, minimizing psychological and physical stress that most users will not tolerate [6]. On the other hand, new approaches on using the immersive VR, such as interactive Worlds-in-Miniature (WIM) [64], may pave the way for more applications of the immersive VR.

Nonimmersive VR is a valuable interaction paradigm that will be fruitful in multimedia database applications, as well as in general business applications. When displays and input devices that are easily manageable and not intrusive will be available, immersive VR will become acceptable.

The above categorization can be summarized in Figure 1.1:

Space	Objects	World
Logical Information Space	Abstract	Abstract
Logical Information Hyperspace	Abstract Clustered	Abstract
Physical Information Space	Real*	Abstract
VR Information Space	Real	Real

Fig. 1.1 Summary of information spaces.

*Real objects in the physical information space reflect real-life objects, rather than mimic real-life objects.

1.3 Strategies for Visual Reasoning

Visual reasoning is the process of reasoning and making inferences, based upon visually presented clues. As mentioned in Section 1.2, visual reasoning may help the user find the most desirable query from examples and clues. In this Section, we survey strategies for visual reasoning.

Visual reasoning is widely used in human-to-human communication. For example, the teacher draws a diagram on the blackboard. Although the diagram is incomplete and imprecise, the students are able to make inferences to fill in the details, and gain an understanding of the concepts presented. Such *disgram understanding* relies on visual reasoning so that concepts can be communicated. Human also uses *gestures* [36] to communicate. Again, gestures are imprecise visual clues for the receiving person to interpret.

In human-to-computer communication, a recent trend is for the human to communicate to the computer using visual expressions. Typically, the human draws a picture, a structured diagram, or a visual example, and the computer interprets the visual expression to understand the user's intention. This has been called *visual coaching*, *programming by example* [52], or *programming by rehearsal* [33], [38] by various researchers.

Visual reasoning is related to spatial reasoning, example-based programming, and approximate/vague retrieval. *Spatial reasoning* is the process of reasoning and making inferences, about problems dealing with objects occupying space [27]. These objects can be either *physical objects* (e.g., books, chairs, cars, etc.) or *abstract objects* visualized in space (e.g. database objects). Physical objects are tangible and occupy physical space in some measurable sense. Abstract objects are intangible but nevertheless can be associated with a certain space in some coordinate system. Therefore, visual reasoning can be defined as spatial reasoning on abstract objects visualized in space.

Example-Based Programming refers to systems that allow the programmer to use examples of input and output data during the programming process [52]. There are two types of Example-Based Programming: *Programming by Example* and *Programming with Example.* "Programming by Example" refers to systems that try to guess or *infer* the program from examples of input and output or sample traces of execution. This is often called "automated programming" and has been an area of AI research. "Programming with Example" systems require the user to specify everything about the program (there is no inferencing involved), but the programmer can work out the program on a specific example. The system executes the programmer's commands normally, but remembers them for later re-use. Halbert [35] characterizes Programming with Examples as "Do What I Did" whereas inferential Programming by Example might be called "Do What I Mean". Many recently developed visual programming systems utilized the example-based programming approach [33], [53], [63]. The approach described in Section 1.4.1 combines presentation of visual clues (programming by example) with query augmentation techniques (programming with example).

We now discuss visual reasoning approaches for databases. Most research in database systems is based on the assumptions of precision and specificity of both the data stored in the database, and the requests to retrieve data. In reality, however, both may be imprecise or vague. Motro characterizes three categories of imprecision and/or vagueness: (1) the data stored in the database is imprecise; (2) the retrieval request is imprecise; and (3) the user does not have a precise notion of the contents of the database [51].

Imprecision in stored data can be dealt with by applying fuzzy sets theory to provide a linguistic description of the stored imprecise data. Fuzzy queries also allow the user to give imprecise retrieval requests. Such techniques are generally applicable when the source of imprecision is quantifiable into numbers, for example, "the age of a person is somewhere between 40 and 45" (imprecision in stored data), "retrieve all middle-aged employees" (imprecision in queries). However, when the source of imprecision is not easily quantifiable, for example, "find persons with faces similar to Einstein's face", the above techniques are less well suitable. Recent research in content-based retrieval may lead to techniques to address such problems.

Imprecision in the user's model may be classified as follows [50]: incomplete knowledge of the data model, imprecise information on the database schema and/or its instance, vagueness of user goals, and incomplete knowledge about the interaction tools.

To deal with imprecision in user's model, several approaches have been investigated: (i) *browsing* techniques to provide different views of the database [51]; (ii) *heuristic interpretation of user' query* to transform the user' query by a connective approach [25], [66], [14]; (iii) *example-based techniques* to generalize from selected examples [68], or to modify the original query if the answer is not considered satisfactory [67], [51]. The modification is done either interactively or automatically.

Browsing is generally effective and widely used but may be very wasteful on the user's time. Heuristic interpretation of user's query can lead to "false drops" or "false hits". Example-based techniques work well for some applications but are hard to generalize. In addition, two common limitations of these approaches [26] are worth mentioning here: (1) the browsing environment and the querying environment are usually distinct, thus separating the learning and the querying activities. (2) knowledge about the user must be gathered to build the user profile (user model). The approach described in Section 1.4.1 integrates the querying environment (using the visual query) and the browsing environment.

1.4 Applications and Techniques

1.4.1 *Application Example: Digital Library*

In this and the next two sections, we look at three application examples. The first example is the digital library. To support multimedia information access we need a multiparadigmatic visual interface that supports progressive queries – The Visual Query and Result Hypercube (*VQRH*) [16].

We have experimented with information retrieval using VQRH in two application domains: (a) the medical databases, and (b) the library databases. The subjects are students with no previous experience in using VQRH. We will not describe VQRH in details here. We just recall its basic features, namely: (1) the screen is divided into two main windows, in the left one the user formulates its query, and the results are shown in the right window; (2) both query and results can be visualized in any of the available paradigms for query and data representation; (3) the queries formulated during an interaction section are stored, with the corresponding results, as successive slices of the Hypercube, so each slice can be easily recalled.

The preliminary experiments indicate that the users have little difficulty in learning VQRH, and they can formulate queries after half an hour of interaction. They generally like the idea of progressive querying, and find it useful to be able to recall any past query-and-result slice. From such experiments, it is already clear that the visualization of the retrieved result is very important for the success of this approach. While in the initial design of VQRH only physical information spaces were used for presenting the data, in a second version of the prototype a VR information space was added. VR is established as a query paradigm, that is, the user selects with the mouse the items of this 3D space he or she is interested in.

When performing a query, the admissability conditions to switch between a *logical paradigm* (our previous paradigms are all logical paradigms) and a *VR paradigm* (such as the Virtual Library) can be defined as follows. For a logical paradigm, a *VR-admissable query* is an admissable query whose retrieval target object is also an object in VR. For example, the VR for the Virtual Library contains stacks of books, and a VR-admissable query could be any admissable query about books, because the result of that query can be indicated by blinking book icons in the Virtual Library. Conversely, for a VR paradigm, an *LQ-admissable query* is a VR where there is a single marked VR object that is also a database object, and the marking is achieved by an operation icon such as *similar_to* (find objects similar to this object), *near* (find objects near this object), *above* (find objects above this object), *below* (find objects below this object), and other spatial operators. For example, in the VR for the Virtual Library, a book marked by the operation icon *similar_to* is LQ- admissable and can be translated into the following query: "find all books similar to this book." An example of a VR-admissable logical query is illustrated in Figure 1.2. The query is to find books on bicycles. It is performed with the iconic paradigm. The result is presented as marked objects in a Virtual Library. The user can then navigate in this Virtual Library, and switch to the VR query paradigm. Figure 1.3 illustrates an LQ-admissable query. The query is to find books similar to a specific book about bicycles that has been marked by the user. The result is again rendered as marked objects in a Virtual Library. If we switch to a form-based representation, the result could also be rendered as items in a form. This example illustrates progressive querying can be accomplished with greater flexibility by combining the logical paradigms and the VR paradigms. The experimental VQRH system supports VR paradigms, but the similarity function must be supplied for the problem domain.

The experiment was useful for understanding the limitations of the screen design and their impact on system's usability. Some interesting characteristics of the VR paradigm emerged, which led to a revised screen design. Indeed, the distinction between query space and result space does not make sense in VR, since a query is performed by acting, with either the mouse or another pointer device, in the environment the user is in. The result of the query usually determines some modification of such an environment, and this new situation is that one on which a successive re-

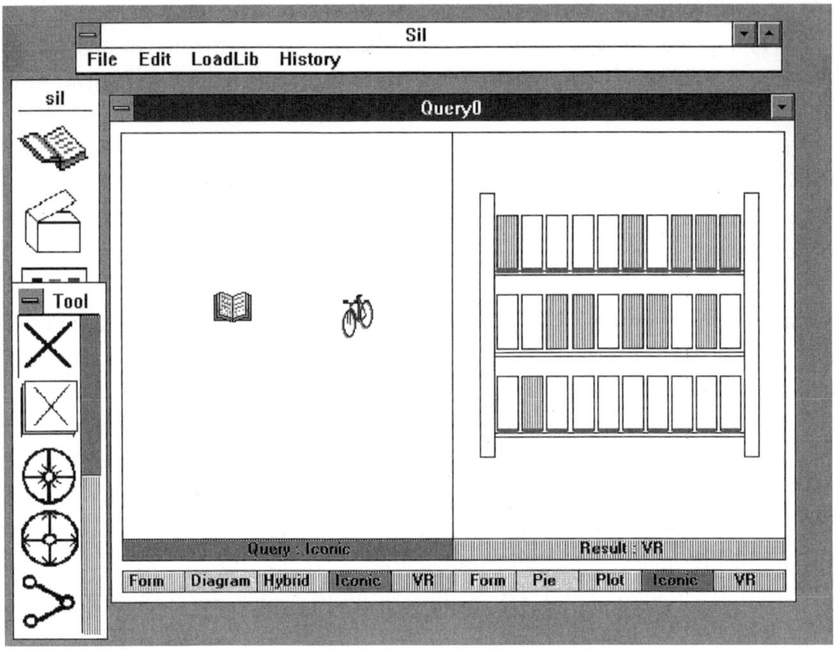

Fig. 1.2 A VR-admissable logical query.

quest has to be performed. As a consequence, when working with the VR paradigm, the user gets confused by the separation of the query window and the result window. This is easily understandable by looking at Figure 1.2 and Figure 1.3. The situation depicted in Figure 1.2 does not create any problem for the user, who is formulating a query in the iconic paradigm but wants to see the result in VR, since VR actually provides visual indication of where the requested books can be found. Moreover, showing the results in separate windows, gives the user the possibility of viewing them in a different representation, providing the user the full advantage of viewing the data in different ways [5]. For example, while VR gives immediate indication about physical location of a book, in a form-based representation more details can be provided at once, such as title of the book, authors, exact number of pages, etc. Therefore, in a situation involving a change of paradigm between query and result representations, the user is perfectly

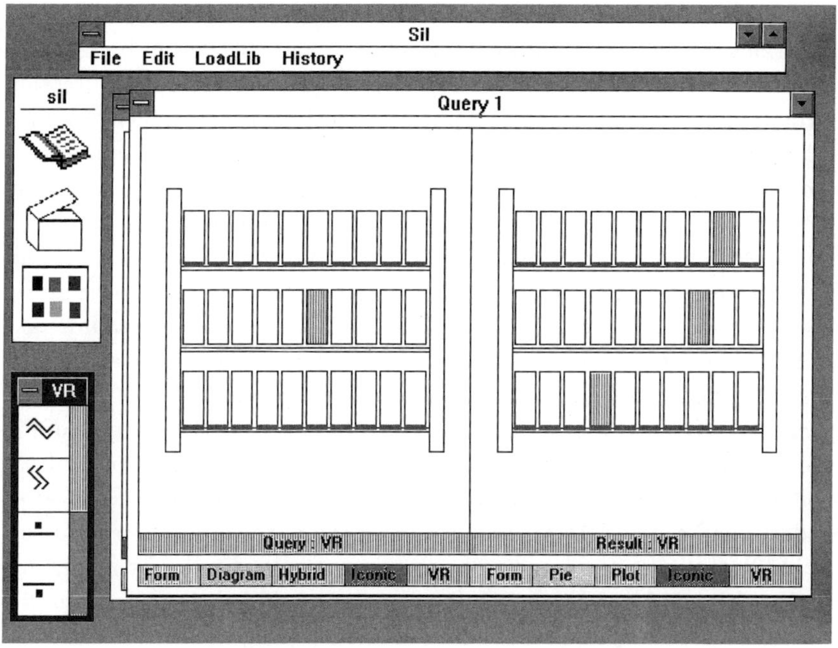

Fig. 1.3 An LQ-admissable query.

comfortable with the two windows shown on the screen.

However, the user gets confused when working in VR, in the situation depicted in Figure 1.3. The two windows both show the book shelf, but the left-side window shows the VR query and the right-side window shows the VR result. When the user is visualizing the VR result, it is unnatural to go to a different window to modify the query. There should be only one window, showing both the VR result and the VR query. Therefore, in the new version of the VQRH prototype, the computer screen displays only one view of the Virtual Library at a time. The user first navigates in the Virtual Library and clicks on a bookshelf. The user then proceeds to click on individual books, and uses operators such as "near", "similar_to", "above", etc. to retrieve other books.

Extending the Virtual Library metaphor, we can consider map as a metaphor for navigation in an information space. Hypermaps, short for cartographic hyperdocuments, fill the gap between hyperdocuments and spatial information so that knowledge pertaining to several kinds of applications can be organized in a very elegant and efficient ay by means of anchors linking words to spatial zones and vice versa, or by linking literal information to coordinates [45]. Applications include urban and environmental planning, architecture and mechanical designs, building maintenance, archeology, tourism and geographic information systems. Hypermaps can be used advantageously as a metaphor for the representation of all the multimedia hyperbase elements [8]. In GeoAnchor, a map can be built dynamically as a view of the multimedia hyperbase [8]. As shown in Figure 1.4, each displayed geometry is an anchor to either a geographic node or to a related node. Hence, the map on the screen acts both as an index to the nodes and as a view to the multimedia hyperbase. With this metaphor, *semantic filtering* can be accomplished as illustrated by the example of Figure 1.5, where user behavior determines the semantic weight of both the nodes and the links of the road network. If the access frequency of a secondary road such as 'D751' is much lower than that of a major road such as 'A10', the secondary road will not appear on the display for readability.

In a Virtual Library a hypermap can also be used as a metaphor to link the most frequently accessed items such as reading rooms, book shelves, etc. to present different views to the end user. This combined metaphor of *Hypermapped Virtual Library* (which is a combination of the VR information space and the logical information hyperspace) may lead to efficient access of multimedia information from a digital library.

1.4.2 *Application Example: Medical Information Fusion*

The framework for human- and system-directed medical information retrieval, discovery and fusion [40] is best illustrated by Figure 1.6. As shown in Figure 1.6, we envision a three-level model for information: *data*, *abstracted information*, and *fused knowledge*. Information sources such as camera, sensors or computers usually provide continuous streams of data, which are collected and stored in medical databases. Such data need to be abstracted into various forms of abstractions, so that the retrieval, processing, consistency analysis and combination of abstracted information becomes possible. Finally, the abstracted information needs to be integrated and transformed into fused knowledge. These three levels of information form a hierarchy, but at any given moment there is the continuous transformation of data into abstracted information and then into fused knowledge.

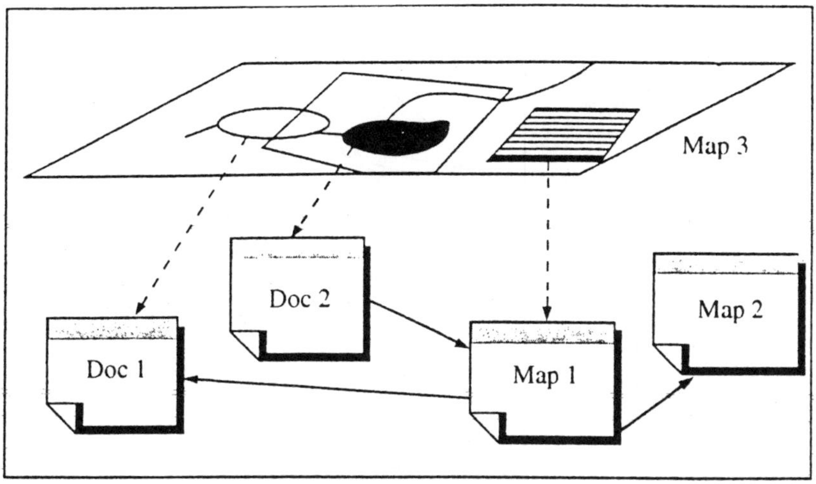

Fig. 1.4 A GeoAnchor hypermap example.

Figure 1.6 illustrates the relationships among data sources, data, abstracted information and fused knowledge, with emphasis on diversity of data sources and multiplicity of abstracted representations. For example, a video camera is a data source that generates video data. Such video data can be transformed into various forms of abstracted representations:

1) text (video-to-text abstraction by human agent or computer), 2) keyword (video-to-keyword abstraction by human agent or computer), 3) assertions (logical representation of abstracted facts), 4) qualitative spatial description (abstraction such as the symbolic projection [20]), and 5) time sequences of frames (abstraction where both spatial and temporal relations are preserved).

In Figure 1.6, a potentially viable transformation from data to abstracted representation is indicated by a small circle. Thus, from video it is possible to transform into qualitative spatial description or time sequence of frames. A supported transformation is indicated by a large circle in Figure 1.6. Thus the image data will be transformed into keywords, assertions (facts) and qualitative spatial description. It should be emphasized that there are more types of abstracted representations than what are shown in Figure 1.6. Conversely, certain information systems may only support text, keywords and assertions as the three allowable types of abstractions. The

Hyperbase

Node	Weight Initial	Weight Current
A10	10	10
N152	9	9
D675	2	5
D102	2	5
D751	2	2
D62	2	2
Tours	10	10
Blois	9	9
Chambord	8	8
Cheverny	7	7
Amboise	7	7
Herbault	2	2
Contres	2	1

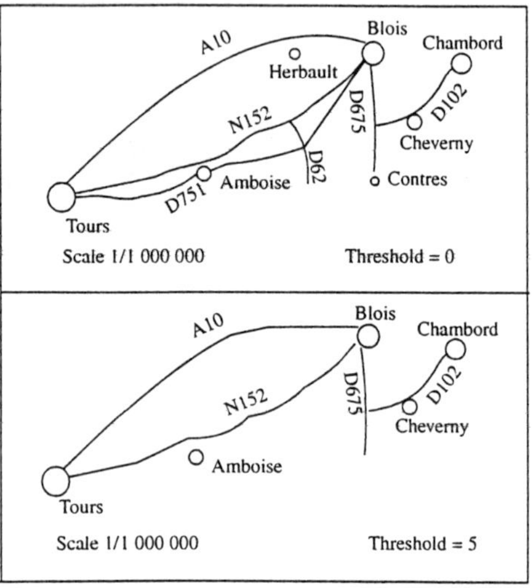

Fig. 1.5 An example of GeoAnchor semantic filtering.

information sources in Figure 1.6 may include hard real-time sources (such as the signals captured by sensors), soft real-time sources (such as pre-stored video), and non-real-time sources (such as text, images and graphics from a medical database or a web site).

The transformation from data to information and then knowledge is effected by the coordinated efforts of the *User*, the *Active Index System* and the *Decision Network*. As shown in Figure 1.6, the user interacts with the Active Index System and the Decision Network to obtain information and create fused knowledge. The user can request the Active Index System to collect information from the sources. Since the active index can perform actions in response to the user's requests, [17] the user is capable of controlling the sources to influence the type of data being collected. For example, the user may turn on or turn off the video camera or manually control the positioning of the camera. Moreover, the user can also provide missing information and evaluate the diagnosis produced by the Decision Network.

The Active Index System receives input data as messages, processes them and sends abstracted information as its output to the user or the Decision Network. Data are transformed into abstracted information through the active index cells which also serve as filters to weed out unwanted data. Some index cells can also perform spatial/temporal reasoning [19] to generate spatially/temporally abstracted information in the form of assertions. An active index contains index cells that can be attached to *sources*, while a conventional index is for data already stored in the database. For example, index cells on sensors, web sites or web pages can be created so that an Active Index System can obtain information from selected sources and send it to the user or the Decision Network.

The Decision Network is a neural net called LAMSTAR [34] capable of storing knowledge, fusing knowledge and posing requests to the Active Index System to collect more information from the sources. The Decision Network can send messages to the Active Index System to activate index cells which then take appropriate actions to generate abstracted information. The Decision Network can also interact with the user. It can, for example, solicit the user's evaluation of its diagnosis to reorganize its internal knowledge base.

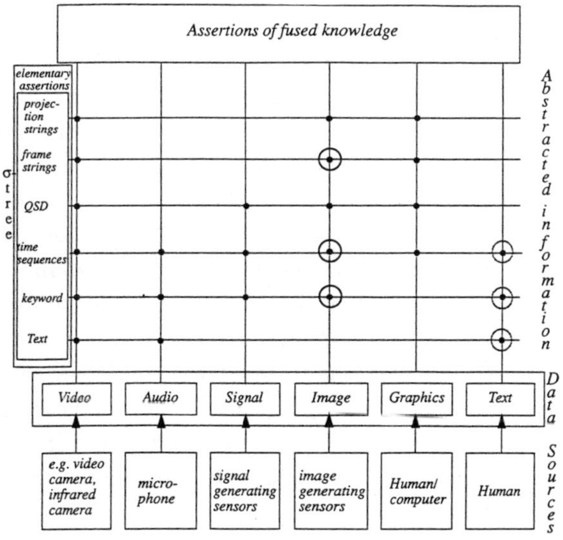

Fig. 1.6 A framework for information retrieval, discovery and fusion from multiple sources.

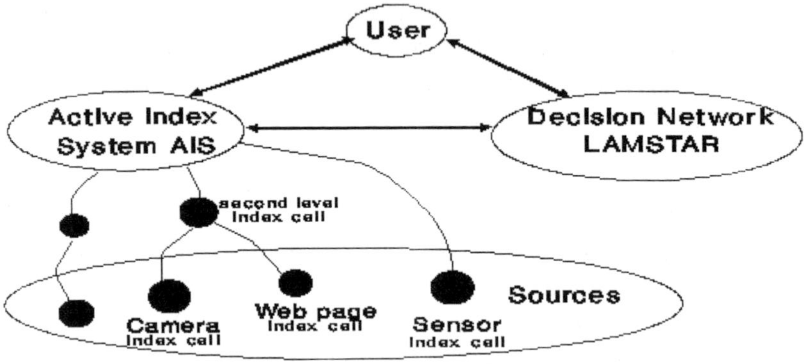

Fig. 1.7 Relationships among the user, the Active Index System, the Dec ision Network and the sources.

1.4.2.1 *A Formal Definition of Semantic Consistency*

A prototype of the experimental system AMIS2 [22] is at

http://www.cs.pitt.edu/~jung/AMIS2.

It can be used to check for consistency in information retrieval, discovery and fusion. To do so, a more formal definition of consistency is necessary. Our definition of consistency is based upon the transformational approach illustrated by the framework of Figure 1.6. It is different from the usual definitions of consistency in database theory or in AI theory, because we believe the problem of consistency for information discovery and fusion must be first addressed at the level of characteristic patterns detected in medical objects. This is where the active medical information system can make the most impact in drastically reducing the amount of medical information that ultimately must be handled by human operators.

We define consistency functions to check the consistency among media objects of the *same* media type, by concentrating on their characteristic patterns. For example, two assertions "there is a tumor in the left lung" and "there is no tumor in the left lung" can be checked for consistency, and two images of the same left lung can also be checked for consistency. These consistency functions are media-specific and domain-specific. For example, to check whether two medical images are consistent, the consistency function will verify whether the two images contain similar *characteristic patterns* such as arteries, bone structures, tissues. For different application domains, different consistency functions are needed.

To check whether media objects of *different* media types are consistent, they need to be transformed into media objects of the same media type so that the media-specific, domain-specific consistency function can be applied. Our viewpoint is that each object is characterized by some characteristic patterns that can be transformed into characteristic patterns in different media type. For example, the characteristic pattern is a tumor in the image media, which is transformed into the word "tumor" in the keyword media. The consistency function can then be applied to the characteristic patterns of objects of the same media type.

Let o^i_j be the jth object of media type M^i. Let c^i_k be the kth characteristic pattern detected in an object o^i_j of media type M^i. Let C^i denote the set of all such characteristic patterns of media type M^i. Let $\phi_{1,2}$ be the transformation that maps characteristic patterns detected in objects of media type M^1 to characteristic patterns of media type M^2.

For each media type M^i there is a consistency function K_i which is a mapping from 2^{C^i} (the space of all subsets of characteristic patterns in media type M^i) to $TorF$. In other words it verifies that a set of characteristic patterns of media type M^i are consistent.

A characteristic pattern c^1_k of media type M^1 is consistent with respect to media type M^2 if the transformed characteristic pattern $\phi_{1,2}(c^1_k)$ is consistent with the set C^2 of all characteristic patterns of media type M^2, i.e. $K_{2(\phi_{1,2}(c^1_k) \cup C^2)} = T$. A characteristic pattern c^i_k is consistent if it is consistent with respect to all media types M^j.

Finally, a multimedia information space is consistent at time t if every characteristic pattern of every media type is consistent at time t, and a multimedia information space is temporally consistent if it is consistent at all times.

As an example, an image of media type M^1 is examined and a possible tumor-like object is detected. This is a characteristic pattern c^1_1. The keywords describing findings by the medical doctor is of media type M^2. The transformation $\phi_{1,2}$ maps characteristic pattern c^1_1 to $\phi_{1,2}(c^1_1)$, which could be the keyword "tumor". If the consistency function K_2 verifies that the finding "tumor" is consistent with other findings, then the characteristic pattern c_1^1 is consistent with respect to media type M^2. If we can also verify that c_1^1 is consistent with other patterns detected in media M^1, and suppose the information space contains only objects of these two media types, then we have verified that c_1^1 is consistent.

The information space is temporally consistent if all such findings are consistent at all times. This can be verified only after we run the entire diagnostic procedure. For example, if the "tumor" characteristic pattern is detected at time t_1 but absent at time t_2 and again detected at time t_3, and $t_1 < t_2 < t_3$, then there may be temporal inconsistency. (This temporal inconsistency may lead to the discovery of an important event.)

In this example the transformation function is simply the labeling of characteristic patterns. The "tumor" characteristic pattern is the pattern detected by a pattern recognizer. There are image processing algorithms which will produce characteristic patterns. As for the consistency function, we can use similarity functions which accept as inputs the characteristic patterns in some media space (the simplest being keywords) and produce the output to verify whether the inputs are consistent [61]. In other words, we can use similarity functions to determine whether the inputs are all within a certain distance. As will be explained in the next section, we can also use the neural network for consistency checking. For different media, we need to find the most suitable consistency functions.

1.4.2.2 *Consistency Checking by Horizontal/Vertical Reasoning*

As illustrated in Figure 1.6, information fusion is feasible when information from different sources can be converted into similar representations, indicated in Figure 1.6 by several large circles in the same horizontal row. For example, the system may support the transformation of image, text and web pages into assertions (facts), so that consistency checking among assertions is feasible. We call such reasoning *horizontal reasoning* because it combines information abstracted from different media encoded in the same uniform representation.

Another type of reasoning is applicable to data from similar media with different abstracted representations so that they can be combined and checked for consistency. We call such reasoning *vertical reasoning* because it combines information having different representations at different levels of abstraction.

Horizontal reasoning can be accomplished with the help of an artificial neural network due to its ability to combine information abstracted from different media and adequately encoded in the same uniform representation. Once a horizontally uniform representation is obtained, an artificial neural network can check for consistency. If the neural network's reliability R is less than a predefined threshold, then the inputs are regarded as inconsistent. In other words, the consistency function K is derived from R.

The active index can be used in vertical reasoning due to its ability to obtain information from different sources and actively connecting them by dynamic linking (using index cells). For example, we can link an image to a keyword to an assertion (fact), and then domain-specific algorithms can be applied to check their consistency. Vertical reasoning is associative and combines information in different representations. An artificial neural network with fixed connections is not as appropriate as an active index with flexible connections.

We now use AMIS2 to illustrate information fusion by horizontal/vertical reasoning. Patient information are abstracted from different media sources, including imaging devices, signal generators, instruments, etc. *(vertical reasoning)*. Once abstracted and uniformly represented, the neural network is invoked to make a tentative diagnosis *(horizontal reasoning)*. Using the active index, similar patient records are found by the Recursive Searcher *(vertical reasoning)*. A retrieved patient record is compared with the target patient record *(horizontal reasoning)*. If similar records lead to similar diagnosis then the results are consistent and the patient record (with diagnosis) is accepted and integrated into the knowledge base. If the diagnosis is different then the results are inconsistent and the negative feedback can also help the decision network learn.

In the vertical reasoning phase, in addition to comparing patient data, we can also compare images to determine whether we have found similar patient records. Therefore, content-based image similarity retrieval becomes a part of the vertical reasoning. Depending upon the application domain, image similarity can be based upon shape, color, volume or other attributes of an object, spatial relationship among objects, and so on.

This example illustrates the *alternating application of horizontal reasoning (using the neural network for making predictions) and vertical reasoning (using dynamically created active index for making associations)*. Combined, we have an active information system for medical information fusion and consistency checking.

The research challenge is to find the appropriate visual querying mechanism to express horizontal/vertical reasoning in medical information fusion. One possibility is the *Hypermapped Virtual Clinics* metaphor, where virtual clinical laboratories are linked using horizontal reasoners, and lab test results are then linked to clinical databases using vertical reasoners.

1.4.3 *Application Example: Intelligent Web Searcher*

The issue of providing the user with a powerful and friendly query mechanism for accessing information on the Web has been very recently widely investigated. In particular, one of the most critical problems is to find effective ways to build models of the information of interest, and to design systems capable of integrating different and heterogeneous information sources into a common domain model. Popular keyword-based search engines can be regarded as first generation of such systems, that use feature-based representations (or keyword representations), modeling documents through feature vectors. Such representations make it easy to automatically classify documents, but offer limited capabilities for retrieving the information of interest, still burying the user under a heap of nonhomogeneous information.

In order to overcome such limitations, more sophisticated methods for representing information sources have been proposed by both the database and the artificial intelligence community. Such methods can be roughly classified as being based on database or knowledge representation techniques. The differences between the two approaches is mainly in defining either materialized or virtual views of the data extracted from the web sites, and in providing or not automatic (or semi-automatic) mechanisms for individuating such data.

Typically, in a database approach (see, e.g., [3], [23]) a model of the information sources has to be explicitly specified by the user and there is no automatic translation from the site information to the data in the corresponding database. However, relying on well-established database techniques carries a number of advantages in the ease and effectiveness of access once the data is stored in the database.

On the other hand, in a knowledge based approach the idea is that the system handles an explicit representation of the information sources (which has again to be provided to the system), but the information requested by the user are retrieved at query time, by exploiting planning techniques which introduce a certain degree of flexibility in exploring the information sources and extracting information from them (see, e.g., [4], [46]), and in some cases even deal with incomplete information [29]. A serious drawback of such approaches is obviously the response time.

The problems still existing in both approaches lead us to propose an integrated solution in the WAG system [11], which relies on a conceptual modeling language equipped with a powerful visual environment and on a knowledge representation tool which is meant to provide a simpler representation of the information, but the ability to reason about it. Differing from the other database approaches, WAG attempts to semi-automatically classify the information gathered from various sites based on the conceptual model of the domain of interest (instead of requiring an explicit description of the sources). However, the result of such a classification is materialized and dealt with by using effective database techniques. To illustrate this approach, we first describe an idealized scenario for intelligent information retrieval from the Web:

A user poses a few queries to locate information of interest. The user may also navigate to the web site to select some objects of interest. After this preliminary interaction, when the user is inactive or away, an intelligent information retrieval system will search the web sites to find all the relevant web pages which constitute a virtual site. It then builds conceptual views containing the information relevant to the specific domains. The information, even if originally expressed in different formats, will be presented in a unified way. The views will be conceptualized and populated in two different phases: a) an on-line phase*during browsing sessions of the user; b) an* off-line phase*by the intelligent information retrieval system, which will visit related sites applying the existing search engines to populate the database. The user poses precise database queries and develops a deeper understanding of the problem domain. After a careful analysis of the database, the user again poses imprecise web queries and navigates the web to locate objects of interest, leading to the next cycle of intelligent information retrieval.*

In the above scenario, the intelligent information retrieval system will structure the information in the web sites and present the relevant information to the user or store the relevant information in a database whose conceptual view is constructed by the system. To accomplish the objective suggested by this scenario, we propose the *WAG* (*W*eb-*A*t-a-*G*lance) system which can assist the user in creating a customized database by gleaning the relevant information from a web site containing multimedia data. WAG performs this task by first interacting with the user to construct a customized conceptual view of the web pages pertinent to the user's interests, and then populating the database with information extracted from the web pages.

The WAG system can be realized as an active index which contains multiple index cells (ic's) to perform various tasks. The most important components (realized as index cells) of WAG are the *Searcher ic*, the *Page Classifier ic* and the *Conceptualizer ic*. Each ic will in turn activate other ic's to cooperatively accomplish the objective. WAG could be used by different users. For each of them the active index builds a "personal environment" containing the user's profile, the conceptual views of the domains and the corresponding knowledge bases. However, a user who just starts interacting with WAG is allowed to import and possibly merge the personal environments of previous users (unless marked as reserved) so as to take advantage of the information they already discovered. The new personal environment resulting from the importing operations can be modified, extended, or even rejected by its owner. A further possibility could be to ask the web sites the permission to be marked as visited by a WAG user, and add to them link(s) to the conceptual base(s) of the corresponding WAG user(s) (also in this case the users' authorization is mandatory). This leads to the concept of BBCs and LBCs.

The prototyping of WAG components as web pages enhanced by active index cells has the advantage that the user can easily enter information to experiment with the prototype WAG system. Moreover, whenever the user accesses an html page, an associated ic can be instantiated to collect information to be forwarded to the WAG ic's, so that flexible on-line interaction can be supported for the Searcher, the Page Classifier and the Conceptualizer. In the current version of the light-weight WAG, the Conceptualizer is not included. Thus the user will pose an information retrieval request to search the web sites, observe the results produced by the Page Classifier, and formulate another request to search the web sites, and so on.

The experimental light-weight WAG can be accessed by anyone with a browser. The home page is at http://www.cs.pitt.edu/~jung/WAG. The following scenario describes how to use it:

Step 1 Initialize the WAG system

If this is the first time the user is using the WAG, the user must initialize it. If the user has previously initialized the WAG system, the user need not reinitialize it; the user can create more BBCs and LBCs, or move on to perform the search without creating more index cells. If the user wants to delete all previously created index cells, or if the system seems to have some problems, the user can reinitialize and create a new WAG index cell.

Step 2 Create Big Brothers BBCs

Big Brother index cells (BBCs) are search engines to search web sites on a global scale. Generally speaking, these are commercially available search engines, which will return URLs as the results of keyword searches. The user can create "yahoo" and "lycos" or the user's own BBCs. The user can enter the name of a search engine and click the button below to create a new BBC index cell.

Step 3 Create Little Brothers LBCs

Little Brother index cells (LBCs) monitor individual pages located at any web site. To create a little brother to monitor an individual page, the user can input the page's URL, followed by a positive integer, as shown in the following example:

http://www.cs.pitt.edu/~chang/index.html 3

where the page's full URL must be given explicitly. The LBC will be created, with three most frequently found keywords assigned to it. The user can also assign the user's own keywords to a page specifically. If the user inputs the URL followed by a list of keywords, then the LBC will be assigned these keywords.

Step 4 Perform the Search

The Searcher accepts the URL of the target page, or a keyword, and performs the search by sending messages to all the LBCs and BBCs. For the LBCs that monitor individual pages, those similar to the target page or having a matched keyword will respond, and the URLs of the corresponding pages are returned. For the BBCs that are commercially available search engines such as Yahoo and Lycos, the returned page is processed to yield a list of URLs, and only those URLs who pages are similar to the target page or having a matched keyword will be retained. To calculate similarity, the frequencies for keyword occurrence are first computed. Then the similarity measures between that page and the target page are calculated. Currently we compute three statistical similarity measures: Jaccard, Cosine and Dice. The similarity measures obtained by these three methods are averaged, and the result value (the average) is used as the similarity between this page and the target page. The thresholds for similarity measures can be set by the user. If the user does not set the various thresholds for similarity retrieval as well as the number of keywords to be matched in a page, default values will be used in the search.

Step 5 Classify Pages for Recursive Search

The user can classify the retrieved pages using the Page Classifier to decide whether the user wants to follow a page recursively. First the user displays the results. Then the user chooses those pages to be followed. The user can give a search width and a search depth. The search width is the maximum number of pages to be retrieved similar to a target page in one search step. The search depth is the number of search steps. The Searcher will then perform the recursive search. The recursive search is very powerful and may yield a large number of URLs, which can be regarded as the virtual site to be classified by the Page Classifier.

The ideal user interface for the WAG may allow the user to visualize the BBCs and LBCs in a physical information space. The user interface may also provide a hypermap (a logical information hyperspace) so that the BBCs and LBCs can be associated with the target documents. The combined metaphor is thus a *Hypermapped Virtual World of Big Brothers and Little Brothers.*

1.5 Integrated Technology Comparison

1.5.1 *Taxonomy of Visual Querying Paradigms*

As discussed in Section 1.2, the information stored in a multimedia database is organized in a logical information space. Such logical information needs to be materialized in the physical information space in order to allow the user to view it. We are particularly interested in materializations performed by using visual techniques. Therefore, visual query systems, as defined in Section 1.1, are needed. A survey of VQSs proposed in the last years is presented in [5]. In that paper the VQSs are also compared along three taxonomy criteria: 1) the visual representation, that is adopted to present the reality of interest and the applicable language operators; 2) the expressive power, that indicates what can be done by using the query language; 3) the interaction strategies, that are available for performing the queries.

The query paradigm, which settles the way the query is performed and represented, is very much dependent on the way the data in the database (that are the query operands) are visualized. The basic types of visual representations analyzed in [5] are form-based, diagrammatic, and iconic, according to the visual formalism primarily employed, namely forms, diagrams, and icons. A fourth type is the hybrid representation, that uses two or more visual formalisms.

A form can be seen as a rectangular grid having components that may be any combination of cells of groups of cells (subform). A form is intended to be a generalization of a table. It facilitates the users by exploiting the usual tendency of people to use regular structures for information processing. Moreover, computer forms are abstracted from conventional paper forms familiar to people in their daily activities. Form-based representations have been the first attempt to provide users with friendly interfaces for data manipulation, taking advantage of the bidimensionality of the computer screen. QBE has been a pioneer form-based query language [68]. The queries are formulated by filling appropriate fields of prototypical tables that are visualized on the screen.

Representations based on diagrams are widely adopted in existing VQSs. We use the word diagram with a very broad meaning, referring to any graphics that encodes information using position and magnitude of geometrical objects and/or shows the relationships among components. Referring to the different types of visual representations analyzed in [48], our broad definition of diagram include graphs (such as bar, pie, histogram, scatterplot, etc.), graphic tables, network charts, structure diagrams, process diagrams. An important and useful characteristics of a diagram is that, if we modify its expression by following certain rules, its content can show new relationships [28]. Often, a diagram uses visual elements that are one to one associated with specific concept types. Diagrammatic representations adopt as typical query operators the selection of elements, the traversal on adjacent elements and the creation of a bridge among disconnected elements.

The iconic representation uses sets of icons to denote both the objects of the database and the operations to be performed on them. In an icon we distinguish the pictorial part, i.e. the image shown on the screen, and the semantic part, i.e. the meaning that such an image conveys. The simplest way to associate a meaning to an icon is by exploiting the similarity with the referred object. If we have to represent an abstract concept, or an action, that does not have a natural visual counterpart, we have to take into account different correlation modalities between the pictorial and the semantic part [5], In iconic VQSs, a query is expressed primarily by combining icons. For example, icons may be vertically combined to denote conjunction (logical AND) and horizontally combined to denote disjunction (logical OR).

All the above representations present complementary advantages and disadvantages. In existing systems, only one type of representation is usually available. This significantly restrict the database users that can benefit from the system. An effective database interface should supply multiple representations, in order to provide different interaction paradigms, each one with different characteristics. Therefore, each user, either novice or expert, can choose the most appropriate paradigm to interact with the system. Such a kind of multiparadigmatic interface for databases has been proposed in [10], where the selection of the appropriate interaction paradigm is made with reference to a user model that describes the user's interest and skills. Another interesting query paradigm is introduced in [16]. It is based on the idea that a Virtual Reality representation of the database application domain is available. An example was presented in Section 1.4.1.

The research on multiparadigmatic visual interfaces is conceptually similar to the research on multimodal interfaces for multimedia databases [7]. *Multimodal interfaces* support multiple input/output channels for human-computer interaction. The rationale for providing different input and output mechanisms is to accommodate user diversity. Humans, by their very nature, have unpredictable behavior, different skills and a wide range of interests. Since we cannot obtain a priori information on how each user wishes to interact with the computer system, we need to create customizable human-computer interfaces, so that the users themselves will choose the best way to interact with the system, possibly by exploiting multiple input and output media.

Effective user interfaces are difficult to build. Multimodal and multimedia user interfaces are even more difficult to build. They have further requirements that need to be fully satisfied. The qualities for multimodal and multimedia interfaces have been studied in [37], where the authors identified the following for consideration by the interface designer: (1) blended modalities, (2) appropriate resolvable ambiguity and tolerable probabilistic input capability such as whole sentence speech and gesture recognition, (3) distributed control of interaction among interface modules using protocols of cooperation, (4) real-time as well as after-the-fact access to interaction history, and (5) a highly modular architecture. In our view, one such quality, "blended modalities", requires special emphasis. Blending of modes means that at any point a user can continue input in a new, more pragmatically appropriate mode. The requirement "at any point" is not easy to achieve. In the multiparadigmatic interface described by [10], conditions for allowing a paradigm switch during query formulation are carefully demonstrated. The problem needs to be investigated both from the system's and from the cognitive viewpoint. Besides any model that can help predict user behavior, extensive experimentation is needed with users in order to make sure that the presence of several modes does not create mental overload.

Another issue of great importance to multiparadigmatic interface design is that the expressive power achievable in the different modes, i.e. the kind of database operations that can be performed, may not be the same. For the different visual paradigms analyzed above, form-based and diagrammatic paradigms often provide the same expressive power as the relational algebra [5], but VR only allows selection of objects and retrieval of objects for which similarity functions have been specified. This is even more evident when we consider interaction through different media. A database expert will be very comfortable when performing queries with SQL. The same expressive power cannot be achieved, with the current technology, if we use either speech or stylus-drawn gesture; such modes have the further disadvantage of providing ambiguous or probabilistic input. Until now the design of interfaces avoids the use of such kind of inputs, because their ambiguity is unmanageable. Next generation interfaces should include such input modes, if appropriate to the task the interface is for, and provide means to resolve specific ambiguities. One possibility is changing the interaction mode, so that in the new mode a certain operation is no longer ambiguous.

1.5.2 *Media Interaction Techniques*

The computer technology is providing everybody the possibility of directly exploring information resources. One the one side, this is extremely useful and exciting. On the other side, the ever growing amount of information at disposal generates cognitive overload and even anxiety, especially in novice or occasional users. The current user interfaces are usually too difficult for novice users and/or inadequate for experts, who need tools with many options, and consequently limiting the actual power of the computer.

We recognize three different needs of people exploring information: 1) to understand the content of the database, 2) to extract the information of interest, and 3) to browse the retrieved information in order to verify that it matches what they wanted. To satisfy such needs, the user-interface designers are challenged to invent more powerful search techniques, simpler query facilities, and more effective presentation methods. When creating new techniques, we have to keep in mind the variability of the user population, ranging from first- time or occasional versus frequent users, from task-domain novices versus experts, from naive (requesting very basic information) versus sophisticated users (interested in very detailed and specific information). Since there is not a technique capable to satisfy the need of all such classes of users, the proposed techniques should be conceived as having a basic set of features, while additional features can be requested as users gain experience with the system.

A user interacting the first time with an information system should be allowed to easily navigate into the system in order to get a better idea of the kind of data that can be accessed. Since the information systems become larger and larger, while each user is generally interested in only a small portion of data, one of the primary goal of a designer is to develop some kind of filters to reduce the set of data that need to be taken into account. At Xerox in recent years a group of researchers has developed several information visualization techniques, with the aim of helping the users understand

and process the information stored into the system [59]. They have created the "information workspaces", i.e. computer environments in which the information is moved from the original source, such as networked databases, and where several tools are at disposal of users for browsing and manipulating the information. One of the main characteristic of such workspaces is that they offer graphical representations of information that facilitate rapid perception of the overall patterns. Moreover, they use 3D and/or distortion techniques to show some portion of the information at a greater level of detail, but keeping it within a larger context. These are usually called fish eye techniques, but it is clearer to call them "focus + context", that better gives the idea of showing an area of interest (the focus) quite large and with detail, while the other areas are shown successively smaller and in less detail. Such an approach is very effective when applied to documents, and also to graphs. It achieves a smooth integration of local detail and global context. It has more advantages of other approaches to filter information, such as zooming or the use of two or more views, one of the entire structure and the other of a zoomed portion. The former approach shows local details but looses the overall structure, the latter requires extra screen space and forces the viewer to mentally integrate the views. In the "focus + context" approach, it is effective to provide animated transitions when changing the focus, so that the user remain oriented across dynamic changes of the display avoiding unnecessary cognitive load.

Shneiderman points out that the perfect search paradigm that retrieves all and only all of the desired items is unattainable [62]. Still, he suggests some ways for achieving flexible search. A first possibility for searches within documents is to allow "rainbow search". It is based on the fact that most word processors support several features (different fonts, sizes, styles, etc.) and text attributes (footnotes, references, etc.), therefore it could be useful to allow a search of all words in italic or a search through only footnotes. Another new technique is "search expansion": when looking for documents using some term, the system can also suggest more general (or specific) terms, synonyms, or related terms from a thesaurus or a data dictionary in order to perform a more complete search.

Search techniques applicable to multimedia data are very interesting. For instance, sound is included among data types of multimedia databases, and it could constitute both an output (as a response of the system) or an input (as a query). Some existing electronic dictionaries already provide both the meaning of words as well as their pronunciation, so offering full information on every requested word. In [49] the authors present "sonification", i.e. the mapping of data to sound parameters, as a rich but still unexplored technique for understanding complex data. The current technology has favored the development of the graphical dimension of user interfaces while limiting the use of the auditory dimension. This is also because the properties of the aural cues are not yet well understood as those of visual signals. Moreover, sound alone cannot convey accurate information without a visual context. The tool described in [49] uses sound to complement visualization, thus enhancing the presentation of complex data. Sound can be useful in some situations, for instance to set up an alarm when working with the computer to remember to do something at a certain time. The opposite is also true, i.e. visualization can help in analyzing sound. For example, it is useful for an expert performing a detailed analysis of a certain sound to look at the graphics of its amplitude in a given time interval.

We can think of a sound search in a music database. The user hums some notes and the system provides the list of symphonies that contain that string of notes. This is not difficult to achieve provided that the user input the notes in an unambiguous way (for example entering the notes on a staff connected to the computer) and the search is performed on the score sheets of symphonies stored with the music.

A system called Hyperbook uses sounds as an imitation of bird calls (either in the melody or in the tone) to retrieve specific bird families within an electronic book on birds [65]. The user can also retrieve a bird by drawing a silhouette of the bird. The descriptions provided by both techniques are incomplete since it is difficult for the user to give an exact specification. Hyperbook solves such queries on the basis of a data model, called metric spatial object data, which represents objects in the real world as points in a metric space. In order to select the candidate objects, distances are evaluated by the system, enabling the user to choose those objects (birds) which have a minimal distance from the query in the metric space.

Interesting and useful techniques can be exploited for searching images in a database on the basis of their pictorial contents. Given a sketch of a house, the user may want to find all pictures that contain that house. With the visual query system called Pictorial Query-By-Example (PQBE), Papadias and Sellis proposes an approach to the problem of content-based querying geographic and image databases [55]. PQBE makes use of the spatial nature of spatial relations in the formulation of a query. This should allow users to formulate queries in a language close to their thinking. As in the case of the well-known Query-By-Example, PQBE generalizes from the example given by the user, but, instead of having skeleton relational tables, there are skeleton images.

Several researchers are proposing interaction environments exploiting different techniques than the visual ones. In [58] an interactive multimedia prototype is shown that allows users seating in front of a terminal to experience with a virtual reality environment. The system integrates a number of key technologies and the purpose of the prototype is to experiment such new interaction possibilities. The users communicate with each other and with artificial agents through speech. The prototype also includes audio rendering, hand gesture recognition and body- position-sensing technology. The authors admit that their system is limited by the current technology, but they are confident that in a couple of years what is today expensive or yet impossible will be commonplace.

Traditional languages such as SQL allow the user to specify exact queries that indicate matches on specific field values. Non-expert and/or occasional users of the database are generally not able to directly formulate a query whose result fully satisfies their needs, at least in their first attempts. Therefore, the users may prefer to formulate a complex query by a succession of progressive simple queries, i.e. step by step, by first asking general questions, obtaining preliminary results, and then revisiting such outcomes to further refine the query in order to extract the result they are interested in. Since the results obtained up to a certain point may not converge to the expected data, a nonmonotone query progression should be allowed. During this process of progressive querying, an appropriate visualization of the preliminary results could give a significant feedback to the user. Moreover, it will provide hints about the right way to proceed towards the most appropriate final query. Otherwise, the user will immediately backtrack and try a different alternative path. Often, even if the user is satisfied with the result, he or she is also challenged to further investigate the database, and as a result may acquire more information from it.

The above described advantages of performing a progressive query through visual interaction, also displaying, in a suitable representation, the obtained partial results, has lead to the Visual Querying and Result Hypercube (VQRH), which is a tool that provides a multiparadigmatic approach for progressive querying and result visualization in database interaction [16].

Using the VQRH tool, the user interacts with the database by means of a sequence of partial queries, each displayed, together with the corresponding result, as one slice of the VQR Hypercube. Successive slices on the Hypercube store partial queries performed at successive times. Therefore, the query history is presented in a 3D perspective, and a particular partial query on a slice may be brought to the front of the Hypercube for further refinement by means of a simple mouse click.

Another powerful technique for querying a database is "dynamic query", that allows to do range search on multi-key data sets. The query is formulated through direct manipulation of graphical widgets such as buttons and sliders, one widget being used for every key. The result of the query is displayed graphically and quickly on the screen. It is important that the results fit on a single screen and that they are displayed quickly, since the users should be able to perform tens of queries in a few seconds and immediately see the results. Giving a query, a new query is easily formulated by moving with the mouse the position of a slider. This gives a sense of power but also fun to the user, that is challenged to try other queries and see how the result is modified. As in the case of the progressive query, the user can ask general queries and see what the results are, then he or she can better refine the query. An application of dynamic queries is shown in [62] and refers to real-estate database. There are sliders for location, number of bedrooms, price of homes in the Washington, D. C. area. The user moves these sliders to find appropriate homes. Selected homes are indicated by bright points of light on a Washington, D. C. map shown on the screen.

1.6 Research Challenges

As mentioned earlier, the key to content-based access of multimedia is the efficient and effective creation, encoding and maintenance of associations among media objects. The interaction metaphors employ multiple paradigms to facilitate making these associations. Virtual library, hypermap, vertical/horizontal reasoners, big/little brothers, etc. are some of the useful interaction metaphors to accomplish this goal. Although the metaphors themselves are conceptual, their effective incorporation into the user interface for multimedia often dictates the use of visual querying mechanisms. As discussed in Section 1.2, the appropriate interaction metaphor may involve a combination of several information spaces. To support visual querying, a challenge is to integrate the user's view of the information spaces with the underlying semantic model such as the InfoSleuth's ontology model. In fact, it seems that the *Hypermapped Virtual World* metaphor is quite compatible with the ontology model, so that an integrated model with four or five layers may do the job.

The use of visual interfaces combining different query mechanisms represents a step toward a truly effective utilization of multimedia information systems by large classes of users. The query mechanisms include speech, sound, gestures, etc., but the user interface should be highly visual to enable the user to gradually grasp the database contents, the navigation technique, the visual reasoning strategy, as well as the querying process. As it was pointed out in [9], in the last ten years the research on visual query systems passed from conceiving merely hypothetical and vague ideas to building real systems. Yet, much more need to be done, both from the theoretical and the application-oriented point of view. Since the success of a complex application is largely due to the way it matches the users' expectations as well as their skills and learning ability, more efforts should be devoted to experimenting and validating the proposed interfaces, in order to provide an accurate evaluation of their usability, which is a crucial factor to the practical utilization of such interfaces for multimedia information systems.

Multimedia interface design involves various issues [7]. In determining the criteria for the evaluation of visual and multimedia user interface we should also take into consideration similar criteria for evaluating visual programming languages [42]. For content-based access of multimedia, we need also ask: Can relevant associations be easily discovered? Can new an associations be easily created? How are the associations encoded and maintained? These are some of the critical issues to be evaluated.

Although visual interfaces are supposedly "universal", the meanings of visual symbols (icons) do shift across cultural boundaries. There is no internationally accepted standard of visual symbols. An approach to solve this problem is to provide multilingual interfaces so that the user can shift to the user's native language in an interactive session. AMIS2, for example, allows the user to switch between English and Chinese any time during the interaction. This could be further augmented by speech feedback to enhance user's understanding. Again, it may be possible to integrate all these multilingual, multimodal, multiparadigmatic aspects in the unified information model.

Bibliography

Ahmed, Z., L. Wanger, and P. Kochevar, "An Intelligent Visualization System for Earth Science Data Analysis," Journal of Visual Languages and Computing, vol. 5, no. 4, pp. 307-320, December 1994.

Anupam, V. and C. L. Bajaj, "Shastra: Multimedia Collaborative Design Environment," IEEE Multimedia, pp. 39-49, 1994.

The Araneus Project, http://poincare.inf.uniroma3.it:8080/Araneus/ araneus.html, 1996.

Arens, Y., C. A. Knoblock, and W. Shen, "Query reformulation for dynamic information integration," Journal of Intelligent In formation Systems, 1996.

Batini, C., T. Catarci, M. F. Costabile, and S. Levialdi, Visual Query Systems, Technical Report N. 04.91, Dipartimento di Informatica e Sistemistica, Universit' di Roma "La Sapienza", Italy, 1991 (revised in 1993).

Beaudouin-Lafon, M., Beyond the Workstation: Mediaspaces and Augmented Reality, pp. 9-18, in Blattner, M. M. and R. B. Dannenberg (Eds.), Multimedia Interface Design, Addison-Wesley, 1992.

Blattner, M. M. and R. B. Dannenberg (Eds.), Multimedia Interface Design, Addison-Wesley, 1992.

Caporal, J. and Y. Viemont, "Maps as a Metaphor in a Geographical Hypermedia System," Journal of Visual Languages and Computing, vol. 8, no. 1, pp. 3-25, February 1997.

Catarci, T. and M. F. Costabile (Eds.), "Special Issue on Visual Query Systems," Journal of Visual Languages and Computing, vol. 6, no. 1, 1995.

Catarci, T., S. K. Chang, M. F. Costabile, S. Levialdi, and G. Santucci, "A Graph-based Framework for Multiparadigmatic Visual Access to Databases," IEEE Transactions on Knowledge and Data Engineering, vol. 8, No. 3,, 1996, 455-475.

Catarci, T., S. K. Chang, L. B. Dong, and G. Santucci, "A Prototype Web-At-a-Glance System for Intelligent Information Retrieval," Proc. of SEKE'97, pp. 440-449, Madrid, Spain, June 18-20, 1997.

Chang, H., T. Hou, A. Hsu, and S. K. Chang, "The Management and Applications of Tele-Action Objects," ACM Journal of Multimedia Systems, vol. 3, no. 5-6, pp. 204-216, Springer Verlag, 1995.

Chang, H., T. Hou, A. Hsu, and S. K. Chang, "Tele-Action Objects for an Active Multimedia System," Proceedings of Second Int'l IEEE Conf. on Multimedia Computing and Systems, pp. 106-113, Washington, D.C., May 15-18, 1995.

Chang, S. K. and J. S. Ke, "Translation of Fuzzy Queries for Relational Database System," IEEE Transactions on Pattern Analysis and Machine Intelligence, vol. PAMI-1, no. 3, pp. 281-294, July 1979.

Chang, S. K., "Visual reasoning for information retrieval from very large databases," Journal of Visual Languages and Computing, vol. 1, no. 1, pp. 41-58, 1990.

Chang, S. K., M. F. Costabile, and S. Levialdi, "Reality Bites Progressive Querying and Result Visualization in Logical and VR Spaces," Proc. of IEEE Symposium on Visual Languages, pp. 100-109, St. Luis, October 1994.

Chang, S. K., "Toward a Theory of Active Index," Journal of Visual Languages and Computing, vol. 5, pp. 101-118, 1995.

Chang, S. K., G. Costagliola, G Pacini, M. Tucci, G. Tortora, B. Yu, and J. S. Yu, "Visual Language System for User Interfaces," IEEE Software, pp. 33-44, March 1995.

Chang, S. K., "Active Index for Content-Based Medical Image Retrieval," Journal of Computerized Medical Imaging and Graph ics, Special Issue on Medical Image Databases (S. Wong and H. K. Huang, eds.), pp. 219-229, Elsevier Science Ltd., 1996.

Chang, S. K. and E. Jungert, Symbolic Projection for Image Information Retrieval and Spatial Reasoning, Academic Press, London, 1996.

Chang, S. K., "Extending Visual Languages for Multimedia," IEEE Multimedia Magazine, vol. 3, no. 3, pp. 18-26, Fall 1996.

Chang, S. K., D. Graupe, K. Hasegawa, and H. Kordylewski, "An Active Multimedia Information System for Information Retrieval, Discovery and Fusion," International Journal of Software Engineering and Knowledge Engineering, vol. 8, no. 1, World Scientific Pub. Co., March 1998.

Chawathe, S. and et al., "The TSIMMIS Project: Integration of Heterogeneous Information Sources," Proc. of IPSJ Conference, pp. 7-18, 1994.

Chen, P. W., G. Barry, and S. K. Chang, "A Smart WWW Page Model and its Application to On-Line Information Retrieval in Hyperspace," Proc. of Pacific Workshop on Distributed Multimedia Systems DMS'96, pp. 220-227, Hong Kong, June 27-28, 1996.

D'Atri, A., P. Di Felice, and M. Moscarini, "Dynamic query interpretation in relational databases," Information Sciences, vol. 14, no. 3, 1989.

D'Atri, A. and L. Tarantino, "From Browsing to Querying," Data Engineering, vol. 12, no. 2, pp. 46-53, June 1989.

Dutta, S., "Qualitative Spatial Reasoning: A Semi-Quantitative Approach Using

Fuzzy Logic," Conference Proceedings on Very Large Spatial Databases, pp. 345-364, Santa Barbara, July 17-19, 1989.

Eco, U., A Theory of Semiotics, Indiana University Press, 1975.

Etzioni, O. and D. Weld, "A Softbot-Based Interface to the Internet," CACM, vol. 37, no. 7, 1994.

Faloutsous, C. et al., "Efficient and Effective Querying by Image Content," IBM Research Division Almaden Research Center Technical Report RJ9543 (83074), August 1993.

Faloutsous, C., R. Barber, M. Flickner, J. Hafner, W. Niblack, D. Petkovic, and W. Equitz, "Efficient and Effective Querying by Image Content," Journal of Intelligent Information Systems, vol. 3, pp. 231-262, 1994.

Fox, E. A., "Advances in Interactive Digital Multimedia Systems," IEEE Computer, vol. 24, no. 10, pp. 9-21, October 1991.

Gould, L. and W. Finzer, "Programming by Rehearsal," Byte, pp. 187-210, June 1984.

Graupe, D. and H. Kordylewski, "A Large-Memory Storage and Retrieval Neural Network for Browsing and Medical Diagnosis," Proc. ANNIE Conf., St. Louis, Missouri, 1996.

Halbert, D. C., "Programming by Example," Xerox Office Systems Division, TR OSD-T8402, Dec 1984.

Hanne, K. and H. Bullinger, "Multimodal Communication: Integrating Text and Gestures," Multimedia Interface Design, pp. 127-138, Addison-Wesley, 1992.

Hill, W., D. Wroblewski, T. McCandiess, and R. Cohen, "Architectural Qualities and Principles for Multimodal and Multimedia Interfaces," Multimedia Interface Design, pp. 311-318, Addison-Wesley, 1992.

Huang, K. T., "Visual Interface Design Systems," Principles of Visual Programming Systems, Prentice-Hall, 1990.

Ignatius, E., H. Senay, and J. Favre, "An Intelligent System for Task-Specific Visualization Assistance," Journal of Visual Languages and Computing, vol. 5, no. 4, pp. 321-338, December 1994.

Jungert, E. and S. K. Chang, "Human- and System-Directed Fusion of Multimedia and Multimodal Information using the Sigma Tree Data Model," Prof. of VISual'97: Second International Conference on Visual Information Systems, San Diego, California, Dec 15-17, 1997.

Kawata, Y., A. Kawasaki, W. Udomkitwanit, A. Yabu, H. Kobayashi, P. Wijayarathna, and M. Maekawa, "EVE: A visual specification environment with support for formal descriptions of physical properties," Proc. of First Int'l Conf. on Visual Information Systems, pp. 518-529, Melbourne, Australia, February 5-6, 1996.

Kiper, J. D., E. Howard, and C. Ames, "Criteria for Evaluation of Visual Programming Languages," Journal of Visual Languages and Computing, vol. 8, no. 2, pp. 175-192, 1997.

Kovacevic, S., "A Compositional Model of Human-Computer Dialogs," Multimedia Interface Design, pp. 373-404, Addison-Wesley, 1992.

Lang, L., "GIS Comes to Life," Computer Graphics World, pp. 27-36, October 1992.

Laurini, R. and F. Milleret-Raffort, "Principles of Geomatic Hypermaps," Proceedings of the 4th International Symposium on Spatial Data Handling, pp. 642-651, Zurich, Switzerland, June 23-27, 1990.

Levy, A.Y., A. Rajaraman, and J.J. Ordille, "Querying-Answering Algorithms for Information Agents," Proceedings of the Thirteenth National Conference on Artificial Intelligence (AAAI-96), 1996.

Little, T. D. C. and D. Venkatesh, "The Use of Multimedia Technology in Distance Learning," Proceedings of IEEE Int'l Conference on Multimedia Networking, pp. 3-17, Aizu, Japan, September 1995.

Lohse, G. L., K. A Biolsi, N. Walker, and H. H. Rueter, "A Classification of Visual Representations," Communications of the ACM, vol. 37, no. 12, pp. 36-49, 1994.

Madhyastha, T. M. and D. A. Reed, "Data Sonification: Do You See What I Hear?," IEEE Software, vol. 12, no. 2, pp. 45-56, March 1995.

Motro, A., "BAROQUE: An exploratory interface to relational data bases," ACM Trans. on Office Information Systems, vol. 4, no. 2, pp. 164-181, April 1986.

Motro, A., "VAGUE:A User Interface to Relational Database that Permits Vague Queries," ACM Trans. on Office Information Systems, vol. 6(3), pp. 187-214, July 1988.

Myers, Brad A., "Visual Programming, Programming by Example, and Program Visualization: A Taxonomy," Proceedings of SIG CHI'86, pp. 59-66, Boston, MA, April 13-17, 1986.

Myers, B. A., Creating User Interfaces by Demonstration, Academic Press, Boston, 1988.

Niblack, W. and M. Flickner, "Find me the Pictures that look like this: IBM's Image Query Project," Advanced Imaging, April 1993.

Papadias, D. and T. Sellis, "Pictorial Query-By-Example," Journal of Visual Languages and Computing, vol. 6, no. 1, pp. 53-72, 1995.

Rau, H. and S. Skiena, "Dialing for Documents: An Experiment in Information Theory," Journal of Visual Languages and Computing, vol. 7, no. 1, March 1996.

Reis, H., D. Brenner, and J. Robinson, "Multimedia Communications in Health Care," New York Academy of Sciences Conference on Extended Clinical Consulting by Hospital Computer Networks, March 1992.

Rich, C., R. C. Walters, C. Strohecker, Y. Schabes, W. T. Freeman, M. C. Torrance, A. R. Golding, and M. Roth, "Demonstration of an Interactive Multimedia Environment," IEEE Computer, vol. 27, no. 12, pp. 15-22, 1994.

Robertson, G. G., S. K. Card, and J. D. Mackinlay, "Information Visualization using 3D Interactive Animation," Communications of the ACM, vol. 36, no. 4, pp. 57-71, 1993.

Robertson, G. G., S. K. Card, and J. D. Mackinlay, "Nonimmersive Virtual Reality," IEEE Computer, vol. 26, no. 2, pp. 81-83, 1993.

Santini, S. and R. Jain, "The Graphical Specification of Similar ity Queries," Journal of Visual Languages and Computing, vol. 7, no. 4, pp. 403-421, December 1996.

Shneiderman, B., Designing the User Interface, Addison Wesley Publishing Company, 1992.

Smith, D. C., Pygmalion: A Computer Program to Model and Stimulate Creative Thought, Birkhauser, Stuttgart, 1977.

Stoakley, R., M. J. Conway, and R. Pausch, "Virtual Reality on a WIM: Interactive Worlds in Miniature," Proc. of CHI-95, pp. 265-272, Denver, Colorado, May 7-11, 1995.

Tabuchi, "Hyperbook," Proc. of International Conference on Multimedia Information Systems, Singapore, 1991.

Wald, J. A. and P. G. Sorenson, "Resolving the query inference problem using Steiner trees," ACM Trans. on Database Systems, vol. 9, no. 3, pp. 348-368, 1984.

Williams, M. D., "What makes RUBBIT run?," International Journal on Man-Machine Studies, vol. 21, no. 4, pp. 333-352, October 1984.

Zloof, M. M., "Query by Example," IBM Systems Journal, vol. 16, no. 4, pp. 324 343, 1977.

ATM BASED NETWORKING APPLICATIONS: A BC TEL ADVANCED COMMUNICATIONS PERSPECTIVE

ELEANOR JANG, P.ENG

BC TEL Advanced Communications
Suite 2600 - 4720 Kingsway
Burnaby, B.C. V5H 4N2
Email: eleanor_jang@bctel.net

Abstract

This paper discusses a Service Providers' perspectives on business strategy and network architecture for the delivery of value added services across an ATM infrastructure.

1 Telecommunications Industry Issues

The Telecommunications industry is evolving from a regulated monopoly to a highly competitive set of businesses. The industry is faced with balancing market demands and technology evolution with social policies, subsidies and content. For the incumbent carriers, the future is one of reduced market share but for a new service provider, the opportunity for growth is exponential. In either case, there are significant challenges regardless of one's starting position.

For an incumbent carrier such as BC TELECOM, a Line of Business (LOB) approach was adopted to evolve a monopoly culture to an entrepreneurial culture by establishing arms length divisions to compete in new markets.

2 Background

BC TEL Advanced Communications (BCTAC) is a Service Provider within BC TELECOM, the regional Telephone Company for the Province of British Columbia. BCTAC was established in 1991 to provide unregulated high speed network services in a fully competitive environment. In 1994, BCTAC merged with the regulated Data and Integrated services division to become a single Business Unit responsible for all data services for BC TELECOM.

In this business of early adopters and laggards, BCTAC chose to be early by building a provincial, leading edge Asynchronous Transfer Mode (ATM) network to deliver broadband services.

3 Key Business Strategies

In an immature or evolving market, business practices tend to be short lived. Established service models are ineffective because of the rapidly changing landscape of competitors and technology. The major success factors are flexibility and speed to market in three key areas:

1. innovative solutions,
2. value added services,
3. market driven pricing.

3.1 Innovative Solutions

Solutions to customer business problems require innovation to evolve a core set of standard services and to develop enhanced offerings for major opportunities in industry verticals. The challenge involves constantly leveraging network investment and experience to create the solution.

A solution is different from a service. A solution uses knowledge of the customer's business environment to create a new capability aimed at solving specific customer problems. A service is more generic, typically relying on a customer to determine on his own how to use a new capability to solve business problems. This distinction implies uniqueness from a customer perspective and complexity from a service provider perspective. In addition, re-engineering of existing processes may form part of the solution. Customers tend to under estimate the amount of their input and involvement required to successfully implement a solution. Ultimately, service providers take a leadership role when developing the solution with the customer.

This approach to business redefines the meaning of network standards. The definition changes from a standard being a common platform or network element and configuration to a level of options and flexibility available on the network to be optimized for the customers' requirements.

3.2 Value Added Services

Moving from commodity services to value added services enables a service provider to position solutions in the market that have an improved rate of return or in the case of BC TELECOM, create new revenue opportunities and use the value proposition to a customer as a major differentiator in a competitive market.

Improving rates of return is not an easy exercise. Value added services combined with innovative solutions pose challenges of scale to a service provider. One must adopt a "learning culture" to be able to take a solution developed for one customer and apply it to the next. In addition, gaining operational efficiencies requires not only a learning culture but also advancements in networking technology.

For a telephone company moving from a monopoly to a competitive environment, market share can only decrease as new entrants enter the business and drive prices down. To maintain growth and to find replacement revenue streams, BC TELECOM through BCTAC created a new set of services that reached further into the customer environment and moved higher in the value chain. Customers must recognize the value a service provides before they will pay a premium.

As in any competitive business, differentiation is another key to success. The more one can differentiate from the competition and add value to the customer, the higher the market value.

3.3 Market Driven Pricing

Pricing for all services must be aggressive. Not only against the competitors' services but also to offset any business justification for a customer owned and managed infrastructure. In any situation where customers have mission critical applications, convincing a customer to outsource can be difficult. Ultimately, the service provider must have a cheaper and more reliable solution to even be considered. In many cases, customers may under-estimate their internal costs to support their infrastructure and are subjective in determining costs and value.

4 Network Architecture

Designing a network architecture to deliver on these key business strategies is a major challenge. The traditional circuit switched architecture for the Public Switched Telephone Network (PSTN) and digital data services is proving to be inadequate for virtual, multimedia, interactive and collaborative applications which form the basis of value added services. A fast packet architecture using ATM is the approach many service providers such as BCTAC are pursuing today. Figure 1 shows a tiered switching architecture.

4.1 Tier 1

Tier 1 is based on a star architecture with redundant links to Tier 2. The primary purpose of Tier 1 is service adaptation. Service adaptation at the network edge simplifies the network architecture while maintaining flexibility and scaleability for multiple services on a minimal number of switching platforms. This tier contains the "service intelligence" i.e. the service characteristics from a customer perspective. By having the service functionality close to the customer and in a single network tier, service providers are better positioned to manage the network. Maintenance and operations personnel are better equipped to troubleshoot service problems as devices in this tier tend to have specialized diagnostics.

The service adaptation devices in the initial architecture are service specific i.e. not an integrated switching platform but smaller, cost effective specialized elements. Typically, technology advances at different rates so by having discrete devices per service, one can get to market faster with a lower initial investment. In a leading edge environment where technology evolves rapidly, the low initial investment and speed to market is highly desirable. The equipment in this tier is typically amortized over short time frames and is seen more as a throw away investment. As technology matures, this tier will evolve to an integrated, multiple services platform.

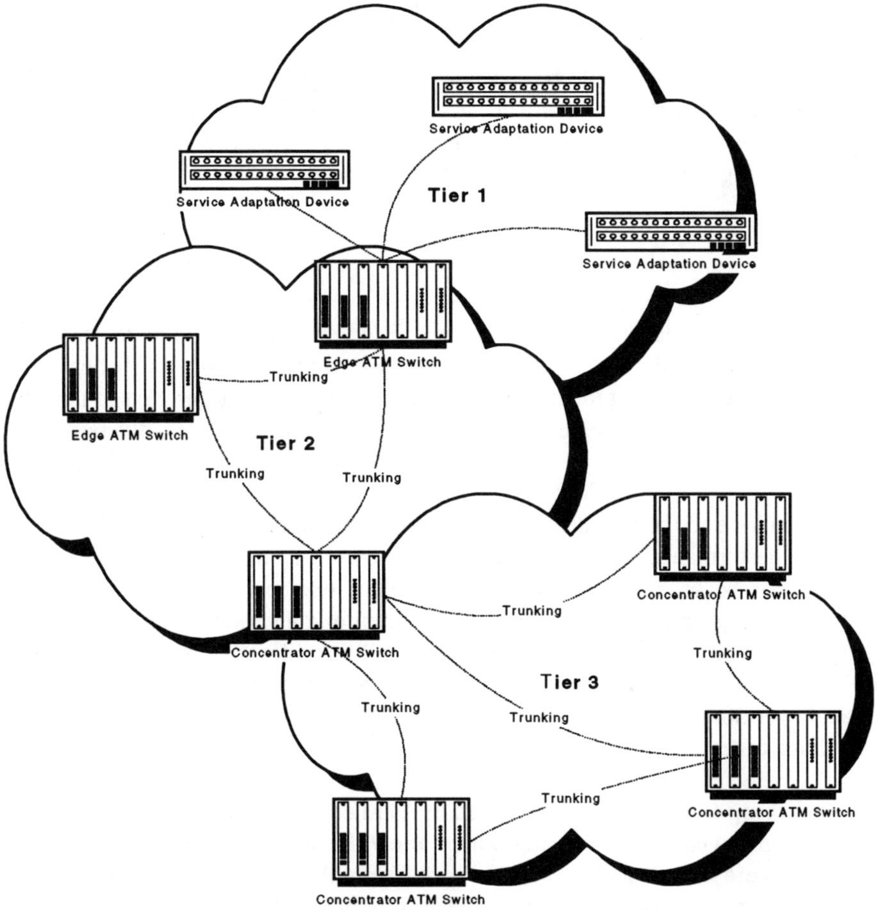

Figure 1: Tiered Switching Architecture

This tier is analogous to a distributed processing model versus a centralized processing one. The service intelligence and network resources in this tier are distributed at the network edge based on customer requirements. Utilization of the network elements may not be as efficient in a distributed model however, this is the tradeoff to gain flexibility and improved performance. In addition, having intelligent edge devices may create efficiencies in the core i.e. traffic management capabilities utilizing buffering and queuing techniques at the edge enable better utilization of the core network resources.

Service adaptation at the edge also allows a service provider to create uniqueness by serving area. The advantage here would be to selectively offer unique services cost effectively. These could be specialized high end services for a small market or a specific solution to compete against a regional carrier such as cable companies. Other advantages include being able to go to market faster in key areas without having to upgrade or evolve the entire network.

4.2 Tier 2

Tier 2 is the first level of concentration. Edge switches are used to "fan out" service adaptation devices, switch locally and within regions for better trunk utilization by minimizing the need to back haul. The ring configuration of the edge switches also increases network availability through route diversity and redundancy.

This tier allows for better latency characteristics within the region. Latency can be a major performance issue for some applications. In many ring architectures, latency can be an issue depending on whether one has bi-directional or uni-directional rings over large distances. By maintaining a regional ring, the effective distances are minimal. Tier 2 is a series of small ring-like islands that connect to a host switch. Depending on market demand and geography, these islands can extend over a metropolitan area or through a series of communities. They are not long haul systems.

The switching elements in Tier 2 are small ATM edge switches. They are typically upgraded first generation switches which allow the service provider to extend the life of the core infrastructure. The network capabilities of second generation ATM core switches are generally not required in this tier. This tier may evolve to the integrated, multiple services platform of Tier 1 which will further simplify the overall architecture to just core and edge tiers.

Tier 2 is a pure ATM switching environment. It introduces minimal overhead in terms of network performance and provides a cost effective means to increase reach and network reliability.

4.3 Tier 3

Tier 3 is the second level of concentration, connects to other carriers' ATM networks and houses gateways to other non-ATM networks. Gateways typically are required for service or network interworking of the service adaptation devices to non-ATM networks.

Regional carrier class core switches are connected together with high capacity trunks in a meshed or ring configuration. This represents the core of the network where fast switching and minimal latency are critical design parameters. The maximum number of hops end to end in this architecture is also important in minimizing network latency. Generally, trunk utilization is higher in Tier 3 than Tier 2 and higher in Tier 2 than in Tier 1.

The traffic management capabilities of the core switches are extremely important in this tier. Of all the tiers, efficiency in this tier is very important from a cost containment perspective. Trunking costs between Tier 3 concentrator switches tend to be high because underlying SONET transport systems are typically used to carry the traffic from concentrator switch to concentrator switch.

The trunks in this tier will vary from OC3c to OC12c depending on network requirements. Typically, high capacity trunks are cost effective due to port density limitations in first and second generation ATM switches. These limitations will disappear as technology progresses.

4.4 Access Architecture

The access architecture from the customer premise to the network edge is shown in Figure 2. The data termination unit converts different media types in the access loop. It is typically a non-intelligent device, however the Customer Interface Unit (CIU) is intelligent. It acts as a physical demarcation for the service and it has operations, maintenance, administration and provisioning features. The CIU can be remotely monitored by the service provider's network operations center to ensure service integrity.

In today's architecture, the role of the CIU is extremely important as it interacts with intelligent devices in the customer network for layer 3 routing. The CIU in turn, communicates over the ATM network to other CIUs within the customer's Closed User Group (CUG) to provide network routing. The CIU does not interact directly with the ATM network for any routing functionality. The CUG configuration is controlled through the Tier 1 network elements. From a CIU perspective, it views the core as a static private network.

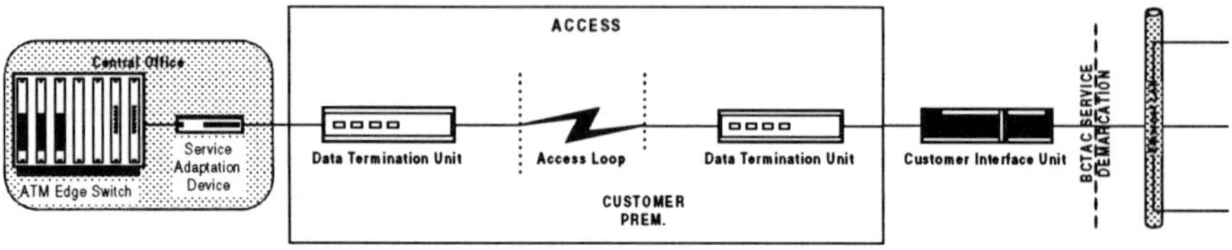

Figure 2: Access Architecture

Because the CIU is a layer 3 device, it requires much processing power. It also has multiple higher layer capabilities and options such as packet filtering that can be customized based on the customer's network requirements. With these complexities, the CIU is typically the bottleneck in the service trading off features and functionality with throughput.

Because the CIU interacts with the customer's network directly, enhanced surveillance features are necessary. Not only will the service provider's operations center monitor this element, customer's may also want some form of monitoring capability by their own operations center or network management application. This level of network visibility can pose a security risk to the network however more and more customers want some form of visibility.

As technology evolves, the network elements in Tier 1 are becoming as rich in capabilities and functionality as the layer 3 CIUs. Over time, the layer 3 routing will migrate to the integrated, multiple services platform of Tier 1. Instead of the intelligent access architecture of today, the service provider will have a simple, non-intelligent access to the customer premise leaving the intelligence in the network edge.

5 Network Centered Services

Conceptually, a network centered service is one which involves interaction between the service provider's network infrastructure and the customer network infrastructure. The service provider's network governs the delivery of service to the end customer. The service can be an application available on the network and/or connectivity controlled by the network.

5.1 Connectivity Services

One advantage of an ATM-based network is the ability to carry multiple types of traffic over a single switching architecture. This capability enables a service provider to deliver various connectivity solutions. For network centered services, the CIU in conjunction with the core network and the customer network can control the feature set associated with the service i.e. routing, bandwidth on demand, etc. Several connectivity services are available today: Native Speed LAN, Internet access and Video Conferencing. These services involve some form of network interaction with the customer.

Today's ATM-based network architecture is capable of delivering wide area connectivity at local area network speeds i.e. Native Speed LAN. Another common term for this type of service is Transparent LAN Service (TLS). The options range from 10 Mbps Ethernet to 100 Mbps Fast Ethernet in wide area network or metropolitan area network configurations. Variations of layer 3 routing are also possible using the CIU on the customer premise. Internet access is a form of specialized connectivity using a layer 3 protocol. Connectivity options for this service range from 1.544 Mbps to 155 Mbps (OC3c speeds).

Video conferencing is a connectivity service that delivers streams of data in point to point, point to multi-point or broadcast configurations across the ATM network. The conference controller resides in the network so for this particular service, there is full interaction with the CIU which allows an end user to dynamically set up the service on demand.

Another variation of connectivity is a virtual leased line service. Connectivity in this network centered model is not like the circuit switched network. There are minimal physical constraints in the network. Most limitations on speed and throughput are logical constraints which are controlled through network management applications on an end to end basis. For dynamic connectivity services, a customer controlled application would interface with the network management applications to logically configure connectivity solutions on a customer demand basis. The value to the customer is to allow him to control and optimize the use of his network service. This level of flexibility and sophistication is not a full reality today but certainly attainable in the near future.

Connectivity services are not just about variations in speed and throughput, they must also have service interworking and network interworking capabilities. In any enterprise network, different types of services exist. In a network centered service model, it would be unrealistic to assume that customers' needs could be served by a homogenous end to end environment. Interworking of various services is a more realistic network requirement that provides a logical evolution path for existing networks.

5.2 Application Services

Application services are an overlay to the network infrastructure. These services are accessible to the customer through some form of connectivity service that provides both access and service interworking. The service adaptation function of ATM is important to enable multiple application types to be accessible to a customer from the network. Some examples of application services are security/firewall, content, and Customer Network Management.

Basic security services is a network centered application. A centralized security/firewall server which applies security rules per connection resides in the network. This is a shared network resource that is generally not flexible. As security can be unique to each customer, enhanced security/firewall services are provisioned in the access as a CIU.

Content is really a form of network centered data that is made available to customers on the network on a subscription basis. Caching strategies are typically used to distribute content across the network to minimize latency because many of the content applications valued by users are very sensitive to latency e.g. gaming. The public Internet is a good example of where content plays an important role.

Customer Network Management services is a value add version of Native Speed LAN. The value add component is pro-active network analysis. By monitoring and reporting network statistics and trends in real time, customers are able to watch their network service performance. In addition, customer elements may also be monitored by the network which provides enhanced visibility to the customer on an end to end basis beyond the network demarcation. This applications reaches through the network into the customer's network.

5.3 The Cloud Model

In a network centered architecture, telecommunications becomes a definition of how people communicate versus how they physically connect. Figure 3 shows a typical view of a cloud model of communications.

The traditional network consisted of leased lines in a point to point configuration. Lines were physically meshed to enable any point to any point communications.

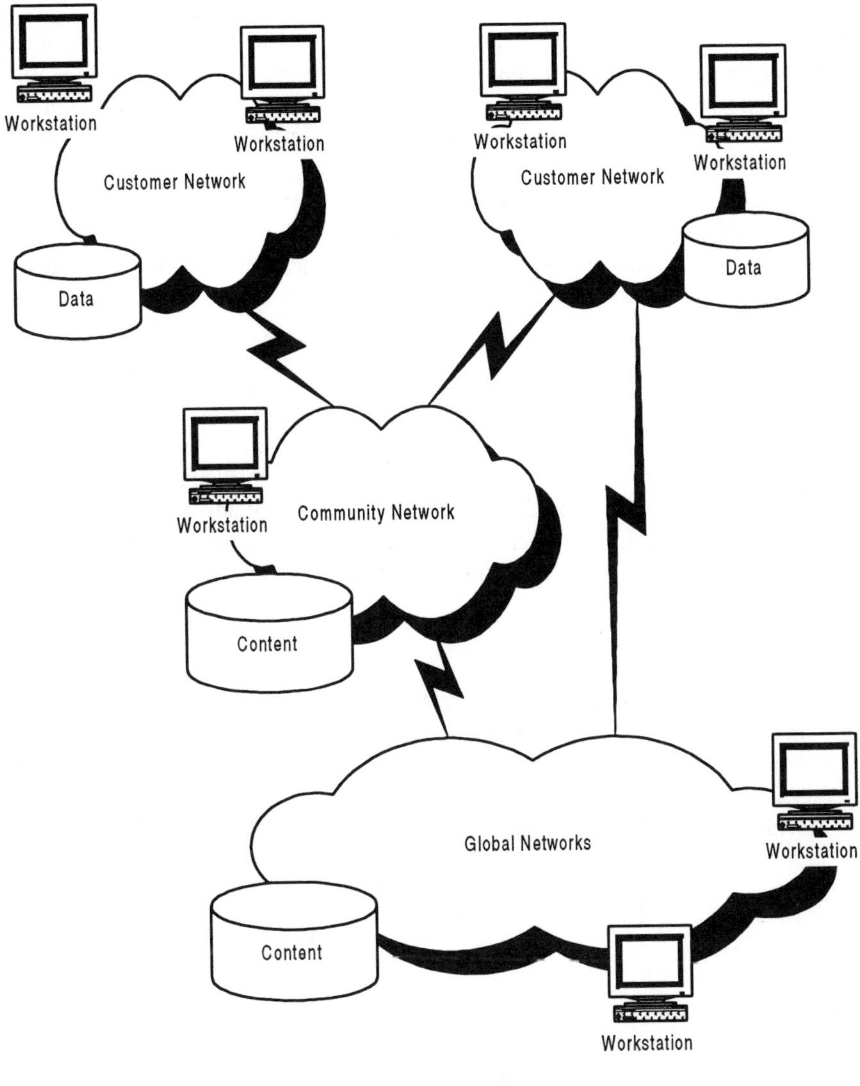

Figure 3: The Cloud Model

Each connection was "nailed up" and static. This model was similar to trunking techniques to move massive amounts of data between locations.

The cloud model eliminates geographical boundaries and physical constraints by enabling the network to create virtual networks of communication. Virtual connections within a cloud replace the traditional leased line. In addition, a single physical connection can be used to communicate simultaneously to any cloud.

Each cloud is a set of network attributes that provides the service interworking and access functions for workstation to workstation and/or workstation to application communication. The physical connections become logical connections that are administered by the network.

6 Summary

Developing network services that evolve with customer applications is a key strategy for any service provider. The business strategy and network architecture adopted by BCTAC have proven to be successful in enabling service overlays and minimizing technical risks and uncertainties. The key success factors can be summarized as follows:

1. link customer evolution with the network architecture evolution,
2. design the network in tiers to provide greater flexibility and manageability,
3. design the architecture to facilitate change and evolution,
4. leverage intelligence at the edge to be closer to the customer and to provide a solution,
5. replicate how people communicate or how they want to communicate.

DISTRIBUTED MULTIMEDIA LEARNING ENVIRONMENTS

TOM CALVERT

Technical University of BC, Surrey, BC, Canada, V3R 7P8

CHRISTIAN PANTEL

IBM Pacific Development Centre, Burnaby, BC, V5A 1S6

The World Wide Web (WWW) provides the basis for a global distributed learning environment that implements virtual classrooms. This chapter will first discuss the principles involved in creating an effective virtual learning environment and then will illustrate this with a description of the web-based *Virtual-U* system developed at Simon Fraser University with support from the Canadian TeleLearning Network of Centres of Excellence.

1 General

The World Wide Web (WWW) provides the basis for a distributed learning environment that extends around the globe. This chapter will first discuss the principles involved in designing and implementing an effective virtual learning environment. This includes a brief review of the theories of learning on which a design will be based and presentation of a framework that can be used to guide the design and evaluation of web-based learning environments. We will then illustrate this with a description of the web-based *Virtual-U* system developed at Simon Fraser University as part of the research program of the Canadian TeleLearning Network of Centres of Excellence (http://www.telelearn.ca).

The term *distributed learning* is used here in distinction to *distance learning;* the latter typically refers to a situation where the learners are separated from the instructor and from each other – communication with the instructor is by often by mail, possibly supplemented by telephone or email. Usually there is little or no communication with other students. In contrast, in distributed learning, students and instructors may or may not be in the same place at the same time, but they can communicate freely using a rich networked multimedia learning environment. Such distributed virtual learning environments can support the collaborative learning and knowledge building necessary for a successful virtual classroom or seminar room. Web technologies running over the internet or intranets are prime candidates to support such environments (Hiltz and Wellman, 1997).

2 Learning Theories in the Design of Virtual Learning Environments

The design of a learning environment must take account of the theories of learning that the course authors and instructors will apply. While learning theories can have many variations, they can be very roughly considered in two classes: the classical behavioural and information processing theories and the contemporary constructivist and socio-cultural theories (Harasim and Stockley, 1997).

2.1 Behavioral and Information Processing Theories:

These theories underlie the instructional models used in most of the schools, colleges and universities around the world. In simple terms, it is assumed that learning takes place when information is transferred to the student from the instructor and from instructional materials (Mayer, 1996). This can be accomplished when a student receives information in a lecture, for example. The role of the teacher consists of setting learning goals, planning learning outcomes, preparing and sequencing learning materials, delivering instruction to learners, assigning activities, evaluating the student's products and giving feedback. The behavioral theory, based on a stimulus-response model, assumes that learning takes place when associations are strengthened between a stimulus and a correct response (Mayer, 1992). While almost any learning environment will make some use of methods which can be explained in terms of these theories, there is strong evidence that virtual learning environments can be more effective if they do not try to recreate the classical information transmission - lecture model.

2.2 Constructivist and Socio-cultural theories:

These theories are an alternative to the classical learning theories and were developed following the work of Piaget (1954) and others in the 1950's and 60's; they have gained popularity in the 80's and 90's. Constructivist theorists do not believe that knowledge is a constant for each object or event but rather that it is constructed by individuals as they interact with an object or an event, in relation to their past experiences, their beliefs and their current mental structures (Black and McClintock, 1995; Honebein, Duffy and Fishman, 1997). For constructivists, learning is the process by which information is transformed into personal knowledge (Jonassen et al, 1997). Socio-cultural theories extend these basic principles to the development of the collective knowledge of a community as opposed to the development of individuals' knowledge within the community.

In a learning environment based on constructivism teachers serve as coaches and guides and learners are given significant cognitive responsibilities - analysis, synthesis, problem solving and creativity. It is believed that learner activities should be authentic - i.e. they should be realistic, meaningful, relevant to a community of practice, complex and information rich (Jonassen et al, 1997). Particular features of a learning environment which can support learning include facilitating with scaffolding and fading, cognitive apprenticeship and collaboration.

3 A Framework for the Design and Evaluation of Web-Based Learning Environments

The learning theories discussed briefly above are complex and difficult to translate into system design features. In addition, there are many other factors such as user interaction, network characteristics, and cost which influence a system design. In an attempt to provide a consistent basis for the design and evaluation of such systems, a comparison framework comprising 17 design dimensions has been developed. The full framework is available as a Technical Report (Pantel, 1997) and only a summary is provided here.

The comparison dimensions are set out in turn - each is intended to capture an important feature of the pedagogical design, the user interface design, the technical characteristics or the economic or business aspects. It is recognized that the dimensions are not orthogonal - i.e. the different features overlap and in some cases are contradictory. However, by considering a design against these features a consistent evaluation profile can be obtained.

3.1 Comparison dimensions

- Facilitating learning - Does the system provide direct tools to facilitate learning, tools with support for facilitation, and tools for scaffolding and fading?
- Cognitive apprenticeship - Can learners participate in a community of practice, engage in authentic activities, and engage in legitimate peripheral participation?
- Collaboration - Are there facilities that enable learners and teachers at a distance to communicate and work together?
    - Asynchronously? – using different kinds of discussion - email, listserve, and conferencing systems;
    - Synchronously? – using chat, Internet phone, video conference, shared whiteboards, shared applications.
- User Interface - Is the design based on established UI principles? Do the metaphors used support the learner? Does the workspace support awareness and help to create a virtual learning environment?
- Personal workspace - Are tools provided to support the learner in concept mapping, annotations, semantic associations, document upload, etc. ?
- Course authoring - Are facilities available to assist the author in planning and structuring a course, in assembling materials, etc. ?
- Assessment - Are there tools to assist in assessing knowledge acquisition and retention (exams, tests and quizzes), and to evaluate the students' learning processes?
- Tracking - Can student participation be tracked from log files?
- Ethical and social issues - Does the design contribute to the depersonalization of learning? Are issues of privacy, monitoring and fair accessibility handled ethically? Are there methods to protect intellectual property?

- System requirements - What are the client, server and network requirements? What is the quality of service?
- Robustness and security - Does the design use proven technology?
- Integration - Is there sound internal integration? Does the system integrate into existing environments?
- Customizability - Can the system be easily customized for the needs of a particular client?
- Support - Does the vendor provide support and upgrades?
- Training - Is training available on how to use, how to teach and learn?
- Business - What is the target market? What are the total costs including those of hosting the learning environment?
- Future direction - What are the vendor's development plans for the product?

4 Summary of Design Features

Based on the principles of constructivist learning, the goal in designing a web-based virtual learning environment is to create virtual-classrooms, seminars, discussion groups, laboratories and problem sessions which support student centred approaches to collaborative learning, and knowledge building (Harasim, Hiltz, Teles and Turoff, 1995). A primary prerequisite for the environment is that it must allow rich discourse between students and instructors and between individual students. This can be achieved with both synchronous and asynchronous conferencing systems. Experience suggests that for most purposes asynchronous conferencing supports the most effective discussions (Hiltz and Wellman, 1997). Another highly desirable feature for the environment is that it should support hypermedia. In this way students can build rich links between their own notes, other students' notes, instructors' comments, course resources, etc. The resulting learning takes place as the students build their ideas and knowledge (Harasim, Calvert and Groeneboer, 1996).

5 Designing and Implementing *Virtual-U*

5.1 Background.

The *Virtual-U* system has been developed to achieve the objectives set out above. *Virtual-U,* one of the Beacon Technologies of the Canadian TeleLearning Network of Centres of Excellence (http://www.telelearn.ca), is a World Wide Web-based networked learning environment customized for the design, delivery, and enhancement of post-secondary education. *Virtual-U* is designed to provide a flexible framework to support advanced pedagogies based on principles of active learning, collaboration, multiplicity, and knowledge building. *Virtual-U* is described briefly and preliminary evaluation results are presented (http://virtual-u.cs.sfu.ca).

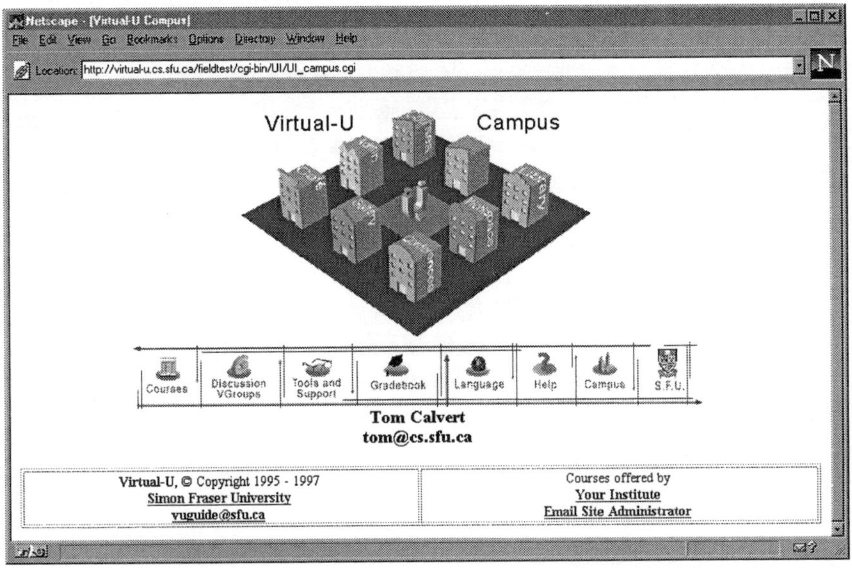

Figure 1. A spatial metaphor is used for the virtual campus.

Based on a decade of field research in online course delivery, the design and development of the system now known as *Virtual-U* was initiated in 1994. The goal was to provide a flexible framework to support advanced pedagogies in varied content areas including sciences and the arts, and in varied instructional formats including seminars, tutorials, group projects, and labs. The framework consists of tools to support core activities including course design, individual and group learning activities, knowledge structuring, class management, and evaluation. The attention to pedagogy is what distinguishes *Virtual-U* from many other virtual universities. The Web has typically been used as a publishing environment characterized by a correspondence course model or a broadcast model of learning in which faculty post lecture notes or students post assignments online.

5.2 *Overall Design.*

As shown in Figure 1, a spatial metaphor is used to enhance the sense of presence on a virtual campus. In the Courses Building (Figure 2), students access the courses in which they are enrolled as well as learner support tools. A hyperlinked Course Syllabus sets out the course content and provides hyperlinked access to course resources and materials (local and remote) as well as course activities (e.g. virtual labs) and assignments (Figure 3). Virtual seminars and other class discussions take place with the support of the VGroups conferencing system (Figure 4). Other tools allow students to upload multimedia materials to a shared workspace and to upload assignments to the instructor's workspace. A gradebook records student grades and makes these selectively available (Figure 5).

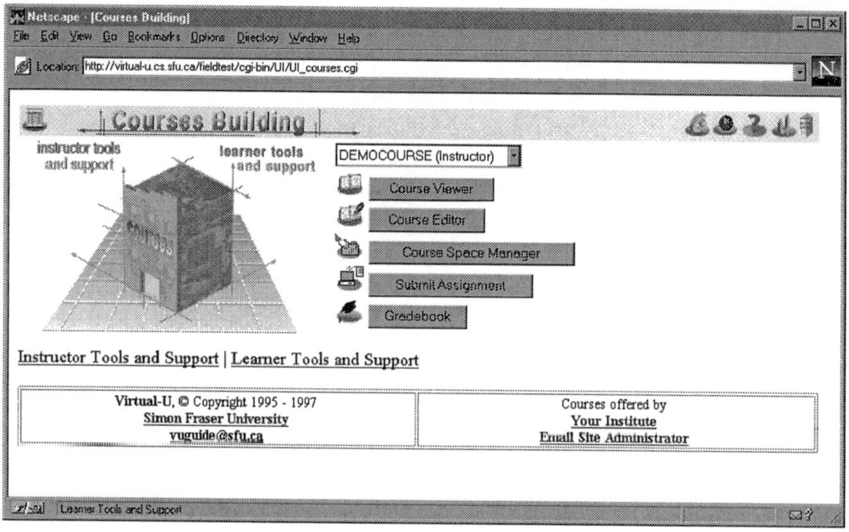

Figure 2. An instructor view of the Courses Building.

The initial design of *Virtual-U* is based on networked multimedia workstations (PC's or Macs) and a UNIX or WindowsNT server. The decision was made to build on widely available World Wide Web (WWW) tools since there is active interest in developing these tools for multiple platforms. Thus the students and instructors using *Virtual-U* need only a Java capable browser on their workstation because all of the *Virtual-U* software resides on a central server.

5.3 User Interaction Issues.

Until recently online learning environments were completely text based; in this situation, the participants form their own imagery of the virtual environments, much like the situation when one reads prose. With multimedia, which provides 2-dimensional images of 3-d scenes, and even video or animation, it is possible to provide the students with explicit cues which help them orient themselves, both in terms of navigating around the virtual environment as well as in setting social norms for the appropriate behaviour expected in each virtual space (Turoff, 1997).

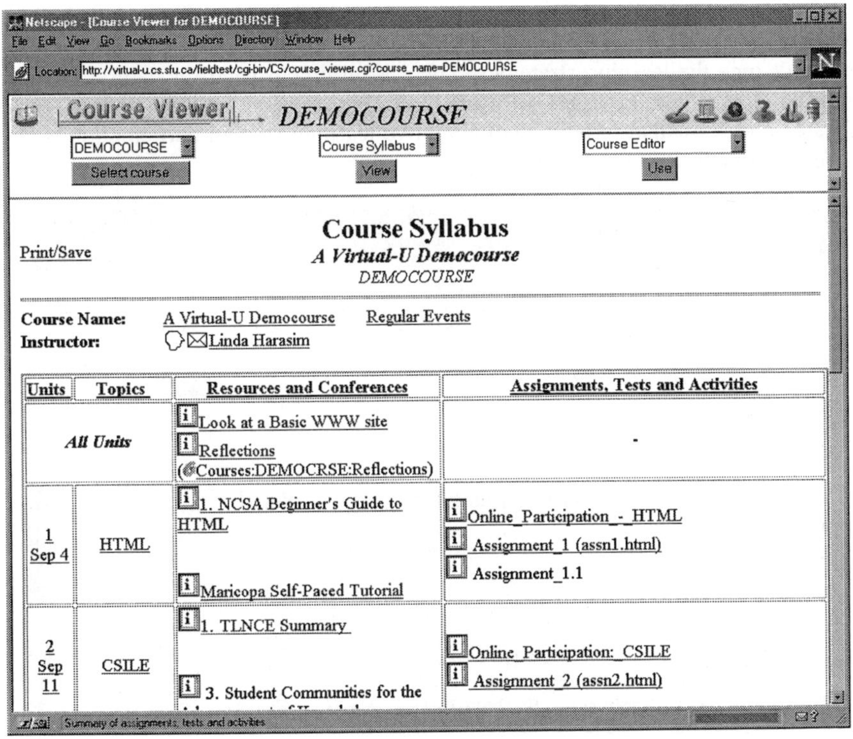

Figure 3. The interactive Course Syllabus

While the key spaces are instructional, (virtual classrooms for seminars and discussion groups and spaces for team projects, labs, etc.), the *Virtual-U* environment also includes spaces for academic advice, for administrative activities such as registration and fee payment, for access to library and other information resources (including an art gallery) and for social interchange (the virtual café). Another major component of *Virtual-U* is the set of tools to support core activities such as course design, individual and group learning activities, knowledge structuring, class management, and evaluation.

5.4 Fieldtest Evaluations.

The first field trials began at Simon Fraser University in September 1995. In the Spring Semester of 1997 12 courses were offered on *Virtual-U* at Simon Fraser University and there were numerous other offerings at 12 field sites across Canada. The data collected from the field sites consists of basic statistics for the courses concerned, pre- and post-questionnaires and computer logs of all student interactions. The questionnaire data and the basic statistics are relatively straightforward to analyse. The transcripts of the student interactions in the virtual seminars, etc. are currently analysed by hand to track the discourse and arguments and to deduce the learning strategies. There is an urgent need for natural language understanding tools to assist this analysis. Preliminary results confirm earlier research and show that in online collaborative learning student participation is even more effective than in face to face.

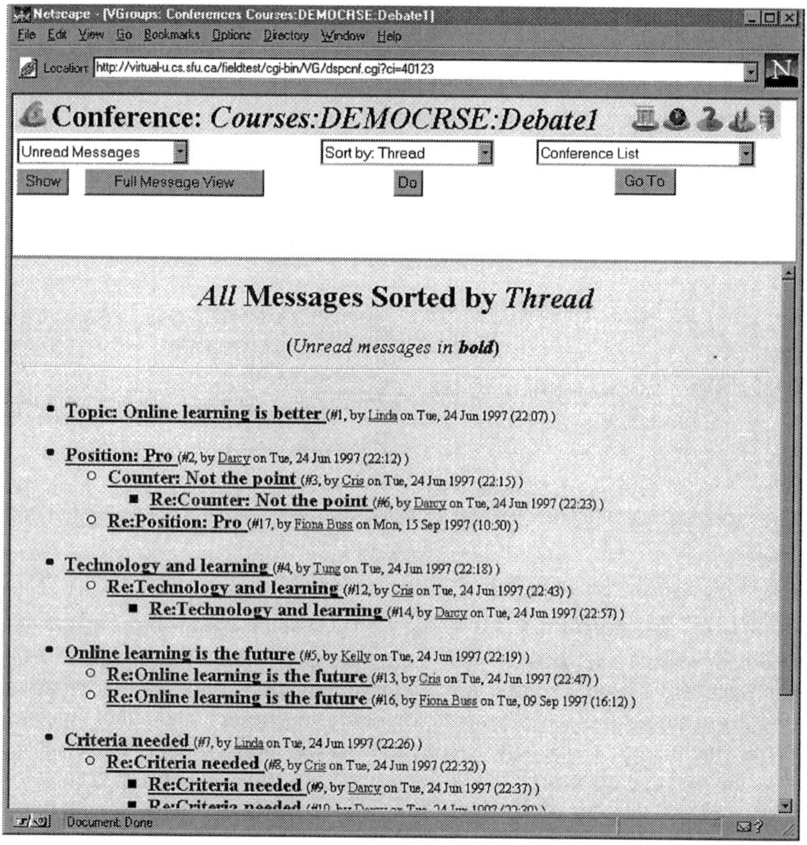

Figure 4. A view of a threaded discussion in the VGroups conferencing system.

New tools are being developed and evaluated which allow an objective analysis of discourse and which may indicate cognitive change and learning - an example is Latent Semantic Analysis (LSA) (Landauer, 1997). It is too early to give a definitive assessment of these tools but the results are encouraging.

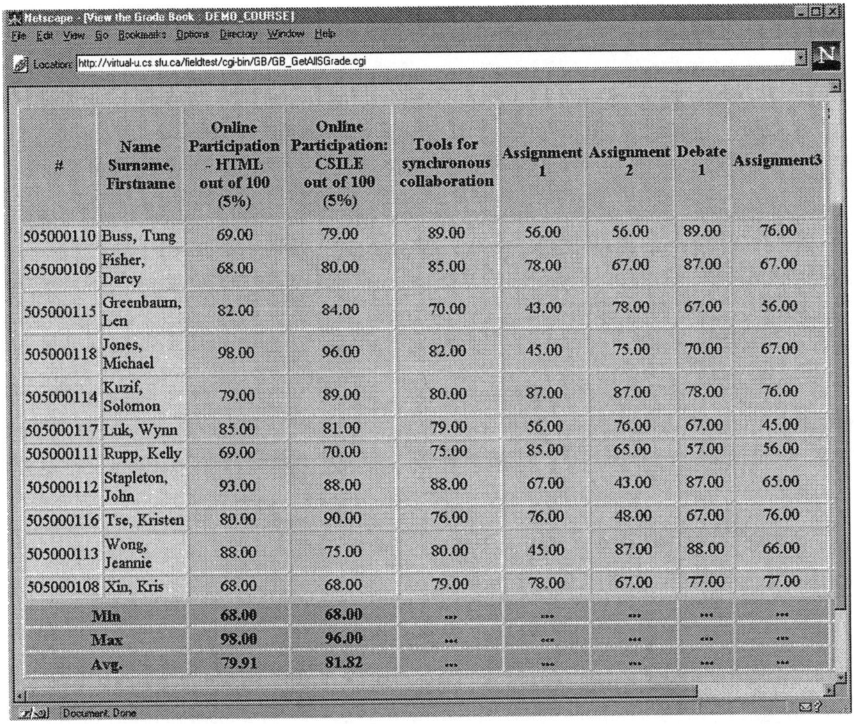

#	Name Surname, Firstname	Online Participation - HTML out of 100 (5%)	Online Participation: CSILE out of 100 (5%)	Tools for synchronous collaboration	Assignment 1	Assignment 2	Debate 1	Assignment3
505000110	Buss, Tung	69.00	79.00	89.00	56.00	56.00	89.00	76.00
505000109	Fisher, Darcy	68.00	80.00	85.00	78.00	67.00	87.00	67.00
505000115	Greenbaum, Len	82.00	84.00	70.00	43.00	78.00	67.00	56.00
505000118	Jones, Michael	98.00	96.00	82.00	45.00	75.00	70.00	67.00
505000114	Kuzif, Solomon	79.00	89.00	80.00	87.00	87.00	78.00	76.00
505000117	Luk, Wynn	85.00	81.00	79.00	56.00	76.00	67.00	45.00
505000111	Rupp, Kelly	69.00	70.00	75.00	85.00	65.00	57.00	56.00
505000112	Stapleton, John	93.00	88.00	88.00	67.00	43.00	87.00	65.00
505000116	Tse, Kristen	80.00	90.00	76.00	76.00	48.00	67.00	76.00
505000113	Wong, Jeannie	88.00	75.00	80.00	45.00	87.00	88.00	66.00
505000108	Xin, Kris	68.00	68.00	79.00	78.00	67.00	77.00	77.00
Min		68.00	68.00	...	...	...	...	...
Max		98.00	96.00	...	...	...	...	...
Avg.		79.91	81.82	...	...	...	...	...

Figure 5. An instructor's view of the online gradebook.

User interface evaluation is included in the field trials but is also conducted in the laboratory prior to the release of the system. The major user interaction problem has been to design within the constraints of the web browser and html capabilities, and with consideration for students who may be using a laptop with a small VGA interface.

6 Discussion and Conclusions

Distributed learning environments are now a reality. Based on the Internet and the open architecture world wide web, learners have easy access to courses offered by institutions throughout the world. One example of what is possible is a course offered on Virtual-U from Simon Fraser University in 1997 and again in 1998. This course, FPA 229-3, *Dancing in Cyberspace*, was offered by Professor Iris Garland of the SFU School for the Contemporary Arts. The course was taught over 13 weeks and was totally online. In each offering there were about 20 enrollees who were regular, continuing students at the university, but in addition there were about 15 special students from around the world - Australia, Hong Kong, United States,

Spain and the United Kingdom. The students had no serious technical problems and judged the course a major success.

Although effective global learning environments are becoming available, they can be substantially improved and extended. In particular, there is a need to implement more pedagogical tools, such as concept maps (Niguma, 1997), to better support advanced models of learning. There is also scope for improved tools which automatically assess the learning through discourse analysis and provide timely feedback to the learners and instructors. Many of the current systems, such as *Virtual-U*, which is described here, make use of web tools that are currently available. While supporting easy access and an open architecture, these tools substantially limit the interaction that is possible. To address this, *Virtual-U* is currently being reimplemented using Java and other systems to avoid the limitations of html and cgi scripts.

There is every reason to expect rapid progress in this field. The distributed learning environments of tomorrow promise to provide advanced pedagogical tools and extensive access. The impact on learning can be substantial.

7 Acknowledgments

The research reported here was supported in part by grants from the Canadian TeleLearning Network of Centres of Excellence. The development of *Virtual-U* as a product was supported by contracts from CANARIE Inc. to FPM Services and Virtual Learning Environments Inc. The authors acknowledge the contributions of all members of the *Virtual-U* team. Specific thanks to Chris Groeneboer, Osmar Zaiane, Rick Rupp, Bonita Tse, Denise Stockley, Brian Fisher, Ken McIntosh and Project Leader Dr. Linda Harasim.

References

1. Black, J.B. and McClintock, R.O. "An interpretation construction approach to constructivist design", in *Constructivist Learning Environments: Case Studies in Instructional Design*, B.G. Wilson, editor, Educational Technology Publications, Englewood Cliffs, NJ, USA, 1995.
2. Harasim, L. and Stockley, D.B., "Virtual-U: An analysis of instructional practices for teaching online". Paper presented at the *Annual Conference of the American Educational Research Association*, Chicago, Illinois, March 1997.
3. Harasim, L., Calvert, T, and Groeneboer, C., "Virtual-U: A Web-based Environment Customized to Support Collaborative Learning and Knowledge Building in Post Secondary Courses". *International Conference on the Learning Sciences*, Evanston, Ill. July 25-27, pp.120-127, 1996.

4. Harasim, L., Calvert, T. and Groeneboer, C., "Virtual-U: A web based system to support collaborative learning", in *Web-Based Instruction*, B.H. Khan (ed), pp. 149-158, Educational Technology Publications, 1997.
5. Harasim, L., Hiltz, S.R., Teles, L. and Turoff, M., editors, *Learning Networks: A Field Guide to Teaching and Learning Online*, MIT Press, Cambridge, Mass., 1995.
6. Hiltz, S.R.and Wellman, B, "Asynchronous Learning Networks as Virtual Classrooms", *Comm. ACM*, vol. 4, pp. 44-49, September 1997
7. Honebein, P.C., Duffy, T.M. and Fishman, B.J., "Constructivism and design of learning environments: Context and authentic activities for learning", Available at ftp://ithaca.icbl.hw.ac.uk/pub/nato_asi/duf2.txt.gz, 1997.
8. Jonassen, D.H., Dyer, D., Peters, K., Robinson, T., Harvey, D., King, M. and Loughner, P., "Cognitive flexibility hypertexts on the Web: Engaging learners in meaning making. In *Web-Based Instruction,* B.H. Khan (ed), pp. 119-133, Educational Technology Publications, 1997
9. Landauer, T.K., and Dumais, S. T. "A solution to Plato's problem: The Latent Semantic Analysis theory of the acquisition, induction, and representation of knowledge". *Psychological Review*, 104, 211-240, 1997.
10. Mayer, R.E., "Learners as information processors: Legacies and limitations of educational psychology's second metaphor", *Educational Psychologist*, 31(3/4): 151-161, 1996.
11. Mayer, R.E., "Cognition and instruction: Their historic meeting within educational psychology", *Journal of Educational Psychology*, 84(4): 405-412, 1992.
12. Niguma, G.K., "Concept Mapping in a Multimedia, World Wide Web Environment", M.Sc. Thesis, School of Computing Science, Simon Fraser University, Burnaby, BC, Canada V5QA 1S6. April, 1997.
13. Pantel, C.R., "A Framework for Comparing Web-Based Learning Environments", M.Sc. Thesis, School of Computing Science, Simon Fraser University, Burnaby, BC, Canada V5QA 1S6. September, 1997. (Also online at http://fas.sfu.ca/pub/cs/Theses/1997/ChristianPantelMSc.pdf).
14. Piaget, Jean, *The Construction of Reality in the Child*, Basic Books, New York, NY, USA, 1954.
15. Turoff, M., "Virtuality", *Comm. ACM*, vol. 4, pp. 38-43, September 1997

Modeling and Specification

A QoS-Message Directed Adaptive Distributed Multimedia System

Chi-Cheng Lin
Department of Computer Science
Winona State University
Winona, MN 55987, U.S.A.
E-mail: clin@vax2.winona.msus.edu

Shi-Kuo Chang and Taieb Znati
Department of Computer Science
University of Pittsburgh
Pittsburgh, PA 15260, U.S.A
E-mail: {chang,znati}@cs.pitt.edu

Abstract

The environment of distributed multimedia systems is not static. The specification of quality of service (QoS) plays an important role to describe the dynamic characteristics and is used for distributed multimedia systems to adapt to environment changes. We argue that the QoS requirements should be able to be specified from the user's and application's perspectives. Thus, we formally define the concept of QoS-massages that provides a specification interface between applications and the communication network. A framework based on a transformation approach is proposed to transform user/application's QoS requirement specification to QoS-messages that direct the transmission of multimedia information.

Keywords

Distributed multimedia system, G-Net, multimedia schema, quality-of-service, QoS-message

1.1 Introduction

Recent advances in technology, such as high speed communication networks, mass storage, and digital media data compression, have stimulated the research and development of *distributed multimedia systems (DMSs)*. A problem is that the environments of DMSs are dynamic because the components that constitute the environments are not static. The components include users, applications, hardware and operating systems, and communication networks. Different users have different profiles. Various multimedia applications have different quality of service (QoS) requirements. Hardware devices of different machines and operating systems of the machines might be different. QoS supported by different networks is different. Even with all the parameters of these components fixed, time and space are yet contributing factors to the dynamics. For example, a mobile unit may reside at different times in different locations, thereby requiring different needs. Thus, it is important for a DMS to support adaptation not only to the physical components of the environment, but also to the changes in time and space.

Maintaining continuous, adaptive multimedia communication with guaranteed minimum QoS poses a major challenge. The support of the QoS requirements of multimedia applications across a highly heterogeneous environment requires the development of a flexible and adaptable network resource management framework. The framework must support efficient mechanisms in order to bridge the heterogeneity gap, by dynamically accommodating applications with different QoS requirements, in response to network performance degradation. Network resource management alone, however, is not sufficient to provide applications with end-to-end QoS guarantees, especially in distributed environments where multiple end systems with different processing and communication capabilities participate in a distributed multimedia application. The framework must also provide the mechanisms necessary to specify application requirements and translate these requirements into negotiated resource allocations.

Apart from significant differences in the underlying characteristics, multimedia applications may involve QoS parameters that are hard to specify from the user's perspective. For example, it is "natural" for certain users to request a "CD-quality" audio stream, but difficult for them to specify the maximum allowable delay jitter. The problem is that the same set of QoS parameters that is used to describe the characteristics of a communication network cannot be adopted directly by the applications. To effectively support the mapping of QoS between different levels of a DMS, we believe that the modeling of multimedia data and their QoS requirement plays a very important role.

Furthermore, applications are not expected to dynamically monitor the global state of the network and adjust their QoS requirements in response to changes in throughput, delay, jitter or error rate. Consequently, the framework must also provide protocol entities that are capable of gathering information about available network resources and dynamically negotiating network resources for a customized connection, in a manner that is transparent to the users.

A successful DMS must adapt to current changes in time and space and support dynamic QoS. The *Active Multimedia System (AMS)* has been proposed to support dynamic adaptation to environment changes and serve as a bridge between multimedia applications and the communication network in a DMS [C. C. Lin *et al.* (1997)]. In addition, the AMS also provides mechanisms to support composition, integration and synchronization, presentation, and maintenance and management of multimedia objects, as well as multimedia information delivery.

The major objectives of bridging and adaptation of the AMS are based on the provision of protocol entities that can be viewed as providing an application interface, using extensive information and feedback, for QoS customization to specific operating environments. The solution to provide this interface must take into consideration the constantly changing information used for decision-making, the management of applications with a wide variety of QoS requirements, and the support of different types of end systems. The approach in this chapter to address these issues is based on the provision of transformation schemas [C. C. Lin (1997); C. C. Lin *et al.* (1996)] which map a high level specification of QoS requirements into *QoS-messages* [C. C. Lin *et al.* (1997); R. Simon (1996); R. Simon *et al.* (1995)]. The objective is to reduce the user provided QoS parameters to a minimal set of easily specifiable parameters. Based on these parameters, the set of composite multimedia objects can be dynamically transformed into a collection of QoS-messages, which represents atomic communication units between the application and the network.

The rest of this chapter is organized as follows: Section 2 discusses the related work. Section 3 presents the system overview of the AMS, including the architecture, approach, and the active multimedia communication. The definition and specification of QoS-message by G-Net are discussed in Section 4. Section 5 discusses adaptation based on the concept of QoS-message. Section 6 discusses the transformation regarding MCS. Section 7 gives examples of applying the concept of QoS-message to different multimedia applications. Finally, Section 8 gives a conclusion and discusses directions of future work.

1.2 Related Work

To provide the support for the multimedia applications, it is required to guarantee a certain level of performance requirements. A *guarantee* is a contract between an application and the service provider to satisfy a requested level of QoS requirements [D. Ferrari (1990)]. $\mathcal{V}$–NET is a framework that supports the network requirements of real-time applications [B. Field *et al.* (1995); T. Znati and B. Field (1993)]. The objective of $\mathcal{V}$–NET architecture is to provide applications with real-time performance guarantees.

A uniform framework is required to integrate QoS support provided by individual levels of a DMS. This type of frameworks is referred to as the *QoS architecture.* The QoS architectures, such as QoS-A [A. Campbell *et al.* (1994)], OMEGA architecture [K. Nahrstedt and J. M. Smith (1995); K. Nahrstedt and J. M. Smith (1996)], and DIPCS [R. Simon (1996); R. Simon *et al.* (1995)], provide mechanisms, including QoS specification, mapping, and management, to incorporate QoS support that is provided by individual levels of a DMS. Lately, literatures have been published that provide comprehensive surveys and reviews of QoS issues and architectures [C. Aurrecoechea *et al.* (1998); B. Stiller (1995)].

The concept of *QoS-messages* has been proposed [R. Simon (1996)] to serve as a bridge of QoS specification between multimedia applications and communications. The extension of the concept of QoS-messages to support QoS adaptation to dynamic changes in the DMS environment has been proposed [C. C. Lin *et al.* (1997)]. This extension utilizes the hierarchi-

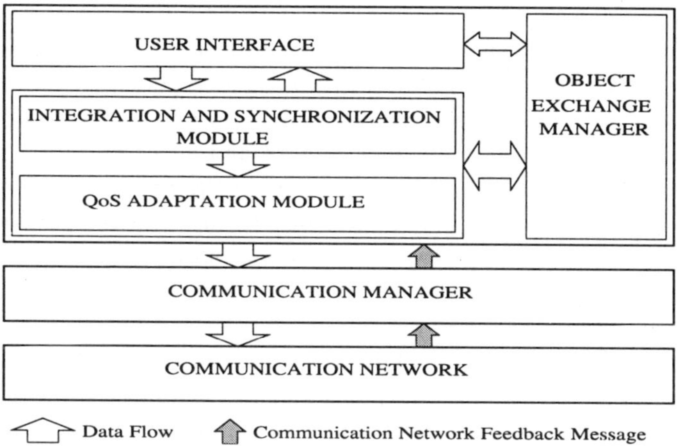

Fig. 1.1 Architecture of the AMS.

cal specification mechanism of the model that represents QoS-messages to provide a uniform solution to QoS adaptation in DMSs.

G-Net is a high-level, executable Petri net which allows multi-level specification of different system components and structures [Y. Deng and S. K. Chang (1990); Y. Deng and S. K. Chang (1991); C. C. Lin *et al.* (1996); T. Znati *et al.* (1993)]. In addition to the features inherited from Petri net such as concurrency, asynchrony, and non-determinism, G-Net also supports modularity and modifiability based on internal switching mechanisms to incrementally refine and construct multi-level system specifications. A G-Net model enhanced with deterministic timing scheme has been proposed in order to perform timing analysis for real-time systems [S. K. Chang *et al.* (1995)].

1.3 System Overview

1.3.1 *Architecture*

The architecture of AMS consists of five major components, namely *user interface*, *G-Net manager*, *object exchange manager*, *communication manager*, and *communication network*. The block diagram of the architecture is shown in Fig. 1.1, and the individual components are described in the following paragraphs.

User Interface:
This component consists of the *composition module* and the *presentation module*. The composition module provides the user with the facilities to edit *multimedia objects* (MMOs), compose MMOs, specify attributes of MMOs, and specify relations such as the structure and synchronization between objects in composite MMOs. The function of the presentation module is to display the composite MMOs according to the temporal attributes associated with individual MMOs and the synchronization relations specified between the MMOs.

G-Net Manager:
This component consists of the *integration and synchronization module* and the *adaptation module*. The integration and synchronization module performs the transformation from the *syntactic* representation of composite MMOs to the *semantic* representation of the MMOs that defines the synchronization and how the components are integrated with each other. The adaptation module transforms the semantic representation of MMOs to a collection of adaptive multimedia presentation and communication units. Those units are used to negotiate with the communication management system in order to establish connections, and to adapt to the changes reported by the feedback messages from the communication network.

Object Exchange Manager:
By adopting the concept of object exchange [F. Colaitis (1994)], the object exchange manager is designed to maintain and manage the information of MMOs represented in an *object exchange format* (OEF) [C. C. Lin *et al.* (1996)] in the distributed environments. The object exchange manager interacts with the other modules in AMS to accomplish its functionality. The information of the MMOs and their representation is maintained in the OEF by the object exchange manager for the purpose of storage, and is also transmitted over the communication network for management and reuse of the MMOs.

Communication Manager:
This component provides the functionalities of session management and the network service as the result of negotiation with the underlying transport service provider. The core of the communication manager is the *QoS-reliable communication module*, whose duties include the admission control and connection establishment with a certain level of QoS guarantee. The main objective in the development of this component is to use a minimal set of QoS parameters which can be specified easily by the user, or implicitly

inferred from the application characteristics.

During the call set-up phase, the communication manager negotiates acceptable values of the QoS parameters with the network call and admission control. As communication progresses, the communication manager monitors the current state of the network, and uses the feedback messages provided by the communication network to adapt QoS requirements to current changes in the communication network.

Communication Network:
The AMS is designed with flexibility which makes it applicable to any network framework that can provide levels of QoS guarantees and feedback. The network framework adopted in our framework is $\mathcal{V}$–NET . A key characteristic of $\mathcal{V}$–NET is its ability to adapt to new environments and traffic requirements as they arise in a dynamically changing environment. The $\mathcal{V}$–NET framework is built to support communication environments where different packet scheduling and admission control policies can co-exist simultaneously. Furthermore, the architecture provides support for end-to-end QoS guarantees based on the current resource usage of the network nodes and the current resource requirements of the application. This flexibility provides the foundation for the development of efficient mechanisms for "on-line" negotiation of traffic rates and end-to-end delay values to support adaptive QoS guarantees in dynamically changing environments. This support is crucial for the integration of wireless subnets which usually limit the qualities of the network service.

1.3.2 *Approach*

The approach is based on two concepts: transformation schemas and algorithms, and the concept of QoS-messages. Schemas are used to represent MMOs so that the components of these objects can be easily manipulated, composed, and adapted to the current environment. The transformation algorithms allow us to translate MMOs and QoS requirements into specific parameters at each level of the architecture.

In the AMS, there are three multimedia schemas, namely *Multimedia Static Schema* (MSS), *Multimedia Data Schema* (MDS), and *Multimedia Communications Schema* (MCS). The MSS specifies the static structure of the composite multimedia data, including the temporal and spatial relations of the data. When a user composes multimedia data in an application, such as a multimedia message/mail system, an MSS is created to represent the

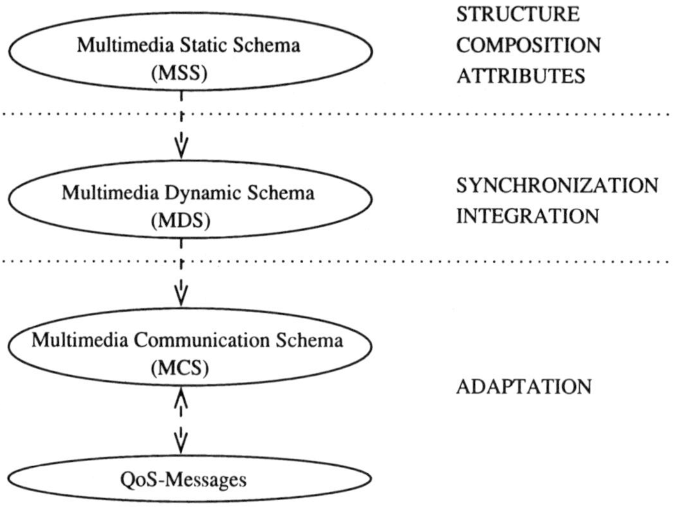

Fig. 1.2 The hierarchical view of the approach of the framework.

composite multimedia data. The MDS is transformed from the MSS, which not only supports the integration and synchronization of the multimedia data, but also conducts the presentation of the data. The MCS is derived from the MDS by adding further communication control and synchronization requirements in order to satisfy the capacity constraint of processors and the bandwidth constraint of the communication network, and therefore to use the service of the communication network effectively.

Adaptation is based on the concept of QoS-messages. The notion of the QoS-message was first introduced as the atomic unit of multimedia communication and presentation [R. Simon (1996); R. Simon *et al.* (1995)], and the formal definition of its structure and semantics was then specified in [C. C. Lin *et al.* (1997)].

Figure 1.2 illustrates the approach at a hierarchical view. At the top level of the hierarchy, the MSS defines structure, composition, and attributes of MMOs. A movie, for example, can be viewed as a composite MMO that consists of video, audio, and data. At the second level of the hierarchy, the MDS defines the dynamics and semantical relationships between the components of MMOs, in terms of synchronization and how these components integrate with each other. Using a movie as an example again, each video frame is associated with an audio frame and the synchronization between these two frames has to be enforced in order to avoid the "lip-sync" problem.

At the third level of the hierarchy, the MCS transforms the representation of MMOs and their requirements, in terms of synchronization and QoS, into a set of adaptive QoS-messages. For example, the MCS of a movie can be viewed as a sequence of QoS-messages that represents a sequence of 1 second long playback units of the movie. The timing delivery guarantee, presentation, and adaptation are then based on the specification of synchronization and QoS requirements of the units.

1.3.3 *Active Multimedia Communication*

The integrated view of the block diagram of the architecture and the transformation schemas in the AMS that support QoS-message-based active multimedia communication is shown in Fig. 1.3. It illustrates where the multimedia schemas reside, as well as where transformation between the multimedia schemas [C. C. Lin *et al.* (1996)] takes place in the system.

Based on the integrated system diagram, a scenario of active multimedia communication is given as follows. A user can invoke the multimedia editor supported in the composition module to compose MMOs into a composite MMO. After the composition, the MSS of the composite MMO is generated and then sent to the integration and synchronization module to be transformed to the MDS. The presentation module can then adopt the MDS to view the presentation of the composite MMO just created.

In addition to conducting the presentation, the MDS is also sent to the adaptation module to be transformed to the MCS. Subsequently, the MCS is sent to the QoS-message manager to attempt to obtain the connection admission from the QoS-reliable communication module. If the QoS-reliable communication cannot guarantee the transmission based on the specification of the QoS-messages in the MCS, the QoS-message manager will negotiate with the QoS-reliable communication module by modifying the MCS. If a negotiation is achieved, a call will be established and the QoS-messages will be injected into the QoS-reliable communication module to direct the transmission of the MMOs. On the other hand, if no agreement is achieved, the call cannot be established.

Once the call is established, if the bandwidth of the established channel changes during the transmission of the MMOs, the communication network will send a feedback message to the QoS-reliable communication module.

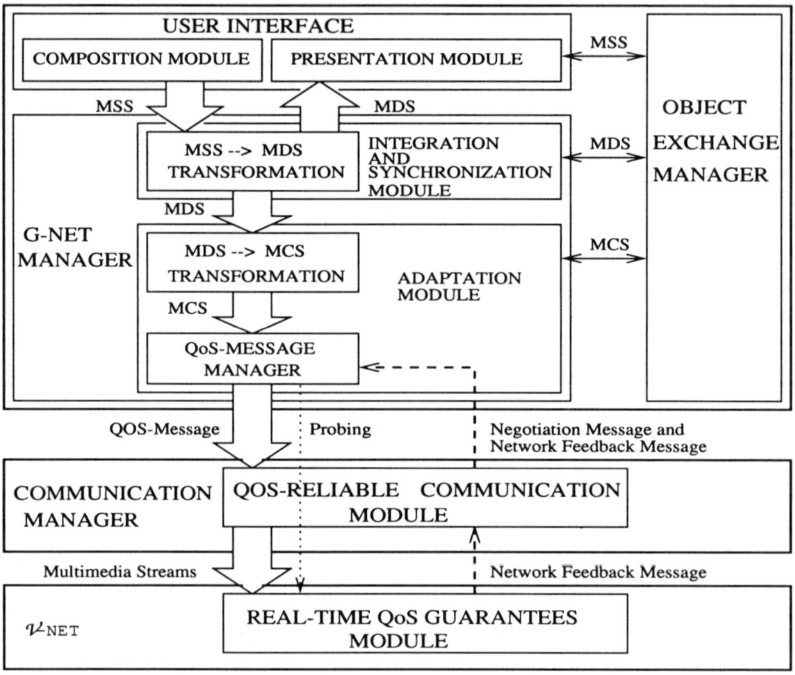

Fig. 1.3 Integrated view of the framework of AMS.

The feedback message is then forwarded to the QoS-message manager, along with a negotiation message, in order to modify the MCS to adapt to the current status.

The conceptual view of QoS-message-directed communication is shown in Fig. 1.4. A communication end point could be a multimedia workstation equipped with audio and video playback devices, a dumb terminal or a mobile unit. The integrated service network (ISN) consists of possibly wired and wireless subnets that could span over local area networks (LANs), metropolitan area networks (WANs), and wide area networks (WANs). The AMS is employed to translate the QoS requirements of multimedia applications to QoS-messages by taking the heterogeneous characteristics of the environment components into consideration. The *QoS-reliable communication channels* are then established with end-to-end QoS guarantees, based on the specification of the QoS-messages. Furthermore, after the channels are established, a QoS-message can adjust its size to adapt to the changing

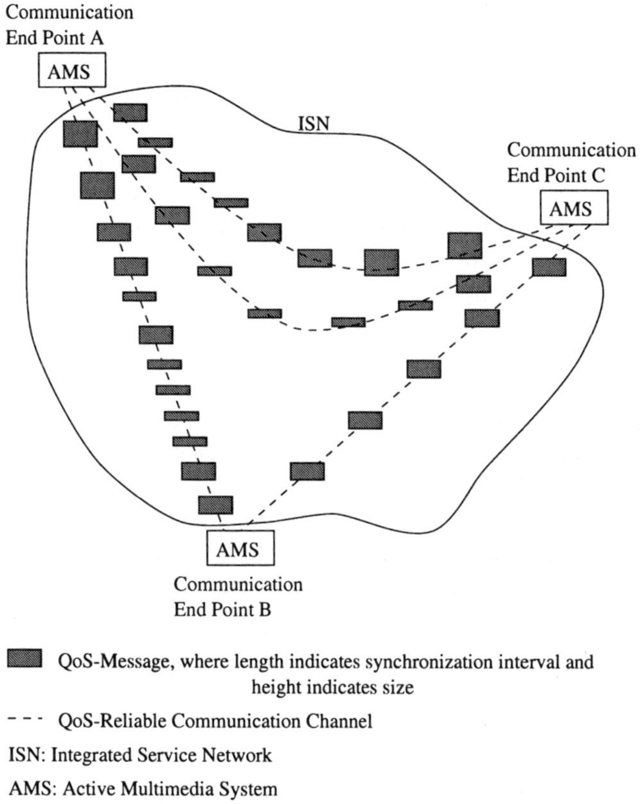

Fig. 1.4 QoS-message-directed QoS-reliable communication on ISN.

environment.

1.4 QoS-Message

1.4.1 *Definition*

Simon defined a QoS-message as "a synchronized, atomic multimedia playback unit containing related information from multiple media streams which must be presented concurrently at appropriate times" [R. Simon (1996); R. Simon *et al.* (1995)]. The term "synchronized" implies that synchronization among the MMOs must be maintained within the QoS-message. The term "atomic" implies that from the presentation perspective, a QoS-message is indivisible into smaller data units. Therefore, the on-time delivery of a QoS-message is "all or nothing" in its effect. This implies that all MMOs associated with a QoS-message must "be presented concurrently at appropriate times" during the presentation. Consequently, if Φ represents the synchronization interval, and Δ represents the acceptable end-to-end delay, a QoS-message Q is on-time if $delay(Q) \leq \Delta$, where $delay(Q)$ is the delay suffered by any data unit generated within the synchronization interval, Φ.

Based on the formal definition of the QoS-message concept, a model for QoS-message specification must take the following characteristics into consideration:

(1) Allow for the implicit or explicit specification of a range of Δ and Φ values to reflect the application's synchronization and on-time reliability requirements.
(2) Preserve the atomicity property of the QoS-message concept.
(3) Enforce the concurrency and synchronization requirements of the QoS-message.
(4) Use the user supplied QoS scaling policy to adjust traffic characteristics in response to network performance degradation and resource availability.

To address the above characteristics, a G-Net based formal model for QoS-message specification is developed. Formally, a G-Net consists of a *generic switch place* (GSP) and an *internal structure* (IS). GSP consists of the G-Net's unique identifier and attributes, as well as the methods that can be applied to the G-Net. IS is a Petri net-based structure that provides an instantiation switching mechanism by *instantiation switch place* (ISP) to invoke another G-Net. See Figure 1.8(b) for an example of G-Net structure and the instantiation switching mechanism. The approach is to model a QoS-message using G-Net as follows:

(1) The allowable ranges of Δ and Φ are stored in GSP as attributes, along with the specified QoS-stream set.
(2) The scaling policy to adapt QoS-message requirements to the current network environment is stored in GSP as methods.
(3) The QoS-message is represented by the G-Net IS, and inherits all characteristics of a Petri net, including concurrency and synchronization.

In this framework, an instance of a distributed multimedia application is modeled as a composite MMO that consists of a set of multimedia *streams*. A stream consists of a set of multimedia objects within the composite MMO to be transmitted over the network. A subset of multimedia objects within a stream form an atomic presentation unit. For example, an MPEG [D. Le Gall (1991)] movie with stereo sound is modeled as one video stream and two audio streams. In turn, the video stream is modeled as a sequence of video frames, while each audio stream is modeled as a sequence of audio objects. A group of MPEG pictures within the video stream represents an atomic presentation unit. The proposed framework uses the following definitions to specify the relationship among streams within the composite MMO, and the concept of a QoS-message.

Definition 1. Given a set S of streams within a composite MMO, a *QoS-stream*, Q, is defined as follows:

(1) $Q \subset 2^S$, and
(2) For any pair $(A_i, A_j) \in Q$, $A_i \not\subset A_j$ and $A_j \not\subset A_i$.

The second condition ensures that the atomicity property of each stream within each element of the QoS stream is preserved. Notice also that in some cases, the union of all the elements in the QoS-stream is not equal to S. This implies that some streams in the composite MMO are not considered part of the QoS-stream. Multimedia objects generated by the left out streams are transmitted in the network conditions permit, i.e. best-effort. To account for this, we define a *best-effort-stream (BE-stream)* as follows:

Definition 2. A *BE-stream set* B of the stream set S of a composite MMO is a set of streams such that

$$B = S - \bigcup_{\forall A_i \in Q} A_i, \text{ where}$$

Q is the QoS-stream of S.

A QoS-message is modeled by a G-Net that is composed of places and transitions. A place in a G-Net that represents a QoS-message can be used to represent an object, a synchronization point, or a delay, and is called *object place*, *synchronization place*, and *delay place*, respectively. Each object place belongs to one, and only one, stream in the composite MMO.

Definition 3. The *place-stream* $S_{G.p}$ of the object places in a G-Net G is defined as:

$$S_{G.p} = \bigcup_{\forall p \in G} \phi(p), \text{ where}$$

ϕ : *place* $\to$ {*stream*}. Given a place, the function ϕ returns a singleton (a set containing only one element) of the stream to which the object that is represented by the place belongs.

Finally, the QoS-message in our framework is defined as follows:

Definition 4. Given the QoS-stream, Q, of a composite MMO, a *QoS-message* is a G-Net, G, such that the following conditions are satisfied:

(1) There is a place p_s representing the starting synchronization point, and another place p_e representing the ending synchronization point in G.
(2) There is no other synchronization place in G.
(3) All places in G are reachable from p_s.
(4) All places in G are not reachable from p_e, except for p_e itself.
(5) The place-stream of G is in QoS-stream.

1.4.2 *Specification of QoS-Stream Set by Visualization*

A prerequisite step to generate QoS-messages for the composite MMO from the application is to specify the QoS-stream set for it. The major issue from the user's perspective is the methodology to aid the specification of a valid QoS-stream set. A two-step approach is devised for this issue. The first step is to use a looser type-based, rather than stream-based, specification to reduce the complexity. The second step is the visualization of validation for a QoS-stream set by the lattice structure.

For a composite MMO with n streams $s_1, \ldots, s_n$. the user/application is free to choose any combination of the n streams to make up m stream sets to compose the QoS-stream set. However, for a QoS-stream set to be valid, it has to be guaranteed that there is no $A_i, A_j \in Q$ such that $A_i \subset A_j$ or $A_j \subset A_i$. A naive and straightforward approach to guarantee this is that the elements of a QoS-stream set is added one by one. When a new element is added into the set, it is verified over the elements already in the set.

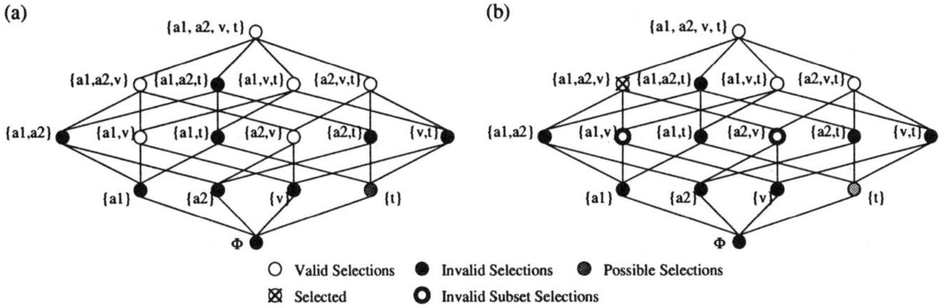

Fig. 1.5 Hasse diagram of example for $C = \{\{audio, video\}\}$.

Another approach proposed here is to provide a visual assistance in choosing valid elements for the QoS-stream set. We propose an approach for visualization based on the lattice structure. For a set S, its power set of 2^S can be represented as a lattice L_S, where $L_S = [2^S, \cup, \cap]$. The graphical representation of L_S, using the *Hasse diagram*, can be adopted to visually assist the specification of a QoS-stream set.

The first step of this approach is to assist the specification of the QoS-stream set by using a looser type-based scheme instead of a stream-based scheme. This approach might reduce the number of potential valid choices in the specification.

Definition 5. The *stream-type set* W of a stream set V is defined as

$$W = \bigcup_{\forall s \in V} \psi(s),$$

where $\psi : stream \rightarrow \{media\ type\}$. Given a stream, the function ψ returns singleton of the media type of the stream.

Definition 6. Given a set of type sets $C = \{T_1, \ldots, T_m\}$, a set of streams $S = \{s_1, \ldots, s_n\}$, a stream set $V \subseteq S$, and the stream-type set W of V, the vertex representing V in the lattice of 2^S is marked as:

(1) *valid*, if $\exists T_i \subseteq W, 1 \leq i \leq m$.
(2) *possible*, if $W \neq \emptyset$ and $\forall T_i \cap W = \emptyset, 1 \leq i \leq m$.
(3) *invalid*, otherwise.

The second step is to specify the QoS-streams by marking a vertex as *chosen*, while still maintaining the atomicity of the QoS-streams. After the first step, a vertex of the lattice is marked as either *valid*, *possible*, or *invalid.* The rules to select QoS-streams based on the marking are described as follows:

(1) Only vertices marked as *valid* or *possible* can be selected.
(2) When a vertex v is selected, it is marked as *selected* and the vertices reachable downward from v are marked as *invalid.*
(3) At least one of the vertices marked as *valid* should be selected.

Therefore, the user is able to know what the valid choices are by visualization.

An example of using lattice structure to aid the specification of the QoS-stream set on the stream set $S = \{a1, a2, v, t\}$, where $\psi(a1) = \{audio\}$, $\psi(a2) = \{audio\}$, $\psi(v) = \{video\}$, and $\psi(t) = \{text\}$, is illustrated. In the first step, stream-type set $C = \{audio, video\}$ is specified, and the markings of the vertices are shown in Fig. 1.5(a).

Suppose the set $\{a1, a2, v\}$ is the first element chosen into the QoS-stream set, then its corresponding vertex is marked as *selected* and the vertices $\{a1, v\}$ and $\{a2, v\}$ are marked as *invalid,* since they are downward reachable from vertex $\{a1, a2, v\}$. The result after this choice is shown in Fig. 1.5(b). The user can then make another choice from the valid vertices left.

1.5 QoS-Message-Based Adaptation

The end-to-end delivery of QoS-messages, based on the specified values of the parameters Δ and Φ, is illustrated in Fig. 1.6. As the value of Δ denotes the maximum tolerable end-to-end delay of the delivery of a QoS-message, it includes the time to prepare the presentation of the QoS-message. If τ denotes the preparation time, then the timing requirement, Δ^*, of transmitting the packets generated within Φ over the communication network can be calculated as

$$\Delta^* = \Delta - (\Phi + \tau).$$

The value of Δ^* is then used to request the resource reservation and negotiate the QoS guarantee.

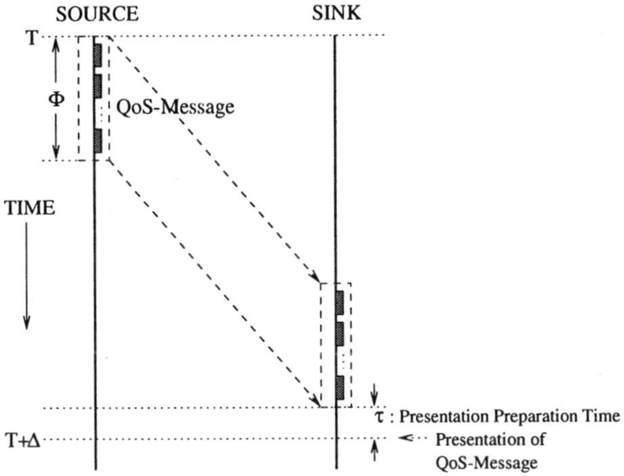

Fig. 1.6 End-to-end QoS-message transmission.

1.5.1 *Rate-Based Feedback*

1.5.1.1 *QoS-message Adjustment*

In a QoS-reliable communication, it is not a good idea to modify Δ and Φ of QoS-messages once the connection is established. The reason for this is that it is not desirable to go through the process of re-establishing the channel, as the process may be time-consuming. Furthermore, there is no guarantee that the effort to re-establish the channel will be successful. Therefore, both old and new channels may be lost. What should be done is an attempt to reduce the number of bits sent by the application during a synchronization interval. This will reduce the network input data rate and will allow a better adjustment to the current situation of the network. The problem that arises is how much reduction can be achieved without totally destroying the qualities of service.

Suppose that the current bit rate at time t, $r(t)$, of the channel that transmits multimedia data is

$$r(t) = \frac{N_\Phi(t)}{\Phi} \mid P \mid, \text{where}$$

$N_\Phi(t)$ is the number of packets generated in Φ, and
$\mid P \mid$ is the packet size.

Assume that the network issues a feedback message at time t^+ to report a rate $r(t^+)$, that

$$r(t^+) = \beta \cdot r(t), 0 < \beta < 1.$$

Then,

$$N_\Phi(t^+) = \lceil \frac{r(t^+) \cdot \Phi}{\mid P \mid} \rceil = \lceil \beta \frac{r(t) \cdot \Phi}{\mid P \mid} \rceil, \text{where}$$

$N_\Phi(t^+)$ is the maximum number of packets that are allowed to be generated in Φ.

Different heuristics, such as media scaling [T. Kapner and L. Wolf (1994)] and media shifting [H. J. Chang (1998)], are then applied to the QoS-message in order to reduce its size, depending on different values of β.

However, before a connection is established, it is feasible to adjust Δ and Φ of QoS-messages. For example, during the establishment of a channel, if an end-to-end delay of two seconds cannot be guaranteed, a looser request, says three seconds, can be specified to establish a channel.

1.5.1.2 *Prediction of Feedback Intervals*

Another issue of feedback messages is the prediction of the feedback interval. It is useful in the case in which the network monitoring mechanism only reports the changes of bandwidth decreases.

Let Ω be the predicted feedback interval. The formula of the prediction is

$$\Omega(t^+) = \alpha\Omega(t) + (1 - \alpha)\bar{\Omega}, \text{where}$$

$\alpha \in (0, 1)$, usually set to around 0.1 to prevent the effect of burst, and $\bar{\Omega}$ is the average of previous feedback intervals.

Two conditions of the timing of receiving a feedback message that can occur are described as follows:

(1) After the period of time $\Omega(t^+)$, if there is no feedback message received and the QoS of the QoS-message can still be improved, the application will increase the bit rate to $r(t^+)$, so that

$$r(t^+) = r(t) + \mu, \mu > 0,$$

to test the capacity of the network.

This approach probes the network *actively*, rather than merely waiting for feedback messages *passively*, and therefore characterizes the feature of *activeness* of our framework,

(2) A feedback message comes back before the end of duration $\Omega(t^+)$, say, after a period of time Ω', to report bandwidth change. In this case, the size of the QoS-message has to be adjusted to adapt to the change. Consequently, a new prediction is calculated starting at the time the feedback message was received.

We assume that the prediction interval, Ω, is a multiple of the synchronization interval, Φ, and is adjustable as time moves along. What is meant by that is to choose an $\Omega = k(t) \cdot \Phi$, where $k(t)$ is a dynamically adjustable factor. The adjustment of k(t) can be based on what is observed from the network. We call this approach the *dynamic probing*. Another approach is called the *static probing*, in which the probing is done periodically, that is, $k(t)$ is a constant, regardless of the network status. We will do experiments by running simulations on both dynamic and static probings in order to verify and evaluate the feasibility of our approach.

1.5.2 *Heuristic-Based QoS Adaptation*

The applying of a different heuristic reduces the size of a QoS-message into a different magnitude. A reduced size can be represented by a ratio of the original size of the QoS-message. Formally, a QoS-message, Q, has a set of heuristics $\mathcal{H} = \{h_1, ..., h_m\}$ and a h_i reduces the size of Q, S_Q, into $S'_Q = \alpha_i \cdot S_Q$, where $\alpha \in (0, 1)$ and $i = 1, ..., m$. Therefore, the heuristic function, f_H, that describes the effect of applying a specific heuristic, in terms of the ratio of the original size, is defined as

$$f_H : \mathcal{H} \rightarrow \alpha, \text{where}$$

$\alpha \in (0, 1]$,
$\mathcal{H} = \{h_1, ..., h_m\}$ such that $h_i = i, i = 0, ..., m$, and
$f_H(h_0) = 1$.

On the other hand, we would like to know the effect on the quality level of Q according to the availability of bandwidth. Suppose that an available bandwidth, B', that is reported by the communication network, is described in the form of a ratio of the original bandwidth requirement, B_Q, of the QoS-message, Q. The quality function, f_Q, that describes the effect of B' is defined as

$$f_Q : \beta \rightarrow QL, \text{ where}$$

$\beta = B'/B_Q$ (and thus $\beta \in (0,1)$), and
$QL = \{q_1, ..., q_m\}$ such that $q_i = i, i = 1, ...m$ and $m = |\mathcal{H}|$.

Notice that f_Q is a decreasing stepwise function that

$$f_Q(\beta) = q_j, \text{ if } f_H(h_j) \leq \beta < f_H(h_{j-1}), j = 1, ..., m.$$

In response to the bandwidth changes of the communication network, we define that the feedback message contains the information of the ratio of the current available bit rate to the previous one.

1.6 MCS Transformation

1.6.1 *Transformation Flow*

There are two transformations regarding MCS in this framework. The first one is the transformation from MDS to MCS, referred to as *MDS-to-MCS transformation.* The second one is an auto-transformation of MCS, referred to as *MCS auto-transformation.* The objective of MDS-to-MCS transformation is to generate from MDS an MCS that consists of a collection of QoS-messages to direct the transmission of MMOs. The objective of MCS auto-transformation is to modify QoS-messages to adapt to the network environment change. There are two cases where MCS auto-transformation takes place. The first case is during the call establishment phase in which the attempt for establishment is rejected, based on the QoS-message specification, and therefore a negotiation is needed between the application and the communication network. The second case happens after a call is established and there is a feedback message from the communication network that initiates a renegotiation between the application and the communication network to adapt to the change.

The steps of MCS transformations during the call establishment phase are described as follows:

MDS-to-MCS transformation

(1) Check system component profiles to determine which objects to transmit.

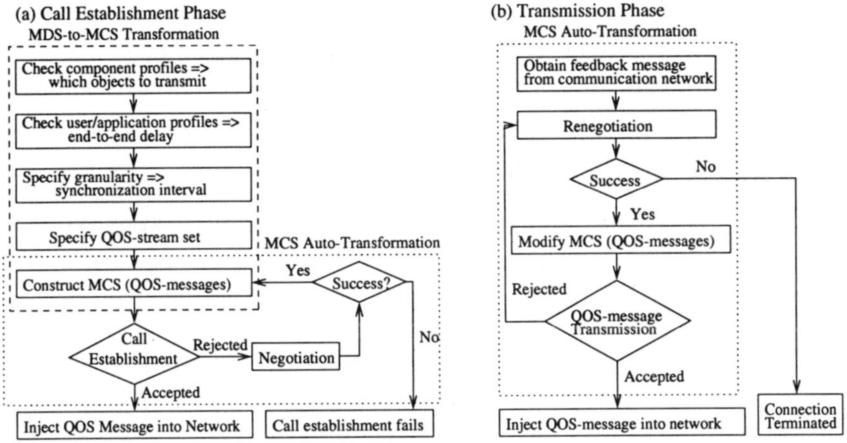

Fig. 1.7 MCS transformations.

For example, check the capability and capacity of the hardware and the user's preferences.

(2) Check user and application profiles to determine the end-to-end delay, Δ.
(3) Specify granularity to determine the synchronization interval, Φ.
(4) Specify QoS-stream.
(5) Construct an MCS that consists of a collection of QoS-messages.

MCS auto-transformation during the call establishment

(1) Attempt to establish the call: If accepted, the transformation is done and QoS-messages are injected into the communication network; otherwise, go to the next step.
(2) Initiate and perform negotiation: If successful, go to the next step; otherwise, the call establishment fails.
(3) Modify MCS and go to step 1.

The flow of the transformations is illustrated in Fig. 1.7(a), where MDS-to-MCS transformation and MCS auto-transformation are enclosed in the dashed-line rectangle and in the dotted-line rectangle, respectively.

After the call is established, the MMOs are transmitted according to the QoS-messages injected into the communication network. During the transmission, if a feedback message is sent back from the communication network to report network bandwidth change, a renegotiation is initiated. This is where the second case of MCS auto-transformation takes place.

The steps of MCS transformation during the MMO transmission phase are described as follows:

MCS auto-transformation during the MMO transmission

(1) Obtain a feedback message from the communication network.
(2) Initiate and perform renegotiation: If successful, go to the next step; otherwise, the transmission is terminated.
(3) Modify MCS.
(4) Attempt to transmit MMOs based on the modified MCS: If accepted, the transformation is done and the QoS-messages are injected into the communication network; otherwise, go to step 3.

The flow of the transformation is illustrated in Fig. 1.7(b).

1.6.2 *QoS-Message Operations*

To support the transformations, a set of operations is needed to construct and modify QoS-messages. *QoS-message operations* (QM-operations) are developed to perform the task. In MDS-to-MCS transformation, QM-operations initialize Δ and Φ, and validate QoS-messages. In MCS auto-transformation, QoS-operations are employed in negotiation and renegotiation in order to adapt to the communication network's bandwidth change, based on the scaling policy.

When transforming MDS into MCS, it must be assured that the derived MCS consists of a collection of QoS-messages. Two operations are useful in this transformation:

- Adjust granularity to adapt to capacities of system components.
- Prioritize elements in the QoS-stream to decompose the composite MMO into QoS-messages.

Additionally, since the QoS-reliable communication is based on the end-to-end delay, the synchronization interval and the media bandwidth, three other types of QM-operations are defined accordingly.

- Change synchronization interval by moving synchronization points, adding synchronization points, and removing synchronization points.

- Change end-to-end delay based on user/application's preference profiles.
- Change the bandwidth requirements by media shifting [H. J. Chang (1995); H. J. Chang (1998)] and media scaling [T. Kapner and L. Wolf (1994); H. Tokuda *et al.* (1992)] to adapt to the changing bandwidth availibility.

1.7 Examples

1.7.1 *Example 1: Video Application*

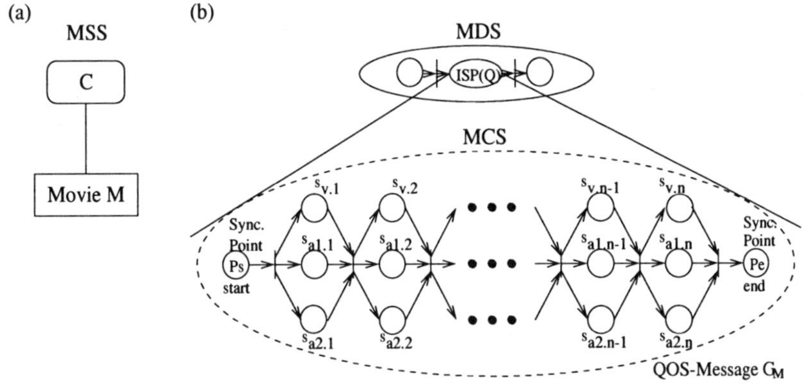

Fig. 1.8 MSS, MDS, MCS of a movie, where the MCS consists of one single QoS-message G_M.

A two-hour-long movie, M, consists of three streams: a video stream, s_v, and two audio streams, s_{a1} and s_{a2}, for the two channels of the stereo audio in the movie, respectively. In this case, the QoS-stream is defined as the set, Q_M, where $Q_M = \{\{s_v, s_{a1}, s_{a2}\}\}$. The whole movie can be modeled by MSS as illustrated in Fig. 1.8(a). The MSS is transformed to MDS and then MCS, where the MCS initially consists of one single QoS-message G_M. The MDS, MCS, and QoS-message are shown in Fig. 1.8(b). It can be verified that G_M is a valid QoS-message directly by definition as follows:

(1) There is a place, p_s, representing the starting synchronization point and there is a place, p_e, representing the ending synchronization

point in G_M.
(2) No other places in G_M represent synchronization points.
(3) All places in G_M are reachable from p_s.
(4) All places in G_M are not reachable from p_e, except for p_e itself.
(5) The place-stream of G_M is in Q_M.

Although G_M is a valid QoS-message, the specification implies that only after the whole movie arrives can it be played back. However, if the receiving end does not have enough buffer to hold the whole movie, the QoS-message should be modified to adapt to the capacity of the buffer. Another consideration is that any packet loss will force the whole movie to be discarded if M is specified as one single QoS-message. Therefore, it is practical to decompose M into a sequence of smaller units, where each unit, for example, consists of MMOs in an one-second interval, or in a group of picture if M is an MPEG movie.

As shown in Fig. 1.9, the subscript n is the number of units after decomposition.

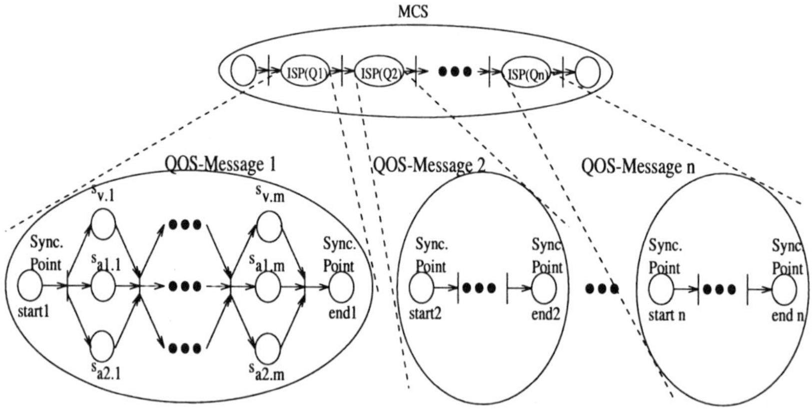

Fig. 1.9 The Decomposition of a movie into a collection of QoS-messages.

During the transmission of MMOs, if a feedback message is reported by the communication network, heuristics such as discarding an audio stream, reducing video frame rate, reducing video resolution or discarding B frames [D. Le Gall (1991)] in an MPEG movie, can be applied to adjust QoS-messages to adapt to the change.

1.7.2 *Example 2: World-Wide-Web Document Retrieval*

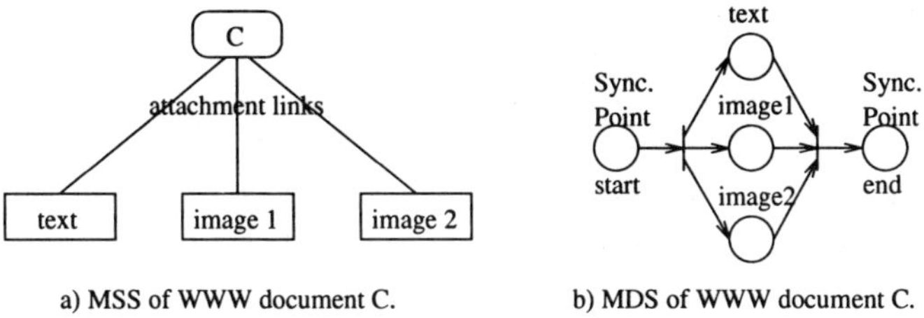

Fig. 1.10 The MSS and MDS of the example document.

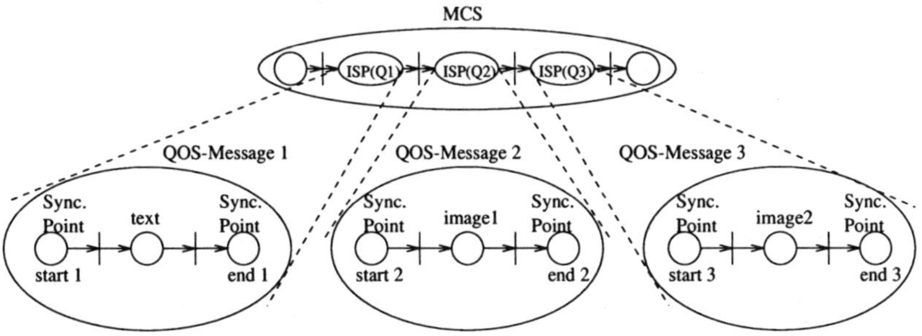

Fig. 1.11 The MCS after prioritization.

A document C in the World-Wide-Web (WWW) consists of a text object, s_t, and two images, s_{i1} and s_{i2}. The MSS and the corresponding MDS transformed from the MSS are illustrated in Fig. 1.10. Suppose that the images are not essential in this document, i.e., the text can be viewed alone without the presence of the images. The QoS-stream can then be defined as a set, Q_C, where $Q_C = \{\{s_t\}, \{s_{i1}\}, \{s_{i2}\}\}$. In the simplest MDS-to-MCS transformation, the MCS is identical to the MDS, and consists of one single QoS-message. However, it can be verified that the QoS-message is not valid, as the stream set of the object places between the two synchronization points $\{s_t, s_{i1}, s_{i2}\}$ is not in Q_C, despite the fact that other conditions are satisfied. In this case, the QM-operation *prioritization* can be adopted in the transformation. Usually the text has the highest priority among the three objects. This is a very common way for most of the Internet browsers to handle the retrieval of documents. Also, assume that the two images are of the same importance (or the same unimportance). As the result, the MCS consists of three QoS-messages, as shown in Fig. 1.11. Note that the tie breaker of the priority is arbitrary.

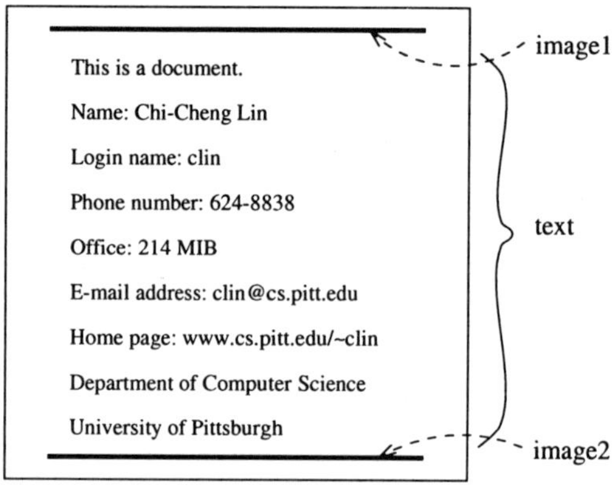

Fig. 1.12 Another example of the WWW document.

Consider another scenario that $Q_c = \{\{s_t\}\}$. Then the best-effort stream set, B_c, is derived as $B_c = S - \{s_t\} = \{s_{i1}, s_{i2}\}$. This implies that only the QoS requirements of the text is specified, while image1 and image2 are two icons that have no QoS requirements and will be sent in the best-effort fashion. This case is also commonly seen in a realistic WWW document such as the one shown in Fig. 1.12, where only the text is important, and the bars at the top and bottom are not important and can be sent in the best-effort fashion.

1.7.3 *Example 3: Telemedicine Application*

We show an example of our proposed work by considering the following scenario that can occur in both civilian and military communities:

(1) At the patient's site, a text file of the patient's information, an audio annotation, and a medical image are to be transmitted over the wireless communication network from a PDA to a mobile hospital that supports a better treatment.
(2) However, at that moment, the communication network between the patient site and the mobile hospital does not have enough band-

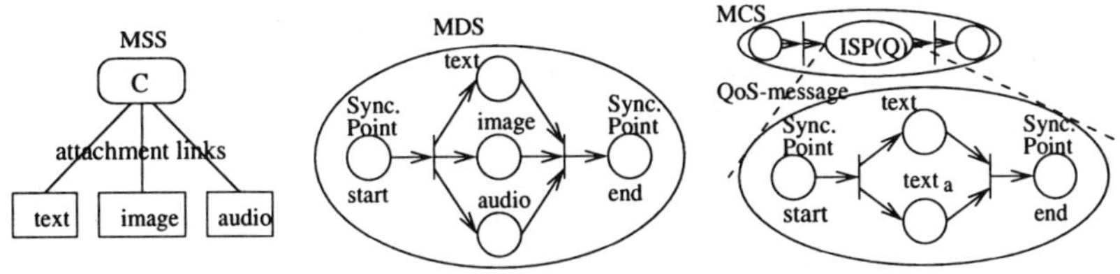

a) MSS. b) MDS. c) MCS and QoS-message.

Fig. 1.13 MSS, MDS, MCS, and QoS-message of a medical record in the example.

width to deliver the data in a specified short period of time.

(3) Originally, the MSS contains all three objects. To adapt to the bandwidth, the audio is media-shifted to a text, and the image is not to be transmitted. Consequently, the QoS-message that is transformed from the MSS contains only the text information and another text file, text_a, that is shifted from the audio, is transmitted to the mobile hospital.

(4) After receiving the QoS-message, the mobile hospital decides that the patient should be transported to a stationary hospital. Therefore, the QoS-message is forwarded to a stationary hospital immediately.

(5) As the QoS-message carries within itself a knowledge to indicate that the QoS-message is not the original set of data intended to be delivered, after the stationary hospital receives the QoS-message, the knowledge will trigger actions to actively request the missing image from the patient site's PDA in order to obtain a complete set of records for diagnosis and/or archiving. The image is then transmitted to the stationary hospital in a looser time constraint.

The MSS, MDS, MCS, and QoS-messages in this example are illustrated in Fig. 1.13.

1.8 Conclusion and Future Work

This chapter presented the architecture and approach of the AMS, a QoS-message-directed adaptive distributed multimedia system. The approach is based on representing MMOs differently at different levels of AMS to support effective manipulation and adaptation. Also presented was the formal definition and specification of the QoS-message, and the multimedia adaptation based on the concept of it. The QoS-messages serve as the atomic presentation, communication, and adaptation units, and when cooperating with schema transformations, they provide an integrated and uniform solution for the issues of presentation, communication, and adaptation for multimedia applications in a distributed environment.

Preliminary simulation based on the schema transformation and QoS-message-based adaptation has been performed [C. C. Lin (1997); C. C. Lin *et al.* (1998)]. The results show the effect of the adaptation and the effectiveness of the running time of the schema transformation. In addition to performing more work on simulation, our future work includes the following:

- the development of cross-disciplinary applications based on the concept of the AMS,
- the investigation of issues related to on-line feedback mechanism of the communication network,
- the investigation of research issues regarding service models and QoS management in the new emerging network environments, such as mobile environments, ad-hoc networks [T. Imielinski and H. F. Korth (1996)], and integrated wired and wireless networks, and
- the extension of the AMS to support the development of multimedia applications in the new network environments.

Bibliography

C. Aurrecoechea, A. Campbell, and L. Hauw. A Survey of QoS Architectures. *ACM/Springer-Verlag Journal Multimedia Systems*, 6(3):138–151, 1998.

A. Campbell, G. Coulson, and D. Hutchison. A Quality of Service Architecture. *Computer Communication Review*, 24(2):6–27, 1994.

H. J. Chang. Dynamic Presentation Scheduling and Media-Shifting of Tele-Action Objects in Distributed Multimedia Systems. *Ph.D.'s proposal*, 1995.

H. J. Chang. *Quality-of-Presentation-based Adaptive Presentation of Tele-Action Objects in Distributed Multimedia Systems*. PhD thesis, University of Pittsburgh, 1998.

S. K. Chang, D. Mossé, and Y. J. Chen. A Framework for Modeling Dependable Real-Time Distributed Systems. In *Proceedings of Second IFAC Workshop on Safety and Reliability in Emerging Control Technologies*, pages 495–510, Daytona Beach, Florida, November 1-3 1995.

F. Colaitis. Opening Up Multimedia Object Exchange with MHEG. *IEEE Multimedia*, 1(2):80–84, 1994.

Y. Deng and S. K. Chang. A G-Net Model for Knowledge Representation and Reasoning. *IEEE Transactions on Knowledge and Data Engineering*, 2(3):295–310, September 1990.

Y. Deng and S. K. Chang. A Framework for the Modeling and Prototyping of Distributed Information Systems. *International Journal of Software Engineering and Knowledge Engineering*, 1(3):203–226, September 1991.

D. Ferrari. Client Requirements for Real-Time Communication. *IEEE Journal on Selected Areas in Communications*, 28(11):65–72, November 1990.

B. Field, T. Znati, and D. Mossé. V-net: A Framework for a Versatile Network Architecture to Support Real-Time Communication Performance Guarantees. In *Infocom 95*, pages 1188–1197, Boston, April 1995.

D. Le Gall. MPEG: A Video Compression Standard for Multimedia Applications. *CACM*, 34(4):47–58, 1991.

T. Imielinski and H. F. Korth. *Mobile Computing*. Kluwer Academic Publishers,

Norwell, MA, 1996.

T. Kapner and L. Wolf. Media scaling in distributed multimedia object service. In *2nd International Workshop on Advanced Teleservices and High Speed Communication Architectures*, Hiedelberg, Germany, September 1994.

C. C. Lin. *An Integrated Framework to Support Dynamic Environment Adaptation in Distributed Multimedia Systems.* PhD thesis, University of Pittsburgh, 1997.

C. C. Lin, S. K. Chang, and T. Znati. QoS-Message Directed Adaptive Distributed Multimedia System. *In Proceedings of DMS'97, 1997 Pacific Workshop on Distributed Multimedia Systems*, 1997.

C. C. Lin, J. Xiang, and S. K. Chang. Transformation and Exchange of Multimedia Objects in Distributed Multimedia Systems. *ACM/Springer-Verlag Journal Multimedia Systems*, 4(1):12–29, 1996.

C. C. Lin, T. Znati, and S. K. Chang. QoS-Message-Directed Adaptive Multimedia Communication. In *The 31st Annual IEEE Simulation Symposium*, pages 157–164, 1998.

K. Nahrstedt and J. M. Smith. The QoS Broker. *IEEE Multimedia*, 2(1):53–67, 1995.

K. Nahrstedt and J. M. Smith. Design, Implementation and Experiences with the OMEGA End-point Architercture. *IEEE JSAC*, 14(3):413–427, 1996.

R. Simon. *An Integrated Communication Architecture For Distributed Multimedia Applications.* PhD thesis, University of Pittsburgh, 1996.

R. Simon, T. Znati, and R. J. Sclabassi. DIPCS: An Interproces Communication Architecture for Distributed Multimedia Systems. *Journal of Multimedia Tools and Applications*, 1(3):263–293, 1995.

B. Stiller. Quality-of-Service Issues in Networking Environments. Technical Report TR380, University of Cambridge, Computer Laboratory, Cambridge, England, U.K., 1995.

H. Tokuda, Y. Tobe, S.T.C. Chou, and J.M.F. Moura. Continuous Media Communication with Dynamic QOS Control Using ARTS with an FDDI Network. In *ACM SIGCOMM'92*, Baltimore, August 1992.

T. Znati, Y. Deng, B. Field, and S. K. Chang. Multi-level Specifications and Protocol Design for Distributed Multimedia Communication. *International Journal in Computer Simulation, Special Issue on Simulation of Communication Systems*, 3(4):355–382, 1993.

T. Znati and B. Field. A Network Level Abstraction for Multimedia Communication in Real-Time Networks. *IEEE Transactions on Knowledge and Data Engineering*, 5(4):590–599, August 1993.

Application of Compositional Petri Nets and PN^3–Tool to the Specification of Distributed Multimedia Objects

NIKOLAY ANISIMOV, ALEKSEY KOVALENKO
PAVEL POSTUPALSKY

Institute for Automation and Control Processes
of the Russian Academy of Sciences, 5 Radio street, Vladivostok 690041, Russia
E-mail: anisimov@iapu2.marine.su

and

SON VUONG

University of British Columbia, Vancouver, Canada
E-mail: vuong@cs.ubc.ca

This paper addresses the problems of specifying synchronization requirements for real-world size multimedia presentations. In particular, we propose a compositional Petri net model, called CoPN, for multimedia synchronization specifications. The salient features of this model, including *macroplaces* and *PN entities*, are presented and the application of the the CoPN model to multimedia specification is discussed via a number of illustrative examples of intra- and inter-stream multimedia synchronizations. This compositional approach enables compact and readable specification of complex, large-scale specifications while preserving the fine granularity as well as supporting user interactions. Preliminary results on incorporating the time stream Petri net (TSPN) in the compositional method for handling time are discussed. The Petri net tool, called PN^3-Tool, is also presented, which can be applied to verify the correctness of specifications of multimedia synchronizations in CoPN.

Keywords: multimedia system, inter-stream, intra-stream synchronization, user interaction, Petri nets, compositional Petri nets, time stream Petri nets, compositionality, modularuty

1 Introduction

An important problem in multimedia communication is the synchronization of both static (data, text) and dynamic (video, audio) objects. To some extent, this problem can be successfully solved with the aid of Petri net models (Reisig, 1985; Brauer *et al.*, 1987) such as Time Stream Petri Nets (TSPN) (Diaz and Senac, 1993; Sénac *et al.*, 1994) and itsextension for user interaction $TSPN_{ui}$ (Cooper, 1995), Object Composition Petri Nets (OCPN) (Little and Ghafoor, 1990), Extended Object Composition Petri Nets(XOCPN) (Woo *et al.*, 1994), Dynamic Timed Petri Nets (Prabhakaran and Raghavan, 1993). A comprehensive review of these models can be found in (Vuong *et al.*, 1995). However, a common problem with the existing specification methods lies in the complexity of the specifications for real-life multimedia application. A viable way to cope with this problem is to apply the notion of compositionality and modularity which was recently introduced in the CoPN model (Anisimov and Koutny, 1996; Best *et al.*, 1992). We should note existing work which addresses similar problems of structured specification, such as the one reported in (Sénac *et al.*, 1996) where the TSPN is extended into the hierarchical TSPN (HTSPN), which has features similar to macronets. Also, the work by Courtiat *et al.* incorporates features for structuring multimedia specification where the real-Time LOTOS is used as the underlining model. Thus, this model inherits both the advantages of existing LOTOS support tools as well as the potential disadvantage of the complexity of LOTOS as a specification language.

The main contribution of our paper rests on the application of the compositional approach developed in (Anisimov,1989; Anisimov, 1991; Anisimov and Koutny, 1996) for the specification of complex real-life multimedia systems. In this paper, we review the salient features of the CompositionalPetri net (CoPN) model: *macroplaces, Petri net entities* and *access points*; and discuss their applications in multimedia synchronization specification via several illustrative examples. In the next section, the notion of of macroplace is introduced and shown how it can simplify large multimedia specifications that involve user interactions. Section 3 defines Petri entity which can be nicely applied to the specification of intra- and interstream multimedia synchronization. In Section 4, we briefly describe a CoPN tool, called PN^3-Tool, which can be used to graphically generate CoPN specifications. To illustrate the viability of the CoPN model, a complete example of multimedia scenario specification is presented in Section 5, followed by some concluding remarks in Section 6. This paper is a revised and extended version of the conference paper (Anisimov *et al.*, 1997).

2 Petri nets with macroplaces

In recent work (Anisimov, 1991; Anisimov *et al.*, 1994; Anisimov and Koutny, 1996) the classic Petri Nets have been extended with the notion of *macroplace*. Such extended nets are called *macronets*. In this section we will show how the use of macroplaces and macronets improves the process of multimedia specification.

Macronet is a regular Petri net augmented with a set of macroplaces. First, we will introduce the *simple macroplace*. Informally, a macroplace is a set of places, called *internal* places, one of which is marked as a *head place* of the macroplace. Macroplaces are connected to/from other (macro)places via transitions in the same way as simple (non-macro) places. So, a macroplace is considered to be marked if at least one of his internal places is marked. Adding the token to a macroplace is defined as putting a token into its internal head place. Removing the token from the macroplace leads to removing the token from one of the internal places of the macroplace. The transition of macronet is considered to be enabled if its each input (macro)place has at least one token. Then, firing of enabled transition involves removing token from each input (macro)place and adding token to each output (macro)place.

Intuitively, the above definition of macroplace makes sense only if its internal places form the state-machine net (SM-net), i.e. a Petri net in which each transition has exactly one incoming and one outcoming arc. A macroplace corresponding to a SM-net will be called *simple macroplace.*

Formally, a macronet is defined as a tuple $N = \langle S, T, F, M_0, Q \rangle$, where:

- $S = S^n \cup S^\mu$, where $S^n \cap S^\mu = \emptyset$. S^n is the set of simple (non-macro) places, and S^μ is the set of macroplaces;
- T is the set of transitions, such that $S \cap T = \emptyset$;
- $F \subseteq S \times T \ \cup \ T \times S$ is a flow relation;
- $M_0 : S^n \rightarrow \{0, 1, 2, \ldots\}$ is an initial marking;
- $Q : S^\mu \rightarrow \mathcal{P}(S^n) \times S^n$, such that $\forall s \in S^\mu$: $Q(s) = (S', s_0) \Rightarrow s_0 \in S'$. Q is a function that associates with each macroplace $s^\mu \in S^\mu$ a set of internal places S' and a head place s_0.

Graphically, a macroplace is depicted as a large circle surrounding the part of the net formed by its associated internal places. Incoming and outcoming arcs are attached to a macroplace in the same way as to an ordinary place.

Fig.1 shows an example of a macronet. This net has a macroplace s_7 with internal places $\{s_5, s_6\}$. Macroplace s_7 will be marked if either s_5 or s_6 has a token. Firing t_5 then will lead to putting a token into the head place s_5. Transition t_4 will be enabled if s_3 and s_7 are marked. In other words, t_4 can fire if either the set s_3, s_5 or s_3, s_6 have tokens.

The specification paradigm depicted in Fig.1 can be quite handy for designating a stream as the multimedia master stream among other streams. For example, part of the stream s_5, s_6 can be "disrupted" by the transition t_2 at any time.

Macronets also allow the specification of a complex system in a more compact and natural way than regular Petri nets. For instance, the macronet in Fig.2 models the repeated background stream (e.g. audio, video, etc.) which can be terminated by the master stream regardless the state (marking) this background stream may be in.

It should be noted that macronets are merely a compact representation of classic Petri nets of complex internal structure. It is relatively straightforward to transform

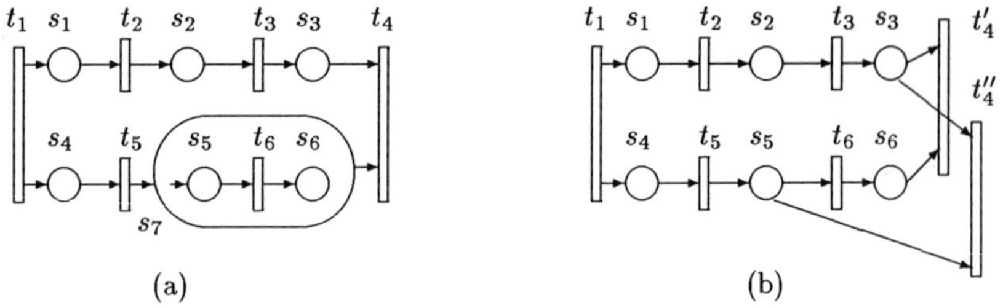

Fig. 1 (a) Macronet with simple macroplace (b) Equivalent regular Petri net

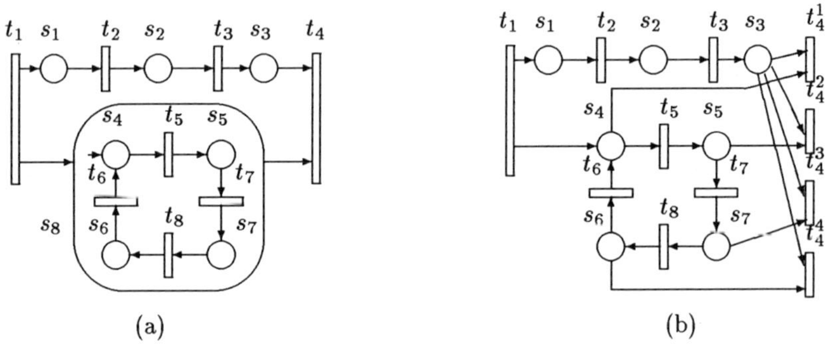

Fig. 2 Cyclic background specification.

a macronet to its equivalent regular Petri net. For example, the macronet shown in Fig.1(a) can be easily transformed into the Petri net shown in Fig.1(b). We can see that transition t_4 is split into two copies t_4', t_4'', each corresponds to the possible marking of either s_5 or s_6.

So far, we have addressed only simple macroplaces whose internal places form a SM-net. We can define a general form of macroplace which consists of the parallel composition of SM fragments. In this case we have to designate a head place for each SM fragment. Respectively, putting (or removing) the token in a general macroplace leads to putting the token in each head place (or removing the token from each SM fragment). A formal definition of the general form of a macroplace can be found in (Anisimov, 1991; Anisimov and Kovalenko, 1995).

Using a general form of macroplace, we can define the operations of user interaction such as `terminate`, `restart`, and `forward`. In Fig.3, executing transition $t_{terminate}$ causes a termination of all activities in the internal net corresponding the the macroplace, i.e. all internal tokens (from both upper and lower streams) are removed. Transition $t_{forward}$ has similar effect on the internal net. The difference between these two actions is that in the future $t_{forward}$ and t_{end} will together be merged with the first transition of next stream whereas $t_{terminate}$ will be merged with a special termination transition. The execution of $t_{restart}$ will remove a token from $s_{7_{macro}}$, i.e. all tokens from the internal net, and then reinitialize all its head places, s_1 and s_4. The macronet Fig.3 can be transformed into a classic Petri net, but it will lead to an extremely messy specification, e.g. the transition $t_{restart}$ will be split into 16 copies. The above user interaction functions would be very useful for video-on-demand applications.

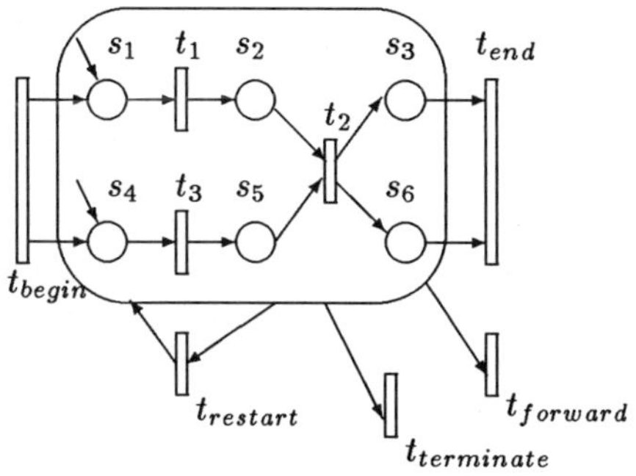

Fig. 3 User interaction: restart, terminate, forward.

Thus, we can see that macronets offer a way of multimedia synchronization specification with more descriptive power while maintaining the compactness of the specification. Using macronets it becomes possible to specify new types of constructs such as cycles as illustrated in Fig.2. Moreover, some user interaction operations such as restart, terminate and forward can be specified in a natural and compact way.

3 Petri net entity.

In this section, we will present the notions of *Petri net Entity* and *access points* used in CoPN to specify compositionality, and show via a number of examples how they can be nicely applied to the compositional and hierarchical specification of multimedia scenarios. The notions of Petri net entity and access points were first introduced in (Anisimov, 1989), and further developed in (Anisimov, 1991a; Anisimov, 1991c; Anisimov and Koutny, 1996).

Petri net entity is a generalization of well-known labeled Petri nets where instead of a single labelling function we allow several ones. These labeling functions are called *access points*. Formally, a Petri net entity (or entity for short) is defined as a tuple $E = \langle N, G \rangle$, where:

- $N = \langle S, T, F, M_0 \rangle$ is a Petri net;
- $G = \{g_1, g_2, \ldots, g_n\}$ is a set of access points $g_i = \langle id_i, Alph_i, \sigma_i \rangle$ where:
  - id_i is the identifier of the access point g_i;
  - $Alph_i$ is an alphabet (set of labels).
  - $\sigma_i : T \to Alph_i \cup \{\tau\}$ is a labeling function, where τ is a special symbol corresponding to an invisible action.

Graphically, an entity can be represented in two complementary ways: in a Petri net form and in a diagram form. In the first case, each transition of a classic Petri net is labeled by the set of expressions of the form $id_i : \xi;$. This means that the transition is visible as (interaction) ξ at access point (gate) names id_i. A transition may have several labels, i.e. it may be visible at different access points by different names. If a transition is labeled at g_i as τ it considers to be invisible at the access point g_i. Furthermore, labels such as $id_i : \tau$ will be omitted. In the diagram form, an entity is represented as a rectangle with small bold-face markers placed on its perimeter, where each marker represents an access point.

In Fig.4 the entity is shown in both forms. As shown in diagram form, the entity E has three access points L, R, and U, where L and R indicate the beginning and the end of the entity execution, respectively, whereas access point U is used for user interaction functions (in this case, only *advance*). In the Petri net form, transitions t_1 and t_3 are visible through L and R access points, respectively. The universal symbol — λ is used for development a composition on entities. The transitions t_3 and t_4 are visible through U as *advance*. Other transitions are not visible at all.

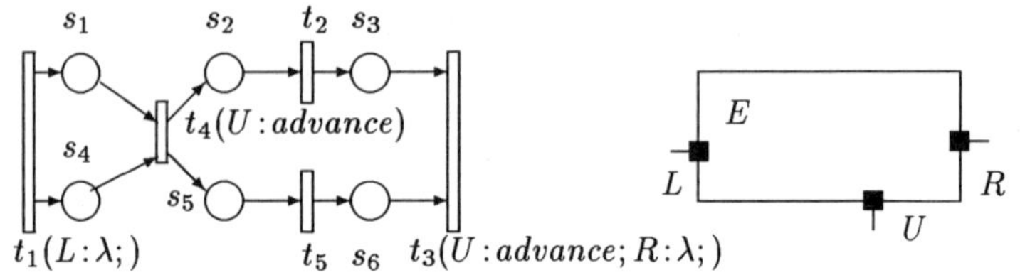

Fig. 4 Petri net entity example.

Composition of entities can be defined through their access points. The composition of two entities E_1 and E_2 through α and β produces a new entity $E_n = E_1 \,_{\alpha}\|_{\beta}\, E_2$. The operation involves disjoint union of corresponding nets N_1 and N_2, and then merging of transitions visible at α and β with the same names. The new set of access points will be $G = G_1 \cup G_2 \setminus \{\alpha, \beta\}$. The complete formal definition of the composition operation can be found in (Anisimov *et al.*, 1994). In the diagram form this operation is represented by connecting the appropriate access points of entities, as shown in Fig.5. For example, it is possible to specify the sequential behavior of the streams (i.e. intrastream synchronization) using the composition of entities. Fig.5 shows the new entity $E_r = E_1 \ {}_R||_L \ E_2$ in the diagram form, composed by connecting the access points R and L, and in Petri net form by merging the transitions that are visible at R and L. In the simplest case, when only one transition in each entity is visible at R and L, respectively, these corresponding transitions will be merged. The result entity will inherit the set $\{L, R, U, T\}$ of access points while the connected R and L will be eliminated due to participation in the composition.

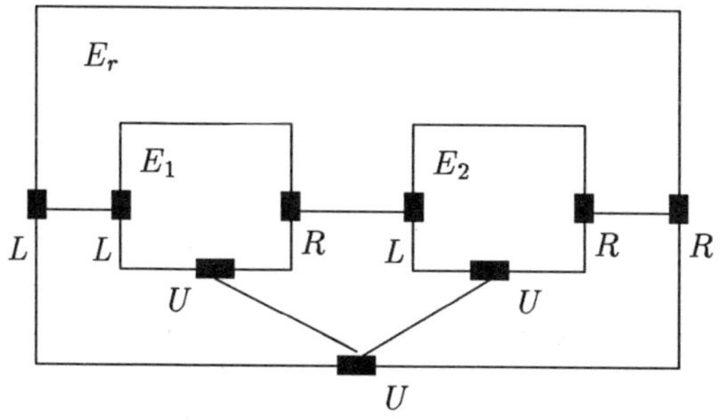

Fig. 5 **Sequential composition of entities.**

On the architectural level, a specification on CoPN consists of the set of hierarchical composed Petri net entities where the lowest level entities have the Petri net equivalent representation. Such level of specification can be view as a conceptual one. A formal semantic of such specification is defined as the result of performing all the entity compositions in the Petri net form. In general, the resulting Petri net can be unwieldily complex. However, it can either partially or fully processed for useful protocol engineering tasks such as verification, test generation and automatic implementation.

The main advantage of compositional specification, i.e. specification at the architectural level, is that it allows description of complex systems in terms of blocks and their interconnections which is more convenient for most practitioners then a single complex Petri net. But at the any phase in the protocol engineering process, the compositional specification can be converted to a Petri net for suitable processing.

Examples. We now present two simple examples to illustrate the applicability of the entity composition in the specification of interstream synchronization, as shown in Fig.6, and of a multimedia scenario with user interactions, as shown in Fig.7. Fig.6 shows two streams which are synchronized at every other transitions. The synchronization is shown by the same interaction label at the respective transitions. The Petri net corresponding to each entity is placed in an entity box. The Petri net corresponding to the composition of the two entities E_a and E_v through the access points A and V is shown on the right-hand side of Fig.6.

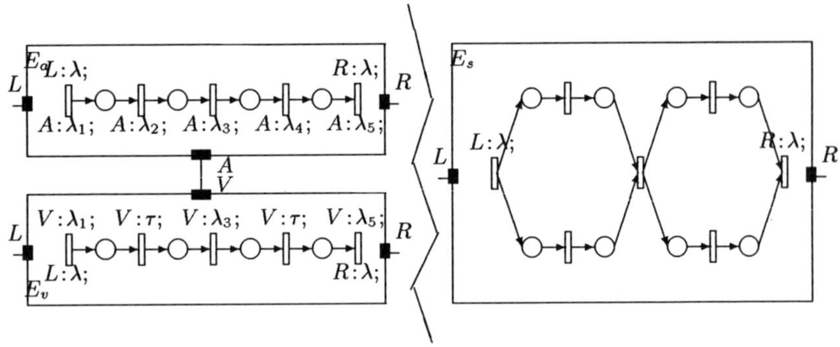

Fig. 6 Interstream synchronization.

User interaction operations such as **stop** and **resume** can be specified in a very elegant way via an extra controller entity, as shown in Fig.7. Each transition of the net which must be controlled (i.e. it may be affected by user interactions) must be visible at the access point by the respective user interaction label in order to be synchronized with the corresponding transition in the controller entity. In this example, every transition in the net is visible through U access point as ζ; they are synchronized with the (self-loop) transition with the same label ζ in the controller entity. After firing the **stop** transition in the controller entity, every (synchronized) transition in the net will be disabled until the **resume** transition is executed.

4 TSPN in entity composition.

We have so far considered Petri net entity composition to provide inter-stream synchronization without time constraints. However, since time constraints plays a key role in multimedia presentation, they must be taken into account during the composition of streams. In this section, we discuss the handling of time constraints by incorporating a basic time Petri net model with into the entity compositional approach. Among the various time Petri net models, we choose the Time Stream Petri Nets (TSPN) (Diaz and Senac, 1993) as the basic model, where the time supports for multimedia presentation are well elaborated. In TSPN, each input arc to a transition is associated with an interval $[\tau^{min}, \tau^{max}]$. Each transition is attributed with one of the firing disciplines: $\mathcal{R}$ = {and, weak-and, or, strong-or, master, or-master, and-master, weak-master, strong-master}, as illustrated in Fig.8. Using arc intervals and transition firing discipline, we can calculate the transition enabling interval. For example, when the token reaches a place s_i, $i \in \{1,2,3\}$ at the moment τ_i^{tok} (Fig.8) the (s_i, t_i) timer for the input arc is started and the

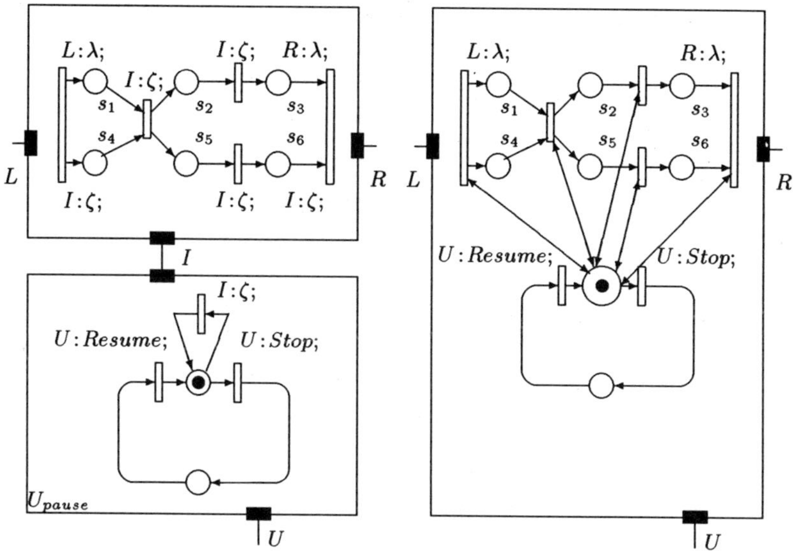

Fig. 7 Example with user interactions: stop and resume.

arc becomes enabled in the interval $[\tau_i^{tok} + \tau_i^{min}, \tau_i^{tok} + \tau_i^{max}]$. According to firing discipline and, the transition t_1 is enabled within the intersection of three intervals $\bigcap_{1 \le i \le 3}[\tau_i^{tok} + \tau_i^{min}, \tau_i^{tok} + \tau_i^{max}]$. For transition t_2 in Fig.8 with associated firing discipline or, the enabling interval is defined as the union of the arc's intervals. Other firing disciplines are discussed in details in (Diaz and Senac, 1993).

Let us now examine the time issues in context of the compositional approach. Suppose, we wish to perform an inter-stream synchronization of two streams that results in the merging of two transitions t_1 and t_2 to yield a new transition (t_1, t_2), as shown in Fig.8. The question arises is which firing discipline should be attributed to the new transition. Intuitively, we would expect the firing discipline in each stream to be preserved in the new transition. Moreover, we need an additional piece of information about the interplaying of the two streams. For example, we may want to synchronize t_1 as the master role. Thus, we can easily see that more than eight rules listed above will be needed.

We suggest a technique for the derivation of firing disciplines within the framework of our compositional approach. The main idea of our approach is as follows. Each firing discipline in $\mathcal{R}$ will be considered as a binary function which maps two intervals into a resulting interval. For instance, and(int_1, int_2) gives us a new interval which is the intersection of intervals int_1 and int_2. This resulting interval can be used as an argument in another function, e.g. strong$-$or(and$(int_1, int_2), int_3)$. Thus it is possible to define firing disciplines of transitions as a superposition of

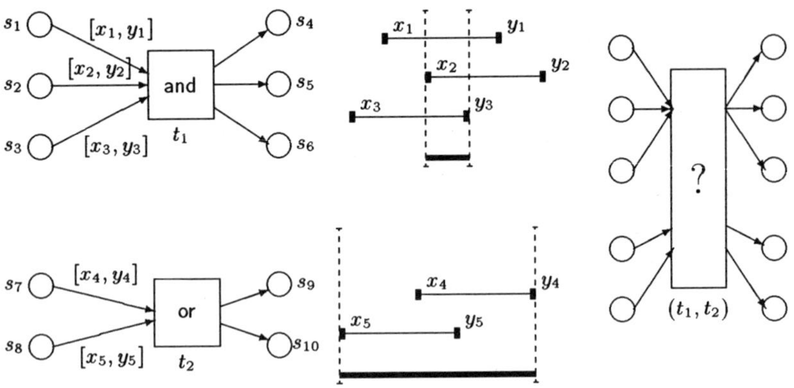

Fig. 8 A TSPN example.

functions whose arguments contain intervals of input arcs.

We note that in formulating the rules for composite firing disciplines, it is more convenient to manipulate with arcs than with its intervals. Thus, for each transition we assign a *firing discipline expression* (FDE).

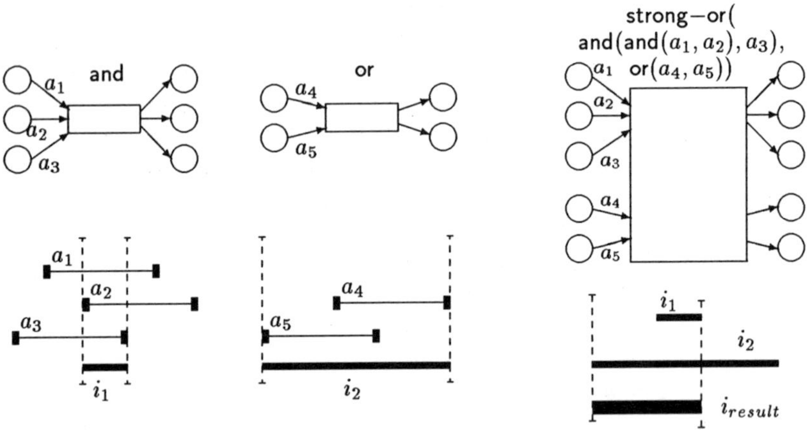

(a) Operands for the composition. (b) Resulting interval.

Fig. 9 Calculating the resulting interval in a TSPN composition.

Let *ex* be an FDE, *a* be an input arc of transition *t*. Let *rule* vary over $\mathcal{R}^* = \{\mathsf{and},\ \mathsf{weak{-}and},\ \mathsf{or},\ \mathsf{weak{-}master}_i,\ \mathsf{strong{-}master}_i\}$, $i \in \{1, 2\}$. We will write

$a \in ex(a \notin ex)$ if a is (not) participating in ex. Here, the index of a master participated discipline will indicate the master operand. We now define the FDE for a transition t recursively as follows:

(1) the empty string is a FDE;
(2) $rule(a_1, a_2)$ is a FDE if $a_1 \neq a_2$;
(3) $rule(ex, a)$ is a FDE if $a \notin ex$
(4) $rule(a, ex)$ is a FDE if $a \notin ex$
(5) $rule(ex_1, ex_2)$ is a FDE if there does not exist a such that $a \in ex_1$ and $a \in ex_2$.

The expressions $\mathsf{or}(a_1, a_2)$, $\mathsf{strong{-}or}(\mathsf{or}(a_1, a_2), a_3)$, $\mathsf{master}_1(\mathsf{weak{-}and}(a_1, a_2), \mathsf{or}(a_3, a_4))$ are examples of FDEs. The expression $\mathsf{weak{-}and}(a_1, \mathsf{strong{-}}\ \mathsf{master}_2(a_2, a_1))$ is not a FDE because it has two instances of the arc a_1.

Since every arc has an appropriate temporal interval, the FDE allows for the unique calculations of the enabling transition interval. For example, the transition (t_1, t_2) is the result of the $\mathsf{strong{-}or}$ FDE of the arcs of the transitions t_1 and t_2, respectively, as illustrated in Fig.9(a). The resulting enabling transition interval is calculated as shown in Fig.9(b).

It should be noted that the graphical representation of transitions with firing discipline expressions is combersome because it clames identification of all incoming arks. For example, in the resulting transition (t_1, t_2) on the Fig.9(b) we have to label all five incoming arks $a_1, ..., a_5$. Less cumbersome representation of the transition is depicted in Fig.10(a) where the transition with FDE is substituted by the cascade of transitions corresponding to FDE*.

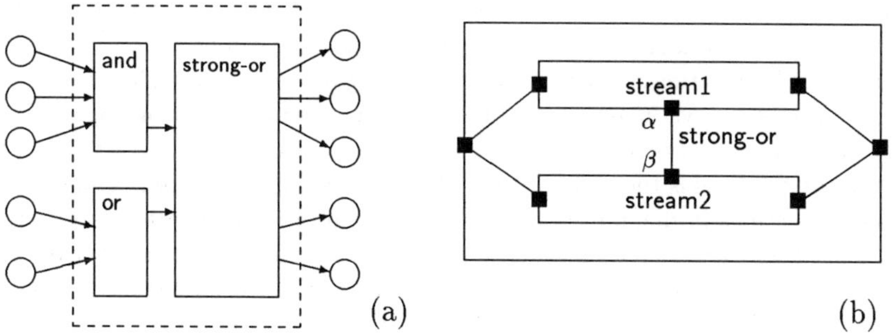

(a) (b)

Fig. 10 Graphical representation of firing discipline expression

Information about the rule for an inter-stream synchronization may be used as a parameter for a Petri net entity composition. Instead of one operation of entity composition with access points α and β we will get several ones: ${}_{\alpha}||_{\beta}^{\mathsf{or}}$, ${}_{\alpha}||_{\beta}^{\mathsf{and}}$, ...,

*Here we use the obvious equation $\mathsf{and}(a_1, \mathsf{and}(a_2, a_3)) = \mathsf{and}(\mathsf{and}(a_1, a_2), a_3)) = \mathsf{and}(a_1, a_2, a_3)$.

${}_{\alpha}||_{\beta}^{\mathsf{master}_i}$, etc .... In this case such composition rules can be easily represented as it is shown on Fig.10(b).

5 PN-Tool.

The compositional specification model , CoPN, described in this paper is supported by a special Petri net tool called PN^3-Tool. The detailed description of the tool can be found in (Anisimov it et al., 1994). In this section we will present the main features of PN^3-Tool which can beapplied to multimedia specifications.

PN^3-Tool has been developed on PC/MS Windows 3.x. Structurally, PN^3-Tool consists of three levels: basic, algebraic and architectural editors.

The basic editor allows explicit creation of specifications in Petri net form. The editor includes standard Petri net editing facilities such as adding, removing, resizing Petri net elements (place, transitions, arcs, marking, labels). The possibility of referencing from either transition or place to another Petri net window, called *page,* allows for the specification of hierarchical structures. The example of basic Petri net editor is presented in Fig.11.

The second level is the algebraic editor, which presents the set of algebraic operations for Petri net specification. In the editor, pages are considered as operands for operations. The first and the most atomic operation is adding an atomic net which consists of a transition with an incoming and an outcoming place. These places are called *head* and *tail*, respectively, see (Kotov, 1978). On the basis of place merging, the following operations were implemented: sequential composition, choice, iteration, and disabling. The parallel composition can be performed either as a pure synchronization or as a transition merging operation through access points. So, the algebraic level makes it easy to construct a complex Petri net specification with from entities of regular structure.

At the top level is the architectural editor, which allows the user to manipulate Petri net entities in diagram form, i.e. in the form of interconnected boxes. Each Petri net entity must either refer to another entity configuration (another page) or directly to a Petri net. The editor of this level enables the designer to think in terms of entities which are represented by boxes. To compose two entities one only needs to connect corresponding access points. The user can produce specifications by either top-down or bottom-up approaches.T he example of architectural editor is depicted on Fig.12.

Useful additional features have also been implemented, which include the visual simulation of Petri nets, which can used for better understanding of the dynamic behavior and for analysis; and verification for several important safety properties (e.g. boundedness and freedom from deadlocks, etc.) by means of the Petri net cover tree building.

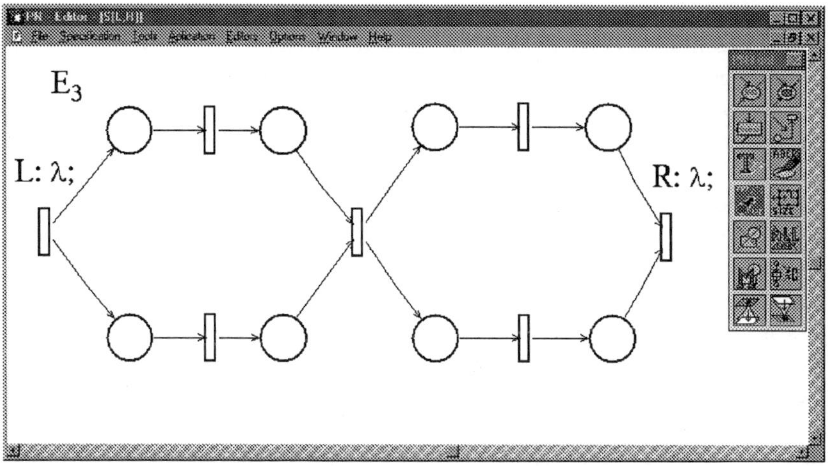

Fig. 11 Basic Petri net editor

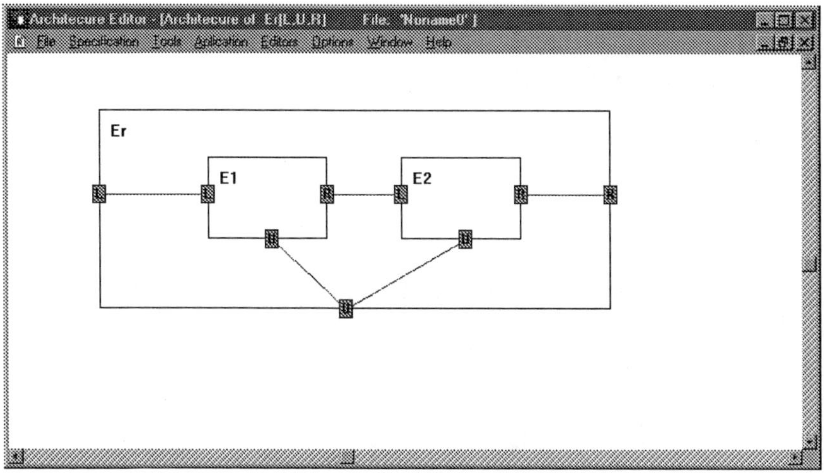

Fig. 12 Architectural editor

6 Example: Specification of multimedia scenario.

To illustrate the practical applicability of the CoPN model in the specification of complex multimedia scenarios, we have developed a CoPN specification of the multimedia scenario example which was presented in (Vuong *et al.*, 1995). This example is interesting since while not overly complex, it involves several important multimedia synchronization requirements, including user interaction functions. In order to simplify the specification we have mixed both Petri nets and diagram forms of representation. Fig.13 shows the top-level specification, which consists two independent parts: multimedia streams (**mms**) and user interaction modules (**uim**). While a designer may develop each part separately, at the end he must synchronize them together. First, we specify the internal representation of **mms**, and then deal with uim.

Multimedia streams. The scenario consists of two main streams, as shown in Figure 14(a): dynamic video and audio data, specified as entities VA_i; static data, specified as entities I_i and T_i. The static data includes two images I_1, I_2 and two texts T_1, T_2, shown in Fig.14(d). The pairs, image I_i with text T_i, must be "intra-synchronized" by means of head l and tail r access points.

The part of the scenario with dynamic data is represented by two sequential video clips (video streams) and one audio stream, as shown in Figure 14(b). The first video stream consists of a set of video frames $\{video_1, \ldots, video_n\}$, and the second stream, $\{video_{n+1}, \ldots, video_{2n}\}$, as shown in Figure 14(c). The audio stream is formed by the set of $\{audio_1, \ldots, audio_{2n}\}$. The specification resulting from intra-stream synchronization between VS_1 and VS_2 must in turn be inter-synchronized with the audio stream AS through the d and u access points, respectively. In inter-stream synchronization, transitions with the same labels (in this case, numbers from 0 to $2n+1$) will be merged. Each transition in the MM entity has an additional access point m:p; necessary for stop/resume primitives.

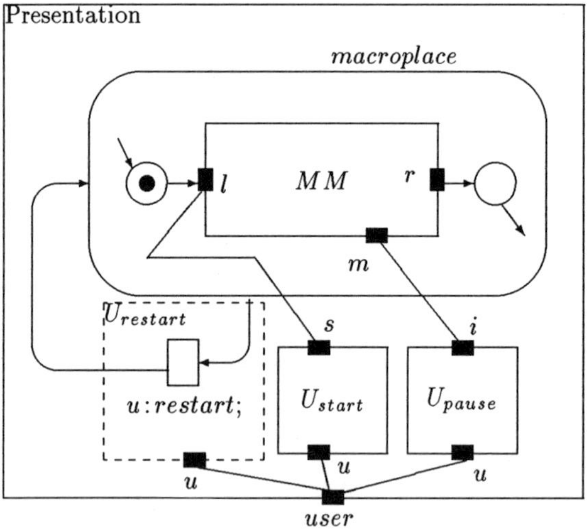

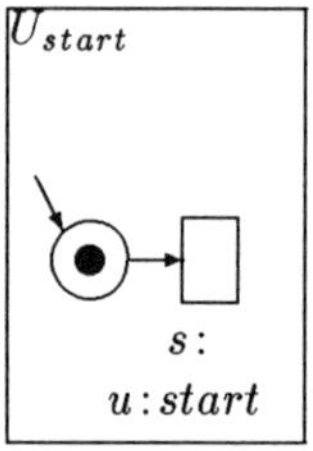

Start entity

Fig. 13 Example of multimedia scenario specification with user interaction.

User interaction. As shown in Fig.13, the entity *Presentation*, is controlled via the following types of user interactions at access point *user*:

- `start`: to perform an initialization and initiate the start of the multimedia streams. Entity U_{start} consists of one marked place and one transition which have to synchronize with the first transition of `mms`.
- `restart`: to allow the user to stop current multimedia presentation and start it from the very beginning. The *macroplace* can disrupt the activities of the MM entity at any time and restart the playing by means of the u:*restart* transition.
- `stop` and `resume`: to specify the possibility to make a pause at any time and resume from where it was left of. The internal structure of the entity U_{pause} is specified in the left bottom corner of Figure 7.

The above example demonstrates the methodology for multimedia scenario specification by means of Petri net entities and macronets. This CoPN model allows the independent creation of separate parts of the specification and then their algamation into an overall specification in a compositional and hierarchical manner.

7 Conclusion.

In this paper, we propose a compositional and hierarchical approach to multimedia scenario specification using a compositional Petri net model, so called CoPN. This compositional approach enables the compact and readable specification of complex, large-scale specifications while preserving the fine granularity as well as supporting user interactions. While discussing the features of CoPN, we have focused on the compositional aspects of the multimedia synchronization specification, without explicitly addressing the time parameters of the specification. Preliminary ideas on incorporating the time stream Petri net (TSPN) in the compositional method for handling time are discussed. We are currently examining further the interplaying of times and compositions in Petri nets, and expect to report the complete results in a future report.

The PN^3-Tool can also be enhanced in order to successfully support the specification of multimedia scenarios. The most significant modifications would include explicit implementation of macroplace operation "unwrapping"; flexible screen managing functions such as scaling and picture rotation; as well time constraint handling accordingly to the time model used.

8 Acknowledgments

The work performed by the first three authors was supported by the Russian Fund for Basic Research (Project No. 96-01-001773) and the NATO Networking Grant

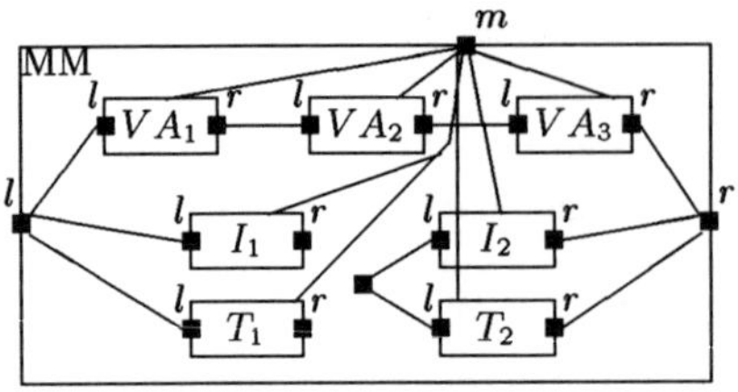

(a) The main multimedia entity and component entities.

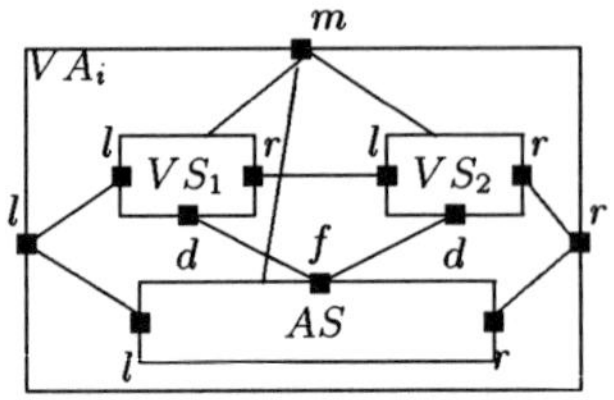

(b) Internal representation of VA_i streams.

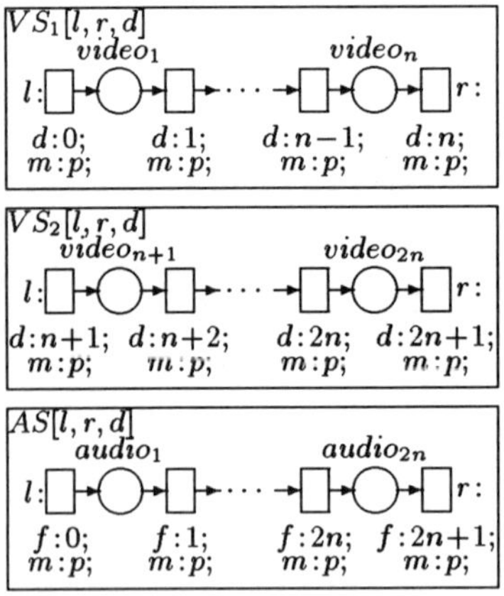

(c) VS_i (video) and AS (audio) streams.

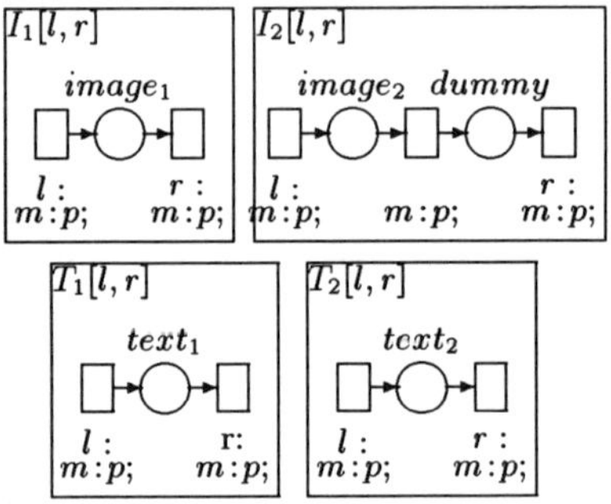

(d) I_i (image) and T_i (text) streams.

Fig. 14 Specification of multimedia streams.

SA.12-5-02(CN.NIG 960067)454/JPN/098. The work performed by the last author was supported in part by a joint grant from Motorola/ARRC and NSERC/IOR.

Bibliography

Anisimov, N. A. (1989) "A Notion of Petri Net Entity for Communication Protocol Design", *Institute for Automation and Control Processes.*

Anisimov, N. A. (1991a) "A Petri Net Entity as a Formal Model for LOTOS, a Specification Language for Distributed and Concurrent Systems", in *Parallel Computing Technologies,* ed. N. N. Mirenkov (World Scientific), 440–450.

Anisimov, N. A. (1991b) "An Algebra of Regular Macronets for Formal Specification of Communication Protocols", *Computers and Artificial Intelligence,* **10**, 541–560.

Anisimov, N. A., (1991c) "A Notion of Entity Based on Petri Nets", in *Proceedings of the 1991 IFAC Workshop on Discrete Event System Theory and Applications in Manufacturing and Social Phenomena,* ed. Yu-Chi Ho, Ying-Ping Zheng, Shenyang, P. R. China, (International Academic Publisher) 142–147.

Anisimov, N.A., Kovalenko, A.A., Postupalski, P.A. (1994) "Compositional Petri Net Environment", in *Proc. of the 1994 IEEE Symposium on Emerging Technologies & Factory Automation: ETFA'94,* 420–427.

Anisimov, N.A., Kovalenko, A.A. (1995) "Towards Petri Net Calculi based on Synchronization via Places", in *Proc. of the 1995 IEEE Symposium on Parallel Algorithms/Architecture Synthesis* (Aizu, Japan) 264–270.

Anisimov, N.A., Koutny, M., (1996) "On Compositionality and Petri Nets in Protocol Engineering", in *Protocol Specification, Testing and Verification, XV.,* eds. P.Dembiński, M.Średniawa. (Chapman & Hall, 1996) 71–86.

Anisimov, N.A., Kovalenko, A.A., Postupalsky, P.A., Vuong, S.T., (1997) "Application of Compositional Petri Nets in the Specification of Multimedia Objects", in *Proceedings of the Fourth Pacific Workshop on Distributed Multimedia Systems (DMS'97),* Vancouver, Canada, (Knowledge Systems Institute) 52–59.

Best, E., Devillers, R., Hall, J.G. (1992) "The Box Calculus: a New Causal Algebra with Multi-label Communication", in *Advances in Petri Nets 1992,* ed. G.Rozenberg, *Lecture Notes in Computer Science,* **609** (Springer–Verlag) 21–69.

Brauer, W., Reisig, W., Rozenberg, G., (eds) (1987) "Petri Nets. Part I and II. Proc. of an Advanced Course, Bad Honnef", *Lecture Notes in Computer Science,* **254/255** (Springer–Verlag).

Cooper, K., (1995) "TSPN$_{ui}$: A Petri Net Model for Specifying User Interaction in Multimedia Presentations", *MASc Thesis, The University of British Columbia,* Canada.

Courtiat, J.-P., De Oliveira, R.C., Andriantsiferana, L., "Formal Modeling and verification of Multimedia Documents".

Diaz, M., Senac, P., (1993) "Time Stream Petri Nets: a model for multimedia streams synchronization", in *Proceedings of the International Conference on Multi-Media Modelling,* Singapore.

Kotov, V.E. (1978) "An Algebra for Parallelism Based on Petri Nets", *Lecture Notes in Computer Science,* **64** (Springer–Verlag) 39–55.

Little, T., Ghafoor, A., (1990) "Synchronization and storage models for multimedia objects", *IEEE Journal on Selected Areas in Communications,*Volume **8**, No **3**, 52–61.

Prabhakaran, B., Raghavan, S., (1993) "Synchronization Models Multimedia Presentations With User Interaction", *ACM Multimedia '93*, CA, 157–166.

Reisig, W. (1985) "Petri Nets: An Introduction", *EATCS Monograph on Theoretical Computer Science,* (Springer–Verlag).

Sénac, P., Diaz, M., Saqui-Sannes, P. (1994) "Toward a formal specification of multimedia synchronization scenarios", *Annals of Telecommunications,* Volume **49**, No **5-6** 297–314.

Sénac, P., Diaz, M., Léger, P., Saqui-Sannes, P., (1996) "Modeling Logical and Temporal Synchronization in Hypermedia Systems", *IEEE Journal of Selected Areas in Communications*, Volume **14**, No **1**, 84–103.

Vuong, S., Cooper, K., Ito, M. (1995) "Formal Methods for Modeling Multimedia Synchronization Requirements", in *Proc. of ICNP'95 - Int. Conf on Network Protocols,* (Tokyo, Japan).

Woo, M., Qazi, N., Ghafoor, A. (1994) "A synchronization framework forcommunication of preorchestrated multimedia information, multimedia objects", *IEEE Network,*.

FLUID-FLOW MODEL FOR VARIABLE-BIT-RATE VIDEO IN ATM NETWORKS.

NASSER-EDDINE RIKLI,

Department of Computer Engineering, King Saud University, P.O. Box 51178, Riyadh 11543, Saudi Arabia.
E-mail: n.a.rikli@ieee.org

A generalized video source model will be presented, where a video source is assumed to operate in two modes with both variable relative rate intensities and durations. A fluid-flow model will be used to assess the performance of an ATM statistical multiplexer fed with various categories of these video sources. We will consider both calm and violent scenes with either impulsive or persistent states. The results will show the effects not only of the ratio of the two modes average duration but also the effects of the magnitude of the holding times in either mode.

1 Introduction

Any advances in distributed multimedia systems rely heavily for their effective implementation on the developments achieved in communication networks. This includes efficient audio and video coding standards for communication of multimedia signals, higher speed networks, and fast switching technology [2].

ATM networks are expected to be the perfect, if not the only viable, carrier of the anticipated multimedia traffic. A major part of this traffic will be in the form of video signals. The ATM forum proposes in TM v4.0 [1] five types of video traffic, namely: constant bit-rate (CBR), real-time variable bit-rate (rt-VBR), non-real-time variable bit-rate (nrt-VBR), unspecified bit-rate (UBR), and available bit-rate (ABR). The specification [1] also defines four parameters for the characterization of any video traffic, namely: peak rate, average rate, cell delay variation (for the peak rate), and the maximum burst length.

In [4], video sources were modeled with a single mode source. In [3], the previous model of [4] was improved by using two modes of equal average holding time durations. The system considered here is a further improvement of the work in both [3] and [4], which can be used in the VBR case (rt or nrt). We will introduce new parameters that may be related to the ones presented in [1].

Our model will correspond to situations where the activity levels of a live scene are alternating between two modes: a low-rate and a high rate. This may correspond for instance, to a single scene of a person alternating between a listening and a talking period. It may also correspond to two different scenes: one during the rush hour in the downtown of a big city, and the other showing a calm scenic view (although, our model fits best the former case).

In both cases we may use two new parameters: one as a measure for the intensity of the source activity, and the second as a measure for the duration. In the first example, the levels of activity in the two modes will be close, and the durations will be short; while in the second, the difference in activity levels may be huge, and last for longer durations.

We will start our paper by defining the parameters that will be used to model a video source. Then, we will present the equivalent mathematical model using the major statistical measures. Using these measures, we will derive the parameters that will match some experimental data. These parameters will be then used to evaluate the cell loss probability, which will be derived using a fluid-flow model. We will end the paper by presenting the major results of our work, and our conclusions.

2 Source Model

A statistical multiplexer will be considered with N independent and identically distributed video sources. As shown in Fig. 1, each video source is assumed to alternate between two activity modes: a *high-rate* and a *low-rate*. The first parameter to be used, as in [3], is the ratio γ_1 of the average rate in the *high-rate* mode $\overline{R}_h$ to the average rate in the *low-rate* mode $\overline{R}_l$. It will be used as a measure of the activity level of the source, i.e. calm or violent.

The second parameter to be introduced here, is the ratio γ_2 of the average duration in the *high-rate* mode $\overline{T}_h$ over the average duration in the *low-rate* mode $\overline{T}_l$. This parameter will give us a measure of the activity endurance, e.g. persistent or impulsive. Furthermore, we will see from the results that it is important to consider scenes with variable average mode durations.

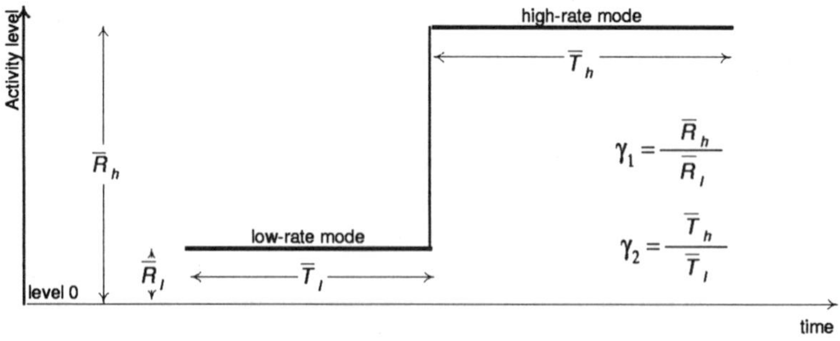

Figure 1. Parameters describing the VBR source two modes.

3 Source Model

3.1 Transition State Diagrams

Each video source will be replaced by the aggregate of two types of ON/OFF mini-sources. The first type is used to model the local fluctuations within a mode, and consists of N_1 mini-sources (low-rate) with states *0* and A_l (Fig. 2-i). The second type is used to simulate changes of mode, and consists of one mini-source (high-rate) with states 0 and A_h (Fig. 2-ii). Hence, we can represent one video source with N_l low-rate mini-sources and one high-rate mini-source.

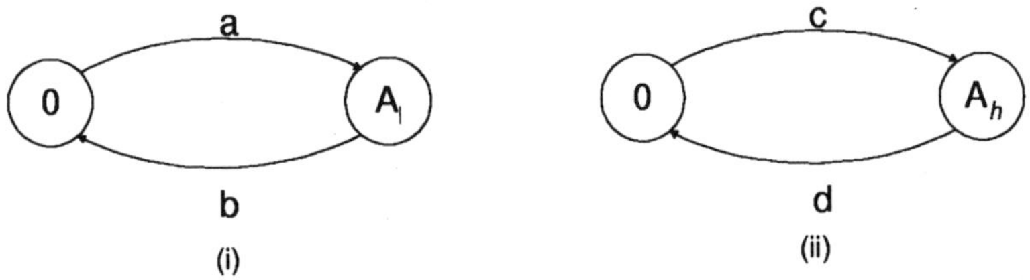

Figure 2. Mini-source model: (i) low-rate, (ii) high-rate.

If we statistically multiplex N_2 such video sources, then we get an aggregate of:

- N_2 high-rate mini-sources;
- N_lxN_2 low-rate mini-sources.

The resulting state diagram corresponds to a birth-death process, as shown in Fig. 3.

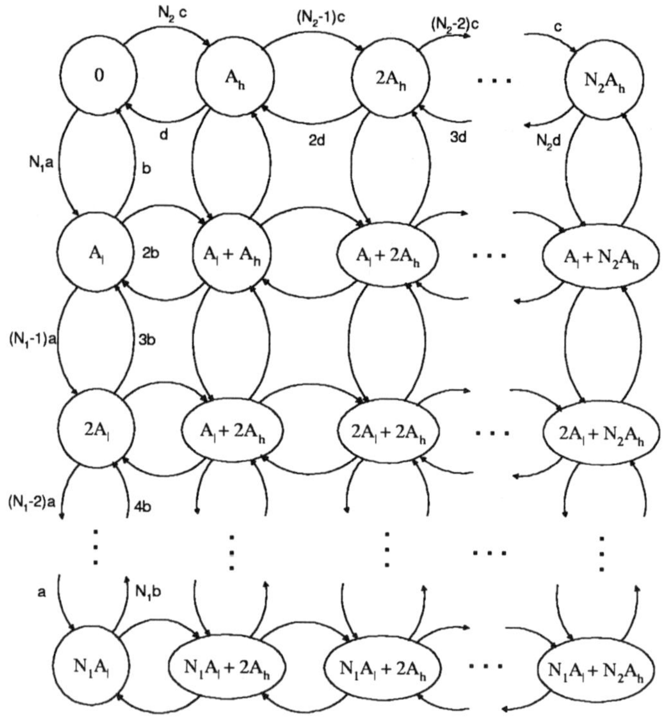

Figure 3. State transition diagram for the aggregate source model.

3.2 Parameter Definition

Let us first define the following parameters for a single video source with N_l quantization levels:

- the exponent of the autocovariance function for a low-rate mini-source:

$$\sigma_l = a + b \tag{1}$$

- the exponent of the autocovariance function for a high-rate mini-source:

$$\sigma_2 = c + d \tag{2}$$

- the ratio of the high-rate mode average intensity over the low-rate average intensity of a modeled video source:

$$\gamma_1 = 1 + \frac{\sigma_1}{aN_1}\left(\frac{A_h}{A_l}\right) \tag{3}$$

- the ratio of the average durations in high-rate mode to that in low-rate mode:

$$\gamma_2 = \frac{c}{d} \tag{4}$$

The statistical equations to be used in finding the matching equations are:

- the autocovariance function for N_1 *i.i.d.* low-rate mini-sources:

$$C_l(\tau) = C_l(0)e^{-\sigma_1\tau} \tag{5}$$

where:

$$C_l(0) = N_1 \frac{ab}{\sigma_1^2} A_l^2 \tag{5a}$$

- the autocovariance function for a high-rate mini-source:

$$C_h(\tau) = C_h(0)\, e^{\sigma_2\tau} \tag{6}$$

where:

$$C_h(0) = \frac{cd}{\sigma_2^2} A_h^2 \tag{6a}$$

- the overall mean bit-rate per video source:

$$\overline{\lambda} = \frac{a}{\sigma_1} N_1 A_l + \frac{c}{\sigma_2} A_h \tag{7}$$

the conditional variance of a video source in either mode:

$$\overline{\lambda}^2 = C_l(0) \tag{8}$$

3.3 *Parameter matching*

We start the parameter matching process by considering some experimental data taken from [4]: the exponent of the autocovariance function in either mode $\sigma_1 = 3.9$ s^{-1}, the overall average rate for a video source is $\overline{\lambda} = 3.9$ *Mbps*, and the conditional variance for a video source in either mode is $\overline{\lambda}^2 = 3.015$ *Mbps*^{2}. In addition, we will use as free parameters: γ_1, γ_2, and either one of the holding times: $\overline{T}_l = 1/c$, or $\overline{T}_h = 1/d$.

The matching equations may be solved by expressing A_h, A_l, and a as functions of the free parameters and of the experimental data. We obtain the following results:

using (3) and (7) we get:

$$A_h = \frac{\overline{\lambda}}{\dfrac{1}{\gamma_1 - 1} + \dfrac{c}{\sigma_2}} \tag{9}$$

using (8), (5a), and the value computed (9) we get:

$$A_l = \frac{A_h}{N_1(\gamma_1 - 1)} + \frac{\bar{\lambda}^2(\gamma_1 - 1)}{A_h} \tag{10}$$

from (3), and the values from (9) and (10) we get:

$$a = \frac{\sigma_1}{N_1(\gamma_1 - 1)}\left(\frac{A_h}{A_l}\right) \tag{11}$$

4 System Differential Equation

The cell loss probability, which will be used as our performance measure, has been derived using various methods. The matrix geometric method has been used in [5] through the definition of a Markov chain embedded at the phase changes of the process. While in [2], [3], and [6], an autoregressive model has been suggested.

As in [3] and [4], we will use here the fluid-flow model, which was introduced in [7], to evaluate the cell loss probability (CLP) of the system.

Let's first define the joint probability distribution function $F_{ij}(x)$ by:

$$F_{ij}(x) \equiv \Pr\left\{\begin{matrix} i \text{ low - rate mini - sources,} \\ j \text{ high - rate mini - sources, buffer} \leq x \end{matrix}\right\}$$

We can see easily that this function represents also, the steady state of the time dependent joint probability distribution function $P_{ij}(x,t)$.

Then, the Chapman-Kolmogorov forward equations corresponding to the system described in Fig. 3, may be obtained by expressing $P_{ij}(t+\Delta t, x)$ as a function of the following probabilities in a manner similar to [8]: $P_{i-1,j}(t, x)$, $P_{i+1,j}(t, x)$, $P_{i,j-1}(t, x)$, $P_{i,j+1}(t, x)$, and $P_{ij}(t, x - (\mu - \lambda_{ij})\Delta t)$.

Then, after letting $\Delta t \rightarrow 0$ and $t \rightarrow \infty$, we may obtain the following matrix differential equation:

$$\mathbf{D}\dot{\mathbf{F}} = \mathbf{MF} \tag{12}$$

where **D** is a diagonal matrix with elements $\lambda_{ij} - \mu$, and **M** is an appropriate matrix with only five non-zero diagonal elements: the main diagonal, the two just off the main diagonal, and the two at the $(N_2 + 1)^{st}$ elements off the main diagonal. The vector **F** with size $(N_1 + 1) \times (N_2 + 1)$ has as elements the functions $F_{ij}(x)$.

As in [3] and [7], the solution of equation (12) will be given by:

$$F(x) = F(\infty) + \sum_z a_z \Phi^{(z)} e^{zx} \tag{13}$$

where z is an eigenvalue of the matrix $D^{-1}M$ that belongs to the left half complex plane, and $\Phi^{(z)}$ is the corresponding eigenvector. The complete derivation of the equations leading to the computation of these eigenvalues and eigenvectors may be reviewed in [7].

5 RESULTS

Using the fluid-flow model described above, we will assess the system performance trends as a function of γ_2. Also, we will find out in which direction will the system performance go when, for instance, γ_2 is kept constant and either $\overline{T}_l$ or $\overline{T}_h$ is varied.

5.1 Effects of γ_2

In Fig. 4, we are considering the effects of γ_2 for short holding times. We have fixed the average holding time in the high-rate mode to $\overline{T}_h = 2.5$ *secs*, and varied the corresponding time in the low-rate mode. The remaining parameters were the number of sources $N = 5$, the average rate ratio $\gamma_1 = 2.5$, and channel utilization $\rho = 65\%$.

We can see easily that the system performance improves by increasing γ_2 (i.e., decreasing $\overline{T}_l$), and converges to a fixed curve, which corresponds to the equivalent single mode source model.

The reason of this is due to the fact that as γ_2 increases the difference between A_h and A_l narrows down. For example, by keeping $\overline{\lambda} = 3.9$ *Mbps*, we get:

Table 1. Effects of γ_2 on A_h and A_l.

γ_2	A_h	A_l	*Difference*
0.5	3.9	1.7	2.2
2.5	2.8	2.0	0.8

This explains both of our remarks:

- as γ_2 increases, the difference narrows, and we get convergence.
- as γ_2 decreases, A_h increases, which causes the buffer to fill-up quickly.

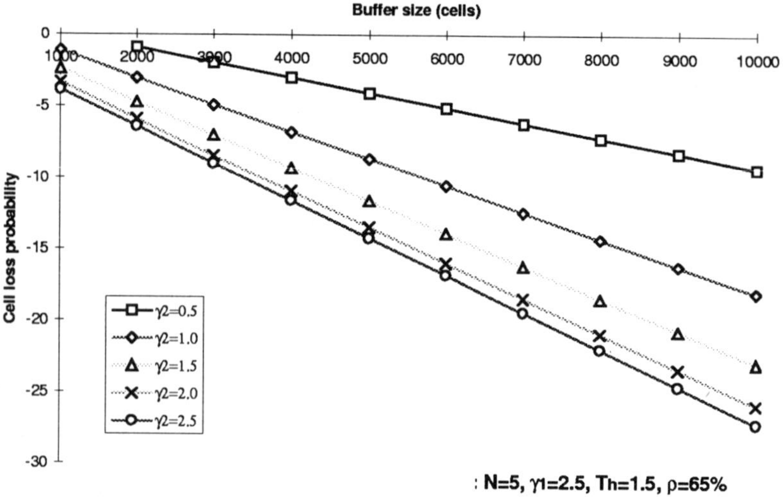

Figure 4. Cell loss probability for varying γ_2.

5.2 *Effects of the holding times $\overline{T}_h$ or $\overline{T}_l$*

As the duration of either mode increases (Fig. 5), while keeping the parameter γ_2 constant, we notice clearly that the performance of the multiplexer decreases and the CLP curves converge to a fixed curve, here also corresponding to the equivalent single mode source model.

The reason here being that the common buffer will have enough time to build as the average duration of the high-rate mode increases.

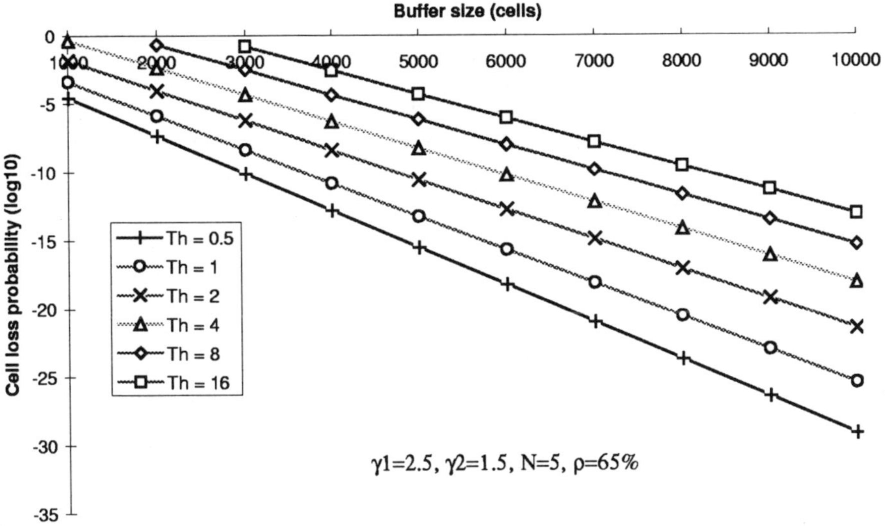

Figure 5. Cell loss probability for varying $\overline{T}_h$.

6 Conclusions

An accurate characterization of the video sources with the right parameters has to be acquainted in order to achieve real advance in the areas of statistical bandwidth allocation and congestion control in ATM networks. In this respect, a new parameter for measuring the activity of VBR video was introduced here. Video sources were modeled with two activity levels of random durations.

The results show that the system performance is a complex function of the average durations in the two modes and of their ratio. Some important conclusions may be enumerated. Firstly, as the parameter γ_2 increases, i.e. higher average mode durations of the sources, the performance of the system improves. This means that a lower charge rate should be imposed on the corresponding user. Secondly, the magnitude of the average duration of either mode should be also taken into consideration. It was found that the effect of γ_2 is more pronounced with shorter durations than with longer ones.

References

1. ATM Forum, *ATM Traffic Management Specification Version 4.0*, Available at ftp://ftp.atmforum.com/pub/approved-specs/atm-0056.000.ps, April 1996.
2. E. Perry and S. Ramanathan, *Network Management for Residential Broadband Interactive Data Services*, IEEE Commun. Mag., vol. 34, No. 11, pp. 114-121, November 96.
3. P. Sen, B. Maglaris, N. E. Rikli, and D. Anastassiou, *Models for packet switching of variable-bit-rate video sources*, IEEE JSAC., vol. 7, No. 5, pp. 865-869, June 1989.
4. B. Maglaris, D. Anastassiou, P. Sen, G. Karlsson, and J. Robbins, *Performance models of statistical multiplexing in packet video communications*, IEEE Trans. Commun., vol.36, pp. 834-844, July 1988.
5. J. N. Daigle and J. D. Langford, *Queueing Analysis for Packet Voice Communication System*, Conf. Rec. IEEE INFOCOM'85, pp. 18-26, March 1985.
6. R. Grünenfelder et *al.*, *Characterization of Video Codecs as Autoregressive Moving Average Processes and Related Queuing Systems Performance*, IEEE JSAC., vol. 9, pp. 284-293, 1991.
7. D. Anick, D. Mitra, and M. M. Sondhi, *Stochastic Theory of a Data-Handling System with Multiple Sources*, Bell System Technical Journal, vol. 61, No. 8, pp. 1871-1894, October 1982.
8. S. Karlin, and H. Taylor, *A First Course in Stochastic Processes*, 2nd ed., Academic Press, New York 1975.

Architecture

A Network Architecture to Support Policing and Scheduling of Tolerant Real-Time and Best-Effort Applications

Michael S. Boykin† and Taieb F. Znati†,‡
†*Department of Computer Science*
‡*Telecommunications Program*
{boykin1, znati}@cs.pitt.edu

Abstract

This paper describes a class-oriented network framework which aims to provide flexible and fair support for both tolerant real-time and best-effort applications. In the literature, tolerant real-time applications have been defined as those applications which require a minimum Quality of Service (QoS) but possess an ability to adapt to transient fluctuations in network support. On the other hand, best-effort applications are those applications that provide the network with no explicit QoS requirements, but for which there is consensus that a portion of the network's resources should be made available for their use. The scheme presented seeks to address the lack of service flexibility usually found in hard real-time frameworks by incorporating the necessary functionalities to provide elastic and predictive service guarantees in a heterogeneous environment. In doing so, the framework strives to ensure that the specified traffic rate of each application class is met, while promoting fair competition among applications for dynamically occuring excess network resource capacity. To achieve this objective, the framework uses an efficient traffic scheduling policy and enforces traffic isolation between different applications.

1.1 Introduction

Recent advances in communication and processing systems have made it possible to provide support for a wide variety of new applications with significantly different characteristics and diverse *quality of service* (*QoS*) requirements. Correspondingly, powerful, distributed multimedia applications continue to be deployed in ways which touch more and more aspects of our daily lives. Increasingly, applications such as distance learning, multisite video conferencing and interactive game play are becoming a part of our home and work environments. The information exchanged by these applications is characterized by a wide range of bandwidth specifications and real-time performance requirements. Supporting these applications, therefore, often requires that a level of performance requirements be guaranteed. A *guarantee* is a contract between an application and the service provider to satisfy a requested *QoS* level [6]. With this contract, the network pledges to ensure sufficient resources will be made available for the applications use according to the agreed upon contract terms. In addition, the application also pledges to consume resources only in accordance with the contracted terms. Lastly, the guarantee permits each party to enforce the contract terms if the other party is found to be in violation.

In the literature, several frameworks [4; 5; 7; 8; 9; 10; 12; 15; 16; 17; 18; 20] have been suggested to support real-time service guarantees for multimedia applications. A class of these frameworks focuses on providing either deterministic or statistical hard real-time guarantees. Deterministic hard real-time guarantees require the network to service all conforming application traffic at the specified *QoS* level barring network component failure. In contrast, statistical hard real-time guarantees require the network to ensure sufficient resources exist in order to provide a statistical percentage of an application's traffic with the specified *QoS* level; barring failure. The literature has shown that while such hard real-time schemes are capable of supporting multimedia application service guarantees, they present several drawbacks [1; 13; 14; 19]. The first of these drawbacks is that the application's role in resource allocation decisions is minimized and limited to connection setup time. Thus, the dynamic variation of some application's resource demand pattern is supported inefficiently at best. However, the ability of many modern applications to dynamically adapt their behavior to changes in network state suggests that such static approaches may be overly conservative. Consequently, by ignoring these factors, hard real time schemes often unnecessarily reject application connection requests due to the potential occurrence of transient network overloads.

A second drawback of hard real-time approaches relates to the fact that such schemes are forced to base their admission decisions upon infeasible or rarely occurring worst case traffic patterns. Such worst case analysis frequently leads to low network utilization as applications rarely submit traffic in accordance with its worst case traffic pattern. Furthermore, the physical implications of multiple connections sharing a common link often makes worst case arrival patterns infeasible. As a result, end-to-end delay guarantees are often much greater than the delay actually experienced by multimedia application traffic [2]. Further, subsequent application connection requests may be rejected due to such conservative delay guarantees.

Lastly, hard real-time schemes limit a network's ability to support best-effort applications. In many schemes, like those employing static priority mechanisms, best-effort applications receive service only when no real-time traffic is eligible for service. This policy leads to the formation of best-effort traffic clusters within the network. Clustering is undesirable because it can negatively impact the retransmission timers used in conjunction with best-effort traffic. In our opinion, such approaches are inherently, and often unnecessarily, unfair to best-effort applications as the delay and loss tolerances of real-time traffic is ignored.

Another class of network architectures focuses on providing applications with predictive service guarantees. Predictive guarantees relax the terms of the contract between the network and the application by permitting the network to fail to fulfill application *QoS* requirements due to transient periods of network overload. During such times, applications are expected to adapt their transmission behavior appropriately. As a result, these schemes solve the issue of the lack of service flexibility afforded by hard real-time schemes by taking a more optimistic approach to resource reservation and admission control. However, the schemes still fail to address the need to support best-effort applications in a "fair" manner. This functionality, nevertheless, is critical to the success of heterogeneous, integrated services networks.

In light of the need to provide a mechanism which affords multimedia applications greater service flexibility without reducing traditional best-effort applications to a second-class status, we have begun construction of a new network architecture. Instead of defining completely new protocols, however, the COPS architecture seeks to incorporate, whenever possible, the approaches recommended by the recognized *B-ISDN* standards. As presented here, the COPS architecture aims at providing flexible and fair support for both tolerant real-time and best-effort applications. To address the needs of both application classes, COPS provides elastic guarantees for tolerant real-time applications and predictive guarantees for best-effort applications. The elastic service guarantees provided within the COPS architecture ensure tolerant real-time applications receive service in accordance with its average rate requirements. This is achieved using resource reservation, traffic isolation, policing and scheduling. Resource reservation enables the system to ensure sufficient excess capacity exists to satisfy the connection's average rate requirements. Further, traffic isolation prevents misbehaving applications from monopolizing a link to the detriment of other, well-behaved ones. A policing mechanism enables the system to identify non-conforming traffic in the event of buffer saturation, while scheduling ensures the effective bandwidth allocation does indeed meet the minimal specified average traffic rate.

The COPS architecture's predictive service guarantees ensure that best-effort applications receives their "fair" share of bandwidth. As best-effort connections are not generally subject to admission control constraints, a connection's fair share of bandwidth is dynamically adjusted to reflect both its average rate requirement and the requirements of other currently active best-effort applications. The total amount of guaranteed bandwidth allocated to all best-effort traffic, however, is never allowed to exceed a predetermined threshold. Consequently, if the demand of best-effort bandwidth is low, a best-effort application may receive its desired average traffic rate. On the other hand, if the demand for best-effort bandwidth is relatively high, a best-effort application may see its fair share reduced below the desired average rate. In either case, the application is provided the minimum of its fair share and its specified rate. Therefore, predictive service guarantees can be viewed as a special case of elastic service guarantees, whereby bandwidth is guaranteed at the class level and fairly shared at the connection level.

To further enhance the effective service received by both classes of applications, COPS supports fair competition for any excess resources currently available in the network. Allowing best-effort traffic to compete for excess resources further reduces the likelihood of best-effort traffic clustering without violating the bandwidth guarantees of tolerant real-time applications. In addition, the fair competition for excess bandwidth enables the network to handle tolerant real-time application traffic bursts more efficiently.

The following sections describe the main components of the COPS architecture and the mechanisms these components use to provide elastic and predictive guarantees. Conclusions and future work are discussed in the last section of this paper.

1.2 *COPS* Architecture

The *COPS* architecture is composed of three main components namely, Call Admission Control (*CAC*), Policing and Run-Time Support. These components support the mechanisms and functionalities required to provide elastic and predictive service guarantees.

1.2.1 *Call Admission Control*

Prior to obtaining a service level guarantee, applications must submit a connection requests so that the network can verify the feasibility of fulfilling its current service commitments along with those of the requesting application. A COPS network connection request specifies the source address, destination address, service class, macro-class, maximum burst size and mean traffic rate in bits per second. For best-effort applications the desired mean transmission rate is used in place of the mean traffic rate. The COPS architecture's *CAC* uses this information and currently available network resources to determine the feasibility of supporting a new connection request while maintaining the requirements of currently supported connections. To facilitate this feasibility test, the *CAC* maintains resource availability at three levels: *link*, *macro-class* and *micro-class.*

At the link level, the *CAC* partitions a link's capacity into *guaranteed transmission capacity* and *enhanced transmission capacity* as illustrated in figure 1.1. A link's guaranteed transmission capacity designates the percentage of that link's total bandwidth which may be used to provide bandwidth to support elastic and predictive guarantees. The enhanced transmission capacity, on the other hand, designates the percentage of the link's bandwidth which may be used to service tolerant real-time traffic bursts or improve the service performance of best effort traffic. *CAC* uses the link level capacity allocation to quantify bandwidth commitments for a new connection and determine the feasibility of extending the level of performance guarantees required by this connection.

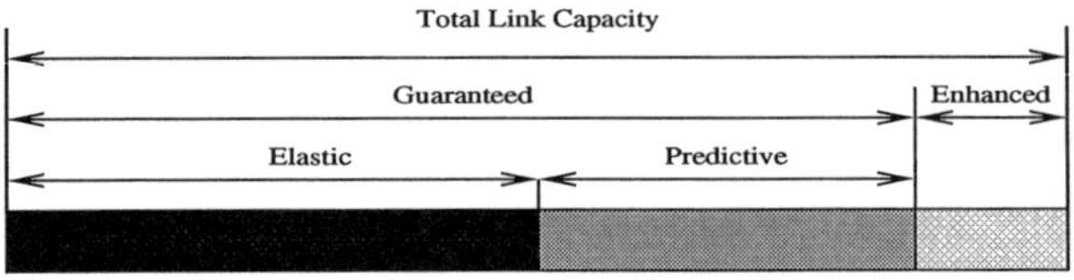

Fig. 1.1 Link Level Bandwidth Partition

At the macro-class level, the *CAC* associates connection requests according to their media types. This level of abstraction provides the ability to exercise control over the amount of bandwidth associated with each media type as may be required to ensure sufficient bandwidth is available during prime time viewing hours. To achieve this control, the COPS architecture supports three macro-classes: real-time video, real-time audio and time-independent media, such as text. The COPS framework associates a maximum percentage of the link bandwidth with each macro-class and ensures, at any point in time, a new connection does not cause the total bandwidth guaranteed to a given macro-class to exceed its maximum percentage. The sum of all macro-class maximum percentages may exceed 100% and can change dynamically to reflect temporally varying demands for media types. These maximum percentages, however, may be carefully selected to ensure that every macro-class can receive a minimal amount of bandwidth at all times.

At the micro-class level, *CAC* classifies connection requests according to their media types, *QoS* requirements and service guarantees. Each micro-class, uniquely identified by these values, belongs to a specific macro-class. The amount of bandwidth guaranteed to all connections within each micro-class is limited by the maximum bandwidth percentage of the associated macro-class. Furthermore, to prevent connections of a single micro-class from acquiring an unfair portion of macro-class bandwidth, the COPS architecture provides the ability to limit the amount of bandwidth consumed by a given micro-class. The limits can be carefully selected to ensure a minimum level of access for each micro-class.

1.2.1.1 *Elastic Call Admission Procedure*

A tolerant real-time application's connection request for an elastic service guarantee can only be accepted if all the links on the route from the source to the destination are capable of supporting the connection's requested *QoS* without violating the *QoS* requirements of the currently supported connections. In addition, *CAC* must ensure that granting the connection its required bandwidth does not cause the network to exceed the bandwidth allocated both at the connection's macro-class and micro-class levels.

A successful connection request causes the network to reserve bandwidth in accordance with the connection's traffic descriptor at each level of the *CAC* hierarchy on each of the connection's link. The *CAC* reserves resources, however, in accordance with the connection's average rate instead of its peak rate. This bandwidth reservation reflects the elastic nature of guarantees provided by *COPS*. The *COPS* framework does not reserve the bandwidth required to support peak rate transmission. Instead, *COPS* uses the average rate to determine the bandwidth necessary to provide elastic guarantees. Consequently, depending upon instantaneous resource requirements, it is possible for the network violate an elastic application's *QoS* guarantee during application bursts. However, as will be described later, the network's policing mechanism helps to minimize the duration of this interval of *QoS* violation.

1.2.1.2 *Predictive Call Admission Procedure*

Because they do not require an explicit *QoS* guarantee, best-effort connection requests are not subject to network admission control tests. The actual amount of bandwidth guaranteed to these connections is limited by the fraction of bandwidth, β, allocated to the time-independent macro-class. Consequently, the COPS architecture does not provide individual best-effort connections with any type of service guarantees, but extends a *predictive* guarantee to the class of best-effort connections as a whole.

A new best-effort connection request causes the *CAC* to update the actual link bandwidth required by all best-effort connections along the routing path by adding the accepted connections' desired average transmission rate. The *CAC*, however, does not always reserve bandwidth at this updated level. Instead, the level of bandwidth reserved at the link and macro-class levels is determined by computing the minimum of the actual bandwidth desired by current best-effort connections and the preallocated best-effort bandwidth defined by β. At the micro-class level, the actual bandwidth requirement is updated to include the new connection's desired bandwidth request and used to determine the fair share of bandwidth to be received by a connection within the micro-class.

1.3 Policing Function

At the network edge, the *COPS* framework employs a Policing Function (PF) which prevents applications from unfairly consuming resources in excess of their traffic contract. During periods of overload, network policing must determine which cells are in violation of its connection's traffic contract and mark them eligible for discard. Marked cells may be dropped, without penalty, to alleviate congestion along the connection's routing path.

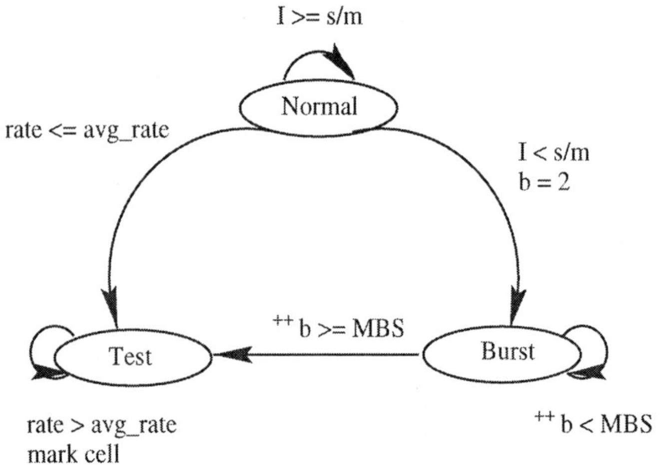

Fig. 1.2 COPS Policing Function State Diagram

On one hand, the *COPS* framework exploits the retransmission tolerance of best-effort applications by marking all traffic from these connections eligible for discard. On the other hand, *PF* measures resource consumption in order to police tolerant real-time connections, or connections with associated elastic service guarantees, based on the actual value of their mean and burst traffic rates. *PF* uses a *mean rate controller* algorithm to police the connection's mean transmission rate, and uses a *bit counter* based algorithm to police its bursts.

Upon acceptance, PF initializes a connection to be in *normal* transmission state. While in this state, the mean rate controller algorithm is used to measure the gap between successive cells originating from the same connection. If s is the network's cell size in bits, and m is the specified mean transmission rate, a connection's minimum permitted intercell gap is computed to be $\frac{s}{m}$. While in normal state, the adherence of a connection to its specified average rate is determined by the conformance of its cells to the minimum intercell gap.

If a connection's intercell gap is less than its lower bound, PF moves the connection into *burst* transmission state. In this state, a bit counter algorithm is used to determine if cells should be marked eligible for discard. PF uses the connection's specified maximum burst size, b, the network cell size, s, (both quantified in terms of bits) to determine the number of cells a connection is permitted to transmit in burst mode without having any of its cells marked eligible for discard. This number is computed as $\lfloor \frac{b}{s} \rfloor$. Upon receipt of the $\lfloor \frac{b}{s} \rfloor + 1^{st}$ cell, PF computes the connection's transmission rate over the current busy period. If the computed rate exceeds the specified mean rate, the cell is marked. PF continues to mark subsequent cells from the connection until the computed transmission rate falls within the connection's specified mean rate. PF then ceases to mark cells and moves the connection back to normal transmission state.

The PF can be easily shown to enforce application traffic arrivals to conform to a *linear bounded arrival process* (LBAP) property. A LBAP is any process in which the number of arrivals, $\mathcal{A}(t)$, over a interval of length t is upper bound by a function:

$$\mathcal{A}(t) \leq (\rho \cdot t) + b$$

where ρ denotes the mean arrival rate and b denotes the maximum burst size denoted in bits. To show PF enforces this property, note that any time in which a connection is in *normal state* its current transmission rate is bound by $m \cdot t$. Therefore, the only time a connection can exceed this rate is when it is in *burst state*. Since the maximum number of bits PF allows a connection to send in *burst state* without being marked eligible for discard is b, then clearly PF must enforce the LBAP property where the number of unmarked cell a connection may transmit over an interval of length t is defined by:

$$m \cdot t + b$$

where m denotes the connection's mean transmission rate and b denotes its maximum burst size. Upon close inspection, it can be noted that the PF marking policy is slightly more stringent than the GCRA algorithm proposed by the ATM Forum [3]. To better understand this fact, observe that GCRA considers any cell which arrives within L units of time from its *theoretical arrival time* (*TAT*) as being compliant. Therefore, given identical mean transmission rates, m, and maximum burst sizes, b, GCRA marks the $\lfloor \frac{b}{s} \rfloor + 1^{st}$ cell only if it violates the LBAP property. The COPS PF, however, marks the $\lfloor \frac{b}{s} \rfloor + 1^{st}$ cell if the connection's rate does not conform to the stricter mean transmission rate, $(m \cdot t)$. This policy is adopted because the architecture is optimistic and attempts to transmit marked cells despite their non-conformance. However, if congestion is encountered, it is fairer to drop such a packet instead of being forced to reduce another connection's *QoS* because of buffer overload.

1.4 Run-Time Support

COPS run-time components support scheduling, buffer management and best-effort traffic flow control. This section describes the policies and mechanisms used by these components to ensure *COPS* service guarantee semantics, fairness and congestion control.

1.4.1 *Traffic Scheduling Policy*

Within the *COPS* architecture, the traffic scheduling policy is responsible for determining the order in which cells from multiple connections are multiplexed to ensure each connection's requested guarantee. *COPS* uses a uniform, hierarchical and work-conserving scheduling strategy to service cells from multiple connections. The strategy uses the *neediness deviation rate first* policy, at the macro, micro and connection levels of the hierarchy, to determine the next connection to be serviced.

The process of selecting the neediest connection starts by first determining the neediest active macro-class*. Once the neediest macro-class is

*A macro-class, micro-class or connection is considered active at a given node n if that

determined, the process continues by selecting the neediest active micro-class within the macro-class. The process completes when the neediest active connection within the selected micro-class is determined. Cells from the selected connection are then serviced in *first-in-first-out (FIFO)* order.

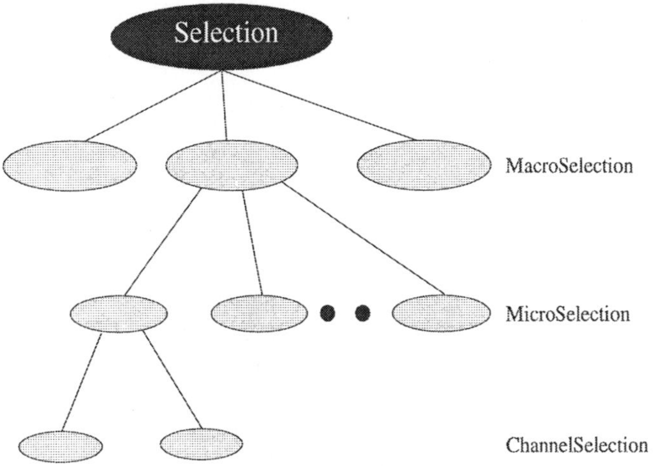

Fig. 1.3 COPS Scheduling Hierarchy

The selection process maintains three parameters for each scheduling entity at each level of the hierarchy where a scheduling entity may be either a macro-class, a micro-class or a connection. The first parameter, *busy start time* usually denoted by t_0, records the start time of an entity's most recent busy interval. *COPS* sets the associated *busy start time* parameter to a negative value when a scheduling entity, at any level, becomes idle. Upon the arrival of a cell, *COPS* updates the *busy start time* for the associated scheduling entities at the macro-class, micro-class and connection levels. The update process sets the *busy start time* to the current time only if the scheduling entity at that level has been idle. The parameter remains unchanged if the entity is active.

The second parameter, *equipartition commitment service rate*, quantifies the service rate a node should have allocated to a scheduling entity in the current busy period. Another way of understanding this parameter's purpose is to view it as an idealized guaranteed service curve for scheduling

(macro-/micro-) class or connection has cells awaiting transmission at node n.

entity m at node n from the *busy start time* until the current time t. The *equipartition commitment service rate*, denoted as $\overline{EQRate_m^n}(t_0, t)$ for a scheduling entity m at node n from time t_0 to t, may be used to compute the number of bits the network should have transmitted on m's behalf between t_0 and t. This value, referred to as m's *equipartition commitment service level* and denoted as $EQ_m^n(t_0, t)$, may be computed as shown in Equation 1.1 below. In the equation, the time t_0 is taken to be the start of m's most recent busy interval.

$$EQ_m^n(t_0, t) = \overline{EQRate_m^n}(t_0, t) * (t - t_0), \tag{1.1}$$

For entities at the connection level, the computation of the *equipartition commitment service rate* and the *equipartition commitment service level* parameters is straightforward. At higher levels of the COPS connection hierarchy, however, the value of the *equipartition commitment* cannot simply be obtained by summing the *equipartition commitment* parameters of the constituent connections. This is due to the fact that a specific connection may have several busy periods within a single busy period of its macro- or micro-class. Furthermore, busy periods of different connections within the same class can overlap.

To account for each of a given connection's busy periods that occur within a single busy period of its macro- or micro-class, *COPS* keeps track of how long each connection is active during its class' active period. These value are referred to as the *macro-class busy length* and *micro-class busy length.* A connection's *macro-class busy length* are *micro-class busy length* parameters are maintained by adding the length of the connection's busy period to the current *busy length* value each time the connection moves from being active to being idle and the macro-class or micro-class remains in active state. The *busy length* values are reset each time a macro- or micro-class changes from idle state to active state. Note that, for the above reset to occur, the connection itself must be idle. Therefore, its *busy start time* is reset also.

For each class, *COPS* uses the appropriate busy length value and the *equipartition commitment service rate* for each connection within that class in order to compute the *equipartition commitment service rate* for the class. This computation of a class' *equipartition commitment service rate* parameter is illustrated in Equation 1.2, where m represents a connection and μ

its associated class.

$$\overline{EQRate^n_\mu}(t_0, t) = \frac{\sum_{m \in \mu} \overline{EQRate^n_m}(t_0, t) * [busy\_length^n_m + (t - t_0)]}{t - t_0} \tag{1.2}$$

Given the micro-class *equipartition commitment service rate*, the micro-class *equipartition commitment service level* can be computed as shown in Equation 1.1.

The final scheduling parameter, *node allocation service rate*, quantifies the actual service rate a node has allocated to a scheduling entity during its current busy period. One may view the *node allocation* parameter as the actual service curve denoting the amount of service received by a scheduling entity m at a node n during the period of time from m's *busy start time* to the current time t. Because nodes service channels sequentially at its maximum rate, the slope of a scheduling entity's *node allocation* curve alternates between zero when it is not receiving service and the server's peak rate, R, when it is.

At a given node n, *COPS* computes an entity m's *node allocation service rate*, $\overline{AllocRate^n_m}(t_0, t)$, according to Equation 1.3 shown below. In the equation, the parameter $Alloc^n_m(t_0, t)$ denotes the actual number of bits node n has transmitted on m's behalf during the interval $[t_0, t]$.

$$\overline{AllocRate^n_m}(t_0, t) = \frac{Alloc^n_m(t_0, t)}{t - t_0} \tag{1.3}$$

Based on the above parameters, scheduling in the *COPS* framework involves two main tasks. The first task consists of selecting the next scheduling entity to be serviced. The second task deals with potential priority inversion caused by the hierarchical nature of *COPS*'s scheduling framework.

(a) Scheduling Entity Selection:

In the *COPS* framework, the selection of the next scheduling entity to be serviced is based on the concept of *neediness*. In order to compute a scheduling entity's *neediness*, *COPS* determines how far ahead or behind the system is in servicing the entity. This is achieved based on the the three scheduling parameters associated with each scheduling entity, namely the *node allocation service rate*, the *equipartition commitment service rate*, and the *busy start time*. *COPS* uses these three parameters to compute the entity's accumulated *neediness deviation rate* from the scheduling entity's *busy start time* to the current time. For a given scheduling entity, m, at a node n, with a starting time, $start^n_m$, the *neediness deviation rate*, N, at a given point in time t, can be defined as:

$$N^n_m(t_0, t) = \frac{\int_{t_0}^{t} \overline{EQRate^n_m}(t_0, x) - \overline{AllocRate^n_m}(t_0, x)\, dx}{(t - t_0)} \tag{1.4}$$

Using the rate, rather than the total accumulated service units since the start time, prevents a scheduling entity from accumulating the need for a large number of service credits during periods of idleness. It has been shown that using the accumulated service units, instead of the rate, may cause a scheduling entity to monopolize a node's scheduling service, thereby resulting in a high degree of instability [11].

It should also be noted that instead of looking merely at the deviation of the *node allocation service rate* from the *equipartition commitment service rate* to calculate an entity's *neediness deviation rate*, the calculation also takes into account how long it took for the deviation to build. Thus, given two entities with the same deviation, the entity which acquired that deviation in the smaller interval of time is assigned a higher priority. This is based upon the idea that it is better to service the entity having the smaller busy period because its *node allocation service rate* is deviating from its *equipartition commitment service rate* at a faster rate. Thus, we limit the total deviation of all the entities being scheduled by servicing the entity whose deviation rate is accelerating fastest.

Positive values of $\mathrm{N}^n_m(t)$ indicate that m is owed service and that node n is behind in servicing it. Negative values, on the other hand, indicate that m has received service in excess of its rate specification and that node n is ahead in servicing entity m. Consequently, the neediest scheduling entity is the one with the largest *neediness* value. The *COPS* scheduler selects this entity for service.

(b) Priority Inversion:

Based on the above scheduling policy, a group of macro- or micro-class scheduling entities may obtain excess service. This, in turn, may cause priority inversion when a new macro- or micro-class scheduling becomes active. To illustrate a case of priority inversion, consider the following example. At time, t_0, nine connections belonging to the same micro-class are admitted with a mean rate specification of 1 unit per second. Assume the network has a capacity of 90 units per second. In this example, each of the nine connections begin bursting at a rate of 10 units per second which keeps the server busy continuously. Since the network has sufficient capacity to service these bursts, each of the nine connections along with their macro- and micro-class *node allocation* parameters is in excess of their respective equipartition values (i.e. their *neediness deviation rate* is negative). Assume at a later time $t_1 > t_0$, two additional connections are admitted. The first of these two connections, connection 10, belongs to the same macro- and micro-class as the earlier nine connections indicating they all have identical requirements. The other, connection 11, belongs to a different macro- and micro-class and specifies a mean rate of 2 units per second.

Upon invocation of the next scheduling computation, the $COPS$ scheduler will select connection 11 because its macro- and micro-class have a priority of zero. Call 10's macro- and micro-class have a negative priority at time t due to their continuously active state and the service rate they have accumulated. Furthermore, let's assume that connection 11 begins bursting at the link rate, starting at time t_1, thereby keeping the server continuously busy. The scheduler services this connection exclusively until the other connection's macro-class and micro-class becomes needier. This occurs to the detriment of connection 10, whereby connection 11 receives service in excess of its mean rate specification while connection 10 is starved.

A closer look at this problem reveals that the inversion occurred because in the interval from $[t_0, t_1]$, connections 1 through 9 are allowed to consume excess service capacity which would have otherwise gone idle. This excess consumption, however, did not occur at the expense of any other connections. To remedy this problem, the COPS framework modifies the neediness definition to account for the fact that no scheduling entity should be considered ahead (have negative need) unless some other entity is behind (has positive need).

The $COPS$ scheduling framework prevents priority inversion by setting a flag when it is computing the macro- and micro-class mean rate parameters defined in Equation 1.2. The flag indicates whether any active connection has a positive need. If no connection possesses a positive need, indicating the node is not behind in servicing any connection, the serviced entity's *node allocation* parameter is set to the minimum of the normal update value and the value of the *equipartition commitment* parameter after the entity's cell is serviced. If some connection does have a positive need value, indicating it is behind in its service, the entity's *node allocation* update is performed in the normal fashion.

1.4.2 *Buffer Management*

In the *COPS* architecture, an important task of *COPS* run-time support is its buffer management. A buffer management function is required to prevent bursty connections from unfairly occupying buffers, thereby causing cells from other connections to be dropped. Indiscriminate dropping of cells may cause *COPS* to fail to meet its elastic or predictive QoS guarantees.

When buffers at a given node become exhausted, *COPS* uses *PF*'s markings to determine whether to drop a currently buffered or newly arriving cell. The arriving cell is dropped if it is marked and no buffers are available. The cell is also dropped if none of the buffered cells are marked. If a subset of the buffered cells are marked and the arriving cell is not, the node uses an algorithm similar to the *COPS* scheduling algorithm in order to decide which connection's cell to drop.

A connection is eligible for cell dropping if it currently has marked cells awaiting transmission. Thus, only best-effort connections and tolerant real-time connections transmitting at an excessive rate are subject to cell dropping. The selection process for cell dropping is performed using a *greediest first* algorithm. The *greediness* of a connection is determined based on its *neediness* relative to other potential victims. However, instead of selecting the connection with the largest neediness value, as performed during transmission scheduling, a congested node selects the connection with the smallest neediness value. Notice that this approach selects as its victim the connection having received the greatest percentage of its *equipartition commitment.*

A tradeoff exists between determining the connection with the smallest neediness value and indiscriminately dropping marked cells. The latter strategy fails to preserve fairness among different connections and may potentially lead to guarantee violation for best-effort connections. The former strategy takes into consideration service fairness and service guarantees, but may result in a larger overhead. To reduce the amount of overhead, *COPS* adopts a strategy by which *greediness* is only computed at the connection level instead of all levels of the hierarchy. This strategy minimizes the selection process time, by not computing *greediness* hierarchically, but still selects the greediest connection for cell dropping.

1.4.3 *Best-Effort Flow Control*

As alluded to in the discussion of the *COPS* admission control procedure, the *COPS* framework does not limit best-effort applications' entry into the network. Instead, it only controls the guaranteed bandwidth best-effort traffic may receive so that it never exceeds the predetermined best-effort bandwidth allocation as defined by the parameter β. This strategy, however, may lead to congestion which causes best-effort traffic to suffer extended queuing delays. Congestion occurs when the arrival rate of best-effort traffic exceeds the available rate defined by the reserved best-effort bandwidth and that unused by tolerant, real-time traffic. To address this problem, best-effort applications and the *COPS* network participate in a symbiotic relationship by which best-effort applications agree to adjust their traffic rate in response to congestion, while *COPS* ensures fair division of the reserved bandwidth among best-effort applications. This is achieved based on an initial rate establishment and procedures to dynamically adjust the application's rate to reflect current state of the network.

(c) Rate Establishment:
As mentioned, best-effort applications submit traffic descriptors to the network prior to connection establishment. Included in the traffic descriptor is the application's desired rate specification. This parameter quantifies the amount of bandwidth the application desires the network to reserve on its behalf. However, this amount of bandwidth may not be available at all times of the application's life span. In order to deal with the potential lack of bandwidth while allowing transmission rates to be as high as possible, the *COPS CAC* determines an initial *throttle rate* for best-effort applications at connection setup time. The initial throttle rate quantifies the level of bandwidth the network can provide at the time of the connection setup request. The application uses the initial value of the *throttle rate* to initiate its transmission rate.

For a given best-effort connection i, a *COPS* node computes the *throttle rate* as defined in Equation 1.5, where $mean\_bw_i$ represents application i's desired mean rate, BE_a represents the actual amount of best-effort bandwidth along i's output link at the local node, BE_r represents the amount of best-effort bandwidth requested along i's output link at the local node and k represents the *rate adjustment step.*

$$TR_i^k = \min\left(\frac{BE_a}{BE_r} * mean\_bw_i,\ mean\_bw_i\right) \tag{1.5}$$

At connection setup time, k is zero, and TR_i^0 represents the initial *throttle rate* of best-effort connection i. Each node along the routing path computes a potential initial *throttle rate.* The actual value selected by CAC represents the minimum *throttle rate* of all the rates computed by the nodes along the routing path. This value is also referred to as the application's actual transmission rate at step zero which is denoted as AR_i^0. The *rate adjustment step k* is incremented for subsequent rate adjustments to TR_i^k and AR_i^k.

The arrival of a new connection that shares any of i's links may cause i's actual transmission rate to decrease. This potential decrease is due to the increase in BE_r at the nodes common to i and the new connection. Similarly, the departure of best-effort connections sharing any of the links along i's route may potentially increase i's actual transmission rate. Because of the dynamic nature of network bandwidth demands, best-effort connections periodically adjust their actual transmission rate according to network load. The procedure for best effort connections adjusting their actual transmission rate is detailed below.

(d) Best-Effort Traffic Management:
COPS nodes manage best-effort traffic by monitoring the length of their best-effort queues over the duration of a *best-effort cycle.* The cycle is initiated with the arrival of the best-effort cell which causes a node's best-effort queue length to grow from zero to one. The cycles are terminated with the departure of the best-effort cell that causes a node's best-effort queue length to shrink from one to zero. The arrival or departure of a best-effort cell is referred to as a best-effort event. While best-effort queue lengths remain beneath independently computed thresholds, *COPS* nodes service best-effort traffic according to the parameters described in Section 1.4.

COPS nodes determine their best-effort buffer thresholds independently and dynamically in order to facilitate a high degree of best-effort application flexibility. This threshold is defined as the maximum between the percentage of a node's buffers currently available for use by best-effort connections and the minimum threshold value guaranteed to best-effort connections.

Equation 1.6 is used to calculate the percentage of a node's buffers that are available for use by best-effort traffic. A node recalculates this parameter each time it admits a new real-time connection.

$$Avail_n(t) = 1 - \frac{\sum_{i \in I}[reserved_i^n + (\epsilon_i^n * l^i)]}{\sum_{i \in I} l^i} \tag{1.6}$$

COPS nodes use Equation 1.6 to compute the percentage of a node's incoming link bandwidth at time t which has not been allocated to the *enhanced transmission capacity* partition or to *elastic* guarantees. In the equation, I represents node n's set of input links. $Reserved_i^n$ represents the number of bits reserved on behalf of guaranteed connections over input link i. The term ϵ_i^n represents the percentage of bandwidth reserved for *enhanced transmission capacity* demands on input link i. Finally, l^i represents link i's transmission rate in bits per second. The summation of the two terms in the numerator of Equation 1.6 equals the number of bits reserved on node n's input links. The denominator is the aggregate bit rate of all node n's input links. The value computed by Equation 1.6 denotes the percentage of node n's aggregate transmission capacity which can be guaranteed for best-effort application use.

Next, Equation 1.7 is used to compute the minimum buffer threshold percentage. This parameter is recomputed any time the macro-class partitions on one of a node's adjacent links are reassigned. This equation's value represents the minimum percentage of node n's buffer which should be reserved for best-effort applications. It is computed by dividing the number of bits reserved for best-effort traffic on each of node n's input links by the total bit rate of these links.

$$min\_pct_n(t) = \frac{\sum_{i \in I}(\beta_i * l^i)}{\sum_{i \in I} l^i} \tag{1.7}$$

By computing the threshold according to the above procedure, *COPS* nodes permit best-effort traffic to consume a larger percentage of buffers when the node has excess capacity due to *elastic* commitments below the maximum possible requirement. As the level of *elastic* commitments increase, the best-effort buffer threshold shrinks to its minimum.

Equation 1.8 shown below computes the maximum percentage of node n's buffers that best-effort cells may occupy at a time t. Thus, where bufs_n

represents the total number of buffers at node n, a $COPS$ node computes the maximum number of buffers that best-effort cells may consume at time t according to Equation 1.9.

$$\text{ThresholdPct}_n(\text{t}) = \max(Avail_n(t), \text{min\_pct}_n(\text{t})) \tag{1.8}$$

$$\text{MaxBufs}_n(\text{t}) = \text{bufs}_n * \text{ThresholdPct}_n(\text{t}) \tag{1.9}$$

$COPS$ nodes monitor the number of buffers consumed by best-effort traffic by calculating the average best-effort queue length at each cell arrival. At each best-effort cell arrival, $COPS$ nodes compare the average best-effort queue length with the node's threshold at that time. If the node discovers the average exceeds the threshold, it sends a *throttle* message to each of the best-effort applications traversing it.

(e) Transmission Rate Reduction:
$COPS$ nodes use *throttle* messages to inform applications when they are suffering congestion. The information contained in the *throttle* message informs the receiving application of the congested node's BE_a and BE_r values. Applications use these two values to determine whether or not they need to reduce their rate. The application uses Equation 1.5 to compute its new *throttle rate*, and then Equation 1.10 to compute its new actual transmission rate.

$$AR_i^{k+1} = \max\left(\frac{AR_i^k}{2}, TR_i^{k+1}\right) \tag{1.10}$$

(f) Transmission Rate Increase:
$COPS$ periodically offers applications the opportunity to increase their actual transmission rate in response to network load reduction. Potential rate increases are based on a *congestion interval* computed by best-effort applications at each step of their rate adjustment. The *congestion interval* defines the period of time an application will transmit at the current rate before attempting to increases its actual transmission rate. To compute the size of its congestion interval, applications use Equation 1.11.

$$\text{Congestion Interval} = v * RTT \tag{1.11}$$

In Equation 1.11, RTT is the current estimated round trip delay, and v is a multiplicative factor greater than or equal to 1. If an application receives a *throttle* message within the congestion interval, it computes a new actual transmission rate according to the procedure outlined in subsection (e) and starts a new *congestion interval*. If no *throttle* message is received within the *congestion interval*, the application computes it new actual transmission rate according to Equation 1.12.

$$AR_i^{k+1} = \min(\alpha * AR_i^k, peak\_bw_i) \tag{1.12}$$

In Equation 1.12, α is a parameter greater than one that defines the magnitude of the application's attempted increase. Notice that α must be selected carefully as a large value of α may trigger a *throttle* message in the near future, while a small value may lengthen the required transmission time.

1.5 Conclusion and Future Work

The $COPS$ scheme described here has suggested a framework intended to provide both elastic and predictive service guarantees for use by tolerant real-time and best-effort applications, respectively. The main components of the $COPS$ architecture, admission control, policing and run-time support, have been discussed. In the discussion of these components, we outline the unique approach $COPS$ uses to service best-effort traffic which allows connections from this class to compete with connections from real-time classes. This approach differs from other approaches where best-effort traffic is only transmitted during idle periods of real-time traffic activities.

Future work will include adding support for deterministic and statistical hard real-time guarantees. This effort not only represents an attempt to provide an efficient integrated environment for hard real-time, elastic and predictive service guarantees, it also seeks to reduce the overhead encumbered providing such guarantees. By dynamically computing the number of scheduling decision required to meet the QoS demands of the supported applications, we are pursuing an approach to reduce system overhead which attempts to service multiple cells per scheduling decision rather than the single cell per scheduling decision approach used at present. In addition, we are also developing a dynamic rate management scheme in order to distribute each connection's load in a fairer manner. Finally, extensive analysis must still be performed to better characterize the performance results provided by the *COPS* framework.

Bibliography

J.C.R. Bennett and H. Zhang. WF^2Q: Worst-case Fair Weighted Fair Queuing. In *Proceedings of INFOCOM '96*, March 1996.

D. C. Clark, S. Shenker, and L. Zhang. Supporting Real-Time Applications in an Integrated Services Packet Network: Architecture and Mechanism. In *SIGCOMM '92*, pages 14–26, 1992.

The ATM Forum Technical Committee. *Traffic Management Specification*. The ATM Forum, 1996.

Alan Demers, Srinivasan Keshav, and Scott Shenker. Analysis and simulation of a fair queueing algorithm. In *Proc. ACM SIGCOMM*, pages 3–12, 1989.

D. Ferrari and D. Verma. A Scheme for Real-Time Channel Establishment in Wide-Area Networks. *IEEE Journal on Selected Areas in Communications*, 8(3):368–379, April 1990.

Domenico Ferrari. Client Requirements for Real-Time Communication. *IEEE Journal on Selected Areas in Communications*, 28(11):65–72, November 1990.

S. Jamaloddin Golestani. A Framing Strategy for Congestion Management. *IEEE Journal on Selected Areas in Communications*, 9(7):1064–1077, September 1991.

S. Jamaloddin Golestani. A Self-Clocked Fair Queueing Scheme for Broadband Applications. In *Proc. IEEE INFOCOM*, pages 636–646, 1994.

Pawan Goyal, Harrick Vin, and Haichen Cheng. Start-Time Fair Queuing: A Scheduling Algorithm for Integrated Services Packet Switching Networks. In *Proc. ACM SIGCOMM*, pages 157–168, August 1996.

Simon Lam and Geoffrey Xie. Burst Scheduling Networks: Flow Specification and Performance Guarantees. In *Proceedings of NOSSDAV '95*, Durham, New Hampshire, April 1995.

Cathy McCann, Raj Vaswani, and John Zahorjan. A Dynamic Processor Allocation Policy for Multiprogrammed Shared Memory Multiprocessors. *ACM Transactions on Computer Systems*, pages 146–178, 1993.

A. Parekh. *A Generalized Processor Sharing Approach to Flow Control in Integrated Services Networks.* PhD thesis, Laboratory for Information and Decision Systems, Massachusetts Institute of Technology, February 1992.

A. K. Parekh and R. G. Gallager. A Generalized Processor Sharing Approach to Flow Control in Integrated Services Networks: The Single Node Case. *IEEE/ACM Transactions on Networking*, 1(3):344–357, June 1993.

A. K. Parekh and R. G. Gallager. A Generalized Processor Sharing Approach to Flow Control in Integrated Services Networks: The Multiple Node Case. *IEEE/ACM Transactions on Networking*, 2(2):137–150, April 1994.

M. Shreedhar and George Varghese. Efficient fair queueing using deficit round robin. In *Proc. ACM SIGCOMM*, pages 231–242, August/September 1995.

Subhash Suri, George Varghese, and Girish Chandranmenon. Leap Forward Virtual Clock: A New Fair Queueing Scheme with Guaranteed Delays and Throughput Fairness. Technical Report WUCS-96-10, Washington University in St. Louis, June 1996.

Anujan Varma and Dimitrios Stiliadis. Design and Analysis of Frame-Based Fair Queueing: A New Traffic Scheduling Algorithm for Packet Switched Networks. In *Proc ACM SIGMETRICS*, May 1996.

D. Verma, H. Zhang, and D. Ferrari. Delay Jitter Control for Real-Time Communication in a Packet Switching Network. In *Proceedings of TriComm '91*, pages 35–43, 1991.

C. Parris H. Zhang and D. Ferrari. Dynamic Management of Guaranteed Performance Multimedia Connections. *ACM/Springer-Verlag Multimedia Systems*, 1:267–283, 1994.

Lixia Zhang. Virtual Clock: A new traffic control algorithm for packet-switched networks. *ACM Trans. Computing Systems*, 9(2):101–124, 1991.

End-to-End QoS Functions Using Dynamic Rate Control Methods

Koji Hashimoto†, Jun Sato‡, Yukiharu Kohsaka‡ and Yoshitaka Shibata†

†Faculty of Software and Information Science, Iwate Prefectural Univ. 152-52 Sugo, Takizawa, Iwate, Japan 020-0173 {hashi, shibata }@iwate-pu.ac.jp

‡Dept. of Information and Computer Science, Faculty of Engineering, Toyo Univ. 2100 Kujirai, Kawagoe, Saitama, Japan 350 {jun, kohsaka}@sb.cs.toyo.ac.jp

With advent of CPU and network technologies, multimedia services such as VOD or teleconferencing system have been feasible. In those systems, however, suitable QoS (Quality of Service) in accordance with user's requirements, available computing and network resources during multimedia services must be guaranteed. In this paper, we introduce end-to-end QoS functions with uses dynamic rate control methods in dual : packet rate control method to reduce packet loss, and frame rate control method to maintain the frame rate at constant under the dynamic load conditions. These dynamic control methods are defined as a media coordinate system and implemented for a prototyped Video-on-Demand system to evaluated the performance of these functions. Through these performance evaluation, we could justify the usefulness of our suggested media coordinate system.

1.1 Introduction

In order to provide continuous media services, such as Video-on-Demand over high speed networks, a suitable QoS(Quality of Service) requested by the user has to be guaranteed by taking accont of the characteristics of offered media data, processing capabilities and load deviations of both client stations and video servers, and the available network bandwidth and its traffic load. Therefore, the system has to include mechanisms which guarantee end-to-end QoS from the application through network layers.

Recently, there are a number of researches concerned with QoS guarantee [1][2] on the transport and network layers [3][4]. However many multimedia applications must have inter-media and intra-media synchronizations between audio and video, audio/video frame rate control functions, data transformation, compression / decompression functions and media flow control functions. In addition, end-to-end QoS protocol and management functions are required to guarantee QoS on top of the transport layer. However, few researchers have paid attention to the end-to-end QoS control functions and mechanisms, although it is very significant.

On the other hand, light and simple protocols such as UDP, is expected to provide higher throughput rather than reliable protocol such as TCP. However, if many users share the same computing and network resources, the provided multimedia QoS might be decresed because of the generation of packet loss, delay and jitter. Therefore, the system must be adapted dynamically and smoothly to the environment under the various extra load conditions. In real-time continuous media transmission, the feedback functions from client station to server station is efficient when the unreliable UDP/IP protocol is used.

In this paper, we introduce client-agent-server system which includes end-to-end QoS management functions and end-to-end QoS negotioation protocols. Also, we introduced two different dynamic rate control methods including packet rate control method which controls the packet interval at the sender side to reduce the packet loss rate under the admissible packet loss rate, and frame rate control method which controls the transmitted frame rate at the sender side to maintain displayed video frame rate at a constant under the various load conditions using the feedback message sent from the receiver side.

We implemented the prototyped VOD system including QoS guarantee functions and dynamic rate control functions to evaluate the performance of these functions. As a result, we could verify the usefulness of these rate control functions.

In the following section, we describe our suggested video-on-demand system in section 1.2. In section 1.3, we introduce a system architecture and specify functional modules and QoS negotiation protocols. In section 1.4, dynamic rate controls which contain packet rate control and frame rate control is described. In section 1.5, a prototyped VOD system and its performance evaluation are discussed.

1.2 Continuous Media Services

In order to provide more user oriented Video-on-Demand system, we introduce client-agent-server system (Figure 1.1). 1) to provide a wide variety of video depending on the user's request, 2) to provide interactive operations(play-out, pause, rewind etc.) capabilities. 3) to guarantee QoS requirements of each client such as video/audio frame rate, pixel resolution, and the number of colors.

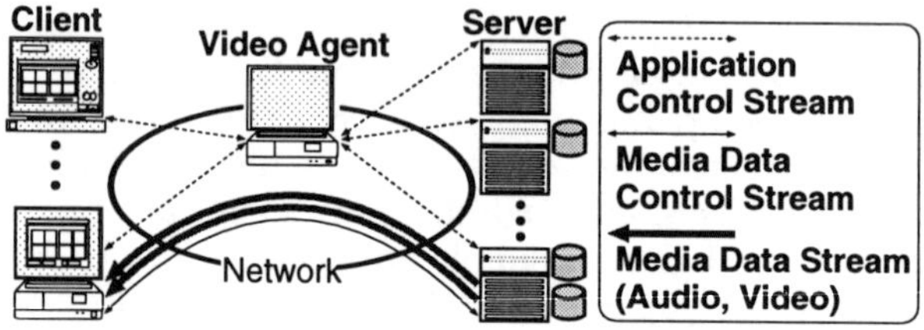

Fig. 1.1 Video on Demand System

The client performs interactive video presentation functions for the user. The client and server process audio and video data via media data stream, and exchange control messages such as feedback of packet loss ratio, frame rate and QoS negotiation via media data control stream to guarantee user's QoS requirement. The video agent receives VOD service requests which include the video title and the QoS requirement by the user from the clients via an application control stream, determines the suitable server according to the client's QoS requirement.

1.3 System Architecture

In order to realize end-to-end QoS functions[1][5] on continuous media transmission service, we introduce new system architecture based on three layers model, including synchronization, data transform and media flow control layers between the applicatin and the transport layers in the OSI reference model (Figure 1.2).

The synchronization layer performs intra and inter-media synchronization functions, the data transform layers performs compression / decompression and data format conversion of audio and video, such as RGB, NTSC format, pixcel resolution, color depth, etc. and the media flow control layers performs variable packet flow control and packet loss rate control functions. We have integrated these three layers into one layer as the media coordinate system[6].

The media coordinate system is furthermore vertically divided into four planes as shown in Figure 1.2: a user plane, a control plane, a QoS maintenance plane and a steream managemant plane, over high speed network such as ATM and adopted to QoS-A model of Lancaster university[1]. In the user plane, synchronization function between different media, such as audio and video, data transform function between different media attributes, media flow control for both constant and variable bit rate transmission for continuous media are performed[7]. In the control plane, connection establishment/release of the media stream and QoS renegotiation to maintain. In the QoS maintenance plane, each entity is responsible for the fine-

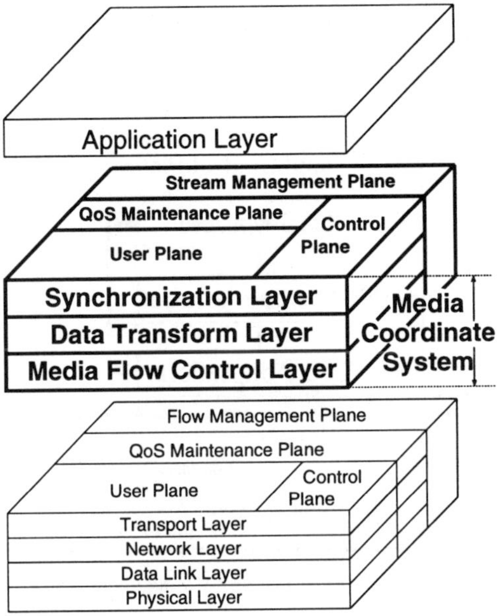

Fig. 1.2 System Architecture

grained monitoring and maintenance of their associated protocol entities. In the stream management plane, the most suitable QoS parameter values on each protocol layer are determined according to the user's QoS requirements, characteriseics of the source media data, output device attributes available computing and network resources.

We also define a media coordinate system to unify these three layers into one layer.

1.3.1 *Stream Management and Control Plane*

Figure 1.3 shows the functional modules of the stream management and control plane.

Stream Manager offers Signaling-MCSAP to application layer for user's interactive operations and QoS requirements, uses a transport layer's Signaling-TSAP and TSAPs to establish and release media data streams with QoS, update QoS requests and interactive operations from application.

QoS Mapper maps the application layer's QoS requirements into synchronization, data transform and media flow control layer's QoS parameters, and computing resources(CPU power, memory size, etc.).

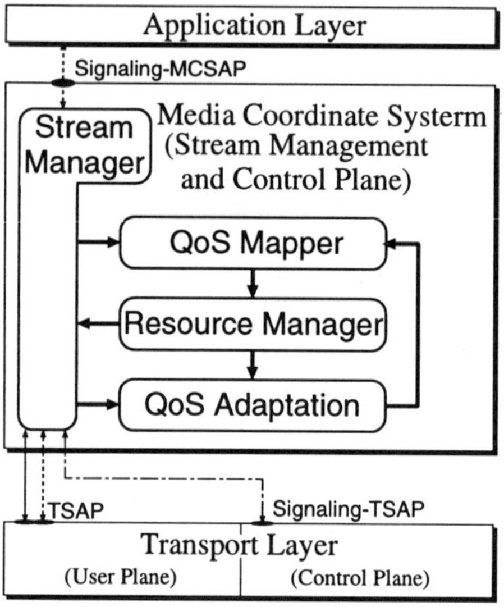

Fig. 1.3 Functional Modules of Stream Management and Control Plane

Resource Manager reserves and release computing resources and performs admission test whether the mapped computing resources are available or not.

QoS Adaptation performs QoS paramater's adaptation according to QoS parameter's priority required from application layer.

The association of these functional modules performs admission control and decides the suitable QoS according to user's QoS requirements on client or server side.

1.3.2 *QoS Negotiation Protocols*

The media coordinate system needs to be associated with functional modules shown in figure 1.3 between client and sever to guarantee end-to-end QoS. Therefore, media coordinate system uses QoS negotiation protocols at the beginning and during of sessions to decide suitable QoS between client and server from the application through transport layers. Figure 1.4 shows QoS negotiation protocol flow at the beginning of session. Figure 1.5 shows control message flow during the session, when the number of sessions varies in the server.

If computing resources necessary to guarantee QoS can't maintain, then the QoS adaptation module adapts QoS for existing all of the sessions. As a result, the media coordinate system performs QoS negotiation during of the session.

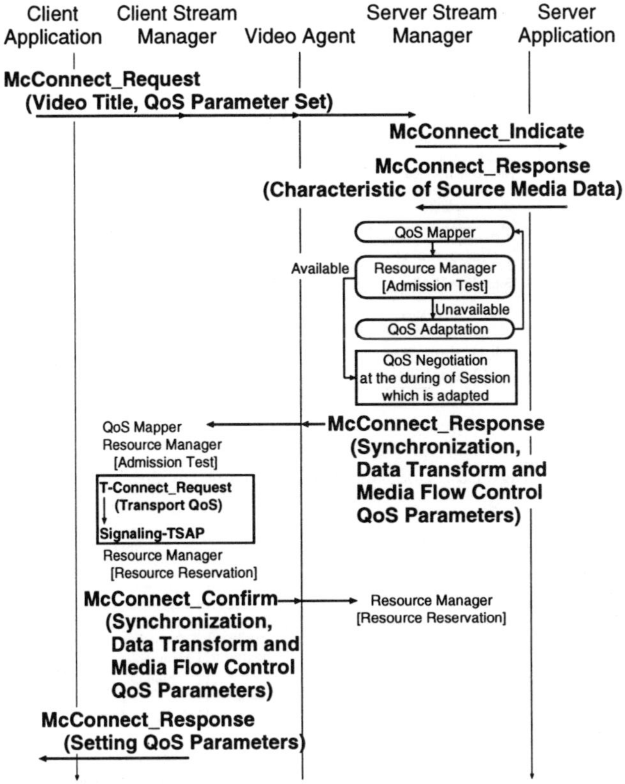

Fig. 1.4 QoS Negotiation at the beginning of Session

1.4 Variable Bit Rate Transmission and Dynamic Rate Control Methods

Figure 1.6 shows the functional modules necessary to realize our suggested dynamic rate control functions. In the packet rate management module, the numbers of packet to be transmitted on server or to be received on client are managed. In the frame rate management module, actual frame rate to be read from hard disk on server or to be displayed on client are managed. In the stream management control module, CPU loads on client and server, and traffic condition of network are periodically monitored and feedback messages between client and server, are managed.

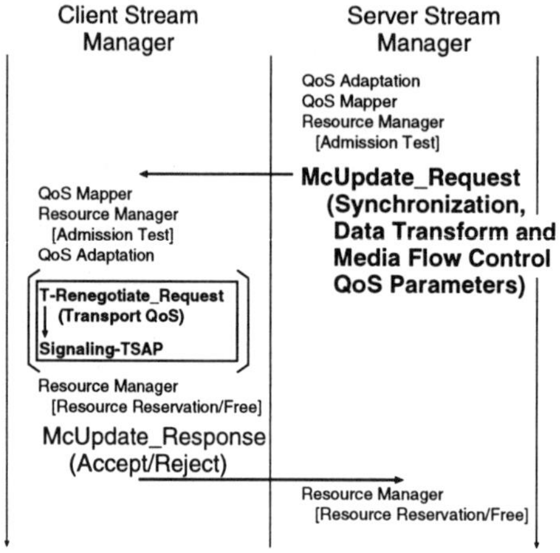

Fig. 1.5 QoS Negotiation during the session

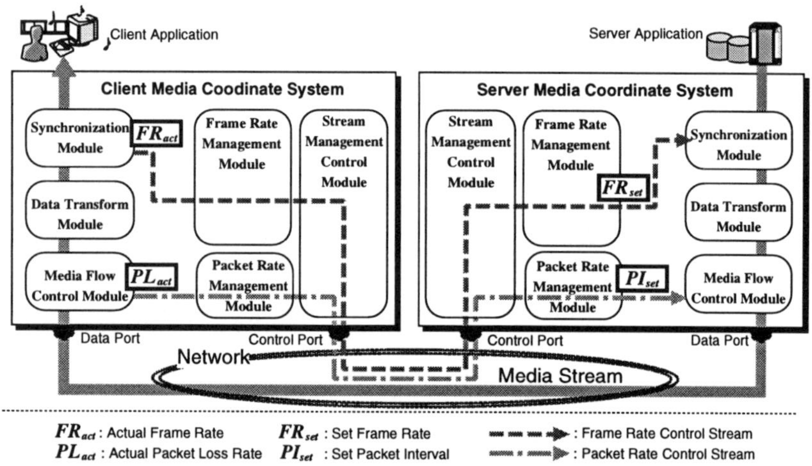

Fig. 1.6 Functional Modules Configuration and Flow of Rate Control

1.4.1 *Variable Bit Rate Transmission*

In order to transmit and display both uncompressed and compressed video frames, we introduce two different variable bit rate methods including Group of Picture(GoP) transmission method and frame transmission method. In both methods, the packet length is assumed to be fixed although the number of the packets in a time unit and the time interval between the packets are controlled according to GoP or frame size.

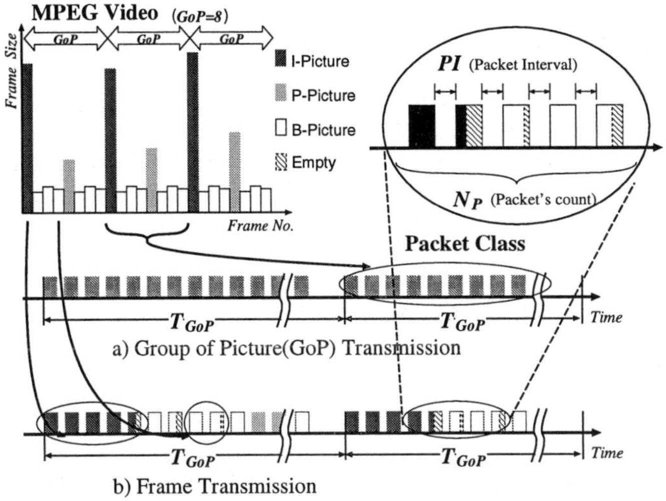

Fig. 1.7 Variable Bit Rate Transmission

In the case of GoP transmission method for the MPEG video depicted in Figure 1.7 a), where one GoP is consisted of 8 frames(1 I-frame, 2 P-frame and 6 B-frames), the multiple packets equivalent to one GoP are generated and transmitted. When we define the time interval for a GoP as $T_{GoP}[sec]$, the number of the packet for a GoP as N_p and data size of a GoP as $L_{GoP}[bytes]$, and transmitted packet size as L_p, then $N_p = \lceil L_{GoP}/L_p \rceil$ packets are generated at video server and transmitted within $T_{GoP}[sec]$ to the client. Thus, constant frame rate with variable data sizes can be attained by generating packets according to the data size of each GoP within T_{GoP}. We define this as GoP transmission method. In this method, since each GoP consisted of multiple frames is regareded as a basic unit for transmission, not only packet overhead can be reduced, but also the processing load of intra-frame and interfame synchronizations can be simplified. However, when one packet is lost, then the multiple frame are influenced.

On the other hand, in the case of the frame transmission method as depicted in Figure 1.7 b), each frame including I-frame, P-frame and B-frames on each GoP is identified and the packets equivalent to each frame are generated on the server and transmitted to the client.

GoP transmission method: since MPEG data can be packetized without considering the type of frames in a GoP, the number of the packet generatedand their packet processing can be reduced. On other hand, when the packet is lost by increasing the CPU and network traffic loads, a number of frames belong to one GoP is lost.

Frame transmission method: since each frame in each GoP is identified and transmitted individually, the number of the packets generated increases, and the complicated packet process on each control module must be implemented. On the other hand, the influence of the lost packet can be restricted within one frame.

1.4.2 *Dynamic Rate Control Methods*

Too much CPU load of the client/server station, and network traffic load causes packet loss, delay and jitter by packet buffer overflow and underflow of client, server and gateway, and eventually transmitted video frame rate is seriously reduced and influenced. In this research, we introduce two dynamic rate control methods in order to adapt to the environment these extra load conditions[8].

In packet rate control, inter-packet time interval is controlled on the server station to reduce the packet loss rate under the admissible loss rate by feedback message from client station including actual packet loss rate. In frame rate control, transmitted frame rate is controlled on the server station to maintain the displayed video frame rate at a constant and keep the time constraint of continuous media data by feedback message from client station including actual value of frame rate. By combining these two rate control methods, audio/video quality couldn't be completely guaranteed, however, these could be adopted quickly and smoothly to environment under the various extra load conditions.

1.4.3 *Packet Rate Control*

In order to reduce packet loss rate under the admissible packet loss rate when the CPU loads in both client and server, and network traffic load has be dynamically changed, packet interval, $PI[msec]$, is updated according to extra load conditions.

In this system, when the packet loss rate, $PL_{act}[\%]$, for a measurement interval, $T[sec]$, is exceeded over the admissible packet loss rate, $PL_{adm}[\%]$, then the packet interval, PI, is immediately increased based on the characteristic curve of packet loss rate for packet interval and dynamically controlled to keep the condition $PL_{act} < PL_{adm}$. Here, the characteristic curve between the packet interval and packet loss rate can be measured as a characteristics curve as depicted in Figure 1.8.

A priori of video service, this characteristic curve is measured in advance, and when extra load increases and packet loss is generated higher

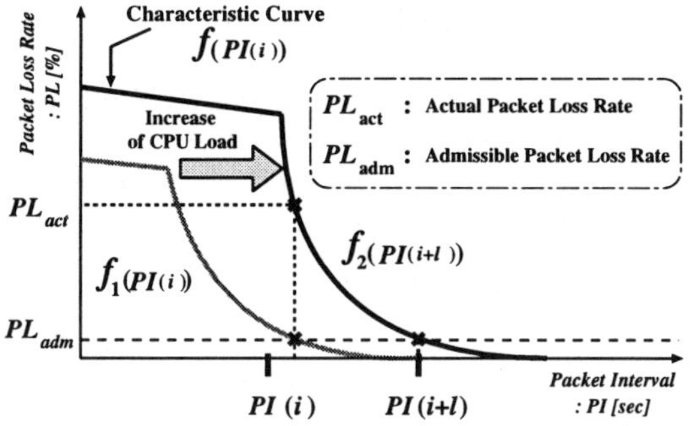

Fig. 1.8 Characteristic Curve of Packet Loss Rate for Packet Interval

than admissible packet loss rate during the audio/video transmission, this characteristic curve moves parallel correspond to extra load conditions. And next packet interval is updated in the point when the packet loss rate could be limited under the admissible packet loss rate in the moved characteristic curve shown Fugure 1.8.

1.4.4 *Frame Rate Control*

In order to normally display video data transmitted from the server at the client station, the frame rate by which the video source was initially stored at the video server must be maintained during video session and displayed on the client. However, in the case when the frame rate of the source video cannot be attained at the client, then sub-sampling of the frame has to be introduced to reduce the source frame rate before transmitting the video data from the server.

The client frame rate controller in the QoS maintenance plane periodically monitors the real frame rate FR_{act} to be displayed and compares it with the set frame rate FR_{set}. If the FR_{act} is smaller than FR_{set} for the interval $T[sec]$, then the counter value for rate difference status, $Miss_{cnt}$, is incremented. When $Miss_{cnt}$ exceeded a threshold, then a rate control message to reduce the current frame rate by ΔFR is sent from the client station to the video server's rate controller. The rate controller at the video server then dynamically updates the current frame rate based on the control message by sub-sampling the source frame rate FR_{src}. The rate controller at the client station also updates the set frame rate FR_{set} to the new value which has been sent to it from the video server's frame rate controller. By periodically adjusting the set frame rate, a constant rate is maintained.

1.5 Prototype and System Evaluation

In order to evaluate the usefulness of our suggested QoS guarantee functions and dynamic rate control methods, a Packet Audio Video System(PAVS) was prototyped based on the combination of FDDI with 100[Mbps] and Ethernet with 10[Mbps], and we implemented the prototyped VOD system.

Through this prototype, we evaluated following three items:

(1) The usefulness QoS functions when the session number on the video server varied and the priority attribute of the application QoS parameters are updated by the user.
(2) The relationship between the packet interval and packet loss rate.
(3) Packet rate and frame rate when the extra CPU load on client station are provided.

1.5.1 *Performance Evaluation of QoS guarantee functions*

We implemeted the media coordinate system which controls video frame rate and frame size as variable QoS parameters, and simple VOD application on four workstatoins for a server, a video agent, client1 and client2 over the FDDI network. Figure 1.9 shows the environment of the prototype.

In the prototype system, TCP/IP protocol was used for application control stream and media data control stream and UDP/IP protocol for media data stream. The effective throughput was observed in advance as available computing resources. Table 1.1 shows characteristics of audio, video data which were used to observe effective throughput and evaluate of QoS functions, desired and admissible QoS requirement by the user. Table 1.2 shows required throughput to guarantee the desired QoS and observed effective throughput in advance.

In order to evaluate QoS functions when the session number on the server and the user varied and the priority attribute of the application QoS parameters ware updated; either smoothness or size during the session 1 (from the period 1 to period 5) on the server – the client 1, the session 2(the period 2 and 3) on the sever – the client 2 is started. Two session's priority was assumed to be equal. Table 1.3 and 1.4 show application QoS parameter's priority attribute requested by the user, setting frame rate and frame size decided the media coordinate system, and necessary throughput at the during these sessions. The media coordinate system decides suitable setting QoS parameter's values according to priority attribute required by the user and the efficient throughput shown Table 1.2.

Figure 1.10 shows the relation between the actually displayed frames and the elapsed time on the client 1. Here the slope shows relation of the actual video frame. If these output times of the displayed frames are close

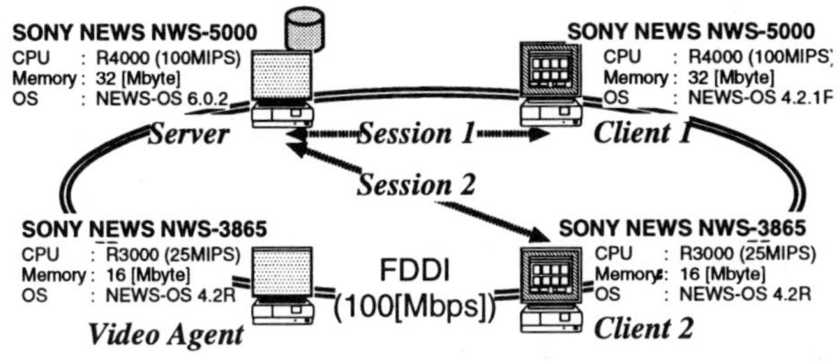

Fig. 1.9 Prototyped VOD System

Table 1.1 Characteristics of Media Data, Desired and Admissible QoS

		Characteristics of Stored Data	Desired QoS	Admissible QoS
Audio Data	Quantized Bit [bit]	8	8	8
	Sampling Frequency [Hz]	8000	8000	8000
Video Data	Frame Size [pixel]	352x240	***352x240***	***160x128***
	Frame Rate [fps]	24	***24***	***4***
	Depth [bit]	8	8	8

Table 1.2 Effective throughput

The Number of Sessions	Necessary Throughput [Mbps]	Measured Efficient Throughput [bps]		
		Server	Client 1	Client 2
1	16.3	11.5	6.3	4.8
2	32.6	10.2	7.7	5.0
3	49.9	9.6	8.1	4.8

to the slope which shows the relation of the stored video frame and logical output time, this means the time constraint of the video frame can guarantee. Therefore, using the QoS functions the media coordinate system can performed better continuous media service with suitable QoS according to user's QoS requirements, compared the case where there is no QoS functions.

In this prototyped VOD, when client, server or networks get CPU and traffic loads, frame output time was not exactly controlled. This is because this prototyped VOD does not have dynamic rate control function for continuous media transmission which is based on the paket/frame rate control. Since have investigated the dynamic rate control methods[8], we will implement this to the media coordinate system to correctly control the frame rate.

Table 1.3 Setting QoS Parameter (Session 1)

Session 1 (Client 1)	Period1	Period2	Period3	Period4	Period5
	Priority is Size		Priority is Smoothness		Size
Frame Rate [fps]	8	4	10	16	8
Frame Size [pixel]	352x240		160x128		352x240
Necessary Throughput [Mbps]	5.41	2.77	1.70	2.69	5.41

Table 1.4 Setting QoS Parameter (Session 2)

Session 2 (Client 2)	Period1	Period2	Period3	Period4	Period5
	——	Priority is Smoothness		——	
Frame Rate [fps]	——	4	4	——	
Frame Size [pixel]	——	352x240	160x128	——	
Necessary Throughput [Mbps]	——	2.77	0.72	——	

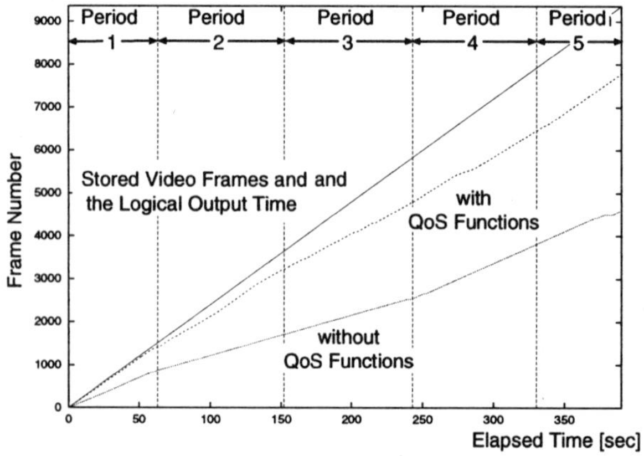

Fig. 1.10 Frame Number and Output Time (Session 1)

1.5.2 *Performance Evaluation of Dynamic Rate Control Methods*

In order to evaluate the usefulness of our suggested dynamic rate control methods, the prototype as shown in Figure 1.11. The characteristics of the source video and other system parameters in the prototyped VOD system are shown in Table 1.5 and 1.6. As video source, we used the one scene from the movie "Back to the Future" which is compressed MPEG-1[9] techniquies. As extra loads on the user client, the number of the processes of MPEG-1 softwere decoder(mpeg_play[10]) was increased from 0 to 2 on the user client. As network traffic load, continuous remote file transfer equivalent to about 7.5[$Mbps$] between the other workstations was intentionally executed.

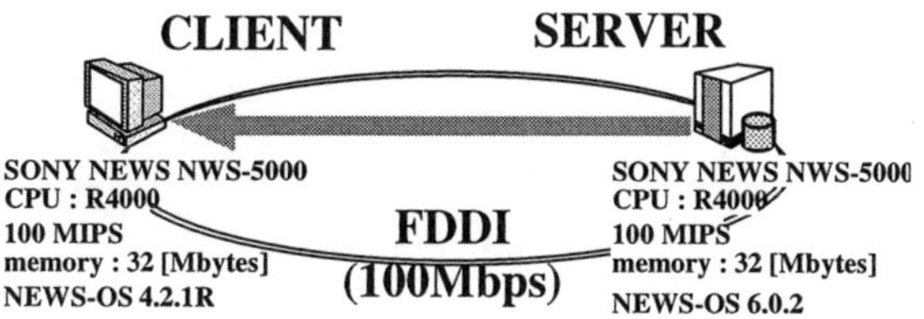

Fig. 1.11 Prototype for Evaluate of Dynamic Rate Control Methods

Table 1.5 System Parameters of Evaluation

Extra Load	Client
Physical Networks	FDDI
Packet Length[byte]	$4K$
Average Video Bit Rate[Mbps]	5.0

Table 1.6 Transmitted Video Parameters

Compression Format	MPEG-1
Average Bit Rate[Mbps]	1.5
Pixel Resolusion[pixels]	640×480
Color Depth[bits]	24
Frame Rate[fps]	30
Number of Frames in GoP	N = 15
I,P Frames Cycle	M = 5

In order to adjust the packet interval when the actual packet loss rate exceed the admissible packet loss rate in the packet rate control, the relation between inter packet interval and the packet loss rate was investigated using the prototype system. The packet loss rate was observed by actually sending the packets with the fixed length from the video server to one of the client station and changing the packet interval for different CPU load conditions as shown in Figure 1.12.

As understood from Figure 1.12, the packet loss rate was gradually

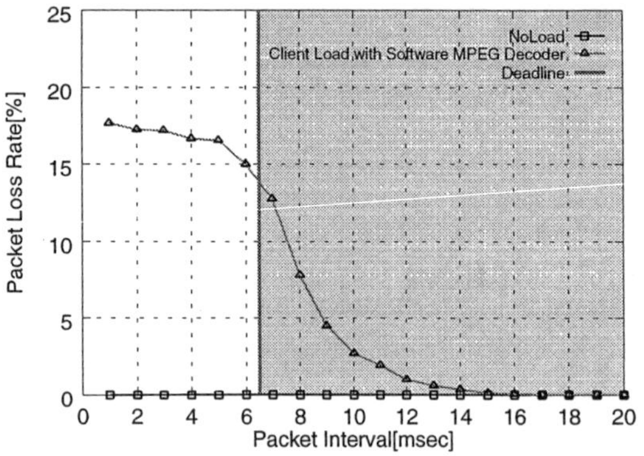

Fig. 1.12 Relationship of Packet Interval and Packet Loss Rate

dereased as the packet interval increases. However, when packet interval is larger than 6.5[*msec*], the time constraint of the source video frame rate with 30[*fps*] cannot be maintained. We define this time interval as "deadline" of the packet interval for this video source. In the case of the packet interval larger than the deadline, the original frame rate cannot be maintained. Because the required average packet throughput for an video frame cannot be attained, the original frame rate cannot be maintained. Therefore, the source video must be sub-sampled and the packet interval must be controlled to maintain the admissible packet loss rate while maitaining the frame rate higher as much as possible. Thus, this characteristic curve with the packet loss rate, PL is expressed by the following equation as a function of packet interval, PI :

$$PL = \begin{cases} -0.37 \times PI + 18.03 (PI < deadline) \\ -3.55 \times PI + 38.86 \; (PI >= deadline) \end{cases}$$

1.5.3 *Evaluation of Dynamic Rate Control*

Figure 1.13 a) and b) show the results of the packet rate control when the extra CPU load on the client station was given during video data transmission.

In the case when the packet rate control was not introduced, the packet loss rate randomly increased from 0[%] to about 13[%] when the extra CPU load on the client station was given between the 28[*sec*] to 152[*sec*] elapsed time while the packet interval was constant at 1[*msec*]. On the other hand, in the case when the packet control function was introduced, the packet interval immediately increased to reduce the packet loss rate

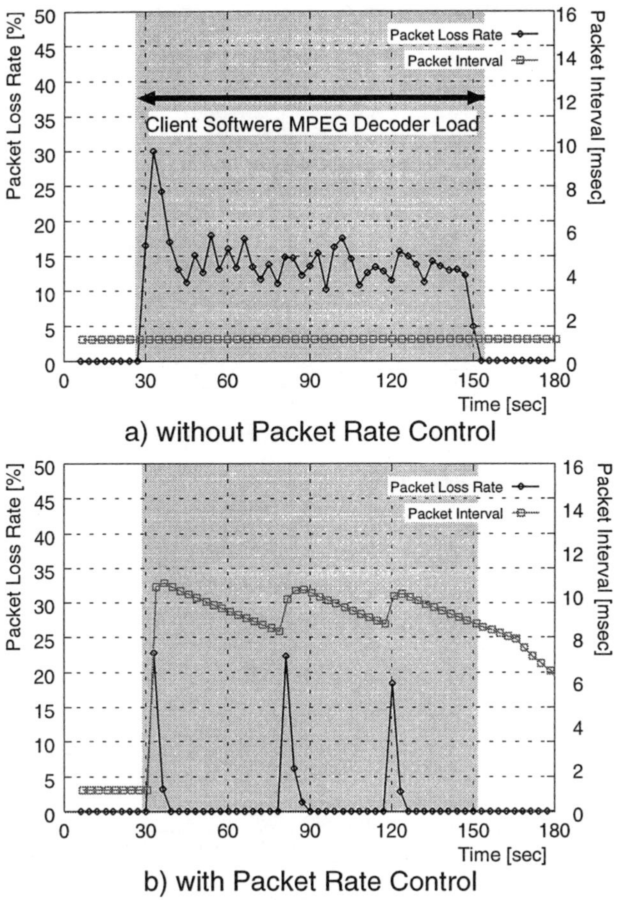

Fig. 1.13 Evaluation of Packet Rate Control with Client Load

when the extra load on the client station was giving and packet loss was generated. After that the packet loss rate could be maintained quickly under the admissible loss rate. However, the packet loss rate could not completely limited because current value of the packet interval was only the feedback message from client station. It is required to improve the always keep the packet loss rate under the admissible packet loss rate combining this feedback message and change value of the CPU load on both client and server, and network traffic load conditions.

Figure 1.14 a) and b) show the result of frame rate control when the

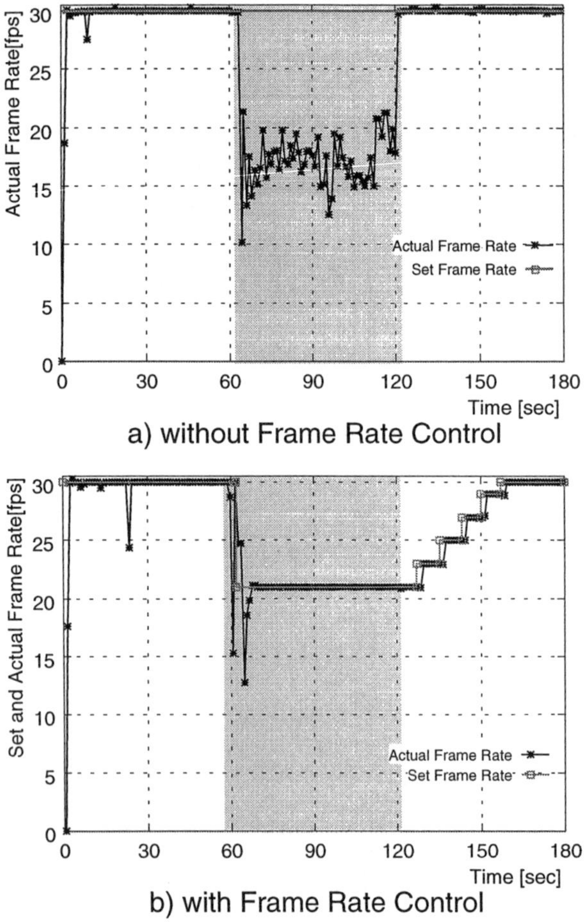

Fig. 1.14 Evaluation of Frame Rate Control with Client Load

client extra CPU load was given during video data transmission. In the case when the frame rate control function was not introduced, the actual frame rate decreased and randomly influenced when CPU load on the client station was giving while the setting frame rate was constant at 30[fps]. On the other hand, in the case when the frame rate control was introduced, the set frame rate on the video server was immediately updated according to the feedback message from the client station. After that the actual frame rate could be maintained at a constant with 15[fps]. After the CPU load was released, the frame rate was gradually increased and approached to the original frame rate 30[fps].

Thus, we could verify the usefulness of the suggested rate control functions through this performance evaluation.

1.6 Conclusions

In this paper, we introduced the Media Coordinate System which provides end-to-end QoS guarantee functions, specify each functions and QoS negotiation protocols. We also introduced two variable bit rate transmission methods, the GoP transmission and the frame transmission when compressed video data were transmitted over networks. The GoP transmission method can provide higher throughput. On the other hand, the frame transmission can expect flexibility packet transmission. At the same time, we suggested packet rate control and frame rate control methods as dynamic rate control when extra loads on client and network are given. We implemented prototyped VOD system which has our suggested functions in this paper, and evaluated these functions. As a result, the media coordinate system performed continuous media service with suitable QoS according to user's QoS requirements using QoS functions. The system also performance has demonstrated the usefulness of our suggested control methods even through the client CPU and network traffic loads are dynamically changed by comparing the performance between with and without these two rate control methods.

As furture works, we will evaluate of these rate control when audio/video syncronization functions mechanism is implemented, and realization of QoS functions with QoS parameters including frame rate and frame size and evaluation of the end-to-end QoS in cases of delay, jitter and packet loss rate will be made.

Bibliography

A. Campbell, G. Coulson and D. Hutchison. "A QUALITY OF SERVICE ARCHITECTURE", *ACM SIGCOM Computer Communication Review*, Vol.24, Number.2, pp.1-27, 1984.

A. Vogel, B. Kerherve, G. Bochmann and J. Gecsei. "Distributed Multimedia and QOS: A Survey", *IEEE Multimedia*, 2(2):10-19, 1995.

S. Fotedar, M. Gerla, P. Crocetti and L. Fratta. "ATM Virtual Private Networks" *COMMUNICATION OF THE ACM*, 38(2):101-109, 1995.

K. Nahrstedt and R. Steinmetz. "Resource Management in Networked Multimedia Systems" *IEEE COMPUTER*, 28(5):52-64, 1995.

K.Nahrstedt and Jonathan M. Smith. "The QOS Broker" *IEEE MultiMedia*, 2(1):53-67, 1995.

K. Hashimoto, M. Katsumoto, M. Watanabe and Y. Shibata. "End-to-End QoS Architecture for Continuous Media Services" *Proc. of ICOIN-10*, pp.578-583, January 1996.

Y. Shibata, N. Seta and S. Shimizu. "Media Synchronization Protocols for Packet Audio/Video System on Multimedia Information Networks" *Proc. of HICSS-28*, pp.594-601, January 1995.

J. Sato, K. Hashimoto and Y. Shibata. "Dynamic Rate Control Methods for Continuous Media Transmission Services" *Proc. of ICOIN-12*, pp.110-116, January 1998.

D.L.Gall "MPEG: A Video Compression Standard for Multimedia Applictions" *Communications of the ACM*, Vol.34, No.4, pp.46-58, Apr.1991.

K.Patel, B.C.Smith, L.A.Rowe: "Performance of a Software MPEG Video Decoder" *ACM Multimedia'93*, pp.75-82, 1993.

AN ARCHITECTURE FOR THE STRUCTURED ANALYSIS AND DESIGN OF PARTICIPATOR DEPENDENT MULTIMEDIA PRESENTATIONS

TIMOTHY K. SHIH, HUAN-CHAO KEH AND JASON C. HUNG
Multimedia Information Network (MINE) Lab
Department of Computer Science and Information Engineering
Tamkang University
Tamsui, Taipei Hsien
Taiwan 251, R.O.C.
E-mail: tshih@cs.tku.edu.tw

We propose a software architecture and a revised DFD/CFD mechanism with an improved Petri net for the analysis and design of multimedia presentations. A number of additional diagram components are introduced in the multimedia DFD/CFD. Unlike mapping a traditional data flow/control flow diagram to a structured chart, the refinement of a multimedia DFD/CFD results in a number of multimedia Petri nets which represent the schedule and navigation of a presentation. The proposed mechanism allows a presentation to change itself. Thus a dynamic multimedia presentation can learn from the audience and act according to the audience's individual background. Using our system, a presentation designer is able to analyze his/her presentation script and design the presentation in a systematic manner.

1 Introduction

Structured analysis and design have been used for quite a while in software development. A system engineer analyzes the requirements of a software system and constructs a system specification. Based on this specification, the engineer uses data flow diagrams or control flow diagrams to design a functional specification and the preliminary design of a software system. The design is then refined stepwise toward a structured chart before the implementation proceeds. This Water Fall paradigm [4] has several benefits. Firstly, with the help of a CASE tool, an engineer is able to clearly organize the data flow and the transition control of a system. The engineer does not need to have the detail at the beginning. The initial design of a system can be refined step by step in a multi-level data flow/control flow diagram. This methodology allows the engineer to focus on a level of detail each time without being loose in the complexity of the system. Moreover, a data flow diagram allows the engineer to precisely specify the type of data each part of the system needs in a data dictionary. This dictionary is then used as a base in the design of a program's data structures. After the structured chart is derived from the data flow diagram, the implementation of the system can be constructed more efficiently. These benefits make a data flow/control flow diagram become a useful tool in the process of software development. The development of a multimedia presentation involves the analysis of a presentation script, the collection of multimedia resources, and the realization of a presentation layout and navigation control flow. In line with the growing needs of multimedia presentations, many authoring systems were developed. However, in the community of multimedia computing, there is no discussion of the need of a good presentation development methodology. We have surveyed a number of presentation design tools. We found that, not many authoring system focus on the concept of stepwise refinement. In this paper, we discuss a new authoring system for this purpose. The proposed system is based on data flow and control flow diagrams, with many enhanced notations especially useful for multimedia presentation designs. The proposed notations and the methodology are implemented in a prototype software run on Microsoft Windows 95/3.1.

This paper is organized as the following. In section 2, we survey a number of well-known authoring packages. To run a multimedia presentation, we have developed a Multimedia Abstract Machine (MAM) which is based on a timed Petri net model. A short discussion of MAM is given in section 3. The proposed multimedia data flow/control flow diagram is discussed in section 4. Section 5 proposes a new direction of multimedia presentation designs. Unlike other systems, which generates static presentations, our system allows dynamic multimedia presentations. We give a short example of multimedia presentation design in section 6. A short conclusion summarizes our contributions is also presented in section 7.

2 Related Works

Before we design our system, we have surveyed both academic researches and industrial software packages. Sony Corporation developed a hypermedia prototype system (SAL) [3] for multimedia authoring, which is based on a link and node model used in most authoring systems. The Layered Multimedia Data Model (LMDM) [5] allows the reuse of presentation templates which is important for improving the efficiency of multimedia presentation designs. LMDM has a number of strengths including the support of a general model of media synchronization, limited system dependencies, and the generalization of a traditional animation model. The work discussed in [1] proposes an architecture and data model for integrated multimedia presentations. The architecture provides a homogeneous strategy to access, process, and exchange multimedia documents generated by different authoring and presentation systems. Diamond [10] is a multimedia message system built on a distributed architecture for creating, editing, transmitting, and managing multimedia documents. Multimedia documents are stored in folders in a distributed database. An open hypermedia system is discussed in [2]. The system supports heterogeneous multimedia data types and allows new types to be added. A platform independent multimedia presentation composition system is discussed in [11]. In the system, a script based approach is used to model the object-oriented presentations as well as user interactions.

We also looked at the following commercial products related to multimedia authoring or presentation designs:

1. Authorware by Macromedia, Inc.
2. Multimedia Viewer by Microsoft
3. Multimedia Toolbook by Asymetrix Corporation
4. Hypermedia Authoring and Playback System by ITRI (Taiwan)
5. Action! by Macromedia, Inc.
6. Audio Visual Connection by IBM
7. Astound by Gold Disk Inc.

Authorware uses an event control flow diagram allowing the presenter to specify presentation objects and controls, which can be decomposed into several levels in a hierarchy structure. The system also provides a simple script language for calculation and data manipulation. Other systems (i.e., 2, 3, and 6 above) also provide script languages and API (application program interface) functions. Hypermedia System and Action! use a time line table allowing actions or objects be dropped in a particular time slot. Most systems allow users to cut and paste presentation objects or actions via button click and drawing. Multimedia Viewer also provides a set of medium editing tools. Presentation objects produced by these tools can be linked together by a script language supporting functions, data structures, and commands.

None of the above system, however, allows dynamic presentations. That is, a presentation generated by the above systems will stay as the form it was created. Different audience watches the same presentation over and over again. If a presentation can take user interactions and mutate itself, the presentation is more diversified. And this is the main strength of our system. Moreover, not many systems focus on the stepwise refinement of presentation designs. A presentation designer who uses the above systems must have his/her presentation script ready before using the systems. On the other hand, our system helps the designer to design his/her presentation step by step until the final version is created.

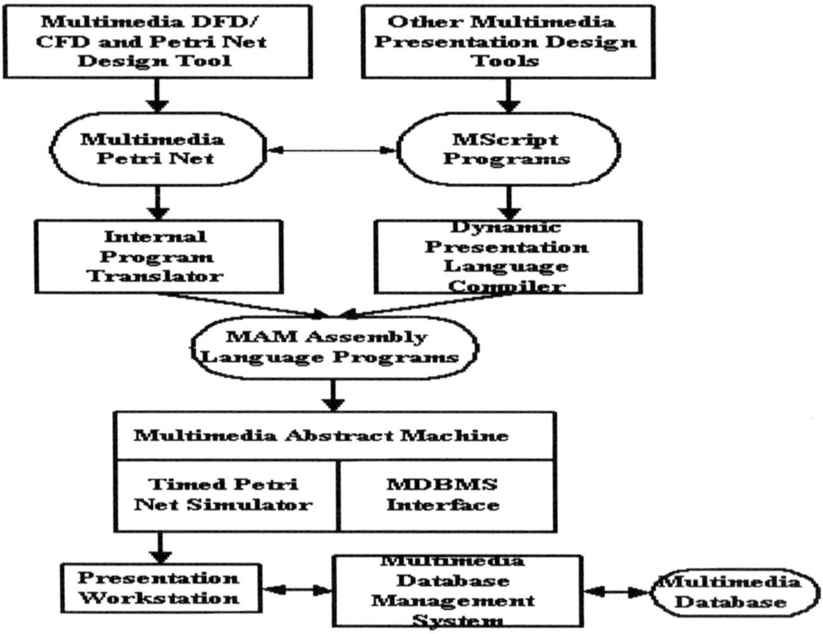

Figure 1: The software environment of our Multimedia Abstract Machine

3 A Multimedia Abstract Machine

The main theme of our system is a timed Petri Net based multimedia abstract machine (MAM). MAM is a software architecture and system for multimedia documentation demonstrations and presentations. We realized that most multimedia information processes consist of a sequence of atomic steps, such as opening a sound channel, transferring a block of video data from buffer to the graphic memory page, closing a MIDI sequencer, etc. These atomic steps, from the perspective of multimedia computing, are non-separable items. This concept is relatively similar to assembly language instructions, which are atomic steps of a procedural program. We have the MAM instruction set defined [6]. Some instructions control multimedia hardware devices while others support user interactions. A multimedia presentation designed by using our multimedia DFD/CFD and Petri net design tool has a number of Petri nets and navigation messages. These Petri nets are represented in a MAM assembly program, which is produced by an internal program translator. Therefore, the designed presentation is executable on the MAM. Figure 1 pictures the overall software environment of the MAM.

The development of MAM has multiple purposes. We have developed a multimedia script language. The language serves as an intermediate representations of various formats of multimedia presentations which we have developed [9,7].

These representations are compiled to the MAM instructions. Thus, it is possible to link multimedia presentations produced by different tools to make an integrated presentation. On the other side of the MAM environment is a multimedia DBMS [8], which we are trying to integrate to the environment. The objective of this MDBMS, from the perspective of MAM, is to assist a presentation to quickly locate the multimedia resources required in the demonstration.

Since MAM is an integrated multimedia programming environment with a relatively large scope, in this paper, we focus on the discussion of the multimedia DFD/CFD and Petri net design tool. Other components in the environment are omitted.

4 Multimedia DFD/CFD

In this section, we propose a revised DFD/CFD mechanism for multimedia presentation designs. The design of a multimedia presentation, utilizing message passing for navigation, has a similar concept to writing a software specification. The proposed multimedia data flow/control flow diagram is based on DFD and CFD, with the extension of some new objects:

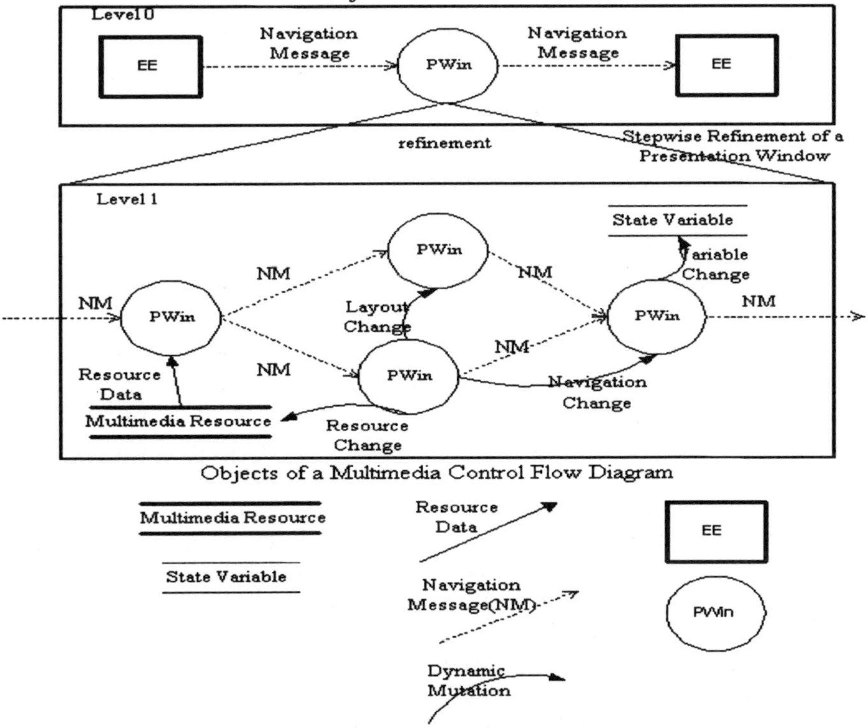

Figure 2: Components of a Multimedia DFD/CFD

- **Multimedia Resource**: similar to the data store in a DFD, a multimedia resource is denoted by a pair of thick parallel lines.
- **State Variable**: besides resources, an interactive presentation may contain state variables store presentation data, such as the audience's name. A state variable is represented by a pair of thin parallel lines. State variables not only keep information, but also control *dynamic presentations* (to be discussed in section 5).
- **Resource Data**: similar to the data link in a DFD, resources are passed to a presentation program by a link with a regular arrow.
- **Navigation Message (NM)**: similar to the control link in a CFD, a navigation message is passed by a link with a light-weighted arrow.
- **Dynamic Mutation**: to support dynamic multimedia presentations, the dynamic mutation link is introduced, which is represented by a curved arrow. There are four types of mutations in a multimedia DFD/CFD:
  - State Variable Change
  - Layout Change
  - Resource Change
  - Navigation Change

  These links mutate the content and appearance of a multimedia presentation. When we discuss the stepwise refinement of a presentation, we will define these mutations in detail.
- **External Entity (EE)**: similar to one in DFD/CFD, an external entity could represent a user, a hardware device, or another system which pass data/controls to the multimedia presentation. An EE is denoted by a box surrounded by thick lines.
- **Presentation Window (PWin)**: similar to a process in a DFD, a presentation window is denoted by a circle.

A multimedia presentation contains a number of presentation windows. Each presentation window contains a layout definition, a collection of multimedia resources (sharable among presentation windows), some state variables, and navigation control messages. Figure 2 illustrates the various types of components of a multimedia DFD/CFD.

A presentation window must be refined. Stepwise refinement of a presentation allows the presentation to be specified in different levels of details. The system allows the user to use multimedia DFDs/CFDs, with the help of a drag and drop mechanism, to design a multimedia presentation. The system also provides a connection to a multimedia database [8]. The multimedia database resource browser [8] allows the user to select multimedia resources needed for a presentation.

A multimedia DFD/CFD of multiple levels is to help a presentation designer to analyze the script structure of a presentation. However, it is not powerful enough to define the precise schedule or layout of a presentation. Incorporated with an interactive multimedia Petri net diagramming mechanism, the last level of a presentation window is refined to a Petri net, which describes the temporal behavior of a presentation window. An example showing the last level refinement is shown in figure 3. Our interactive multimedia Petri net is a variation of timed Petri net, with the addition of *User Transitions* and *Sync Arc*. Since a multimedia presentation is interactive, it is natural for us to introduce the above two objects for participant dependent synchronization.

A timed Petri net is a bipartite graph with two types of nodes: the transition nodes and the place nodes. A transition controls synchronization and a place holds a token and a time duration. A transition is fired only after each place adjacent to the transition releases the token. A place holds a multimedia resource to be played for the time duration. Transitions and places are connected by *sync arcs* in our revised Petri net. We add *user transitions* and *user arcs* to the timed Petri net. A user transition receives a navigation message from the user before it is fired. A user transition is directly connected to some transitions. The activation of the user transition interrupts the demonstration of the presentation window and causes the activation of the connected transitions simultaneously. For instance, in figure 3, the activation of the only one user transition (on the lower-left corner) causes transitions ``c" and ``d" to be fired together, which makes ``Music2", ``Map", and ``Shopping" resources to be demonstrated. Note that, the resulting presentation is missing the ``WallPaper" resource since transition ``a" was not fired. In a normal situation, when transition ``a" is fired, the presentation proceeds according to a pre-defined schedule. However, the existence of a user transition may cause the rearrangement of a presentation schedule. Using these user transitions and navigation messages, the revised Petri net is able to accept user interactions.

The last level of the refinement between a presentation window and a Petri net needs to maintain two types of balances: the navigation message balance and the multimedia resource/state variable balance. That is, the incoming and outgoing messages of a presentation window have to match those of the refined Petri net. Similarly, the multimedia resources and state variables used have to be the same. The last level of a multimedia presentation refinement has a number of interactive multimedia petri nets. The followings are components of the Petri nets:

- **Transition**: is for synchronization control. Transitions are shown as vertical dark bars.
- **User Transition**: accepts a message and causes the activation of connected transitions. User transitions are shown as vertical light bars.
- **Place**: is for playing a multimedia resource. Places are shown as ellipse.
- **User Arc**: connects from a user transition to a transition. User arcs are shown as straight arrowhead lines.
- **Sync Arc**: connects from a place to a transition, or from a transition to a place. Sync arcs are shown as curved arrowhead arcs.

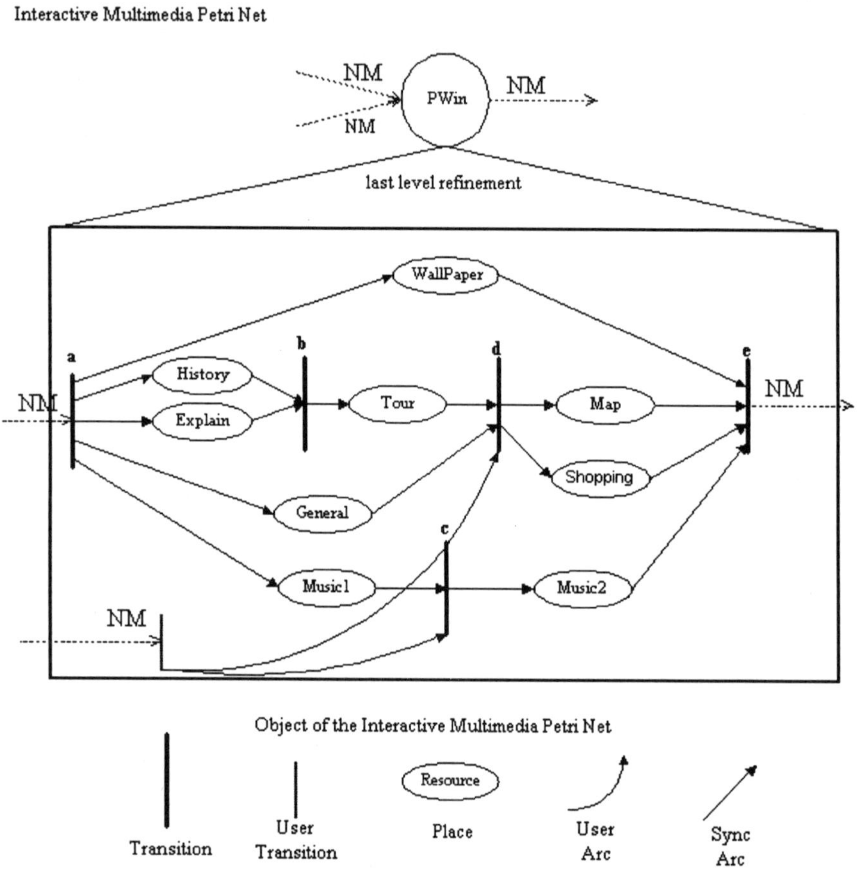

Figure 3: An Interactive Multimedia Petri Net

In the multimedia presentation design system, we allow six type of resources: sound, MIDI, video, animation, picture, and text resources. Some of these resource types are static (i.e., picture and text) while others are dynamic. Dynamic multimedia resources come with a resource duration. Within the time period, repeated steps are performed to load data, such as video frames, from disk to the video memory page. As illustrated in figure 4, we defined four sub-nets for the six type of resources. These sub-nets consists of atomic execution steps, such as preparing a sound card, or writing data to sound buffer. Each of these atomic step is corresponding to an assembly instruction of the MAM. Some of the sub-nets (e.g., the video sub-net) use transitions for synchronization control. All sub-nets of dynamic resources have an iterative counter (IC) calculating the duration of the resource demonstration.

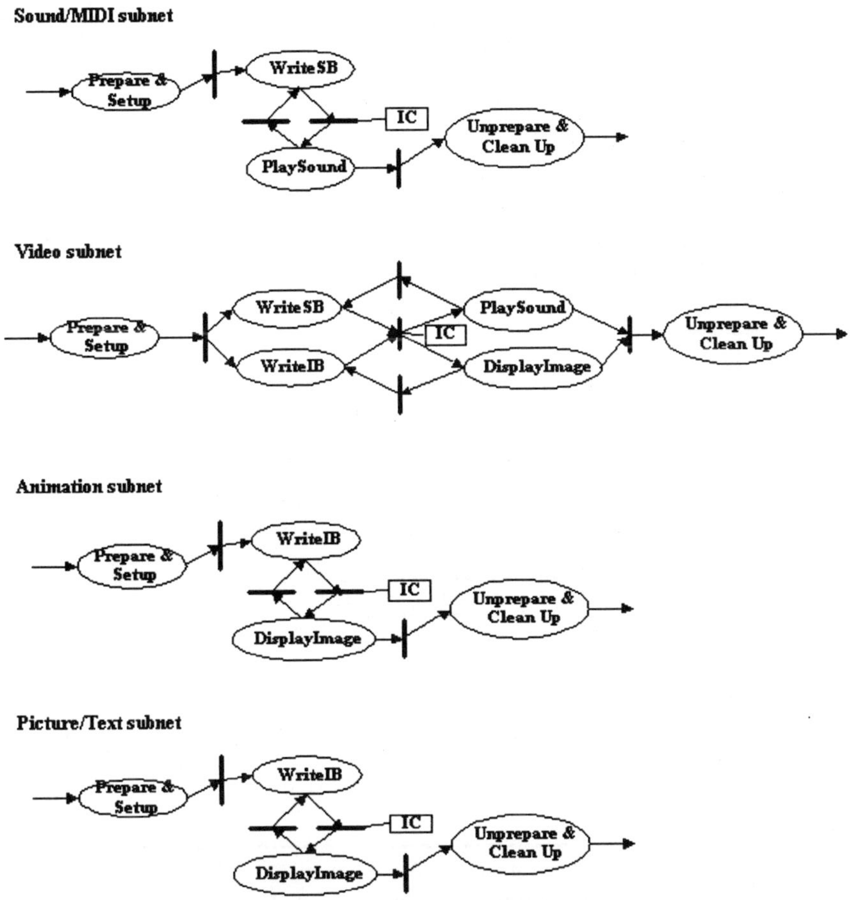

Figure 4: Sub-nets for Different Multimedia Resources

We have discussed the global view of our diagramming mechanism. However, a multimedia presentation in our system is dynamic and mutable. In the following section, we propose other diagramming techniques to achieve our goal – allowing dynamic multimedia presentations.

5 Dynamic Presentations

Usually, when a multimedia presentation is designed, the usage of resources, the layout, and the navigation sequences are all fixed until the presentation is re-designed again. We want to improve this approach by allowing dynamic replacement of resources, layouts, and controls of the presentation. This makes the presentation generator have the ability of computing the presentation representation at the run-time. Possible dynamic events are:

- asserting/retracting of information
- changing resources
- changing layouts
- changing navigation controls

Figure 5 illustrates a mutable Petri net. On the top of the revised timed Petri net (see figure 3), we further add the following components:

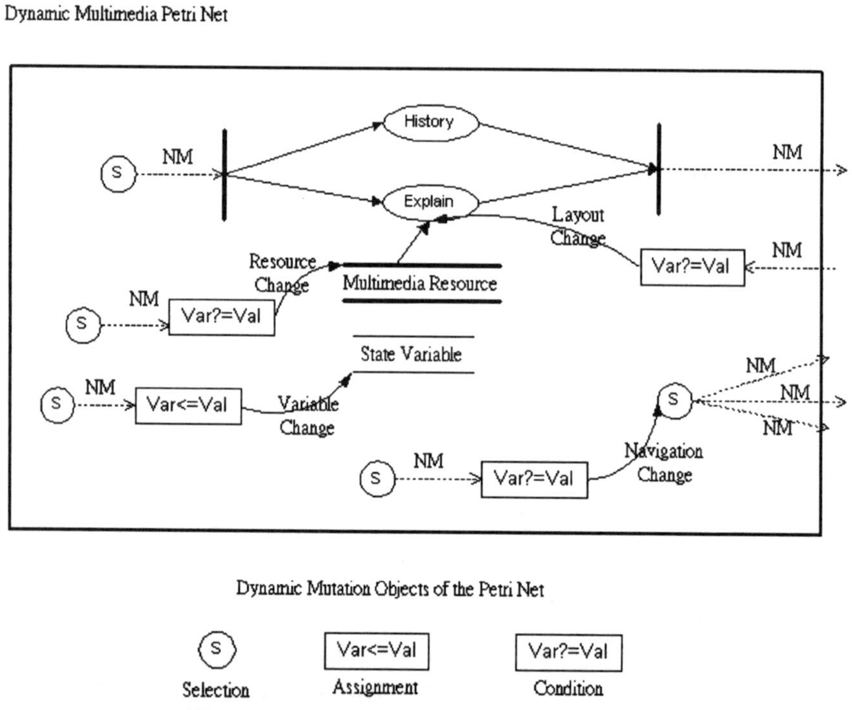

Figure 5 : A Dynamic Mutable Multimedia Petri Net

- **Selection**: selects one of the outgoing navigation messages. A selection could be a push button or a key of the presentation window. A selection holds an internal representation of which outgoing navigation message will be sent upon the activation of the selection. A selection is represented as a circle labeled with an ``S" in the Petri net diagram.
- **Assignment**: assigns a value to a state variable. An assignment is connected to a state variable. When an assignment received a navigation message (with a

parameter holding a value), the assignment set the state variable to the value. An assignment is denoted by a box labeled with the ``Var <= Val" sign.

- **Condition**: decides whether to proceed with a change. A condition is a pair of state variable and value. The value is checked against the value of the state variable. If they match each other, the associated outgoing change is fired. A condition is represented by a box with the ``Var ?= val" sign.

The Petri nets of a presentation may contain a number of selections. Usually, a selection is associated with only a navigation message. However, if the selection is tight to a condition, the selection may have more than one outgoing messages. Which message to send out is decided by the condition's value. We allow an assignment statement to change the value of a state variable. State variables are used in a presentation to hold internal states. These variables will be saved on the disk when the presentation terminates (upon the user's decision), and will be loaded when the presentation starts again. A condition decides whether to proceed with a change or the propagation of a navigation message. A condition may change the execution flow of a Petri net.

The above are semantics of the newly introduced components of our Petri net. Since each Petri net place is associated with a multimedia resource, in order to allow the designer to select and reuse a multimedia resource, we have developed a multimedia object database. A resource contains a number of attributes. In the following subsection, we discuss these attributes. In the section of graphical user interface, we will show a multimedia resource browser.

5.1 The Multimedia Resource Attributes

To make a good multimedia presentation, one has to use a set of multimedia resources. Multimedia resources are recorded or captured via camera, tape recorder, or video camera, converted to their digital formats, and saved on the disk. These resource files can be reused in different presentations. A resource is associated with a number of attributes. We consider the following attributes for multimedia resources:

- **name**: a unique name of the resource.
- **keyword**: one or more keywords are used as the description of a multimedia resource. For instance, name of the city is a keyword of the bitmapped picture of Paris.
- **usage**: how the resource may be used (e.g., background, navigation, or focus).
- **medium**: what multimedia device is needed to carry out this resource (e.g., hardware supports for sound, video, MPEG, or picture resources).

- **model**: how the resource is presented (e.g., table, map, chart, or spoken language).
- **temporal endurance**: how long does the resource last in a presentation (e.g., 20 seconds or permanent).
- **synchronization tolerance**: how does a participant feel about the synchronization delay of a resource. For instance, a user usually expects an immediate response after pushing a button for the next page of text. But, the user might be able to tolerate a video playback being delayed for two seconds.
- **detectability**: the intensity of the resource attracting a listener (e.g., high, medium, or low).
- **startup delay**: the time between sending a message and the presentation of the corresponding resource, especially when the resource is on a remote computer connected via network.
- **hardware limitation**: what kind of hardware is essential for carrying out the resource (e.g., MPC level 1, level 2, level 3, or other limitations).
- **version**: the version of this resource file.
- **date/time**: the date and time this resource file was created.
- **resolution**: the resolution of this resource file, specified by X × Y (or 0 × 0) screen units.
- **start/end time**: for non-permanent resources, the starting cycle and the ending cycle of the piece of video, sound, or other resource that can be used, especially used as a presentation resource. A cycle can be a second, one-tenth of a second, or a frame number of a video/animation.
- **resource descriptor**: a logical descriptor to a physical resource data segment on the disk.

Since each resource has a number of attributes, it would be cumbersome to require each query searching for a resource to contain all of these attributes. Thus, we propose an intelligent mechanism to simplify a query. The system contains several inference rules. Each rule describes an if-then relation between two attributes. For example, the following are some of the rules used in our system:

If usage = focus then
 detectability = high
If model = illustration then
 medium = picture
If medium = picture then
 temporal_endurance = permanent
If medium = MPEG then
 hardware_limitation = MPEG_card
If model = map then
 medium = picture
If ... etc.

Some unspecified attributes can be deduced from others. Thus, a user does not need to specify all attributes of a resource when he/she is using a query to search for the resource.

Recently, Data Mining has become a hot research topic in the community of database systems. The existence of mutual dependence among the above multimedia attributes infers us that it is possible to analyze these dependence and use Data Mining techniques to improve our system. For instance, we found that many presentation designers use a bit mapped picture with a low detectability for background usage. A MIDI medium resource is usually used as a background music. We are constructing an interactive database subsystem to collect the ways that presentation designers use our database. Therefore, the subsystem may later on suggests the user to use a good resource.

6 An Example

In this section, we use our revised multimedia data flow/control flow diagrammatic technique to design a lecture teaching students a course of multimedia computing. The course contains several chapters, including topics such as media file formats, OS supports of multimedia, database, networking, synchronization techniques, etc. The level 0 data flow/control flow diagram (see figure 6) takes as input an external entity of the presenter. And the diagram has an output to another external entity of audiences. The level 1 diagram has a selection presentation window with a state variable (i.e., Visited Topics) keeping the topics selected by the student. This variable is set to a list of numbers representing the topic visited by the student. Depending on the selection, various topics are visited in different presentation windows. Some of the presentation windows are associated with multimedia resources extracted from the multimedia database. In the synchronization presentation window, depending on the synchronization criteria, a bit mapped picture showing database requirements is changed. The synchronization presentation window is then refined to a level 2 diagram with another state variable and a resource. Using our diagrammatic technique, the presentation design is able to organize his/her presentation in a structured manner.

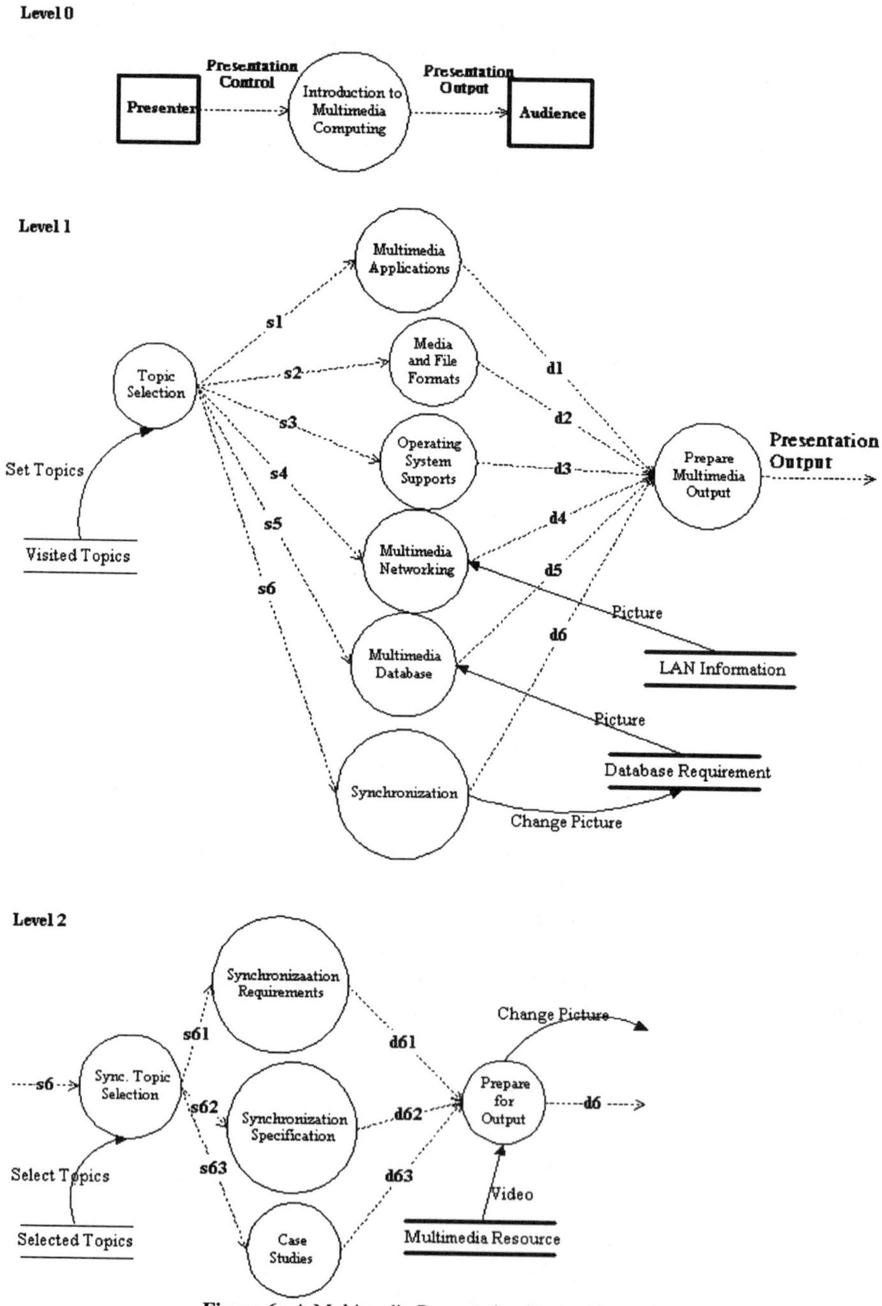

Figure 6 : A Multimedia Presentation Design Example

7 Conclusions

We used Visual Basic and Visual C++ as the implementation languages of our system. The preliminary experiences show that, the proposed multimedia DFD/CFD is easy to learn since data flow diagrams have been used by many engineers and managers for two decades. The concept is easily adapted. Even the implementation is not perfect, we have some contributions in this paper. Firstly, we revised structured analysis/design methodology and data flow/control flow diagrams for the use of multimedia presentation designs. Next, we proposed a multimedia Petri net for dynamic multimedia presentations. Finally, a prototype system was developed on MS Windows 95/3.1 to justify our approach. With this system, we hope to bring the spirit of structured analysis/design methodology to the design of multimedia presentations. The system can be used for general-purposed presentations as well as education software, demonstrations, and others.

References

1. H.Khalfallah and A. Karmouch. "An architecture and a data model for integrated multimedia documents and presentational applications". Multimedia Systems, Springer- Verlag, 3:238-250, 1995.
2. T. Kirsta and W. Hubner. "An Open Hypermedia System for Multimedia Applications".In Eurographic Seminars, Tutorials and Perspectives in Computer Graphics, L. Kjelldahl(ED.) Multimedia Systems,Interaction and Applications Chapter 17, chapter 17. 1991.
3. A. Lundeberg, T. Yamamoto, and T. Usuki. "SAL, A Hypermedia Prototype System". In Eurographic Seminars, Tutorials and Perspectives in Computer Graphics, L. Kjelldahl(ED.) Multimedia Systems,Interaction and Applications Chapter 10, chapter 10. 1991.
4. R.S. Pressman. "Software Engineering: A Practitioner's Approach". McGraw Hill,1992.
5. G. A. Schloss and M. J. Wynblatt. "Presentation Layer Primitives for the Layered Multimedia Data Model". In Proceedings of the IEEE1995 International Conference on Multimedia Computing and Systems. May 15-18, Washington DC, Pages 231-238, 1995.
6. T. K. Shih. "Multimedia Abstract Machine". In Proceedings of the the Third Joint Conference on Information Science,1997.
7. T. K. Shih. and R. E. Davis. "IMMPS: A Multimedia Presentation Design System". IEEE Multimedia, Summer, 1997.
8. T. K. Shih, C.-H. Kuo, and K.-S An. “An Object-Oriented Database for Intelligent Multimedia Presentations”. In Proceedings of the IEEE International Conference on System, Man, and Cybernetics Information, Intelligence and Systems Conference, 1996.

9. T. K. Shih C.-H. Kuo, and H.-J. Lin. “Visual Multimedia Presentation Designs”. In Proceedings of the 1996 Pacafic Workshop on Distributed Multimedia Systems, pages 306-315,1996.
10. R. H. Thomas and e. a. Harry C. Forsdick. "Diamond : A Multimedia Message System Built on a Distributed Architecture". IEEE Computer, December: 65-78, 1985.
11. M. Vazirgiannis and C.Mourlas. "An Object-Oriented Model for Interactive Multimedia Presentations". The Computer Journal, 36(1), 1993.

A The MAM Instruction Set

The MAM has a set of pseudo assembly instructions. The concept of pseudo assembly is because each instruction is a non-separable step in running a multimedia application, which is similar to an assembly instruction serving as a atomic step in running a C program. However, multimedia pseudo instructions are in a relatively higher level. The MAM also has some components. Conceptually, MAM uses a dual bus architecture. Image and audio data are separated. The multimedia Petri net of MAM is controlled by a number of *guard registers*. A guard register serves as a switch controling multimedia synchronization. An instruction is executed only if all of its guarding registers are clear. After the execution, the instruction should release guard registers. This concept is similar to the blocking places in the timed petri nets. The MAM has the following hardware components:

- Guard Register Array: G(n) is a collection of guard registers.
- Sound Buffer Array: SB(n) contains a number of cache buffers for sound data.
- Image Buffer Array: IB(n) contains a number of cache buffers for image data.
- Sound Buffer Index Register: SBI is an index to SB(n).
- Image Buffer Index Register: IBI is an index to IB(n).
- Sound Channel Status Register Array: SCS(n) controls the use of a number of sound channels.
- Image Channel Status Register Array: ICS(n) controls the use of a number of image channels.
- Sound Channel Index Register: SCI is an index to SCS(n).
- Image Channel Index Register: ICI is an index to ICS(n).
- Resource Designator Register: RD is a register holding a pointer to a multimedia resource.
- Device Designator Register: DD is a register holding a pointer to a multimedia device.
- File Handler Register Array: FH(n) is a set of registers holding pointers to multimedia files.
- File Handler Index Register: FHI is an index to FH(n).
- I/O Status Register: IOS controls the input/output status.

The set of instructions are divided into the following categories, with some instructions explained:

- **Instructions for user interactions and interrupts**: include start, restart, stop, pause, resume, skip, reverse, mutate, and exception instructions. These instructions are to support interactive multimedia applications.
- **Instructions for network controls**: include lock, unlock, remote copy, and others. These instructions are to control network activities.
- **Instructions for I/O, presenting resources, and timing controls**: include the following instructions:

  - SetRD R, [Gi's], [Go's]: set resource designator register RD according to resource R. A resource could be a file name or a database descriptor.
  - SetDD D, [Gi's], [Go's]: set device designator register DD according to designator D. A designator could be a Windows 95 DC for image or video, or a sound channel.
  - GetFHI [Gi's], [Go's]: get available file handler. FHI is set to the available file handler, or set to 0 if no available handler is found.
  - PrepRes [Gi's], [Go's]: prepare presentation resource according to the designator specified in RD register, set FH(n) register and IOS register. This step is similar to opening a resource file.
  - GetSCI [Gi's], [Go's]: get available sound channel. SCI points to the available channel, or set to 0 if no available channel is found.
  - GetICI [Gi's], [Go's]: get available image channel. ICI points to the available channel, or set to 0 if no available channel is found.
  - GetSBI [Gi's], [Go's]: get available sound buffer. SBI points to the available buffer, or set to 0 if no available buffer is found.
  - GetIBI [Gi's], [Go's]: get available image buffer. IBI points to the available buffer, or set to 0 if no available buffer is found.
  - PrepSC n, [Gi's], [Go's]: prepare the n-th sound channel, set sound channel status register SCS(n).
  - PrepIC n, [Gi's], [Go's]: prepare the n-th image channel, set image channel status register ICS(n).
  - WriteSB FH(m), SB(n), [Gi's], [Go's]: move data from disk pointed by FH(m) to sound buffer SB(n).
  - WriteIB FH(m), IB(n), [Gi's], [Go's]: move data from disk pointed by FH(m) to image buffer IB(n).
  - PlaySound SB(m), n, [Gi's], [Go's]: move data from SB(m) to the n-th sound channel.
  - DisplayImage IB(m), n, [Gi's], [Go's]: move data from IB(m) to the n-th image channel.
  - WWFC [Gi's], [Go's]: wait till wave function complete.

  - UnPrepSC n, [Gi's], [Go's]: unprepare the n-th sound channel, set sound channel status register SCS(n).
  - UnPrepIC n, [Gi's], [Go's]: unprepare the n-th image channel, set image channel status register ICS(n).
  - UnPrepRes [Gi's], [Go's]: unprepare presentation resource pointed by FH(n) register and set IOS register.
  - Sync [Gi's], [Go's]: synchronization instruction does nothing except blocking other instructions to achieve synchronization. This is similar to the concept of transition in a Timed Petri Net.
- **Instructions for control abstractions**: include conditional and unconditional branch instructions, assignments, and others.

Note that, ``[Gi's]" and ``[Go's]" are incoming and outgoing guard registers. They are represented by lists of integers pointing to guard registers. The integers are assigned by a register relocation algorithm in the multimedia specification language compiler. Using the set of instructions, for example, the video subnet discussed in figure 4 can be coded as the following:

```
   SetRD "Tour.avi", [Gi's], [Go's]
   GetFHI [Gi's], [Go's]
   PrepRes [Gi's], [Go's]
   GetSCI [Gi's], [Go's]
   PrepSC SCI, [Gi's], [Go's]
   GetICI [Gi's], [Go's]
   PrepIC ICI, [Gi's], [Go's]
   GetSBI [Gi's], [Go's]
   GetIBI [Gi's], [Go's]
>/ WriteSB FH(FHI), SB(SBI), [Gi's], [Go's]
-  PlaySound SB(SBI), SCI, [Gi's], [Go's]
   WriteIB FH(FHI), IB(IBI), [Gi's], [Go's]
-\ DisplayImage IB(IBI), ICI, [Gi's], [Go's]
   UnPrepIC ICI, [Gi's], [Go's]
   UnPrepSC SCI, [Gi's], [Go's]
   UnPrepRes [Gi's], [Go's]
```

Note that, we have a number of annotations to the instructions: ``>" is an interrupt arc denotation, ``/" represents interleaving begins, ``\" represents interleaving ends, and ``-" is a synchronize annotation.

Server Design and Implementation

A CORBA-based Distributed Multimedia Collaboration System

JAMES WON-KI HONG
Dept. of Computer Science and Engineering
Pohang University of Science and Technology
Pohang Korea 790-784
Email: jwkhong@postech.ac.kr

Multimedia applications are being developed and used for many aspects of our lives today. New high-speed, broadband networks have emerged and made the operation of these high-bandwidth requiring applications readily feasible. However, the development of distributed multimedia applications and efficient and reliable operation of these applications are still very difficult. This paper presents a flexible and reliable distributed multimedia collaboration system called MAESTRO that provides a rich multimedia collaborative services which can be used to develop a variety of multimedia applications easily. MAESTRO has been designed using OMG CORBA. The system as well as applications running on it are managed and controlled in order to provide a reliable and efficient multimedia operations environment. We validate our claim by developing a number of multimedia collaboration applications (such as video conferencing, whiteboard, electronic notebook, chat, and application sharing) using our distributed multimedia system and by using them for supporting distributed collaborative scientific and engineering research experiments.

[**Keywords**: distributed multimedia collaborative environment, collaboration tools, distributed multimedia services, multimedia communication, operation and management, CORBA, QoS management]

1 Introduction

Multimedia applications are beginning to play an important role in various aspects of our lives, including education, business, health care, publishing, and entertainment. The recent advance in computing and networking technologies has fueled the emergence of these applications requiring real-time processing and high bandwidth. In order for these applications to be truly useful and effective, they must be able to operate in a distributed fashion, covering users possibly located in geographically distant locations. Many national and international information superhighways [1, 2, 3, 4, 5, 6] being developed today can be used to support collaboration of distant users using multimedia applications, exchanging various multimedia data. The real problem in making the national or international users collaborate using multimedia applications, as if they are in a same physical location, is providing a system that can be used to develop multimedia applications easily and supporting the operation of these applications efficiently and reliably.

One of the major problems in supporting the development and operation of such applications lies in the operating systems of the computers being used. Most conventional operating systems running on these computers have not been designed to support multimedia systems that impose stringent constraints. Multimedia applications also require various forms of communication (such as conferencing, collaboration, multicasting and so on). Further, most of these operating systems have not been designed to support applications operating in a distributed fashion. In order for the system and applications to operate efficiently and reliably, they must be monitored and controlled properly at run time. As the number of users increases, the underlying system must be able to cope with the increased resource requirements. What is needed is a solution that is easily scaleable.

Much research work related to multimedia systems has been done [7, 8, 9, 10, 11]. However, most of these systems fall short of meeting the requirements mentioned above. In this paper, we present a distributed multimedia collaboration system called MAESTRO [12, 13, 14, 15] that is flexible enough to support the development of a variety of multimedia collaborative applications easily and that can support efficient and reliable operation of the applications. MAESTRO has been designed to support a wide variety of multimedia applications (such as video/audio conferencing, multimedia-on-demand, whiteboard, electronic notebook, telemedicine, teleshopping, etc.) that can operate in a distributed environment in mind.

The heart of MAESTRO lies in the multimedia collaborative service application programming interface (API) and multimedia collaborative services that can be used to develop, operate and manage various multimedia collaborative applications. The multimedia collaborative service API uses the set of distributed multimedia services MAESTRO provides for the operation and management of distributed multimedia applications. MAESTRO includes *communication service* for supporting various forms of communication (one-to-one, one-to-many, many-to-many), *session service* for managing multimedia sessions, *naming service* for naming and locating objects, *multimedia database service* for storing and retrieving multimedia data, *management service* for monitoring and controlling services and applications, *QoS management service* for controlling quality of service, and *security service* for providing secure environment. The API as well as the underlying services have been modeled and implemented using the distributed object-oriented approach. Specifically, OMG CORBA [16] has been used to design MAESTRO multimedia collaborative services and Orbix [22] (IONA's CORBA implementation) has been used for implementation.

As a validation of our claim, we have developed a number of distributed multimedia collaborative applications (such as video conferencing, whiteboard, electronic notebook, chat, and application sharing) using MAESTRO for a national information superhighway project in Korea. In this project, distant researchers (mechanical engineers, chemical engineers and chemists) collaborate in performing various research experiments simultaneously and collect, analyze and view the results using the multimedia collaborative applications developed using and running on MAESTRO.

The remainder of this paper is organized as follows. Section 2 presents the architecture of MAESTRO. Section 3 presents the multimedia collaborative service application programming interface (API). Section 4 describes the distributed multimedia services provided by MAESTRO. Section 5 presents the implementation details of MAESTRO. Section 6 presents the multimedia collaborative applications we have developed. We summarize our work and discuss some possible future work in Section 7.

2 MAESTRO Architecture

In this section, we present the layered architecture of MAESTRO as illustrated in Figure 1. At the top layer, there exist various multimedia collaborative applications (video/audio conferencing, video-on-demand, telemedicine, whiteboard, electronic notebook, etc.) which use the multimedia collaborative service API.

The second layer provides multimedia collaborative service API that is used by various multimedia collaborative applications. This layer has been designed using the distributed object-oriented approach and consists of class definitions that can be used to generate and transfer multimedia data between multimedia devices. This layer is used by multimedia collaborative application components which are scattered throughout a distributed environment and which collectively form a distributed multimedia application.

The third layer consists of distributed multimedia services that are needed to support the operation and management of multimedia collaborative applications. This layer has also been designed using the object-oriented approach and consists of services, such as Communication Service, Session Service, Naming Service, Multimedia Database Service, Management Service, QoS Management Service and Security Service. These services are used by multimedia collaborative applications at run time such that they allow multimedia collaborative applications to discover their source or destination associations, create/join/destroy sessions, exchange multimedia data, store or retrieve multimedia data, be monitored and controlled, control QoS and provide secure environment.

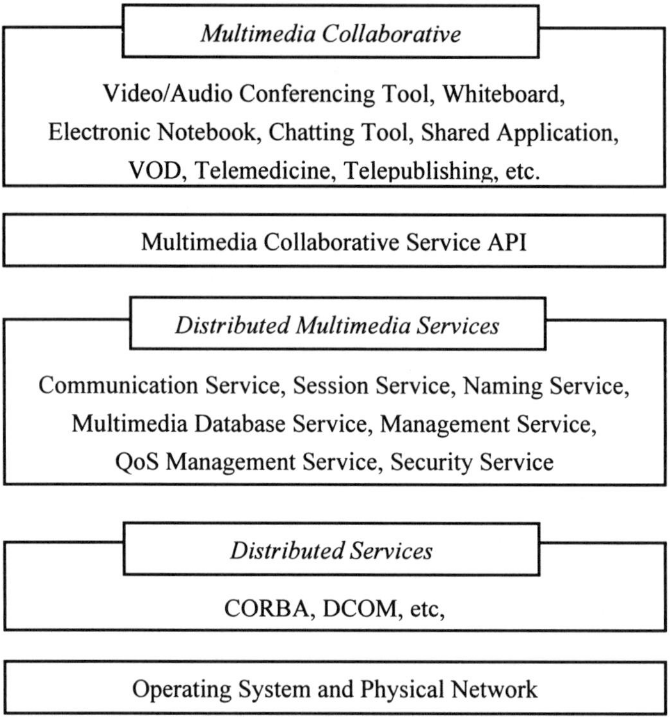

Figure 1. Layered Architecture of MAESTRO

At the fourth layer, there exist distributed services that provide transparency to distributed multimedia services and applications. Although any existing middleware service can be used in this layer, distributed object technologies such as CORBA [16] or DCOM [29] may be suitable. At the lowest layer, there exist various operating systems (such as Solaris, HP-UX, AIX, Digital Unix, IRIX, Linux, Windows NT) and networking technologies (such as ATM, FDDI, SONET, Fast Ethernet, Ethernet, Token Ring) that physically connect the parties involved in a multimedia collaborative application.

The heart of our work is the multimedia collaborative service API of the second layer and the distributed multimedia services of the third layer. We will present more details of those two layers in the following two sections.

3 Multimedia Collaborative Service API

In this section, we describe the purpose of defining multimedia collaborative service API and present the objects that are defined in the multimedia collaborative service API layer.

3.1 Purpose of Multimedia Collaborative Service API

The purpose of defining Multimedia Collaborative Service API is as follows.

- To provide a wide range of multimedia-related class definitions so that multimedia collaborative applications can deal with multimedia-related problems easily and flexibly.
- To provide efficient and reliable methods of collaborative communications for people working together remotely.
- To provide a common programming interface so that the developers of multimedia collaborative applications can develop a new application easily.
- To reuse codes, which are common to many multimedia collaborative applications.
- To support the processing and presentation of various kinds of media such as video, audio, image, and text so that multimedia applications can deal with various kinds of media easily.
- To reduce software development time and unburden application developers from difficulties of low-level programming.

3.2 Object Classes in Multimedia Collaborative Service API

The multimedia collaborative service API is composed of three object class hierarchies, which are *media class hierarchy*, *component class hierarchy* and *device class hierarchy*. The media class hierarchy models various multimedia data being exchanged in multimedia collaborative applications. The component class hierarchy models media producers and consumers, which generate and transmit media from a sender and receive and output the media to the receiver devices on a distributed environment. Finally, the device class hierarchy models various devices (such as camera, microphone, monitor display, speaker) involved in multimedia applications.

There are two main classes in the media class hierarchy. The first class is *Media* which is the root class and has common interfaces for all kinds of media type. The second class is *Temporal* which is a subclass of Media and has common interfaces for the temporal media types. Here, we define a temporal media type as one that is much affected by time factor when they are presented. The subclasses of Temporal include *Audio, Video, Music* and *Animation* classes. Figure 2 shows the media class hierarchy.

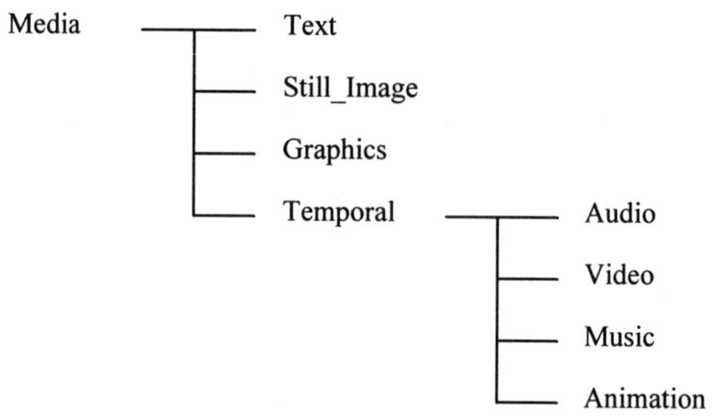

Figure 2. Media Class Hierarchy

In MAESTRO, multimedia collaborative applications use the concept called **component objects** [28] to transmit and receive various kinds of data. Component objects are objects of a special form. That is, they have their own thread of execution.

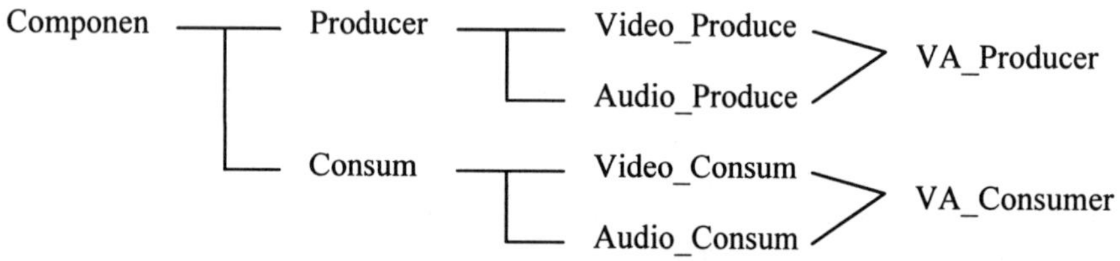

Figure 3. Component Class Hierarchy

Figure 3 shows the component class hierarchy. *Component* is the root class of the component class hierarchy. *Producer* is a subclass of *Component* and models application components that generate data. *Consumer* is also a subclass of *Component* and models application components that consume data generated by *Producer* objects. *Video_Producer* is a subclass of the *Producer*, which is used for generating *Video*. *Audio_Producer* is also a subclass of the *Producer* but it is used for generating *Audio*. Similarly, *Video_Consumer* and *Audio_Consumer* are used to consume *Video* and *Audio*, respectively. The *VA_Producer* inherits both *Video_Producer* and *Audio_Producer* and is used to generate both *Video* and *Audio*. The *VA_Consumer* inherits both *Video_Consumer* and *Audio_Consumer* and is used to consume both *Video* and *Audio*. Video/audio conferencing tools typically use VA_Producer and VA_Consumer objects for generating video and audio data in the sender and consuming them in the receiver. Although the component class hierarchy (illustrated in Figure 3) only shows the hierarchy for video/audio-related producers and consumer, any type of producers and consumers can be modeled and developed.

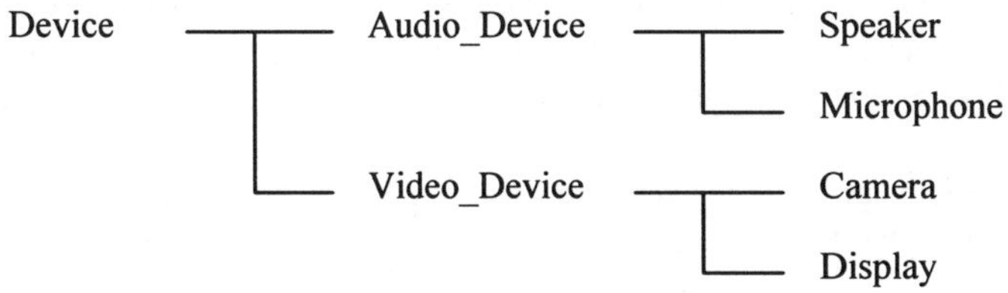

Figure 4. Device Class Hierarchy

Figure 4 shows the device class hierarchy. There are three main classes in this class hierarchy. The first class is *Device* that is the root class. It has common interfaces for all multimedia-related devices. The second class, *Audio_Device,* is a subclass of *Device* and has common interfaces for the audio-related devices. The third class, *Video_Device,* is also a subclass of *Device* and has common interfaces for the video-related devices. *Speaker* is a subclass of *Audio_Device*, which is used to control audio-output device. *Microphone* is also a subclass of *Audio_Device*, which is used to control audio-input device. Similarly, *Camera* and *Display* are subclasses of *Video_Device*, which are used to control video-input and video-output devices, respectively.

4 Distributed Multimedia Services

In this section, we present MAESTRO distributed multimedia services that are essential in supporting the operation and management of distributed multimedia applications. There are currently five distributed multimedia services defined, which include

Communication Service, Session Service, Naming Service, Multimedia Database Service, Management Service, QoS Management Service and Security Service. These distributed multimedia services support multimedia collaborative applications to transmit or receive multimedia each other, to do a collaborative work in a session, to find a service in a distributed environment, to store/retrieve multimedia, to monitor and control services and applications, to control QoS, and to provide secure environment.

Although, we present only five important distributed multimedia services, a new service can be easily defined and incorporated since the services have also been modeled using the object-oriented approach. Now, we describe each distributed multimedia service.

4.1 Communication Service

In this section, we describe Communication Service that is needed by multimedia applications to exchange various kinds of media. The functional requirements of the Communication Service for supporting distributed multimedia communication are as follows.

- It should be possible to exchange various media including temporal and non-temporal media.
- Multi-point communication should be possible to support conferencing, multicasting and collaboration.
- It should control the flow of temporal media and synchronize two or more types of media if necessary.

The Communication Service in MAESTRO has been designed with the functional requirements mentioned above. The unit of data exchange in MAESTRO communication is media object, which can be of any size or type defined using the media class hierarchy. Main features of the communication service include the support of multi-point communication (i.e., one-to-one, one-to-many, many-to-many communication) and intra-domain and inter-domain communication which are essential for supporting multimedia collaborative applications. Below, we present the details of the communication service.

4.1.1 Objects in Communication Service

The objects that are defined and used in the Communication Service are *CommunicationFactory*, *ConnectionManager*, *Port*, *Connector* and *Channel* objects. The role of *CommunicationFactory* is to create, manage or destroy *Port*, *Connector* and *Channel* objects that are used by multimedia collaborative applications in a multi-point communication. If a multimedia collaborative application wants to communicate, it must first create a *Port* using a *CommunicationFactory*. After creating a *Port*, the multimedia collaborative application can communicate with another multimedia collaborative application that also has created its own *Port*. A *Port* alone can not join a multi-point communication because the *Port* can not know all the information about the created *Ports*, *Connectors* and *Channels*. Thus, a *Port* must join a multi-point communication by passing a connection request to a *ConnectionManager* that has all the information about the created *Ports*, *Connectors* and *Channels*. *Connector* is used when an inter-domain communication is needed. The role of *Connector* will be described in more detail in Section 4.1.3. *Channel* keeps all the references of *Ports* that are joining the *Channel*.

There are two kinds of *Ports*. One is one-to-many *Port*, the other is many-to-many *Port*. When a multimedia application creates a *Port*, it should pass an argument that specifies whether the *Port* should be one-to-many *Port* or many-to-many *Port*.

4.1.2 Multi-point Communication

Multi-point communication (i.e., one-to-many, many-to-many communication) is essential when developing multimedia collaborative applications. Thus, the Communication Service in MAESTRO provides multi-point communication. One-to-one communication can be easily achieved by using either one-to-many communication or many-to-many communication.

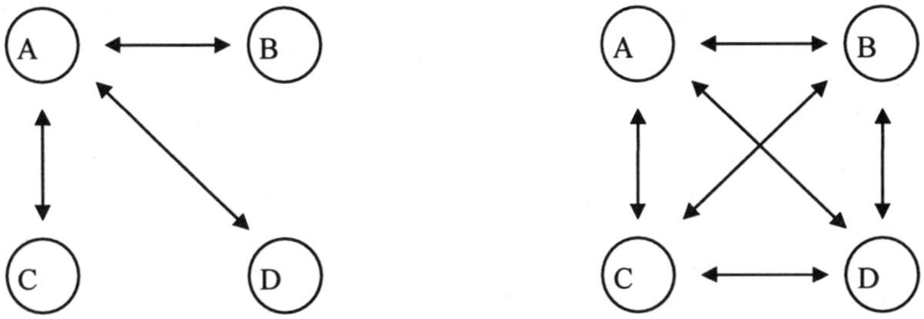

(a) One-to-many communication (b) Many-to-many communication

Figure 5. One-to-many and many-to-many communications in MAESTRO

Before describing the multi-point communication in MAESTRO, we define what we mean by one-to-many and many-to-many communication. Figure 5 (a) illustrates an example of one-to-many communication where component A can send the media to all the other components. The components B, C and D can send the media back to component A only. Figure 5 (b) illustrates an example of many-to-many communication where any component can send the media to all other components.

In MAESTRO, *Ports* and *Channels* are used for multi-point communication. If a multimedia collaborative application component wants to take part in one-to-many or many-to-many communication, it must create a one-to-many or many-to-many *Port* using the *CommunicationFactory*. The multimedia collaborative application component must also create a *Channel* using the created *Port*. Then, other *Ports* that have been created by other participated multimedia collaborative application components can join the created *Channel* by connecting to the *Port* that has created the *Channel*.

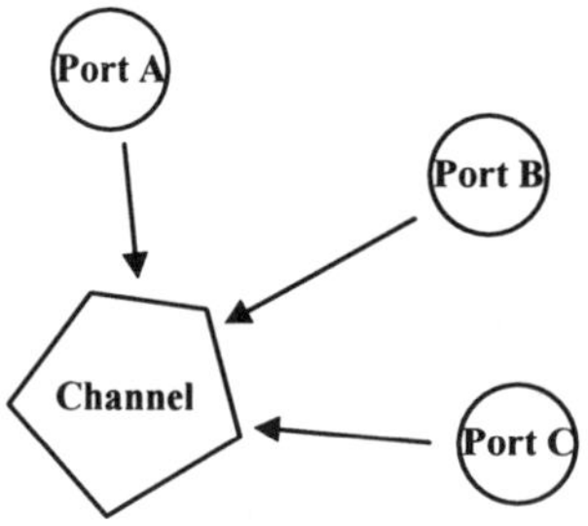

Figure 6. Ports and Channels in Multi-point Communication

Figure 6 illustrates how a multi-point communication is realized conceptually. In the figure, *Port A* created by a multimedia application component creates a *Channel*. *Port A* automatically joins the *Channel* by creating the *Channel*. Then, when *Port B* and *Port C* connect to *Port A*, they automatically get joined to the *Channel*. Thus, there are two ways for a *Port* can join a *Channel*:

1. by creating a *Channel* itself, or
2. by connecting to a *Port* which has already joined a *Channel*.

When a *Port* joins a *Channel* we can make the connection of *Ports* in many ways. For example, a hierarchical tree or a virtual ring of *Ports* can be constructed to make the connection of *Ports*. In MAESTRO, we selected to construct a hierarchical tree when a *Port* joins a *Channel*. Figure 7 illustrates how a hierarchical tree of *Ports* is constructed in MAESTRO. First, *Port A* creates a *Channel,* which makes it possible for other *Ports* to connect to *Port A*. So, *Port B* can connect to *Port A*. Similarly, *Port C* and *Port D* can connect to *Port A*. Now, *Port E* can connect to *Port D* because there is a *Channel* that *Port D* has joined. *Port F* can join likewise. Through this hierarchical tree of *Ports*, multi-point communication between multimedia collaborative application components using the respective *Ports* is possible.

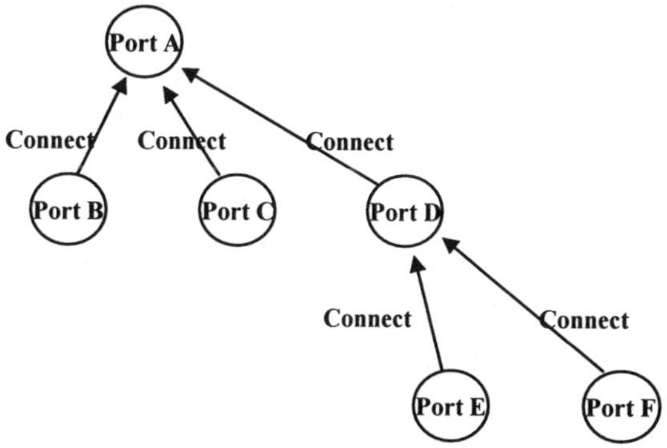

Figure 7. Hierarchical Tree of Ports in Multi-point Communication

The construction process of hierarchical tree is the same in both one-to-many communication and many-to-many communication. The difference lies in the way media flows in the tree. We now describe the difference by using Figure 7.

We describe the case of one-to-many communication first. If the root *Port* sends a media object, all the other *Ports* receive it. For example, if a multimedia collaborative application component sends a media object to *Port A*, *Port A* sends the media object to its children *Ports B, C* and *D*. *Port D* then sends the media object to its children *Ports E* and *F*. If any *Port* except the root *Port* sends a media object, only the root *Port* receives that media object. For example, if a multimedia collaborative application component sends a media object to *Port F*, *Port F* sends the media object to its parent, *Port D*, but *Port D* just passes the media object only to its parent, *Port A*.

In the case of many-to-many communication, any *Port* can send a media object to all the other *Ports*. For example, if a multimedia collaborative application component sends a media object to *Port A*, the media object flows same as in one-to-many communication. If a multimedia collaborative application component sends a media object to *Port F*, then *Port F* sends the media object to its parent *Port D*. And *Port D* sends the media object to its child, *Port E* and parent, *Port A*. Also, *Port A* then subsequently sends the media object to its children *Ports B* and *C*.

4.1.3 Intra-domain and Inter-domain Communication

We define a domain as an area in which distributed multimedia services are provided to multimedia collaborative applications. In MAESTRO, we have used the concept of domain for the ease of administration as well as for the purpose of scalability. There can be no doubt that multimedia collaborative applications should be able to communicate each other in a same domain. But it should be also possible for multimedia collaborative applications in different domains to communicate each other.

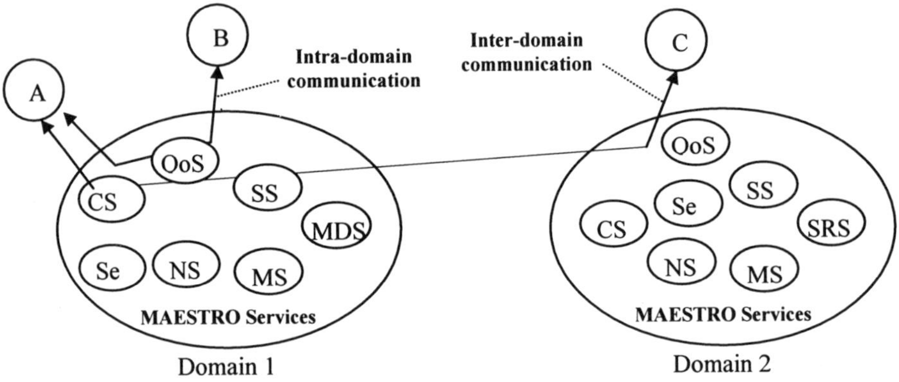

Figure 8. Intra-domain and Inter-domain Communication in MAESTRO

The general concept of intra-domain communication and inter-domain communication is illustrated in Figure 8. Multimedia collaborative application components A and B, which use the distributed multimedia services in the same domain, are participating in an intra-domain communication. Multimedia collaborative applications components A and C, which use the distributed multimedia services in two different domains are participating in an inter-domain communication.

Now, we will illustrate the difference of intra-domain and inter-domain communications in MAESTRO. Suppose a hierarchical tree has been constructed as in Figure 9 (a). If all the *Ports (A, B and C)* are located in a local domain, then the connection of the *Ports* is the same as what we described in Section 4.1.2 using Figure 6. This is shown in Figure 9 (b). However, if *Port A* is located in a local domain, and

Ports B and *C* are located in a remote domain, a *Connector* in the remote domain is needed to connect the *Ports* as shown in Figure 9 (c).

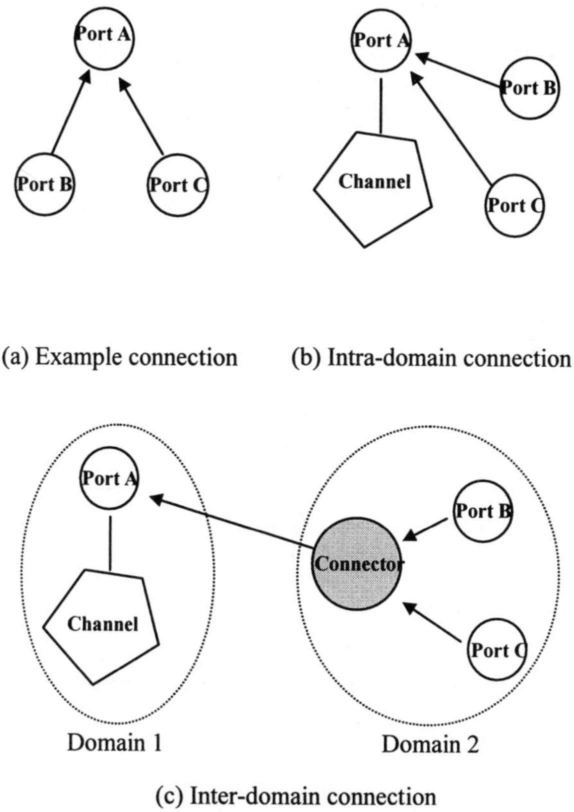

Figure 9. Intra-domain and Inter-domain Connections

Although we can construct a hierarchical tree without a *Connector*, the reason why we use the *Connector* in an inter-domain communication is for transmitting the media object more efficiently across domains. That is, if a media object should be transmitted across different domains, a single copy of the media object is transmitted to the *Connector* only rather than transmitting multiple copies to all the destination *Ports* in a remote domain. The *Connector* would then transmit the media object locally to appropriate *Ports*.

4.1.4 Connection Establishment

Now, we describe the detailed process of connection establishment between *Ports*. First, we describe an intra-domain connection where two *Ports* exist in a single domain. Then, we describe an inter-domain connection where two *Ports* exist in different domains.

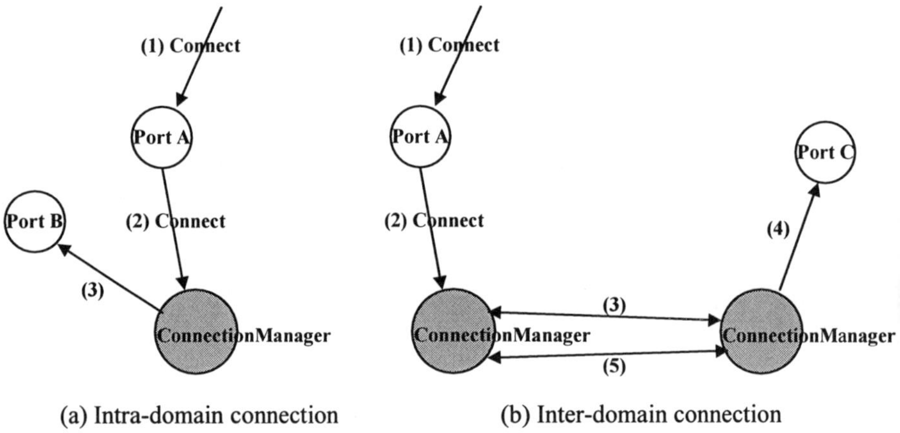

Figure 10. The process of connection establishment

The followings are steps involved in an intra-domain connection. It is illustrated in Figure 10 (a).

(1) A multimedia collaborative application component issues a connection request. When issuing a connection request, the multimedia collaborative application component passes a domain name and port number which identify a unique destination *Port*. Note that a unique port number is given to a *Port* when it is created.

(2) *Port A* passes the connection request to *ConnectionManager*.

(3) *ConnectionManager* finds the destination *Port* in a local domain and makes a tree relationship between the two *Ports*.

An inter-domain connection is explained as follows and illustrated in Figure 10 (b).

(1) A multimedia collaborative application component issues a connection request.
(2) *Port A* passes the connection request to *ConnectionManager*.
(3) After discovering that the destination *Port* exists in a remote domain, *ConnctionManager* communicates with the appropriate remote *ConnectionManager* to carry out the connection request.
(4) Remote *ConnectionManager* finds the destination *Port*.
(5) The local *ConnectionManager* and remote *ConnectionManager* make a tree relationship between the two *Ports* by passing the needed information to each other.

We have presented the details of the most important multimedia service, communication service. In the remainder of this section, we describe the rest of distributed multimedia services that comprise MAESTRO services.

4.2 Session Service

The second multimedia service provided in MAESTRO is the Session Service that keeps track of currently active sessions in MAESTRO. A session is a live activity in which one or more participants can interact using multimedia collaborative applications. In MAESTRO, multiple sessions can exist simultaneously, involving participants from different domains.

Essential functional requirements of the Session Service are as follows. The Session Service in MAESTRO has been designed with these functional requirements.

- A user should be able to create, join, leave or destroy a session.
- A user should be able to discover the users currently participating in a session
- There should be a chairman (i.e., a super user) in a session such that he should have all the rights in a session.
- If needed, the chairman should be able to control the right to speech.
- A user should be able to join and leave a session that is created not olny in a local domain but also in a remote domain.
- If needed, the chairman should be able to forcefully terminate sessions or eliminate participants from a session.

4.2.1 Objects in Session Service

The objects that comprise the Session Service are Session Service Object (SSO), Session, Participant, Application, Registry and ApplicationDB objects. The role of SSO is to create, destroy and search a Session object that has the information of a session. A Participant object has the information of a participant, an Application object has the information of an application a Registry object has the information of the user of an application.

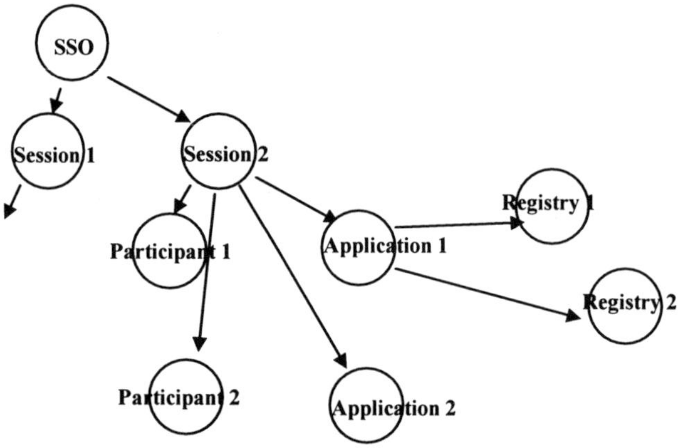

Figure 11. Object Management in Session Service

Figure 11 illustrates how the objects including SSO, Session, Participant, Application and Registry are managed in the Session Service. SSO manages Sessions and a Session manages Participants and Applications and an Application manages Registries. Thus, one can discover which sessions have been created by SSO and which users have joined a session. One can also discover which users are running which applications.

Finally, ApplicationDB has the information about what kind of multimedia collaborative applications can be used with the Session Service. If any multimedia collaborative applications should be integrated with the Session Service, an authorized participant should register the name and the location of those multimedia collaborative applications first before participants can use the applications.

4.2.2 Information in Session

User who is willing to join a multimedia collaborative application session wants to get some information of the session. Those are what session is opened, who joins the session and what application is used in the session. So Session Service must offer those information. Session service maintains the information consistently. Although session service can be accessed from many domains, session service provides the information consistently.

4.3 Naming Service

The objects that comprise distributed multimedia services are distributed in a network. In such an environment, multimedia collaborative applications should be able to find the objects that serve the wanted services. The role of the Naming Service is to allow a name to be bound to an object and to allow the object to be found subsequently by resolving that name within the Naming Service. Thus, if an object wants to provide a service, it should register itself with the Naming Service first, giving it a name that can be used by multimedia collaborative applications to find the object.

The Naming Service provides the following functions.

- Binding a name to an object reference.
- Resolving a name to find an object reference.
- Unbinding a name to remove a binding.
- Listing the names.

There is a Naming Service specification that has been defined by OMG (Object Management Group). The Naming Service specification is one of the many service specifications of the CORBAservices [17]. The CORBAservices is a standard document from OMG, which extend the core CORBA specification with a set of optional services that are useful in many applications. In our current version MAESTRO, we are using the naming service specification defined by OMG.

4.4 Multimedia Database Service

In the multimedia collaborative service API layer, various kinds of media objects have been modeled. The Multimedia Database Service allows these objects to be stored into or retrieved from a common repository. The Multimedia Database Service provides the following basic functions.

- Storing a media object.
- Retrieving a media object.
- Searching a media object.

When storing a media object, the multimedia collaborative application should pass a name with the media object. This name can be used when a multimedia collaborative application wants to retrieve the media object that the name identifies. Also, multimedia collaborative applications can discover what kinds of media objects are stored currently by using the searching function.

4.5 Management Service

In this section, we describe the Management Service that is required to monitor and control MAESTRO services and applications. The Management Service makes MAESTRO services more efficient and reliable so that MAESTRO applications can perform their tasks without problems.

The functional requirements of the Management Service are as follows.

- Various information about MAESTRO services and applications should be provided.
- Relationship information between MAESTRO services and applications should be provided.
- Events and faults which may occur in MAESTRO services and applications should be reported.
- Performance level of MAESTRO services should be measured.
- Users' list and access control list should be managed.

The Management Service in MAESTRO has been designed based on the functional requirements mentioned above [20].

4.6 QoS Management Service

Most of national and international networks being used today in various organizations are neither high-speed nor broadband networks that can satisfy all the requirements of multimedia applications. What is needed is a way to adapt flexibly to the quality of underlying networks so that these applications can run on most of the networks that exist today. QoS Management Service as part of MAESTRO fulfills this need.

Figure 12 illustrates the architecture for QoS Management. QoS Management Service Object (QMSO) performs QoS functions (including QoS control, QoS mapping, resource monitor and control). In addition, QMSO monitors and controls the available host and network resources through the interaction with CSO and SSO. If QoS violation is occurred, QMSO sends an event message to MSO and performs an appropriate QoS control procedure. QoS Management Interface Object (QMIO) is a specialized version of MIO used for accessing management information related to QoS from multimedia service objects. That is, QoS parameters defined in the QoS MIB [32] are instrumented into the managed objects in the form of QMIO.

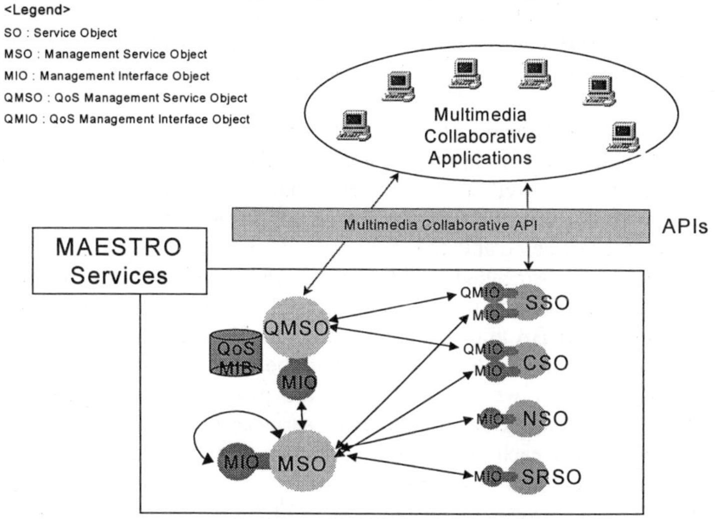

Figure 12. Architecture of QoS Management in MAESTRO

4.7 *Security Service*

The security service is responsible for providing a secure environment for the use of applications. First, when a user makes use of a multimedia collaborative application the security service checks the user in two sides, namely authentication and authorization. Second, the communication data must be protected from an invader. The detailed functions of security service are as follows:

- Allowing all user who present an identification to use multimedia application.
- Allowing a chairman to choose a permission (public/private) of the session.
- Allowing a user to participate a private session by passing a valid password.

5 MAESTRO Implementation

Based on the MAESTRO design architecture, multimedia collaborative service API and distributed multimedia services presented in the previous sections, we have carried out a prototype implementation of the MAESTRO system. This section presents the details of our implementation.

First, MAESTRO multimedia collaborative service API has been implemented using Java [30] and C++ programming languages. This allows the development of Java-based applications as well as more traditional X Windows/Motif GUI-based applications. Java-based applications can be run on any Java-enabled Web browsers and thus have the advantage of being able to run on many Unix and PC platforms.

Second, MAESTRO distributed multimedia services (in the form of distributed cooperative servers) have been implemented using CORBA and C++ on the Sun Solaris platforms. The use of CORBA allows the distributed multimedia services to be defined using CORBA IDL and the body of services to be implemented in a number of programming languages but we chose C++ as the programming language. Thus, MAESTRO distributed multimedia collaborative services have been implemented as CORBA objects interacting each other within a domain or between domains to support the operation of distributed multimedia applications.

There currently exists several freely available CORBA implementations as well as a number of commercially available implementations. We chose to use IONA's CORBA implementations (OrbixWeb 2.0.1 [21] and Orbix 2.2 [22]) that are commercial but known to be the most stable among the ones currently available. IONA OrbixWeb 2.0.1 allows Java-based applications to access MAESTRO multimedia services implemented as CORBA objects and Orbix 2.2 allows C/C++ based applications to access the services.

Using the MAESTRO multimedia collaborative service API and distributed multimedia services, we developed a number of multimedia collaborative applications such as video/audio conferencing tool, video/audio multicasting tool, whiteboard, electronic notebook, chatting tool and session management tool. Most of these applications have been developed using Java and thus they can be run on any platform that supports Java Virtual Environment [31]. For example, the multimedia collaborative applications that we developed can be run on the Web because Web browsers such as Netscape and Microsoft Explorer supports Java Virtual Environment. The multimedia collaborative applications that we have developed will be explained in more detail in the following section.

The hardware we have used are Sun Sparc 20 (running on Solaris 2.4) and Sun Ultra 1 (running Solaris 2.5). We have used SunVideo Card [23] and Solaris XIL

Library [24] for video/audio compression and decompression used in video/audio conferencing and multicasting tools.

6 Multimedia Applications on MAESTRO

In this section, we explain the multimedia collaborative applications developed by using MAESTRO. The developed multimedia collaborative applications include video/audio conferencing tool, video/audio multicasting tool, whiteboard, electronic notebook, chatting tool, shared application and session tool.

6.1 Video/Audio Conferencing Tool

Using a video/audio conferencing tool, researchers in this project can interact each other in real-time without travelling to remote sites. Figure 13 shows the video/audio conferencing tool developed using and operating on MAESTRO. The tool has been implemented using C++ and X Window/Motif library for user interface and Sun Video/Audio Card for capture of video and audio from the source. In this tool, users can control the transmission and reception of video and audio data separately. This is a desirable capability so that when no voice is to be heard, one can shut it off and send/receive the video data only. Further, when audio conferencing is only required, then video signals can be turned off, thus effectively using the tool as an audio conferencing tool.

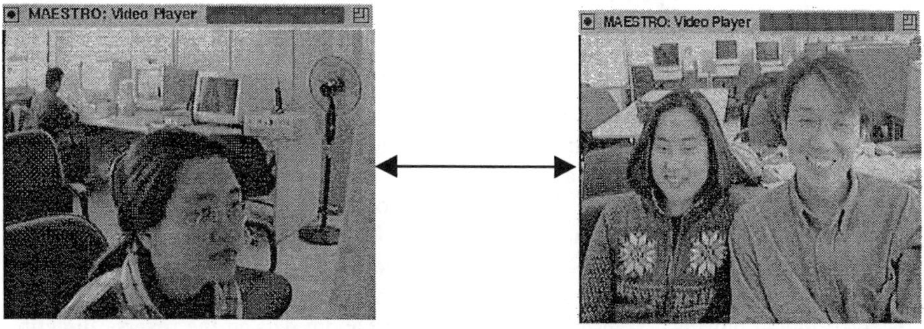

Figure 13. Video/Audio Conferencing Tool

The video/audio conferencing tool has been implemented using the objects in multimedia collaborative service API and one-to-many communication service. Figure

14 shows how objects in the layers of multimedia collaborative service API and distributed multimedia services have been used to implement the video/audio conferencing tool. A video/audio conferencing session is achieved by the use of *VA_Producer* and *VA_Consumer* objects in the multimedia collaborative service API layer (described in Section 3.2) and *Port* objects in the multimedia services layer (described in Section 4.1).

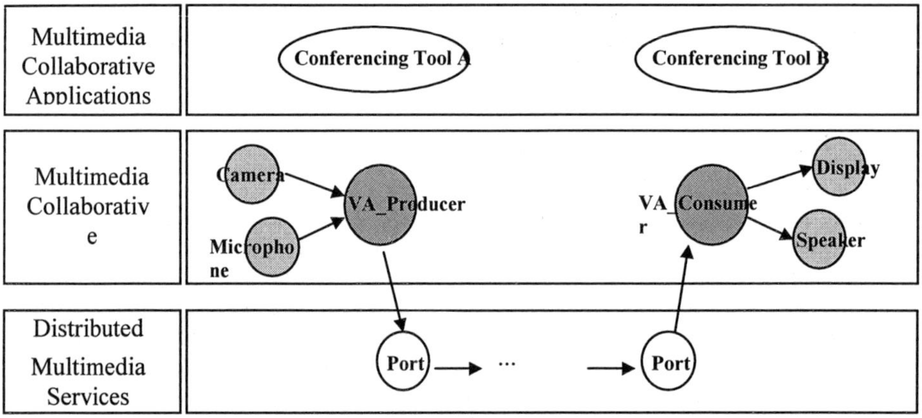

Figure 14. Objects in Video/Audio Conferencing Tool

Conferencing tool A uses a *VA_Producer* object which is an instance of the *VA_Producer* class in the multimedia service API layer. *VA_Producer* has inherited features of the *Video_Producer* and *Audio_Producer* classes. *VA_Producer* generates video and audio data by capturing video data using a camera and audio data using a microphone. The captured data are represented as *Video* and *Audio* media objects and are transmitted to the receiver *Port* objects. Conferencing tool B, in turn, uses a *VA_Consumer* object which is an instance of the *VA_Consumer* class. *VA_Consumer* has inherited features of the *Video_Consumer* and *Audio_Consumer* classes. *VA_Consumer* object uses a display (such as monitor) and speaker to output the received media objects. Transmission of video and audio data in the reverse direction (i.e., tool B to tool A) is achieved using the same objects only in the reverse direction.

6.2 Video/Audio Multicasting Tool and Whiteboard

The video/audio multicasting tool can be used for broadcasting or showing a video tape or equivalent video archive to a participating group of researchers. The tool consists of server and client applications. The server application controls the initiation and termination of multicasting and the client application is used by each of the participating users to receive the multicasting. Like the video/audio conferencing tool, this tool has also been implemented using C++ and X Window/Motif and Sun Video/Audio Card.

Another multimedia collaborative application that has been developed on MAESTRO is whiteboard. Users may use the whiteboard application to aid the discussion with others in real-time by drawing figures and adding texts. This simulates an interactive group discussion using a black or white board in a meeting room. Figures and texts entered by a user are displayed instantaneously to the whiteboards of other participants. Figure 15 illustrates the drawing control and display windows of the whiteboard tool we have developed.

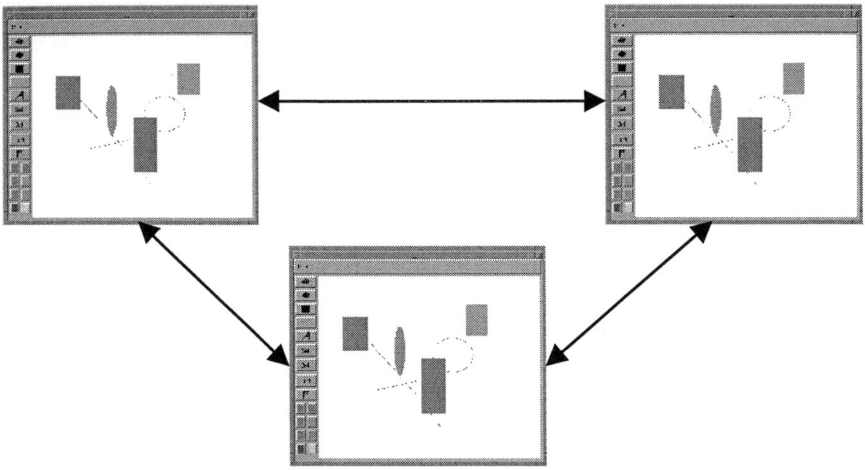

Figure 15. Whiteboard Tool for Interactive Group Discussions

6.3 Electronic Notebook & Shared Application

Electronic notebook can be thought as a normal paper notebook that is made with the help of computer. Thus, we do write on it using a pen by hand but by keyboard and mouse through a graphic user interface. The electronic notebook tool that we have developed can be used by a group of researchers for taking notes during a distant experiment. It can be also used to retrieve the old notes taken during a previous experiment. The tool is capable of inserting graphical images as well as texts, as shown in Figure 16. Note that although Figure 16 shows only two users collaborating, many more users can simultaneously participate in the collaboration.

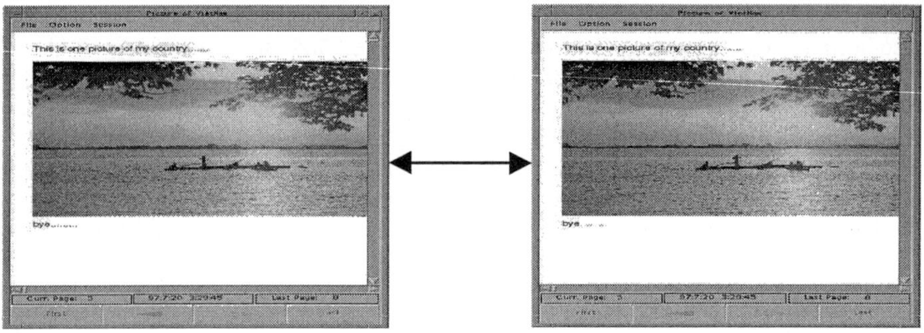

Figure 16. Electronic Notebook

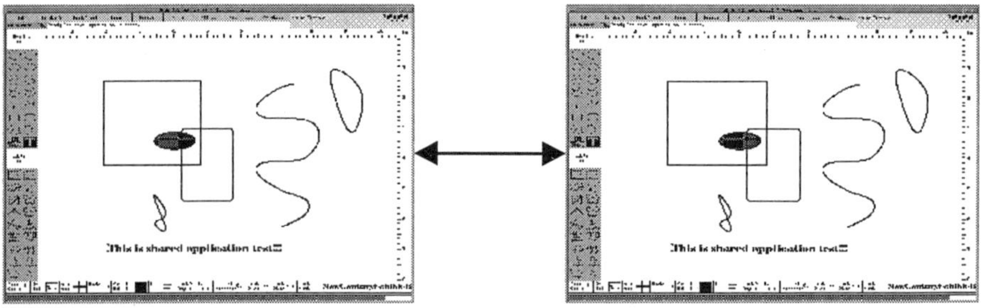

Figure 17. X Window Application (xfig) Sharing

Shared application is another approach to supporting synchronous collaboration such as a distributed, workstation-based conferencing facility. It is a distributed system for sharing existing single-user X Window applications synchronously among a group of remotely-located users at workstations running X and interconnected by the Internet. Using this shared application, all collaborating users can view the output of an X window application simultaneously and interact with it in real-time. X is a standard windowing system in Unix which has the client/server architecture and the server is responsible for the graphic display between client and user. The communication between an X client and an X server is done via message passing.

Shared application is built by inserting a routing object in the connection between a server and a client. This object intercepts all message traffic between client and server, and distributes it properly to make window sharing possible. There are two main communication objects. One is packet switch object which is responsible for distributing the output of the shared application to all of the remote servers. The other is packet translator object which runs on every remote workstation participating in window sharing and is responsible for translating the X protocol for remote X server. This tool is implemented using C++ programming language. Figure 17 illustrates the xfig utility (a popular figure drawing utility in Unix) being shared among users.

6.4 Chatting Tool & Session Management Tool

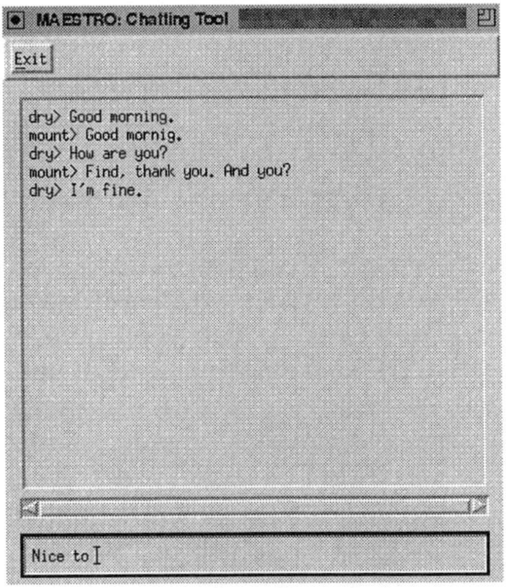

Figure 18. Chatting Tool

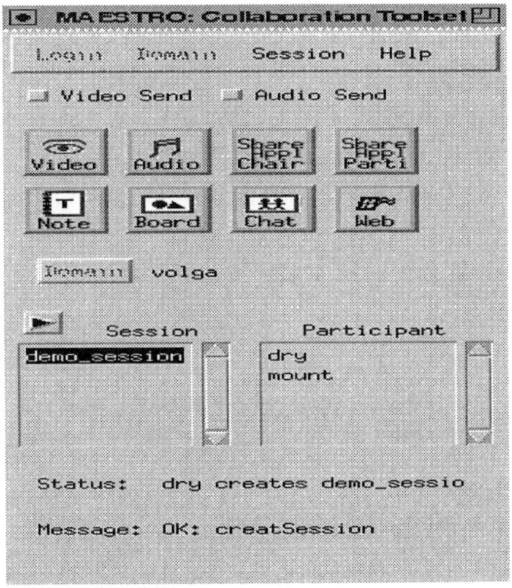

Figure 19. Collaboration Session Management Tool

The chatting tool shown in Figure 18 can be used by a number of researchers when they need to have interactive multi-user discussions or when they wish to simply talk by exchanging texts. This tool may be used in conjunction with video/audio conferencing and whiteboard tools or separately, especially when video/audio conferencing is not available due to problems with camera and/or speakers or due to lack of bandwidth available to support video/audio conferencing. Figure 18 illustrates the user interface of the chatting tool.

Figure 19 illustrates the user interface of the collaboration session management tool that is used to manage and control the sessions in MAESTRO as well as the information on the participants of a session. Using this tool, a user can discover what sessions have been opened in a domain, which users are currently participating in a session, and which applications are being used which by users. It is also possible to do a collaborative work using the session management tool because all the multimedia applications introduced above are integrated with it. That is, using this tool, one can run a video/audio conferencing tool automatically connecting to other video/audio conferencing tool and run a whiteboard automatically sharing the information of whiteboard with other user's whiteboard, and so on.

7 Concluding Remarks

This paper discussed the motivation behind our work on developing a CORBA-based distributed multimedia system called MAESTRO, which can be used to develop, operate and manage a variety of multimedia collaborative applications. We presented its architecture, multimedia collaborative service API and distributed multimedia services.

As a proof of concept, we have developed a number of multimedia collaborative applications that are required for supporting cooperative research experiments among distant users on the Korean national information superhighway. Using such multimedia collaborative applications, researchers can perform experiments using research facilities located in remote institutions, collect and analyze data, and interact with remote colleagues in real-time. This not only can save a lot of money by sharing expensive experimental facilities but also can save a lot of time by not traveling to remote sites. We believe that this type of collaboration will be exercised more commonly in the future and multimedia systems such as MAESTRO can play a key role in making it possible.

We are currently developing other multimedia collaborative applications (such as telemedicine, telepublishing and telecommerce) using MAESTRO. We plan to evaluate our system with the increase the number of users (on the order of thousands or more). We can then truly evaluate the scalability of MAESTRO and it will be a good opportunity to fine-tune the system for even better performance. We also plan to include international sites running multimedia collaborative applications on MAESTRO so that we can extend the underlying network infrastructure from the national information superhighway to an international information superhighway.

References

1. Korea Information Infrastructure Project, http://www.nca.or.kr/NCA97e/index97.html.
2. The ACTS ATM Internetwork, http://www.arl.mil/HPCMP/DREN/testbed/aai.html.
3. Singapore Information Technology (IT2000), http://www.ncb.gov.sg/.
4. CANARIE Information Highway, http://www.canarie.ca:80/eng/main.html.
5. National Information Infrastructure, http://nii.nist.gov/nii/niiinfo.html.
6. Global Information Infrastructure, http://www.gii.org/.
7. Barry K. Aldred, "IBM Lakes Architecture: Introduction and Programmers' Guide", IBM UK Laboratories Ltd., 1993, http://www.hursley.ibm.com/~p2p/.
8. Interactive Multimedia Association, "IMA Recommended Practice Draft", September 1994, http://www.ima.org/forums/imf/mss/.
9. P. Dubois, "Detailed Specification of the BETEUS application platform", BETEUS Consortium, November 1994, http://www.tik.ee.ethz.ch/~beteus/.
10. Electronics and Telecommunications Research Institute (ETRI), *Mux Tutorial*, 1995.
11. M. Arango, et al, "The Touring Machine System", *Communications of the ACM*, 36(1):68-77, January 1993.
12. J. W. Hong, T. H. Yun, J. Y. Kong and Y. M. Shin, "A Flexible and Reliable Distributed Multimedia System for Multimedia Information Superhighways", *Malaysian Journal of Computer Scientce*, Vol. 10, No. 2, December 1997, pp. 1-16.
13. T. H. Yun, J. Y. Kong and J. W. Hong, "Object-oriented Modeling of Distributed Multimedia Services", *Proc. of IEEE International Conference on Communications*, Montreal, Canada, June 1997, pp. 777-781.
14. T. H. Yun, J. Y. Kong and J. W. Hong, "A CORBA-based Distributed Multimedia System", *Proc. of 1997 Pacific Workshop on Distributed Multimedia Systems*, Vancouver, Canada, July 1997, pp. 1-8.
15. T. H. Yun, J. Y. Kong and J. W. Hong, MAESTRO: A CORBA-based Distributed Multimedia System, Technical Report, *POSTECH, PIRL-TR-97-2*, March, 1997.
16. OMG, The Common Object Request Broker: Architecture and Specification Revision 2.0, OMG, July 1995.
17. OMG, CORBAservices: Common Object Services Specification, OMG Document Number 95-3-31, March 1995.
18. OMG, *CORBAservices: EventService Specification*, http://www.omg.org/corba/sectrans.htm, March 1995.
19. J. W. Hong, G. Gee, and M. A. Bauer, "Towards automating instrumentation of systems and applications for management", *Proc. of IEEE Globecom*, Singapore, November 1995, pp. 107-111.

20. Ji-Young Kong and J. Won-Ki Hong, "A CORBA-based Management Framework for Distributed Multimedia Services and Applications", *Technical Report PIRL-TR-97-1*, POSTECH, March 1997.
21. IONA, *OrbixWeb 2.0.1*, IONA Technologies Ltd., Release 2.0.1.
22. IONA, *Orbix 2*, IONA Technologies Ltd., Release 2.0.
23. Sun Microsystems, *Sun Video User's Guide*, August 1994.
24. Sun Microsystems, *Solaris XIL 1.1 Imaging Library Programmer's Guide*, November 1993.
25. H. Lutfiyya G. S. Perrow, J. W. Hong and M. A. Bauer, "The Abstraction and Modeling of Management Agents", *Proc. of the Fourth International Symposium on Integrated Network Management*, pages 466-478, May, 1995, Santa Barbara CA.
26. J. Won-Ki Hong. "Distributed Systems Management Technology", *KISS Review*, 14(1):51-61, January 1996.
27. OMG, "Control and Management of A/V Streams Request For Proposal", August 1996.
28. S. J.Gibbs and D. C. Tsichritzis, Multimedia Programming, Objects, Environments and Frameworks, Addison-Wesley, 1995.
29. Microsoft, "DCOM: A Business Overview", http://www.microsoft.com/ntserver/info/dcom.htm, August, 1997.
30. E. R. Harold, *Java Network Programming*, O'Reilly & Associates, 1997.
31. Sun Microsystems, "The Java Virtual Machine Specification", http://java.sun.com/docs/books/vmspec/index.html.
32. J. S. Kim, J. W. Hong and J. T. Park, "A CORBA-based Quality-of-Service Management Framework for Distributed Multimedia Services and Applications", *Proc. of IFIP/IEEE DSOM '98*, Delaware, USA, October 26-28, 1998, pp. 105-116.

Quality-based Flexible Distributed Objects

Tetsuo Kanezuka, Hiroaki Higaki, and Makoto Takizawa
Tokyo Denki University
{kane, hig, taki}@takilab.k.dendai.ac.jp

Abstract

This paper discusses how to make a distributed multimedia object system flexible so as to satisfy applications' requirements in change of the system environment. The system change is modeled to be the change of not only types of service but also quality of service (QoS) supported by the objects. An object supports methods only by which the object is manipulated. A method changes not only the state of the object but also QoS of the state. We discuss new equivalent and compatible relations among methods with respect to QoS. By using the relations, we newly discuss a QoS-based compensating way to recover the object from the less qualified state.

0.1 Introduction

Units of resources in distributed systems are referred to as *objects* [13]. An object is an encapsulation of data and methods for manipulating the data. CORBA [13] is getting a general framework to realize the interoperable applications. The system is required to be so *flexible* that applications' requirements are satisfied in change of the system environment in addition to supporting the interoperability of autonomous objects.

The service supported by the object is characterized by parameters showing the *quality of service* (*QoS*) like frame rate and number of colors. Yoshida and Takizawa [16] model *movement* of a mobile object to be the change of QoS supported by the object. It is critical to discuss how to support QoS which satisfies applications' requirements in change of QoS supported by multimedia objects. In MPEG-4 [11; 12] and MPEG-7, multimedia data is composed of multimedia objects each of which may support a different level of QoS.

An object supports applications with service through the methods. The method may change not only the state of the object but also QoS supported by the object. Relations among the methods are discussed so far with respect to the states of the objects. For example, a pair of methods are *equivalent* if the states obtained by performing the methods in any order are the same [1]. In this paper, we discuss kinds of relations among the methods with respect to QoS. Here, suppose that a state s_2 is obtained by dropping some frames in a state s_1 of a multimedia object. If the state s_2 satisfies the applications' requirements, s_2 is considered to be equivalent with s_1. In addition, there are two aspects of QoS, i.e. *state QoS* and *view QoS*. The state QoS means QoS which the state of the object intrinsically supports. The applications can view QoS of the object only through the methods. For example, suppose that a multimedia object supports higher quality image data and a method *display*. Here, the application can only view lower quality image if *display* can output only lower quality image. QoS viewed through *display* is the view QoS of the multimedia object.

Effects done by methods performed have to be removed if a state obtained by the methods does not satisfy applications' requirements. For example, if an object is faulty, while multiple objects are cooperating by exchanging messages, the object have to be rolled back. Various kinds of checkpoint and rollback algorithms are discussed so far [4; 7]. The effects can also be removed by the *compensation* [10; 15] of the methods performed. In multimedia applications, it takes time to restore a large volume of high-resolution video data. We can reduce time for recovering the system if data with lower resolution but satisfying the applications' requirements is restored instead of restoring the high-resolution data. In this paper, we discuss a compensation way where an object o may not be rolled back to the previous state at which the object o has been but can be surely rolled back to a state supporting QoS which satisfies the requirements. We can reduce time for rolling back the objects by this way.

In section 0.2, we present a model of the system. In sections 0.3 and 0.4, we discuss relations among the methods and the compensation on the basis of QoS, respectively.

0.2 System Model

0.2.1 *Objects*

A system is composed of multiple objects distributed on multiple computers which are interconnected by reliable communication networks. Each object o is an encapsulation of data and a collection of abstract methods $op_1, \ldots,$

op_l only through which the object o can be manipulated. There are two kinds of objects, *class* and *instance*. A class gives a framework, i.e. set of attributes and collection of methods. An instance is created from the class, which is a tuple of values each of which is given to each attribute of the class. From here, let a term "object" mean an instance in this paper. Each object is uniquely identified by the object identifier (*oid*). The values of the object can be changed by the methods but the *oid* is never changed. A tuple of values of the object is referred to as a *state* of the object.

On recept of a request message with a method op_t, an object o performs op_t. The method op_t changes a state of an object o and outputs data obtained from the state as the response. Let $op_t(s)$ denote a state obtained by performing a method op_t on a state s of the object o. Let $[op_t(s)]$ denote the response obtained by performing op_t on a state s of the object o. For example, $[display(s)]$ shows image displayed on a monitor or printer from a state s of a multimedia object by $display(s)$. $op_t \circ op_u$ means that a method op_u is performed after another method op_t is terminated. Here, a conflicting relation [10] among a pair of methods op_t and op_u supported by an object o is defined as follows: op_t *conflicts* with op_u if $op_t \circ op_u(s) \neq op_u \circ op_t(s)$, $[op_t(s)] \neq [op_u \circ op_t(s)]$, or $[op_t \circ op_u(s)] \neq [op_u(s)]$ for some state s of the object o. For example, a method *record* conflicts with a method *delete* in an object *movie*. A method op_t is *compatible* with a method op_u unless op_t conflicts with op_u in the object o. The conflicting relation is not transitive. In the file, *read* conflicts with *write* and *write* conflicts with *read*. Thus, we assume the conflicting relation is symmetric. Let $\langle s \rangle$ denote a tuple $\langle [op_1(s)], \ldots, [op_l(s)] \rangle$ of the responses obtained from a state s, i.e. *view* of the state s of the object o.

An object can be composed of other objects. For example, suppose one movie scene shows a person driving a car on a road. An object for the scene is composed of four objects showing a person, car, road, and background. In MPEG-4, a multimedia data is composed of multiple objects like audio/video objects (AVOs) and sound object.

The object are hierarchally structured by the inheritance relation in addition to the component relation. If a class c_j is derived from c_i, c_j inherits attributes and methods supported by c_i. An object o_j of c_j also inherit the states and methods of an object o_i of c_i.

0.2.2 *Quality of service (QoS)*

Each object o supports applications with some service. The service can be obtained by issuing methods supported by the object o. Each service is characterized by parameters like level of resolution, number of frames, and number of colors. Quality of service (QoS) supported by the object o is given by the parameters. Even if a pair of objects support the same types of service, they may provide different levels of QoS.

The *scheme* of QoS is given in a tuple of attributes $\langle a_1, \ldots, a_m \rangle$ ($m \geq 1$) where each attribute a_i shows a parameter of the service like frame rate. Let dom(a_i) be a *domain* of an attribute a_i, i.e. a set of possible values to be taken by a_i ($i = 1, \ldots, m$). For example, dom(*resolution*) is a set of numbers each of which shows the number of pixels for each frame. A QoS *instance* q of the scheme $\langle a_1, \ldots a_m \rangle$ is given in a tuple of values $\langle v_1, \ldots, v_m \rangle \in \text{dom}(a_1) \times \ldots \times \text{dom}(a_m)$. Let $a_i(q)$ show a value v_i of an attribute a_i in the QoS instance q. The values in dom(a_i) are partially ordered by a precedent relation $\preceq \subseteq \text{dom}(a_i) \times \text{dom}(a_i)$, i.e. a QoS value v_1 *precedes* another QoS value v_2 ($v_1 \succeq v_2$) in dom(a_i) if v_1 shows better QoS than v_2. For example, $120 \times 100 \preceq 160 \times 120$ [pixels] for the attribute *resolution*. A QoS instance q_1 *totally dominates* QoS instance q_2 iff q_1 and q_2 have the same scheme $\langle a_1, \ldots, a_m \rangle$ and $a_i(q_1) \succeq a_i(q_2)$ for every attribute a_i. Let A be a subset $\langle b_1, \ldots, b_k \rangle$ of the QoS scheme $\langle a_1, \ldots, a_m \rangle$ where $b_j \in \{a_1, \ldots, a_m\}$ ($j = 1, \ldots, k$) and $k \leq m$. A projection $[q]_A$ of the QoS instance q on A is $\langle w_1, \ldots, w_k \rangle$ where $w_i = b_i(q)$ for $i = 1, \ldots, k$. A QoS *instance* q_1 of a scheme A_1 *partially dominates* q_2 of A_2 iff $[q_1]_{A_1 \cap A_2}$ totally dominates $[q_2]_{A_1 \cap A_2}$. q_1 *dominates* q_2 ($q_1 \succeq q_2$) iff q_1 partially dominates q_2 and $A_1 \supseteq A_2$. Let S be a set of QoS *instances* whose schemes are not necessarily the same. A QoS instance q_1 is *minimal* in the set S iff there is no QoS instance q_2 in S such that $q_2 \preceq q_1$. q_1 is *minimum* in S iff $q_1 \preceq q_2$ for every q_2 in S. q_1 is *maximal* iff there is no q_2 in S such that $q_1 \preceq q_2$. q_1 is *maximum* in S iff $q_2 \preceq q_1$ for every q_2 in S. A *least upper bound* (*lub*) $q_1 \cup q_2$ of a pair of QoS instances q_1 and q_2 is some QoS instance q_3 in S such that 1) $q_1 \preceq q_3$ and $q_2 \preceq q_3$, and 2) there is no instance q_4 in S where $q_1 \preceq q_4 \preceq q_3$ and $q_2 \preceq q_4 \preceq q_3$. The *greatest lower bound* (*glb*) $q_1 \cap q_2$ is defined similarly to the least upper bound $q_1 \cup q_2$.

Applications require an object o to support some QoS which is referred to as *requirement* QoS (*RoS*). Let r be an RoS instance. Here, suppose an object o supports a QoS instance $q = \langle v_1, \ldots, v_m \rangle$ where each v_i is a value of an attribute a_i, i.e. $v_i \in \text{dom}(a_i)$ $(i = 1, \ldots, m)$. Here, let A_r and A_q be the schemes of r and q, respectively. The QoS instance q dominates the instance r ($q \succeq r$) iff q partially dominates r and $A_q \supseteq A_r$. If $q \succeq r$, the applications can get enough service from q. Here, q is referred to as *satisfy* r. Otherwise, q is less qualified than r.

0.2.3 *QoS of object*

Real objects in the real world support maximum, possible infinite level of QoS. In order to realize a real object in a computer, we have to reduce QoS of the object. Thus, each state s' of a real object is realized by mapping the maximum level of QoS to a state s with the limited level of QoS depending on the facilities of the computers. That is, $Q(s') \succeq Q(s)$. The state of the real object is referred to as a *super state*. Let super(s) denote a super state of a state s of an object o which is realized in the computer. Here, $Q(\text{super}(s)) \succeq Q(s)$. We assume that there exists exactly one super state for each state s. QoS of every super state is maximum.

[**Definition**] A state s_1 is *state-equivalent* with a state s_2 of an object o iff $\text{super}(s_1) = \text{super}(s_2)$. □

For example, suppose that a state s_1 of the object *video* supports video data of frame rate 30 fps. Suppose a new state s_2 with a frame rate 20 fps is obtained by dropping some frames in the state s_1. If the state s_2 is state-equivalent with the state s_1, s_1 and s_2 are derived from a same super state by reducing QoS but they support different levels of QoS. Let $SE(s)$ be an equivalent set of states which are state-equivalent with a state s. Every state in $SE(s)$ has the same super state.

QoS of an object o has two aspects: *state QoS* which shows QoS of the state of o and *view QoS* which is obtained by performing a method of o. For example, let us consider an object *video* with a method *display* as shown in Figure 0.1. A state s of the object *video* supports video data with a rate 30 [fps], which is a state QoS. $Q(s) = 30$ [fps]. However, *display* can display the view $[display(s)]$ on the monitor of the video data from the state s only at a rate 20 fps. This is a view QoS. $Q([display(s)]) = 20$ [fps]. Here, there is a constraint "$Q([op_t(s)]) \preceq Q(s)$" for every method op_t and every state s of an object o. The object o cannot support the applications with higher QoS than supported by the methods. If $Q([op_t(s)]) \prec Q(s)$ for some state s of the object o, op_t is *less qualified* in the object o. The method op_t is *fully qualified* in the object o if $Q([op_t(s)]) = Q(s)$ for every state s of o. In Figure 0.1, the method *display* is less qualified for the object *video*. Let maxQoS(op_t) show the maximum QoS which op_t can support, i.e. $Q([op_t(s)]) \preceq$ maxQoS(op_t) for every state s of the object o. Here, suppose the object *movie* supports two versions *old-display* and *new-display* of a method *display*. The new version *new-display* can display the same video image as *old-display* while *new-display* can display at a faster rate than *old-display*. The new version *new-display* is considered to be the same as *old-display* because the methods output the same image data and do not change the state of *movie*. However, they support different levels of QoS, i.e. *new-display* is more qualified than *old-display* with respect to the display speed. That is, $Q([\textit{old-display}(s)]) \preceq Q([\textit{new-display}(s)])$ for every state s of *movie*.

[**Definition**] A method op_t is *more qualified* than another method op_u of an object o iff $Q([op_t(s)]) \succeq Q([op_u(s)])$ and $op_t(s)$ is state-equivalent with $op_u(s)$ for every state s of the object o. □

$Q(\langle s \rangle)$ is defined to be a tuple $\langle Q([op_1(s)]), \ldots, Q([op_l(s)]) \rangle$, i.e. view QoS of a state s of an object o which can be obtained through the methods op_1, $\ldots$, op_l. $Q(\langle s \rangle)$ shows the view QoS of the object o which the applications can view through the methods.

The applications cannot differentiate states s_1 and s_2 if data viewed by performing a method op_t on s_1 and s_2 are the same, i.e. $[op_t(s_1)] = [op_t(s_2)]$ in the object o.

[**Definition**] A state s_1 is *op_t-equivalent* with a state s_2 of an object o iff $[op_t(s_1)] = [op_t(s_2)]$ for a method op_t of o. □

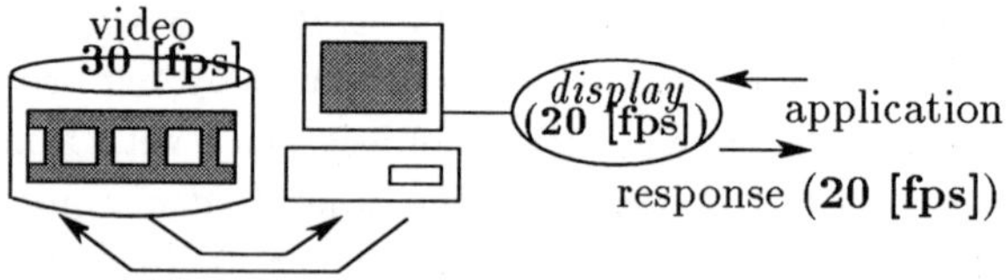

Fig. 0.1 QoS of video object.

[**Definition**] A state s_1 is *method-equivalent* with a state s_2 of an object o iff $\langle s_1 \rangle = \langle s_2 \rangle$, i.e. $[op_t(s_1)] = [op_t(s_2)]$ for every method op_t of o. □

Even if $s_1 \neq s_2$, the applications view a pair of states s_1 and s_2 of the object o to be the same because the applications get the same response through every method. Let $maxQ_o$ and $minQ_o$ denote maximum and minimum QoS to be supported by the object o, respectively. Here, $minQ_o \preceq Q(\langle s \rangle) \preceq maxQ_o$ for every state s of the object o.

There are two aspects of objects to be considered, i.e. states and QoS. Hence, each object supports two types of primitive methods, one for manipulating the state of the object and the other one for manipulating QoS of the object. The former is a *state method* and the latter is a *QoS method*. The method *drop* is a QoS method because *drop* only changes QoS of the object *video*. For a QoS method op_Q, a state $op_Q(s)$ is state-equivalent with every state s of an object o, i.e. super$(op_Q(s))$ = super(s) but $Q(op_Q(s)) \neq Q(s)$. For a pair of QoS methods op_t and op_u, $op_t(s)$ and $[op_t(s)]$ are state-equivalent with $op_u(s)$ and $[op_u(s)]$, respectively, for every state s of an object o because they only change QoS of the object o. On the other hand, for a state method op_S, $Q(op_S(s)) = Q(s)$ while $s \neq op_S(s)$. For example, a method *add* appends some data in *video*. *add* changes the state of *video* but does not change the QoS. Here, we introduce a transition diagram to show the change of states and QoS as shown in Figure 0.2, where a node shows a state and a directed edge indicates a state transition. A horizontally directed edge $s \rightarrow s_1$ indicates that a state s is changed to another state s_1 by a state method which manipulates the state of the object o. Here, QoS of the state s_1 is the same as the state s, i.e. $Q(s_1) = Q(s)$. On the other hand, a vertically directed edge $s \rightarrow s_2$ shows that a state s_2 is obtained from the state s by changing QoS of the state s through a QoS method. For example, s_2 is obtained by increasing number of colors of s. Applications can consider a pair of the states s and s_2 to be the same except for the number of colors. That is, s_2 is state-equivalent with s. A public method is implemented by using these primitive methods, i.e. changes not only the state but also QoS of the state. In Figure 0.2, an edge $s \rightarrow s_3$ denotes that a method op obtains a state s_3 by changing both the state and QoS.

0.3 QoS Relation Among Methods

We discuss how methods $op_1, \ldots, op_l$ supported by an object o are related with respect to QoS.

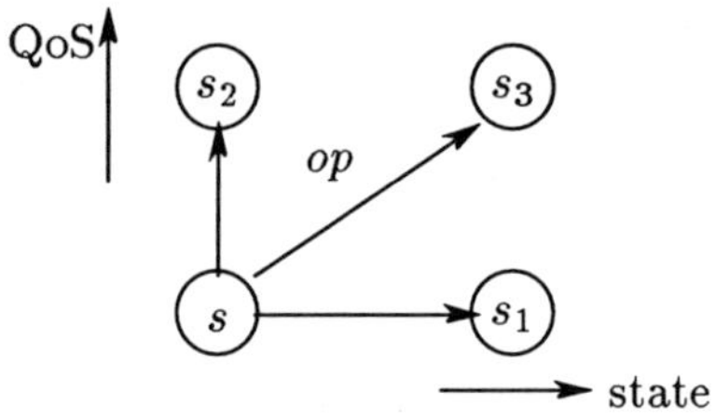

Fig. 0.2 Transition diagram.

0.3.1 *Equivalency*

A method op_t is *equivalent* with another method op_u in an object o iff $op_t(s) = op_u(s)$ and $[op_t(s)] = [op_u(s)]$ for every state s of o. That is, the methods op_t and op_u not only output the same response data but also change the state of the object o to the same state.

Suppose an object *movie* is composed of two subobjects; an *advertisement* object and a *content* object. The advertisement object is removed from the object *movie* by a method *delete*. An application does not care the difference between the original version and the updated version of *movie* since the application is interested only in the content part of *movie*. The updated version is *semantically equivalent* with the original version because the original and updated versions are considered to be the same from the application point of view. That is, the super states of the original and updated versions are considered to be the same in the application. The old and updated versions support the same QoS.

[Definition] A state s_1 is *semantically equivalent* with a state s_2 of an object o iff super(s_1) and super(s_2) are considered to be the same by the application. □

Suppose that a pair of super states s'_t and s'_u of an object o are considered to be the same in some application. Suppose $s_t = op_t(s)$ and $s_u = op_u(s)$ for a state s of the object o. Since s'_t and s'_u are super states of s_t and s_u, respectively, i.e. $s'_t = \text{super}(s_t)$ and $s'_u = \text{super}(s_u)$, the states s_t and s_u are obtained by reducing QoS of the super states s'_t and s'_u [Figure 0.3]. It is noted that $Q(s_t) = Q(s_u)$. The state s_t is semantically equivalent with the state s_u.

[Definition] A method op_t is *semantically equivalent* with a method op_u in an object o iff $op_t(s)$ is semantically equivalent with $op_u(s)$ for every state

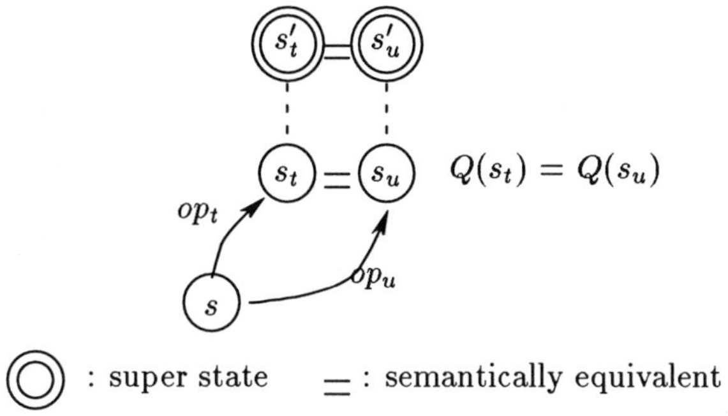

Fig. 0.3 Semantically equivalent methods.

s of o. □

In Figure 0.3, op_t is semantically equivalent with op_u because s_t ($= op_t(s)$) is semantically equivalent with s_u ($=op_u(s)$).

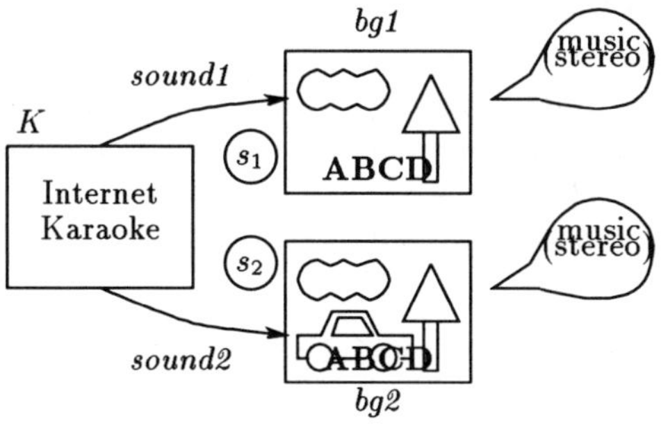

Fig. 0.4 Internet Karaoke object.

Let us consider an Internet Karaoke object K which is realized by using MPEG-4 [12] as an example [Figure 0.4]. The Internet Karaoke object K is composed of multimedia subobjects, i.e. *music*, *text*, and *background* objects (AVOs). Suppose the object K supports a pair of methods *sound1* and *sound2*. The method *sound1* plays sound *music* while displaying a background *bg1* with text. On the other hand, the method *sound2* plays sound *music* while displaying text and background video *bg2* which includes an object *car*. Here, let s_1 and s_2 be states obtained by performing *sound1* and *sound2* on K, respectively. Suppose an application does not care the background objects, i.e. the application is interested only in music and text.

That is, s_1 and s_2 are semantically equivalent. Here, the methods *sound1* and *sound2* can be considered to be the same from the application point of view although s_1 and s_2 are different. The states obtained here support the same QoS. That is, the method *sound1* is *semantically equivalent* with *sound2*.

Let R be requirement QoS which an object is required to support for an application, i.e. RoS. The application does not mind which method *old-display* or *new-display* is performed to display the movie if the application does not care the display speed in the object *movie*. Two methods *old-display* and *new-display* are considered to be equivalent with respect to RoS R if they support QoS satisfying R even if $Q([\textit{old-display}(s_{movie})]) \neq Q([\textit{new-display}(s_{movie})])$ for every state s_{movie} of the object *movie*.

[Definition] A state s_t is *RoS-equivalent* with a state s_u of an object o on RoS R ($s_t -_R s_u$) iff $Q(op_t(s)) \cap Q(op_u(s)) \succeq R$ and $op_t(s)$ is state-equivalent with $op_u(s)$ for every state s of o. □

[Definition] A method op_t is *RoS-equivalent* with another method op_u of an object o on RoS R iff $op_t(s)$ is RoS-equivalent on R with $op_u(s)$ for every state s of o. □

In Figure 0.5, a state s_t ($= op_t(s)$) is state-equivalent with a state s_u ($= op_u(s)$) because super(s_t) = super(s) = s'. If $Q(s_t)$ and $Q(s_u)$ satisfy RoS R, the method op_t is RoS-equivalent on R with op_u. In addition, op_t is more qualified than op_u since $Q(s_t) \succeq Q(s_u)$.

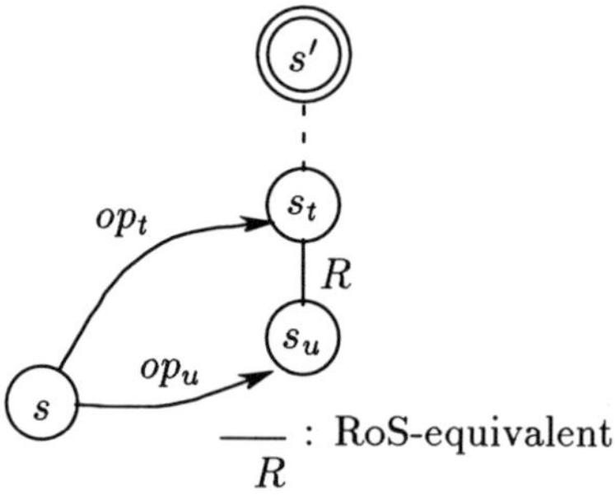

Fig. 0.5 RoS-equivalent methods.

In the example of the object *movie* with two methods *old-display* and *new-display* presented in the preceding section, suppose that the updated version *new-display* supports a higher level of QoS than the original version *old-display*. The versions are not only *semantically equivalent* but also *RoS-equivalent* with one another if *old-display* satisfies the application's requirement.

[**Definition**] A state s_t is *semantically RoS-equivalent* with a state s_u of an object o on RoS R ($s_t \equiv_R s_u$) iff super($op_t(s)$) is semantically equivalent with super($op_u(s)$) and $Q(op_t(s)) \cap Q(op_u(s)) \succeq R$ for every state s of o. □

[**Definition**] A method op_t is *semantically RoS-equivalent* with a method op_u of an object o on RoS R iff $op_t(s) \equiv_R op_u(s)$ for every state s of o. □
The semantically RoS-equivalent relation is symmetric.

In Figure 0.6, $s_t = op_t(s)$ and $s_u = op_u(s)$, and s'_t = super(s_t) and s'_u = super(s_u). The super state s'_t is semantically equivalent with the super state s'_u. $Q(s_t)$ and $Q(s_u)$ satisfy RoS R while $Q(s_t)$ may not be the same as $Q(s_u)$. Here, s_t is semantically RoS-equivalent on R with s_u ($s_t \equiv_R s_u$). Hence, op_t is semantically RoS-equivalent on R with op_u.

According to the definition, the following proposition holds.

[**Proposition**] A method op_t is semantically RoS-equivalent with a method op_u on RoS R if op_t is semantically equivalent with op_u or op_t is RoS-equivalent with op_u on R. □

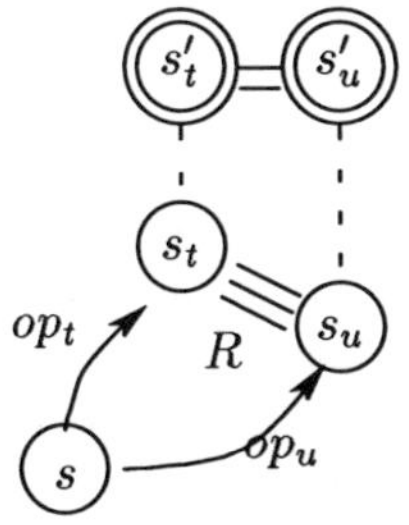

Fig. 0.6 Semantically RoS-equivalent methods.

Here, let us consider the Internet Karaoke object K. Suppose the object K supports two types of methods *sound3* and *sound4* [Figure 0.7]. The method *sound3* plays monaural sound obtained from the object *music* and displays text without background. On the other hand, *sound4* plays stereo sound while displaying text with the background object *bg2*. Here, let s_3 and s_4 denote states obtained by performing *sound3* and *sound4*, respectively. QoS obtained by performing *sound3* is different from QoS obtained

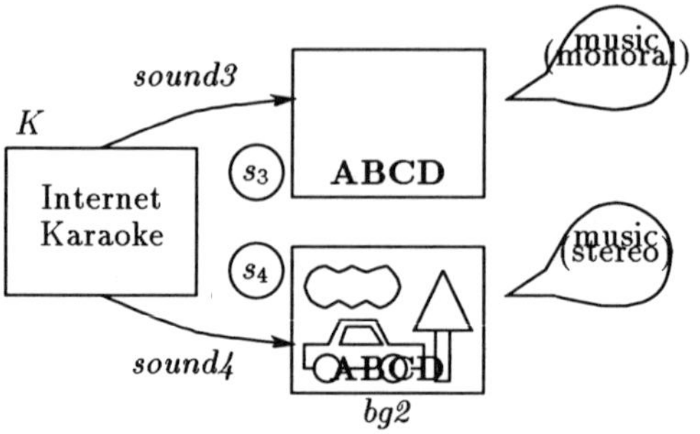

Fig. 0.7 Internet Karaoke object.

by performing *sound4* from an application point of view. That is, *sound4* is not semantically equivalent with *sound3* even if super(s_4) is semantically equivalent with super(s_3). Suppose there is such a requirement QoS (RoS) R that the application does not care whatever the background is and how qualified the music is, i.e. monaural or stereo. The states obtained by performing *sound3* and *sound4* satisfy the application's requirement R. That is, the method *sound3* is *semantically RoS-equivalent* on R with the method *sound4*.

0.3.2 *Compatibility*

We discuss in which order a pair of methods op_t and op_u supported by an object o can be performed in order to keep the object o consistent. According to the traditional theory [1; 10], the method op_t *conflicts* with the method op_u iff the result obtained by performing op_u after performing op_t depends on the computation order of op_t and op_u. op_t is *compatible* with op_u unless op_t conflicts with op_u. Every pair of conflicting methods issued by different transactions have to be performed in the same order [1]. In order to make the computation of the conflicting methods serializable, the concurrency control like locking is used.

A multimedia data is composed of multiple subobjects in MPEG-4. Each object can be manipulated independently of the other component objects. Suppose a multimedia object M displays MPEG-4 data which is composed of two objects showing a colored background and a car. A method *add* of the object M includes an object *car* into the MPEG-4 data. On the other hand, a method *grayscale* changes a colored video object to a white-black gradation video. Suppose an application performs *grayscale* on M after *add*. The MPEG-4 data obtained by performing *add* and *grayscale* is a white-black gradation video with the background and car. However, the MPEG-4 data obtained by performing *add* after *grayscale* is different from one obtained by performing the methods in the reverse order, i.e. *grayscale* after *add*. This MPEG-4 data includes the white-black background and colored car objects. That is, QoS of a state of an object obtained by performing QoS methods depends on the computation order of the methods.

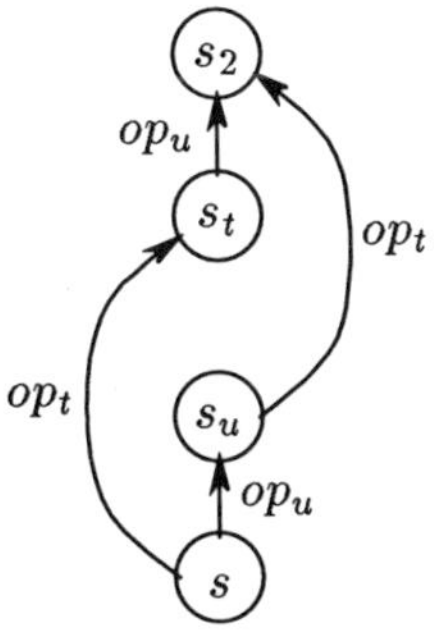

Fig. 0.8 QoS-compatible methods.

[Definition] A QoS method op_t is *QoS-compatible* with a QoS method op_u in an object o iff $op_t \circ op_u(s) = op_u \circ op_t(s)$ for every state s of o [Figure 0.8]. □

If op_t is not QoS-compatible with op_u, op_t *QoS-conflicts* with op_u. In the MPEG-4 example just presented here, the method *add* QoS-conflicts with *grayscale*.

Suppose a multimedia object M displays MPEG-4 data. The MPEG-4 data has QoS of a frame rate 30 fps and 256 colors. A method *mediascaling* of the multimedia object M reduces a frame rate to half of the original one. On the other hand, a method *reduce* decreases a number of colors to 16 colors. The application can obtain the same QoS by performing *mediascaling* after *reduce* as in the reverse order. In any case, the application can get the MPEG-4 data with 15 fps and 16 colors.

[Definition] A method op_t is *semantically compatible* with a method op_u in an object o iff $op_t \circ op_u(s)$ is semantically equivalent with $op_u \circ op_t(s)$ for every state s of o. □

In Figure 0.9, $s_1 = op_t \circ op_u(s)$ and $s_2 = op_u \circ op_t(s)$. Here, the state s_1 is semantically equivalent with the state s_2 if the super states of s_1 and s_2 are equivalent in the application. $Q(s_1) = Q(s_2)$. Here, the method op_t is semantically compatible with op_u. The method op_t semantically conflicts with op_u unless op_t is semantically compatible with op_u.

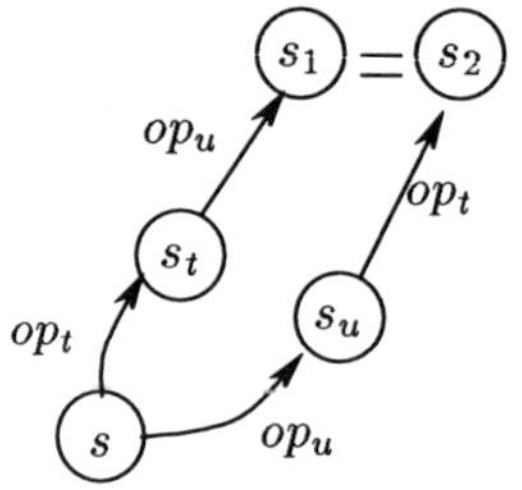

Fig. 0.9 Semantically compatible methods.

[**Definition**] A method op_t is *RoS-compatible* with a method op_u on RoS R in an object o iff $op_t \circ op_u(s)$ is RoS-equivalent with $op_u \circ op_t(s)$ on R $(op_t \circ op_u(s) -_R op_u \circ op_t(s))$ for every state s of o. □
In Figure 0.10, a state s_4 is state-equivalent with a state s_2 because super(s_2) = super(s_4). $Q(s_2) \neq Q(s_4)$ but $Q(s_2)$ and $Q(s_4)$ satisfy RoS R.

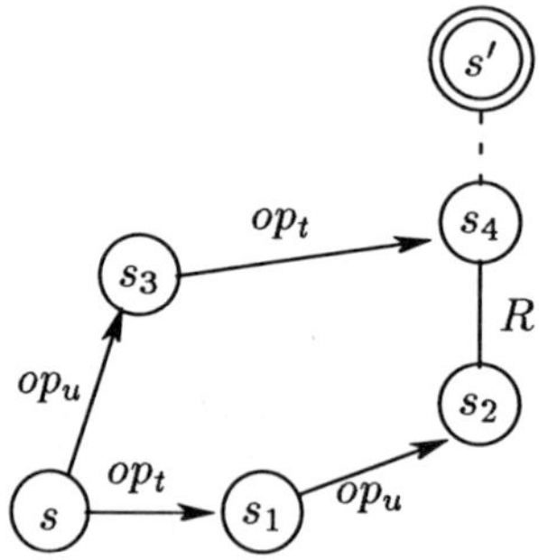

Fig. 0.10 RoS-compatible methods.

The RoS-compatible relation is symmetric. Unless a method op_t is RoS-compatible with another method op_u, op_t *RoS-conflicts* with op_u. In the multimedia object M, the methods *reduce* and *mediascaling* are RoS-compatible. However, the method *add* RoS-conflicts with the method *grayscale*.

Suppose an application is not interested in how colorful movies are. A method *update* changes an object *movie* from a colored version to a monochromatic one. The application sees the colored *movie* m by performing *display*, i.e. $[display(m)]$. If *update* is performed on the state m of the movie, the monochromatic version of m is seen. Since the application is not interested in the color of the movie m, both the versions are considered to satisfy the requirement QoS (RoS) R required by the application. Hence, $Q([display(m)]) \cap Q([update \circ display(m)]) \succeq R$ and $Q(display \circ update(m)) = Q(update \circ display(m))$. *display* and *update* are RoS-compatible. However, they are not semantically compatible because $Q([update \circ display(m)]) \neq Q([display(m)])$.

[**Definition**] A method op_t is *semantically RoS-compatible* with op_u in an object o on RoS R iff $op_t \circ op_u(s)$ is semantically RoS-equivalent with ($\equiv_R$) $op_u \circ op_t(s)$ on R for every state s of o. □

If op_t is not semantically RoS-compatible with op_u on R, op_t *semantically RoS-conflicts* with op_u. For example, suppose the object *movie* is composed of subobjects *background* and *car*. The object *movie* supports a pair of the methods *add* which includes *car* into the MPEG-4 data and *grayscale* which changes a colored video object to a while-black gradation video, respectively. Suppose an application performs the method *add* after *grayscale*. In this case, response data obtained by performing the methods in this order shows white-black gradation *background* and colored *car*. However, the white-black gradation video is obtained if the application performs the methods in the reverse order. Suppose the application is interested in a colored *car*. The response data obtained by performing *add* after *grayscale* satisfies the applications requirement R. However, response data obtained by performing the methods in the reverse order does not satisfy R. That is, the method *add* semantically RoS-conflicts with *grayscale*.

In Figure 0.11, $s_1 = op_t \circ op_u(s)$ and $s_2 = op_u \circ op_t(s)$ for a state s of an object o where $s'_1 = \text{super}(s_1)$ and $s'_2 = \text{super}(s_2)$ are semantically equivalent. In addition, $Q(s_1)$ and $Q(s_2)$ satisfy RoS R. The state s_1 is semantically RoS-equivalent on R with the state s_2. Here, op_t is RoS-compatible on R with op_u.

[**Proposition**] A method op_t is semantically RoS-compatible with a method op_u on RoS R in an object o if op_t is semantically compatible or RoS-compatible on R with op_u. □

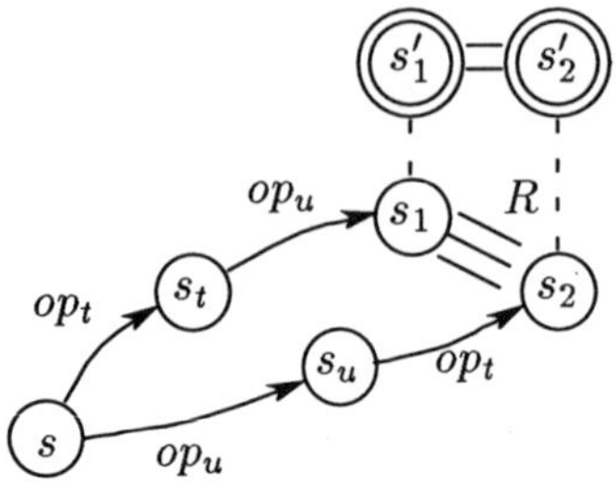

Fig. 0.11 Semantically RoS-compatible methods.

0.4 Compensation

A method op_u is a *compensating* method of a method op_t if $op_t \circ op_u(s) = s$ for every state s of an object o [6; 10]. Let s' be a state obtained by performing the method op_t on a state s of the object o, i.e. $s' = op_t(s)$. Here, the object o can be rolled back to the initial state s from the state s' if the compensating method of op is performed on the state s'. For example, *append* is a compensating method of *delete*.

[Definition] A method op_u is a *semantically compensating* method of a method op_t in an object o iff $op_t \circ op_u(s)$ is semantically equivalent with every state s of o [Figure 0.12]. □

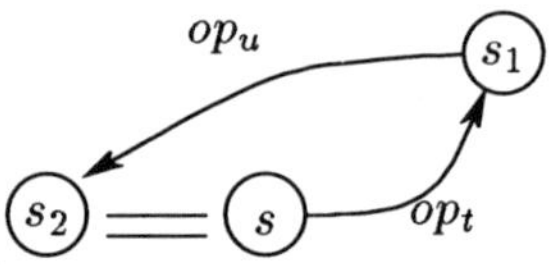

Fig. 0.12 Semantically compensating method.

Let us consider the multimedia object ME with two movie objects A and B at state s_1, where it takes two hours to *play* each of the movies A and B [Figure 0.13]. Suppose that A and B are *merged* into one movie object C at state s_2. Then, C is *divided* into two movies A' and B' at state s_3. It takes one hour and half to *play* each of A' and B' at state s_3. Each of the movie objects A and B is composed of advertisement and content objects of the movie. A' and B' include only the contents of A and B, respectively. The advertisement objects of A and B are merged into one movie object AB. Here, the state s_3 is semantically equivalent with the state s_1 because an application is interested only in the contents of the movies. Hence, *divide* is a *semantically* compensating method of *merge*.

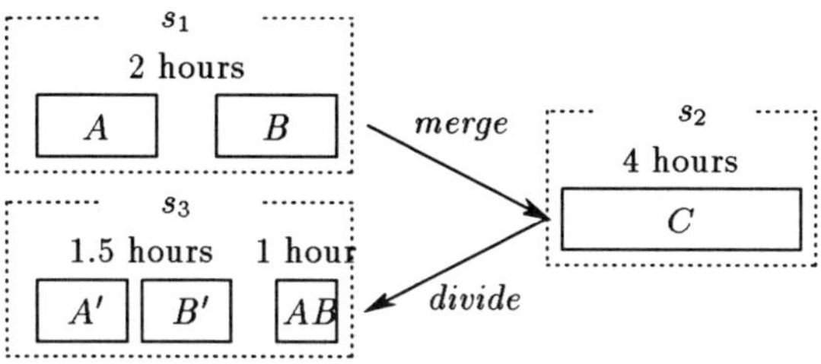

Fig. 0.13 Semantically compensating method.

RoS-compensating methods are defined based on the RoS-equivalent relations.

[Definition] A method op_u is an *RoS-compensating* method of a method op_t on RoS R in an object o iff $op_t \circ op_u(s) \equiv_R s$ for every state s of the object o and the RoS R [Figure 0.14]. □

In Figure 0.14, it is noted that s_2 is state-equivalent with s, i.e. s and s_2 have the same super state s'. However, s and s_2 satisfy RoS R although $Q(s) \neq Q(s_2)$.

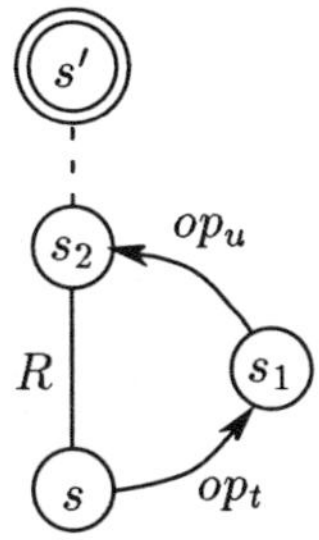

Fig. 0.14 RoS-compensating method.

[Definition] A method op_u is a *semantically RoS-compensating* method of op_t in an object o on RoS R iff $op_t \circ op_u(s) \equiv_R s$ for every state s of o and R. □

Figure 0.15 shows that op_u is a semantically RoS-compensating method of a method op_t on RoS R. A state s_2 $(= op_t \circ op_u(s))$ is semantically RoS-equivalent on R with a state s of an object o.

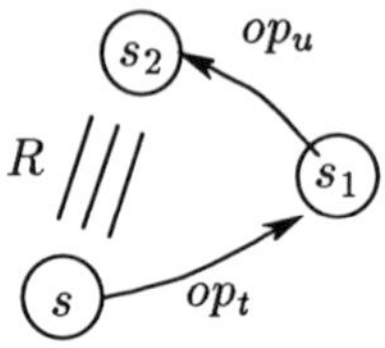

Fig. 0.15 Semantically RoS-compensating method.

Suppose the multimedia object ME supports a method *divide2* which divides the movie C into three subobjects A'', B'', and AB in addition to the methods *merge* and *delete* shown in Figure 0.13. The objects A'' and B'' show the content parts of the movie objects A and B, respectively, which are monochromatic at state s_3. The object AB includes the advertisement objects of A and B. Let s_3 denote a state where the objects A'', B'', and AB are obtained from the objects A and B existing at state s_1. The states s_1 and s_3 are not the same. Furthermore, QoS of s_3 is different from QoS of s_1 because A and B are colored but A'' and B'' are monochromatic. That is, $Q(s_1) \succeq Q(s_2)$. Suppose an application just would like to see the monochromatic one. This is RoS R. Here, $Q(s_3) \succeq R$. Hence, *divide2* is a *semantically RoS-compensating* method of *merge* on R. By performing *divide2*, the object ME can be recovered from the state s_2 to the state s_3 in stead of s_1.

Fig. 0.16 Semantically RoS-compensating method.

From the definitions, the following proposition holds.

[Proposition] A method op_u is a semantically RoS-compensating method of a method op_t on RoS R of an object o if op_u is a semantically compensating or RoS-compensating method of op_t on R. □

0.5 Concluding Remarks

This paper has discussed how to make the distributed system flexible with respect to QoS supported by the objects. We have discussed the novel equivalent and conflicting relations among the methods on the basis of QoS and state, i.e. semantically, RoS, and semantically RoS equivalent and compatible relations. We have also discussed the compensating method to undo the work done. A state semantically equivalent with the previous qualified state with respect to QoS is obtained by performing the compensating methods of methods computed. By using this QoS-based compensation, we can reduce time for recovering the multimedia objects.

Bibliography

Bernstein, P. A., Hadzilacos, V., and Goodman, N., "Concurrency Control and Recovery in Database Systems," *Addison-Wesley Publishing Company*, 1987.

Cambell, A., Coulson, G., Garcfa, F., Hutchison, D., and Leopold, H., "Integrated Quality of Service for Multimedia Communication," *Proc. of IEEE InfoCom*, 1993, pp.732–793.

Campbell, A., Coulson, G., and Hutchison, D., "A Quality of Service Architecture," *ACM SIGCOMM Comp. Comm. Review*, Vol. 24, 1994, pp.6–27.

Elnozahy, E. N., Johnson, B. D., and Wang, M. Y., "A Survey of Rollback-Recovery Protocols in Message-Passing Systems," *CMU-CS-96-181*, 1996.

Gall, D., "MPEG: A Video Compression Standard for Multimedia Applications," *Comm. ACM*, Vol.34, No.4, 1991, pp.46–58.

Garcia-Molina, H. and Salem, K., "Sagas," *Proc. of ACM SIGMOD*, 1987, pp.249–259.

Higaki, H. and Takizawa, M., "Checkpoint-Recovery Protocol for Reliable Mobile Systems," *Proc. of the 17th IEEE Int'l Symp. on Reliable Distributed Systems (SRDS)*, 1998, pp.93–99.

Kanezuka, T. and Takizawa, M., "QoS Oriented Flexibility in Distributed Objects," *Proc. of Int'l Symp. on Communications (ISCOM'97)*, 1997, pp.144–148.

Kanezuka, T. and Takizawa, M., "Quality-based Flexibility in Distributed Objects," *Proc. of 1st IEEE Int'l Symp. on Object-oriented Real-time distributed Computing (ISORC'98)*, 1998, pp.350–357.

Korth, H. F., Levy, E., and Silberschalz, A., "A Formal Approach to Recovery by Compensating Transactions," *Proc. of VLDB*, 1990, pp.95–106.

MPEG Requirements Group, "MPEG-4 Requirements," ISO/IEC JTC1/SC29/WG11 N2321, 1998.

MPEG Requirements Group, "MPEG-4 Applications," ISO/IEC JTC1/SC29/WG11 N2322, 1998.

Object Management Group Inc., "The Common Object Request Broker: Architecture and Specification, Rev2.0," 1995.

Sabata, B., Chatterjee, S., Davis, M., and Syidir, J. J., "Taxonomy for QoS Specifications," *Proc of IEEE WORDS'97*, 1997, pp.100–107.

Takizawa, M. and Yasuzawa, S., "Uncompensatable Deadlock in Distributed Object-Oriented Systems," *Proc. of IEEE ICPADS-92*, 1992, pp.150–157.

Yoshida, T. and Takizawa, M., "Model of Mobile Objects," *Proc. of DEXA'96*, (*Lecture Notes in Computer Science, Springer-Verlag No. 1134*), 1996, pp. 623–632.

ADVANCE RESERVATION SYSTEM IN VOD SERVICES

KAI-HUI LEE AND YIE-TARNG CHEN

Department of Electronic Engineering, National Taiwan University of Science and Technology, Taipei, Taiwan, R.O.C.

e-mail: D8202003@mail.ntust.edu.tw ytchen@et.ntust.edu.tw

Workload for VOD services greatly fluctuates over a given 24-hour period. System resources are scarce during peak hours. Conversely, system resources are under-utilized during off-peak hours. This paper explores a time adaptation approach to achieve load balancing for advanced resource reservation system in VOD services. A new service model is proposed to support the adaptability for reserved resources in the time dimension. Releasable resources are presented as a multi-stage graph and then the optimal adaptation is found on the shortest path of the graph. To assess the performance of the time adaptation approach, we conduct a series of experiments by simulating the network resources in a VOD system under various workloads. Our results show that the proposed approaches make a significant improvement in terms of the accept ratio.

1 Introduction

Since digital video and audio are time-critical, resource reservation is a general approach to provide guaranteed Quality of Service (QoS) for real-time connections. The reservation can also be divided with respect to time when actual resource allocation occurs: (1) immediate reservation (2) advance reservation [1,2,3,5]. Both of scheme reserves resources for flows during a given time period. But, there is a period between reservation and real allocation in the advance reservation service; thus, the design of the advance reservation system can focus on how to optimize the system.

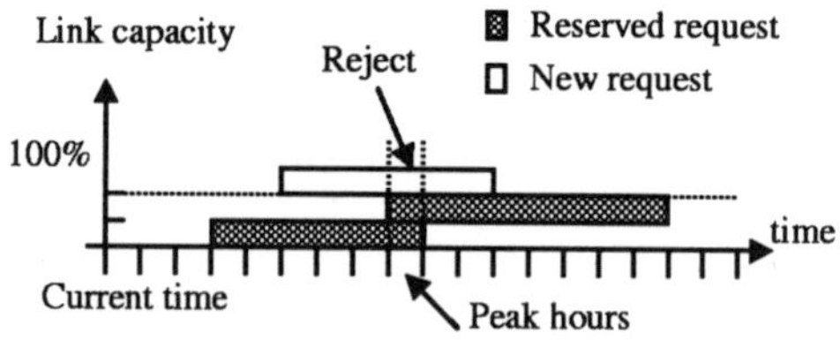

Figure 1. Resource conflicts in an advance reservation system.

In an advance reservation system, it is possible that no new request can be accepted even rough the system utilization is low, as shown in Figure 1. Because available resources are scattered in the time domain, the new request cannot find continuous and sufficient resources. However, if we can reschedule requests, either delay the starting time of the upper request, or change the schedule of the new request, the new request can be accepted.

On the other hand, workload for VOD services is not uniform over a given 24-hour period. The load could be low during the day, increase gradually through the evening and fall off during the night as shown in Figure 2. The great fluctuation of workload poses a problem of the system design for VOD services. During peak hours, high request rate overloads the system. On the contrary, during off-peak hours, system resources are under-utilized, if a portion of load at peak hours can be scheduled to off-peak hours, the system utilization can increase and the rejection ratio decreases respectively. Hence, the objective of this paper is to investigate request rescheduling scheme to improve the performance of the advance reservation system for VOD services.

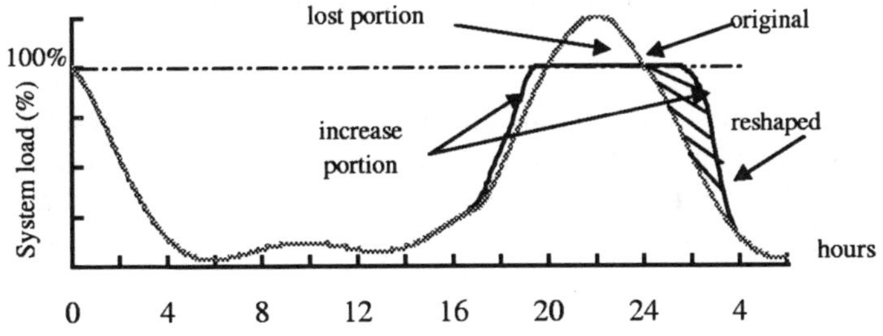

Figure 2. The traffic shape for a video server.

In this paper, we develop a request rescheduling scheme to solve the problem of work load fluctuation in VOD services. An elastic reservation model is proposed to support the adaptability for reserved resources in the time dimension. The releasable resources can be represented as a multi-stage graph. Then, the problem of finding optimal resource rescheduling is equivalent to finding the shortest path in the multi-stage graph.

One of the contributions of this work is to introduce the concept of wait tolerance [4] to advance reservation systems. The rest of the paper is organized as follows: In section 2, we propose an elastic reservation model for the resource reservation in advance. In section 3, we develop optimal solutions for the resource rescheduling problem. Section 4 demonstrates the performance evaluation for the advanced reservation system. Section 5 concludes the paper.

2 Service Model

This section introduces the elastic advance reservation model for VOD systems. In previous research [5], in addition to parameters defined in the immediate reservation, the advance request can be specified by the following two parameters: (i) the starting time and (ii) the duration. In the elastic reservation model, the concept of wait tolerance is introduced to the advance reservation system. Hence, the actual starting time of the request can be scheduled at a range of the wait tolerance.

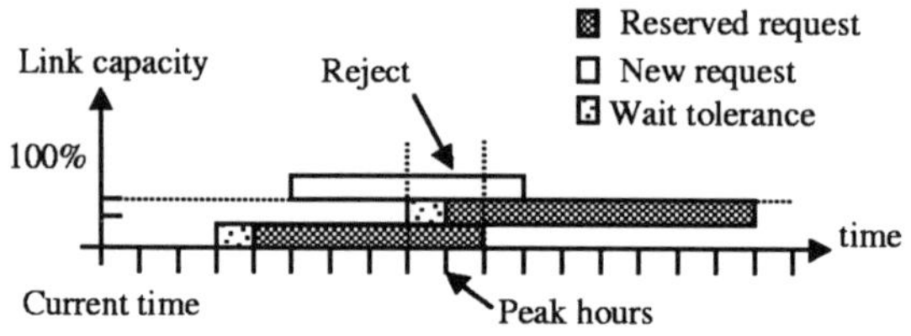

Figure 3(a). A resource reservation with wait tolerance.

In Figure 1, requests specify one time unit wait tolerance and reserve one time unit extra resource in advance. Hence, the actual starting time of existing requests can be delayed for one time unit and extra resources can be released as shown in Figure 3(a). The extra resource can locate either in the end of the reservation or in the beginning of the reservation. Observably, the extra resource reservation can provide adaptability.

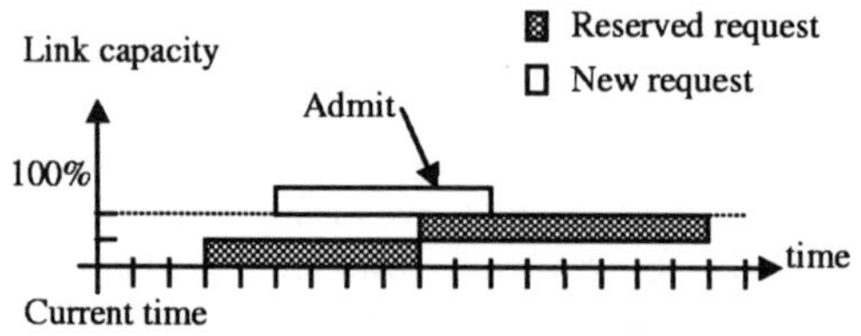

Figure 3(b). Resource rescheduling of Figure 3(a).

Because the starting time of reservations is flexible, a portion of workload can be shifted from peak hours to off-peak hours by rescheduling existing reservations. In Figure 3(a), a new request can not get enough resources at desired interval. With request rescheduling scheme, the starting time of the upper reservation can be postponed. Consequently, extra resources in the beginning of the upper reservation and the end of the lower reservation can be released. Then, the new request can be accepted as shown in Figure 3(b).

2.1 Elastic Reservation Model

In the elastic reservation model, a request can be represented as tuple R_i with the following parameters.

$$R_i = (C, S, M, t_S, t_{Len}, t_w)$$

where,

C	: the client's ID.
S	: QoS requirements.
M	: the movie ID.
t_S	: the starting time.
t_{Len}	: the duration of the movie.
t_w	: the wait tolerance.

In this model, the starting time is flexible in a range of the wait tolerance. The request must reserve extra resources in the temporal dimension. However, the over-served resources can be released if needed. If the duration of a movie is t_{Len} and the wait tolerance is t_w, the duration of resource reservation is $t_w + t_{Len}$.

3 Request Rescheduling

Based on the elastic reservation scheme, if a new request fails in the admission test, the resource manager begins to search for a combination of releasable resources from existing reservations to support the new request. If sufficient resources can be found, the new request is accepted. However, the release of resources from existing reservations will reschedule the starting time of these requests. In our proposed approach, the releasable resources in the advance reservation system can be represented as a multi-stage graph. Therefore, the request rescheduling can be formulated as the problem of finding a minimum cost path in the multi-stage graph. The following example illustrates the request rescheduling. Then, we define the cost function for releasing resources from the existing reservation.

3.1 Example

In Figure 4, the new request R_x fails in the admission test for lacking resources. With request rescheduling, the resource manager finds minimum-penalty

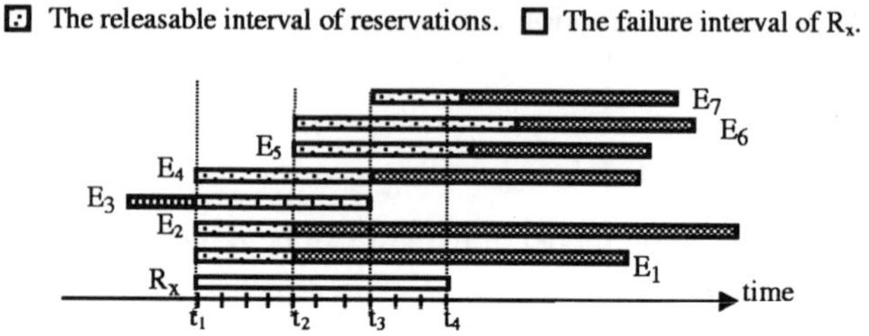

Figure 4. A snapshot of an advance reservation system for VOD.

resources, released by E_1 at $[t_1,t_2)$, E_5 at $[t_2,t_4)$ and E_6 at $[t_2,t_4)$, to satisfy the requirements for R_x. Hence, rescheduling of E_1, E_5 and E_6 is an optimal solution. After request rescheduling, the corresponding requests are shown in Figure 5.

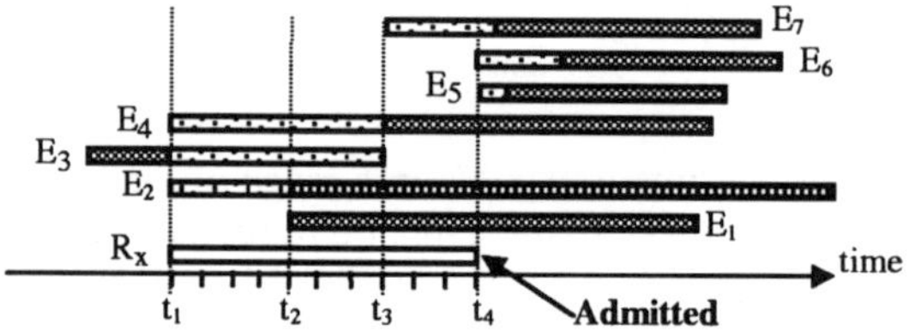

Figure 5. Result of Rescheduling for Figure 4.

3.2 *The Cost Function*

Since rescheduling of reservations can delay the starting time, reshape workload distribution, and change available system resources. An optimal request rescheduling should minimize delay, achieve load balancing and maximize available resources. Therefore, a cost function is defined to represent the penalty of releasing resources from the existing reservation, and it serves as a metric of finding a optimal combination to support the new request. Three major parameters: workload, C_L, time delay, C_D, and elasticity, C_E, contribute to the cost function.

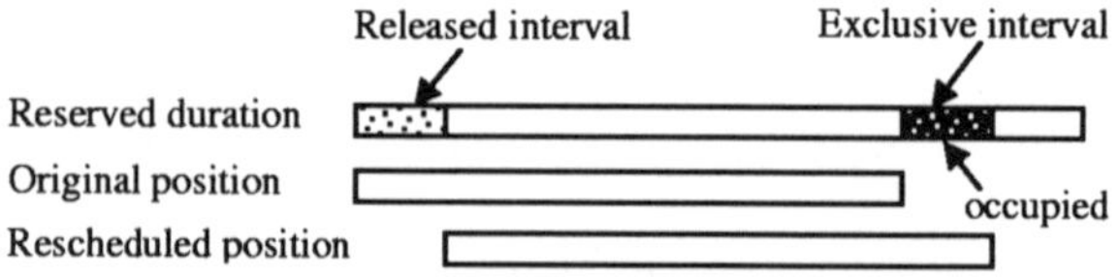

Figure 6. The exclusive interval of a reservation.

The detailed definition of these three parameters will be expressed in the rest of this section.

In the elastic reservation model, a request with a fixed duration and a flexible starting time is similar to a sliding window. When we push the window from one side, the opposite side of the window is occupied. On the other hand, when extra resource is released from the front or the rear of an existing reservation, the opposite side of the reservation, called the exclusive interval is occupied (as shown in Figure 6). The average workload for an exclusive interval, C_L, equals

$$C_L = \left\lceil \frac{1}{N_{TR}} \sum_{t \in \bar{I}_i} L_t \right\rceil$$

where,

N_{TR} : the amount of released time unit.

L_t : the reserved bandwidth in the system at time t.

$\bar{I}_i$: the exclusive interval of I_i.

Elasticity, C_E, expresses the amount of available resources that can be used for request rescheduling. Then, the elasticity of a request, C_E, is defined as

$$C_E = T_{w,\max} - (T_w - N_{TR})$$

where,

$T_{w,\max}$: the maximum wait tolerance of the advance reservation system.

T_w : the wait tolerance of the request.

C_E is directly inversely proportional to remainder elasticity of a request. Thus, the optimal request rescheduling should maximize the elasticity parameters.

The request rescheduling can delay the starting time. Therefore, the delay should be kept as short as possible. We use parameter C_D to represent the cost of time delay. Since the release of extra resource from the front of a reservation, called a forward-shifting reservation, incurs time delay, we give the forward-shifting reservation higher weight.

Hence, the cost of releasing resources from candidate reservation E_i at time interval k, $Cost_k(E_i)$, can be defined as

$$Cost_k(E_i) = C_L{*}w_{CL} + C_E{*}C_D{*}w_{CE}.$$

where,

w_{CL} : the weighting factor for workload.

w_{CE} : The weighting factor for elasticity.

Parameters C_D, w_{CL} and w_{CE} in request rescheduling are shown in Table 1.

If resources released by a single reservation cannot satisfy the new request, the resource manager selects a combination of candidate reservations to support the new request. Therefore, the cost of releasing resources from a combination of candidate reservations α at time interval k, $Cost_k(E_\alpha)$, can be expressed as

$$Cost_k(E_\alpha) = \sum_{E_i \in \alpha} Cost(E_i)$$

Our objective of request rescheduling is to find a combination of existing reservations to minimize cost function $Cost_k(E_\alpha)$.

In this paper, two strategies of selecting releasable resources from candidate reservations are investigated:

- Minimum Load First (MLF).
- Minimize Delay Time (MDT).

Since the major objective of Minimum Load First (MLF) approach is to achieve load balancing. A candidate reservation with minimum workload at the exclusive interval is chosen first to support the new request. If more than one candidate reservations have the same workload at the exclusive interval, we select the backward-shifting reservation, the releasable resource at the rear of the reservation first and then the forward-shifting reservation, the releasable resource at the end of the reservation. Consequently, the workload factor C_L dominates the cost function in MLF.

Table 1. Cost parameters in MLF and MDT approaches.

	Approaches	
Parameters	MLF	MDT
C_D Forward-shifting reservation	15	$T_{w,\max}+1$
C_D Backward-shifting reservation	10	1
w_{CL}	$T_{w,\max}$	1/(link capacity)
w_{CE}	$1/(30T_{w,\max})$	1

The objective of MDT approach is to minimize the delay of the existing reservation. Thus, in selecting candidate reservations we prefer the backward-shifting reservations to the forward-shifting reservations. Hence, a forward-shifting reservation is given higher cost than that of a backward-shifting reservation as shown in Table 1. Consequently, C_D dominates the cost function in MDT.

3.3 The Multi-stage Graph

In the request rescheduling approach, the distribution of releasable resources in time domain can be represented as a multi-stage graph. When the new request can not obtain sufficient resources, the resource manager attempts to find a combination of releasable resources with minimum cost to support to the new request. If a failure interval $I, I = [t_1, t_n)$, i.e. the new request cannot acquire resources at the time interval, is divided into n time units, a $(n+1)$-stage graph can be constructed as follows.

1. Represent a possible combination of releasable resources at time interval t_i that can satisfy resource requirements of the new request as a vertex in stage S^i, $1 \le i < n$. Hence, the vertex set is partitioned into $n-1$ subsets.
2. Add the source vertex as stages 0 and the destination vertex as stage S^n, respectively.
3. Represent a possible combination of releasable resources from stage S^i to stage S^{i+1} as an edge, from a vertex in stage S^i to anther vertex in stage S^{i+1}.
4. Associate each arc with a weight, which indicates the cost of releasing the corresponding resources.

Hence, the shortest path in the multi-stage graph represents a combination of releasable resources at interval I with minimum cost.

The details of the request rescheduling algorithm are expressed as follows.

Step 1: Find candidate reservations

Find all forward-shifting reservations and backward-shifting reservations with releasable resources at the failure interval as candidate reservations. For example, in Figure 4, E_1, E_2, E_4, E_5, E_6 and E_7 are forward-shifting reservations and E_3 is backward-shifting reservation.

Step 2: Interval partition

In failure interval, the adjacent time units with different resource utilization are divided into separate stages. Since the beginning and end of reservation change resource utilization in the system, the beginning and the end of a reservation form boundaries between different stages. Hence, each stage has the same amount of releasable resources. In Figure 4, the failure interval of R_x, $I=[t_1,t_4)$, is divided into 3 stages S^1, S^2 and S^3, to represent three corresponding time intervals, $[t_1,t_2)$, $[t_2,t_3)$ and $[t_3,t_4)$, respectively.

Step 3: Generate vertex

At each stage, a combination of releasable resources, which can satisfy resource requirements for the new request is represented as a vertex. Vertices in the graph can be generated as follows.

Definition 1:

Let $\hat{G}=(\hat{V},\hat{E})$ be an n-stage graph, then the vertex set at the k-th stage, $1<k<n$, can be expressed as

$$V^k = \{ v_\alpha^k \mid \alpha \in (\text{ the power set of } R^k - \{\varnothing\})\}$$

where,

R^k : the set of the releasable resources at the $k-th$ stage.

$B^k(E_i)$: the reserved bandwidth for candidate reservation E_i.

$B^k(request)$: debit bandwidth for the new request at the $k-th$ stage.

$\alpha = \{i \mid \sum_i B^k(E_i) \geq B^k(request), i \in R^k\}$, α is an reservation group set.

The solution space for resource scarcity at the k-th stage is the combination of releasable resources in R^k to exceed the debit bandwidth.

For example, in Figure 4, the set of candidate reservations at stages S^1, S^2 and S^3 are $R^1=\{E_1,E_2,E_3,E_4\}$, $R^2=\{E_3,E_4,E_5,E_6\}$ and $R^3=\{E_5,E_6,E_7\}$ respectively. Suppose that, the sum of any two candidate reservations is larger than the bandwidth requirements for the new request R_x, denoted $B^k(R_x)$, at each stage, we have

$$B^k(R_x) \leq B^k(E_i) + B^k(E_j) \text{ for } 1 \leq k \leq 3,\ i \neq j \text{ and } 1 \leq i,\ j \leq 7.$$

$$B^1(E_1) > B^1(R_x)$$
$$B^1(E_3) > B^1(R_x)$$
$$B^2(E_3) > B^2(R_x)$$
$$B^2(E_5) > B^2(R_x)$$
$$B^3(E_6) > B^3(R_x)$$
$$B^3(E_7) > B^3(R_x)$$

The multi-stage graph has 13 vertices at stage S^1, 14 vertices at stage S^2 and 5 vertices at stage S^3. The vertex sets of stage S^1 are $V^1 = \{v^1_{\{1\}}, v^1_{\{3\}}, v^1_{\{1,2\}}, v^1_{\{1,3\}}, v^1_{\{1,4\}}, v^1_{\{2,3\}}, v^1_{\{2,4\}}, v^1_{\{3,4\}}, v^1_{\{1,2,3\}}, v^1_{\{1,2,4\}}, v^1_{\{1,3,4\}}, v^1_{\{2,3,4\}}, v^1_{\{1,2,3,4\}}\}$.

Step 4: Generate edges and weights

If the continuity of releasable resources at adjacent intervals can remain, a directional edge connects the corresponding adjacent stages. However, the improper combination of releasable resources at adjacent interval can cause resource fragment. For example, a forward-shifting reservation α, releasable resource at the beginning of the reservation consists of two adjacent releasable intervals T_a at time interval $[t_k, t_{k+1})$ and T_b at time interval $[t_{k+1}, t_{k+2})$, respectively. If only the interval T_b has been released, the reservation α becomes fragment. That is, the reservation α is divided into two separate portions, such that reservation α cannot playback continuously. Hence, the connection is called an illegal edge.

Definition 2:

Let α be the reservation group set of stage S^k and β be the reservation group set of stage S^{k+1}, respectively. Edge $< v^k_\alpha, v^{k+1}_\beta >$ is called an illegal edge, if $\forall x$, E_x is a forward-shifting reservation, $x \in \beta, x \notin \alpha$ and $x \in R^k$.

For example, in Figure 4, the reservation $E_4 \in R^1$, $\{4\} \in \{4,3\}$ (the reservation group set of stage S^2) is $\{4,3\}$ and $\{4\} \notin \{2,1\}$ (the reservation group set of stage S^1). Consequently, edge $< v^1_{\{2,1\}}, v^2_{\{4,3\}} >$ is an illegal edge.

If candidate reservation E_γ, which can be represented as vertex v_γ^k in the multi-stage graph, is a forward-shifting reservation and E_γ can release resource at interval $[t_k, t_{k+1})$. Then, the weight associated with edge $< v_\alpha^{k-1}, v_\gamma^k >$ can be expressed as $C_{<\alpha,\gamma>}^k = Cost_k(E_\gamma)$.

If candidate reservation E_γ, which can be denoted as vertex v_γ^k in the multi-stage graph, is a backward-shifting reservation and E_γ can finish before t_k release resource at the end portion of the reservation. Then, the weight associated with edge $< v_\alpha^{k-1}, v_\beta^k >$ can be expressed as $C_{<\alpha,\gamma>}^k = \sum_{i=k}^{m} Cost_i(E_\gamma)$ where $\alpha \cap \gamma = \varnothing$, t_m is the end time of E_γ and $t_m \geq t_k$. Consequently, the weight associated with edge $< v_\gamma^k,\ v_\gamma^{k+1} >$, $C_{<\gamma,\gamma>}^{k+1}$ is 0.

In Figure 4, suppose that the corresponding costs for releasable resources are $Cost_1(E_1)=7$, $Cost_1(E_2)=3$, $Cost_1(E_3)=11$ and $Cost_2(E_3)=7$. We have $C_{<V_S,\{1\}>}^1 = Cost_1(E_1) = 7$, $C_{<V_S,\{3\}>}^1 = Cost_1(E_3) + Cost_2(E_3) = 18$, $C_{<V_S,\{1,2\}>}^1 = Cost_1(E_1) + Cost_1(E_2) = 10$ and $C_{<\{3\},\{3\}>}^2 = 0$.

Step 5: Add null vertices

Two null vertices, source vertex V_s and destination vertex V_d are introduced to construct a complete multi-stage graph. However, source vertex and destination vertex does not represent any releasable resources. Thus, the weight associated with the edge connecting destination vertex is 0.

Figure 7 illustrates part of the corresponding multi-stage graph for reservations in Figure 4. Dotted lines indicate illegal edges and solid lines indicate legal edges. However, all legal except edges from the source vertex or the destination vertex edges are omitted.

Step 6: Find the shortest path

After a multi-stage graph has been constructed, the shortest path on the multi-stage graph is found by dynamic programming. The time complexity of finding the shortest path on a multi-stage graph is $O(v+e)$, where v and e represents the number of vertex and edge on the graph, respectively.

Step 7: Release resources

Finally, we release resources from candidate reservations on the shortest path and then the new request is admitted. Let v_{α}^{k} be a vertex on the shortest path, we release resources that held by reservation group set α in the time interval $[t_k, t_{k+1})$. The starting time of forward-shifting reservations $x \in \alpha$, are changed from t_k to t_{k+1} while resources of backward-shifting reservations $y \in \alpha$, are released from t_k to the end.

If the shortest path $V_s \rightarrow v_{\{1\}}^{1} \rightarrow v_{\{5,6\}}^{2} \rightarrow v_{\{5,6\}}^{3} \rightarrow V_d$ is found in Figure 6, then the new request can be accepted and the schedule for corresponding reservations, is shown in Figure 5 (as mentioned in section 3.1).

4 Simulations

To verify the performance of the request rescheduling approach for advance reservation, we conduct a series of simulation experiments. In this section, we first present the simulation model and performance metrics. Then, we demonstrate the simulation results.

4.1 Simulation model

We simulate a large-scale video file server with 1245Mbps outgoing link (i.e., 2 fiber optic cables of ATM). In addition, the bandwidth requirement for each request is 1.5Mbps. Consequently, this server can serve 830 requests at the same moment. The duration of a video is uniform distribution with mean 120 minutes and deviation 20 minutes. The minimum reservation time unit (i.e., time granule) is 5 minutes. The experiments were performed with various workloads. The requests for video streams are Poisson distribution with dynamic mean arrival rate which is obtained from the Workload of a video server as shown in Figure 2. We summarize simulation parameters in Table 2.

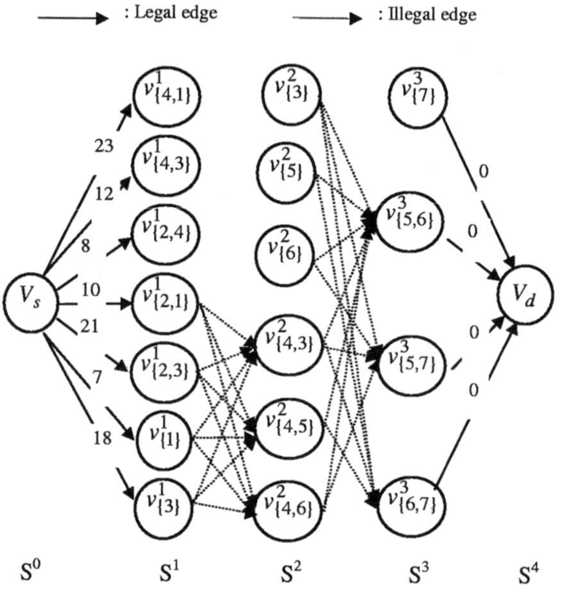

Figure 7. A part of the multi-stage graph for reservations in Figure 4.

Table 2. Simulation parameters.

Factor	Nominal values
Outgoing link capacity	622.5Mbps * 2
Bandwidth requirement	1.5Mbps
Minimum reservation time unit	5 minutes
Request duration	120 minutes
Deviation of request duration (with uniform distribution)	20 minutes
Simulated duration	1 day
Registration behavior	Uniform distribution

Workloads were generated by multiplying various weights by the dynamic mean arrival rate. Moreover, for each workload, wait tolerance ranges from 0 to 60 minutes with 5 minutes/step.

The following three performance metrics are considered in this experiment: the improvement of reject ratio, the acceptance ratio, and the average delay time.

$$\textit{Improvement of reject ratio} = \frac{R_0 - R_{T_W}}{R_0} * 100\%$$

$$Acceptance\ ratio_{[W_1,W_2]T_w} = \frac{A_{[W_1,W_2]T_w}}{A_{[W_1,W_2]0}},\ W_2 > W_1$$

$$Average\ delay\ time = \frac{Amount\ of\ delay\ time}{Number\ of\ accepted\ requests}$$

where,

R_0 : the number of rejected requests without wait tolerance time.

R_{T_w} : the number of rejected requests with wait tolerance T_w.

$A_{[W_1,W_2],0}$: the accept rate for request without wait tolerance and the weight of the workload ranges from W_1 to W_2.

$A_{[W_1,W_2],T_w}$: The accept rate for requests with wait tolerance T_w and the weight of the workload ranges from W_1 to W_2.

4.2 Simulated Results

In our experiments, we compares two approaches to select candidate reservation: Minimum Load First (MLF) and Minimize Delay Time (MDT) as mentioned in the section 3.2.

Table 3: Characteristics of the advance reserved VOD system (T_w=0).

	Weights (range) of the mean arrival rate	
	40% ([40%,50%])	80% ([70%,80%])
# of requests	3875	7759
Reject ratio	4.23%	34.37%
Overloaded zone	[21:05,0:55]	[19:05,3:15]
$A_{[W_1,W_2],0}$	51.50%	24.01%

Table 3, lists characteristics of the advance reservation system for VOD service without wait tolerance. In the overloaded zone, the accumulated traffic load excesses the system capacity. As load increases, the overloaded zone becomes wider and off-peak hours become shorter. Furthermore, under system load the system reaches a very high reject rate (up to 76%) (i.e., weight in the range of [70%, 80%]).

Figure 8-9, demonstrate improvement of the rejection ratio is in proportional to the wait tolerance when weight=0.4 and 0.8. Figure 8 shows that under light system load, Maximum Load First (MLF) approach can achieve up to 100% improvement in reject ratio when the wait tolerance is 30 minutes. In Figures 8-9, the improvement of the reject ratio for Minimum Delay Time (MDT) approach become saturated. The MDT approach selects candidate reservations, with available resources in end portion. Consequently, the MDT approach uses more available resources than the others; hence the available resources disappear rapidly.

Figures 10-11, show the average delay for each request is less than 10 minutes as the wait tolerance reaches 30 minutes. The MDT has minimum average delay. In Figure 11 show that the average delay for MLF is invariant to system load. However, the average delay for the MDT approach is in proportional to the system load.

In Figures 12, as workload increases at range [0.7,0.8] and weight tolerance is 60 minutes, the acceptance ratio for MLF approaches 2.7. In the other word, the accept rate of the system reaches 65%.

5 Conclusion

Workload for VOD services greatly fluctuate over a given 24-hour period. The load would be low during the day, increase gradually through the evening and fall off during the night. Therefore, system resources for VOD services overload during peak hours and under-utilize during off-peak hours. We shows that significant access ratio gain can be achieved by means of request rescheduling. An elastic reservation model is proposed to support high adaptation for VOD services. With the time adaptation approach, releasable resources are presented as a multi-stage graph and then find optimal adaptation is found on the shortest path of the graph. We also investigates two cost functions to evaluate the reserved resources: Minimum Load First (MLF) and Minimize Delay Time (MDT). To assess the performance of the time adaptation approach, we conduct a series of experiments by simulating the network resources in a VOD system under various system loads. Our results show that MLF approach could reduce the reject ratio up to 100% under light system load. Moreover, improvement of the acceptance ratio for MLF reaches to 2.7.

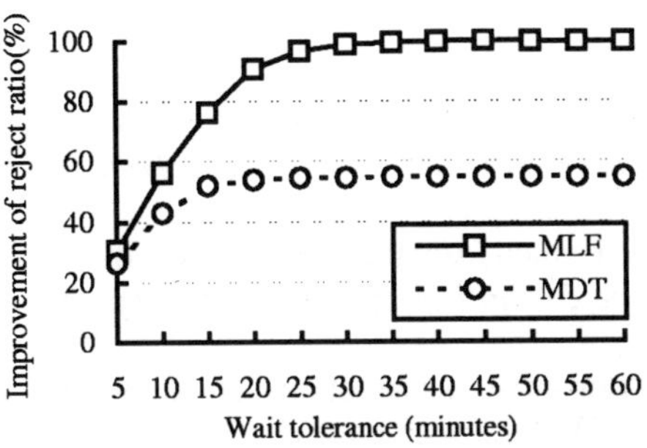

Figure 8. Improvement of reject ratio with weight 40%.

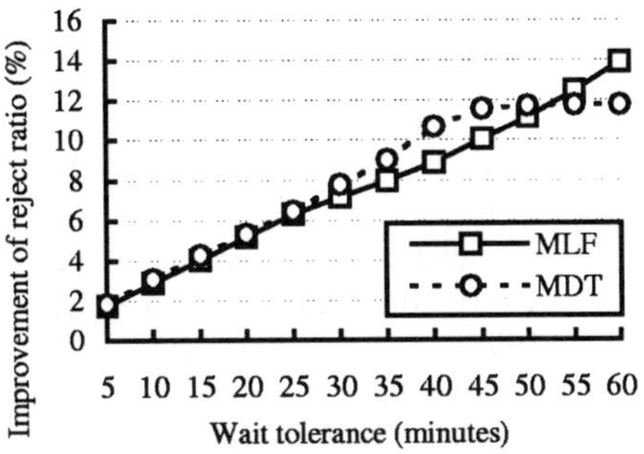

Figure 9. Improvement of reject ratio with weight 80%.

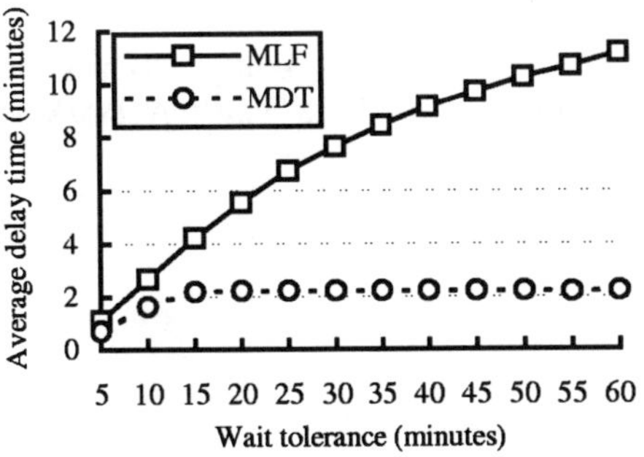

Figure 10. Average delay time with weight 40%.

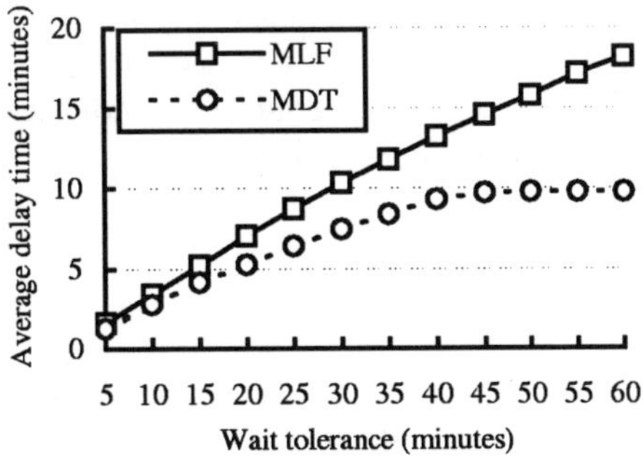

Figure 11. Average delay time with weight 80%.

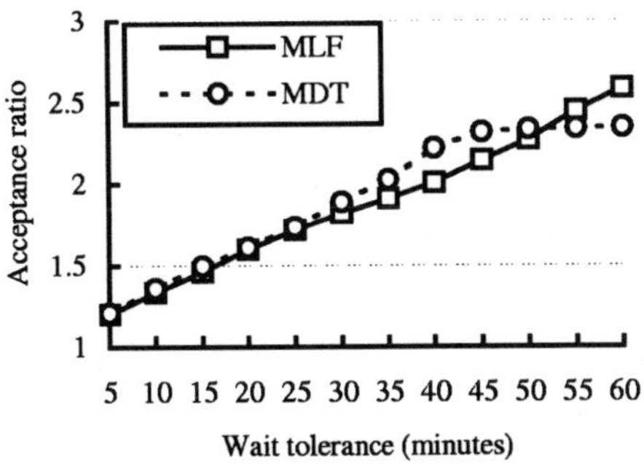

Figure 12. Acceptance ratio$_{[0.7, 0.8]}$ vs. wait tolerance.

References

1. M. Degermark, T. Köhler, S. Pink, and O. Schelén: "Advance Reservation for Predicted Service", *Proceedings of the 5th Int'l NOSSDAV Workshop*, April 1995.
2. D. Ferrari, A. Gupta, G. Ventre: "Distributed Advance Reservation of Real-Time Connections", *Proceedings of the 5th Int'l NOSSDAV Workshop*, April 1995.
3. A. Schill, S. Kühn, F. Breiter: "Resource Reservation in Advance in Heterogeneous Networks with Partial ATM Infrastructures", *INFOCOM '97*, Kobe, Japan.
4. H. Shachnai, P. S. Yu: "The role of wait tolerance in effective batching: A paradigm for multimedia scheduling schemes", IBM Research Division, T.J. Watson Research Center, Yorktown Heights, New York, RC 20038(88607) 04/17/95, Computer Science.
5. L. Wolf, L. Delgrossi, R. Steinmetz, S. Schaller, H. Wittig: "Issues of Reserving Resources in Advance", *Proceedings of the 5th Int'l NOSSDAV Workshop*, April 1995.

Algorithms

Storage-Efficient MPEG-2 Encoding

Jonathan C.L. Liu[1]
School of Electrical Engineering and Computer Science
Washington State University, Pullman, WA 99164

1.1 Introduction

Distributed video-on-demand systems start to become a reality in many cities across the world. With the high-speed network infrastructures, remote users are able to download digital audio and video anytime for listening and viewing. Uncompressed video files require huge amount of space, therefore efficient video compression schemes are essential to reduce the storage requirement. Motion Picture Expert Group (MPEG) compression scheme has recently emerged and became the dominating compression method at the current stage. The first generation of MPEG, MPEG-1, was proposed in early 90s for 1.5 Mbps videos with VHS quality. Just recently in late 90s, the second generation of MPEG family, MPEG-2, was proposed as a new standard for a range between 2 Mpbs to 40 Mbps with broadcasting quality.

One of the driving forces behind the demand for MPEG-2 videos is its higher quality compared to the MPEG-1 videos. The high quality is achieved by using much higher bit rates. Therefore, the storage requirement

*This work is supported in part by the NSF under Grant CDA-9422044.

for MPEG-2 videos is significantly higher than the MPEG-1 videos. For example, a typical MPEG-2 video with 90-min length can still occupy up to 5 Gbyte disk space. Therefore, reducing the storage requirement for MPEG-2 videos can be a great benefit to store more MPEG-2 video files within a video storage system. Our experimental results presented in this paper indicate that up to 43.8% reduction can be achieved with our proposed scheme compared to the conventional MPEG-2 scheme.

Both JPEG (Joint Picture Expert Group) and MPEG compression schemes are bases on Discrete Cosine Transform (DCT) algorithms. The major components of JPEG compression include (1) Preparation: A/D conversion and sub-sampling, (2) Discrete Cosine Transform (DCT), (3) Quantization, and (4) Entropy Encoding: Zigzag scan, Run-length and Huffman encoding. MPEG scheme further increase the compression ratios using motion estimations by eliminating the redundancy of similar images within a video shot. An I-frame (as *Intra-frame*) is encoded as a still image without using any motion estimation. A P-frame (as *Predicted*) is encoded using the motion estimation from the previous I-frame. A B-frame (as *Bidirectional*) is encoded using the motion estimation from the previous and future I- or P-frames. We assume the readers are familiar with the basics of the MPEG schemes. Further detailed information on MPEG basics can be found in [2; 4; 11; 16; 17].

Since MPEG-2 is targeted for the broadcasting-quality video [19], it has to deal with many different kinds of content. Typical broadcasting programs include news, sports, musical videos and films. These different video contents have different styles and characteristics. For example, news content usually have a pattern with the repeating mixtures of anchors and on-the-site video shots; Sport videos can be further subdivided into football, basketball, baseball, tennis and golf, which has also different styles individually. We started our investigation with the popular news videos in this paper. We intend to extend the study for further investigating other kinds of content such like sport videos. Nevertheless, even a news video can contain many independent video shots†. Depending on the different styles, the length of a video shot can be varied widely on the number of frames. The objects in a video shot may has different degrees of spatial im-

†In this paper, we use the 'shot' and 'scene' of a video file equivalently. We loosely define a shot of video file is a number of sequential frames which represent a unit of semantic meaning. In order to simplify the discussion, special effects between shots are ignored in this study.

age complexity. Some of the objects are easy to handle by MPEG (actually by the core DCT operation in MPEG), while other objects may be difficult. Various degrees of motion activity also potentially hinder the performance of MPEG compression. To the best of our knowledge, the impact of these factors has currently not been fully investigated in experimental settings.

The specifications of MPEG compression scheme leave an unanswered optimization problem on the determinations of the various parameters for the compression. For example, while the I, P and B frames are recommended, it is not clear what is the typical setting for a GOP (will be explained in the next paragraph) in order to achieve the best compression ratios. This process is usually left to the vendor implementation [11], but usually it is left to the users to specify this important parameter in the beginning of the encoding process. The users usually suffer from the bad results by try-and-error process in order to fine-tune the visual quality in the final compressed video files. Note that most MPEG compression schemes are performed off-line because the significant computation time needed for the compression process. Therefore, the trial-and-error process may take the users a couple days to encode a feature-length video file with acceptable results because of the usual 90-min video duration. In order to solve this problem, we need a systematic method to recommend the right parameters to the users for many video contents with different characteristics.

We started our investigation with two common parameters, (N, M), in the MPEG-2 scheme. N is the distance between any two I frames, and M is the distance between the reference frames (i.e., either between P and P frames or between I and P frames). These two parameters thus determine the Group-Of-Pattern (GOP) in the MPEG-2 scheme. A typical GOP is as I,B,B,P,B,B,P,B,B,P,B,B,I where the N=12 and M=3. The conventional MPEG scheme usually applies this GOP to the whole video files independently of the video characteristics. The mis-match of the shot boundary and GOP boundary is our particular concern since it will happen frequently by using the conventional MPEG compression method. From our experiences, if they are not coincident (usually they are not) in the current fixed GOP encoder, many consequenced effects on the encoding performance can happen. For instances, instead of using the right P and B frames, I frame may be chosen mistakenly resulting a larger-than-it-should-be size. The final compression ratio thus can be significantly lower than it should be if this scenario does happen frequently.

We thus developed an integrated MPEG-2 system which include the preprocessing methods to detect the shot boundaries, and to measure the degrees of motion activity and image complexity. We have particularly chosen the motion variance as the major factor of considerations. In addition, we propose to slightly augment the conventional MPEG-2 compression scheme in [1] to investigate the performance impact of our design considerations. Our idea laid upon one argument that *each shot should be assigned with different (N,M) combinations depending on the shot characteristics like degree of motion variances.* With this thought and our augmented MPEG-2 scheme, it becomes widely open on how to determine the proper GOP selection and assignments. Given a video shot's characteristics on the image complexity and motion activity after the preprocessing, should the system choose 2 GOPs for a particular shot? or should the system choose N=12, M=3? (why not N=20, M=4 or other combinations?) for a repetitive GOP? or should the system choose a single (and long) GOP for this shot? These questions are important since the answers/recommendations directly benefit the end-users. In the current practice, these questions are usually left to the end users to determine. Therefore, a systematic study on possibly answering these questions is very valuable.

We have presented the problem nature, and analyzed the expected ratio reductions on the design parameters of (N,M). We have shown that the sizes of compressed MPEG-2 videos can be reduced by increasing the values of N. However, the ratio of reductions is not always linear with the values of N. It is predicted (and later verified by the experimental results) that when the values of N are relative small (e.g., up to 32) the ratios of reduction can be significant. We also predicted that increasing the values of M should be able to reduce the number of P frames while at the same time increasing the number of B frames. Because of this behavior, the reduction on the compressed sizes is not always guaranteed. Depending on the sizes of P and B frames, and the decreasing and increasing numbers of P and B frames, increasing the values of M may potentially increase the compressed sizes instead of decreasing the compressed sizes. Nevertheless, by joint considerations with both N and M parameters together, we expect that a close-to 50% reduction ratio on the compressed sizes is quite possible.

With the implemented proposed MPEG-2 scheme and a news video with 903 uncompressed video frames, we have justified the predicted outcomes from the analysis. We have observed the performance improvement on the reduction ratio up to 43.8% compared to the conventional MPEG-2 scheme with fixed GOP. The experimental results also verified the (steady) gain by increasing the number of N. Most of the shots in the test video did experience the positive reduction of the compressed sizes when the values of M was increased up to 5. However, one shot with complex special effects did indicate the counter-effect (i.e., the compressed size was increased instead of reduction) when the M was increased to 5. In addition to make the final recommendations on the proper (N, M) parameters on each shot, we illustrate the correlation between the reduction ratios and the degrees of motion variances. These findings can be served as guild-lines for multimedia system designers.

For the last several years, we have observed a significant research effort on improving the MPEG-2 encoding performance. For examples, Chan and *et al* in [5] investigated the different block-matching techniques. Because the encoding process is time consuming, parallel solutions such like [3; 20] were proposed for the possible real-time MPEG-2 encoding. Hardware solutions were also proposed recently as in [6]. To the best of our knowledge, our study is perhaps the first one to explore the relationships between the nature of video shot and the proper setting of the GOP parameters. The most-related previous study is from [9]. However, they only considered one parameter, and the potential gain on the reduction ratios of the compressed sizes was not reported (the authors only concerned on the PSNR performance). Thus, our study presented here paper should impose a great contribution.

The rest of this paper is organized as follows. We introduce the problem statement in Section 2. Further discussion on the preprocessing methods is addressed in Section 3. Section 4 provides the analysis on the possible effects on choosing the (N, M) parameters. We then describe the experimental performance measurement and discussion the correlation between reduction ratios and degrees of motion variances in Section 5. Finally, the conclusion is included in the last section.

1.2 Problem Statement

We have found that MPEG compression scheme left a very big room on optimizing the system performance. Performance tradeoffs certainly exist on the visual quality and achieved compression ratios. It is also exciting to note that by exploring the characteristics of a video shot, we may be able to find a great balance between these performance tradeoffs.

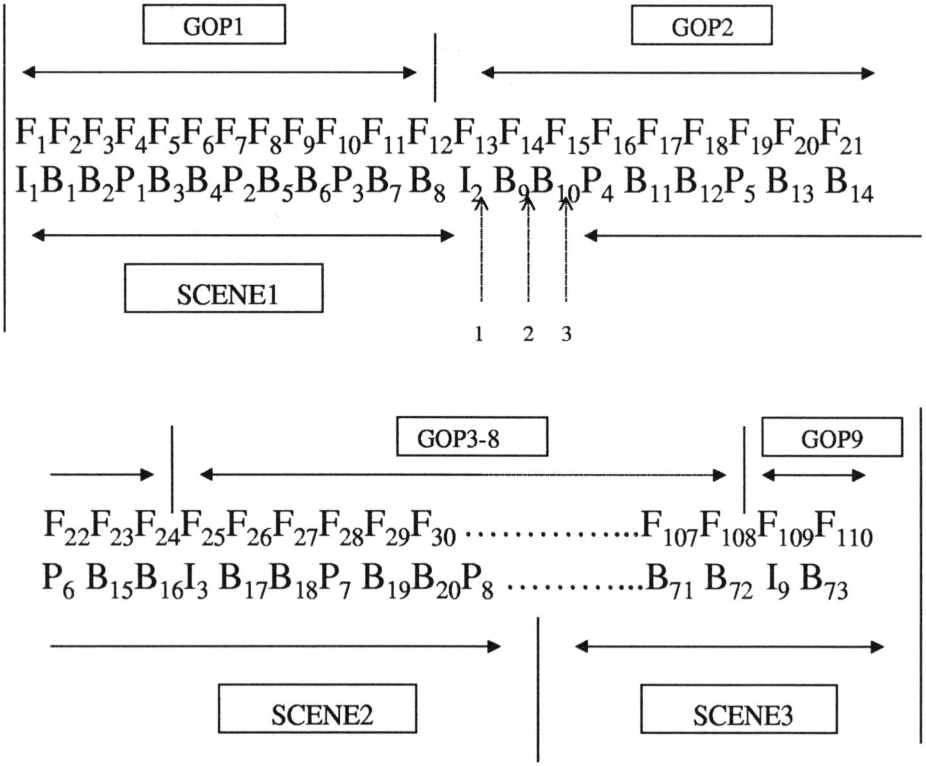

Fig. 1.1 An Example to Illustrate Current Fixed GOP Scheme

We consider an example in Figure 1.1 to demonstrate the possible image degradation scenarios at each scene boundary with current fixed GOP encoders. In Figure 1.1, each GOP consists of an I frame, three P frames, and eight B frames. MPEG specification for N : M ratio is as follows. While N represents the distance between two adjacent I frames, M represents the distance between two adjacent reference frames (I or P). A fixed 12 : 3

(N:M) ratio is applied in this video sequence. Imagine that the first video shot is terminated between Frame 13 and 14 (i.e., the position labeled as '1' in the Figure 1.1). Let us analyze the consequences of this mismatching:

- It can be observed that Frame 13 (i.e., F_{13}) will be encoded as an I frame (i.e., I_2). Since I frames are encoded independently, the resulting I_2 will have a larger size than the other alternatives such as P and B frames. The compression ratio thus can be low than it supposed to be if this scenario does happen frequently.
- The F_{16} coded as P_4 does not obtain a benefit from ME/MC. This is because there is no tight image correlation between F_{13} and F_{16}. F_{16} (P_4) thus generates more encoded output.
- Video frames such as F_{14} (B_9) will be sacrificed on bit assignments. Since the F_{14} is the beginning of the next video shot. This mismatching causes image degradation of the frame, B_9. Note that instead of having the F_{14} encoded as the bigger I frame, it was encoded as B frame with a smaller bit budget caused by the future P frame. This effect can propagate to all of the following frames which reference F_{13} (I_2) and F_{16} (P_4).

Intuitively, F_{14} should be encoded as an I frame (i.e., I_2) to reduce prediction error propagation at the new scene. It will increase the compression ratio and at the same time prevent the quality degradation. In the next sections, we propose our shot-dependent GOP allocation. The nature of our proposed scheme causes the resulting encoder to become VBR-like, where image degradation does not propagate to the next frames because VBR encoders do not control the bit budget with a feed-back loop.

1.3 Preprocessing Methods

Depending on the scene characteristics, to improve image quality, we place proper picture types and assign a shot-dependent N : M ratio. However, some preprocessing tasks are implied in order to carry out the performance evaluation of our proposed scheme.

We consider an integrated system as depicted in Figure 1.2 to complete the proposed experiments. An 900-frame uncompressed video was captured using special video equipment to be stored on a hard drive. System then applies the ***scene boundary detection algorithm*** to determine number of shots

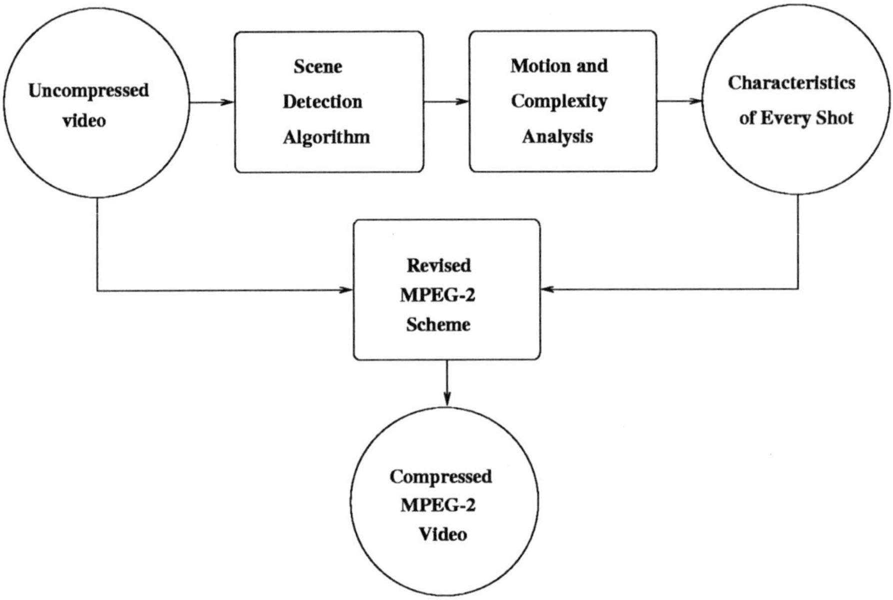

Fig. 1.2 An Integrated System to Determine GOP Allocations

and the boundaries. The results along with the uncompressed video were further analyzed on the degrees of image complexity and motion variances for video shot. The characteristics of each video shot are then saved as shown in Table 1.2. All these analyzed characteristics in addition to the uncompressed video will be processed by our revised MPEG-2 to augment the shot information, and choose the proper parameters for the encoding process. Note that our revised MPEG-2 scheme can be compatible with the conventional MPEG-2 video bit-stream since we only use the *session layer* (which remain unused for conventional MPEG-2 bit-streams) to tag the shot information.

1.3.1 *Scene Boundary Detection Using Motion Estimation*

Using the basis from [10; 12; 13; 22; 23], we have created our own scene boundary detection method. Our method works as the following: all video pictures in sequence are set as a P frame except the first I frame. Forward ME/MC is processed for the whole sequence. If the current macro-block does not find a similar macro-block from previous picture, it is encoded as an intra-macro-block. However, the current macro-block finds a similar macro-block from the previous picture, it is encoded as a forward reference macro-block. If the ratio of intra-macroblocks to the entire macroblocks in a picture is above a given threshold, we assume that there is a scene boundary.

We have applied the detection process to our test video sequence. If the threshold is larger than 60, then it is considered to have a new scene. This method is accurate in general for abrupt scene changes. It is not affected by camera motion for detecting the scene boundary. This method gives us scene boundary information and valuable information to measure image complexity and motion activity.

1.3.2 *Measurement of Motion Activity and Image Complexity*

During the scene boundary detection process, the following two components are measured - (1) motion activity and (2) image complexity.

Motion activity can be measured in two different ways:

- Average size of motion vectors in each picture.
- The ratio of motion macroblocks to the entire macroblocks

Each motion vector for a macro-block and number of motion vectors for each picture are computed and quantified as a picture motion activity measurement unit.

The motion vector size for the coded intra-macroblock is set to the maximum search window size because it does not find a similar macroblock within the search window size of the reference picture. We can interpret it as an active macroblock. A motion vector for each macroblock represents two directions, horizontal and vertical motion displacement. We have measured the average horizontal motion vector and the average vertical motion vector of each picture. We have found that the first method has some degree of flaw. In general, several macroblocks with object movement can be observed within a frame while most background macroblocks do not change. Therefore, large motion displacement of several macroblocks can be interpreted as a very active scene.

We thus adopted the second method to compute motion activity of each picture. Instead of computing motion displacement, we can compute the ratio of motion macroblocks to the entire macroblocks in a picture. A large motion activity because of the camera motion can be successfully measured by the second method. We thus measured the motion variance which represents the motion fluctuation within the scene. The image variance of a spatial domain can be measured as an unit of coding difficulty. High variance represents that the image is difficult to compress, and we define variance as the following:

$$Variance = \frac{1}{W*H}\sum_{i=0}^{i=W-1}\sum_{j=0}^{j=H-1}[x(i,j)]^2 - \left[\frac{1}{W*H}\sum_{i=0}^{i=W-1}\sum_{j=0}^{j=H-1}x(i,j)\right]^2 \quad (1.1)$$

W is the width of a picture, H is the height of a picture, and $x(i,j)$ is a pixel value at the position (i,j). The range of $x(i,j)$ is 0 to 255. Variance of input video sequence can be obtained using Equation 1.1.

We have applied the motion analysis to our test video on the variance of a residual image after ME/MC has been performed. Table 1.2 illustrates the motion activity, image complexity and motion variance for the analysis of our test video shots. We will discuss them in details later.

1.4 Proposed Methods to Improve MPEG Performance

With the preprocessing in place, we were able to find the shots which are difficult to compress because of the complexity from the nature of images. The analysis later in this section gives us some realistic expections on the possible outcomes.

The shot-dependent GOP scheme is thus proposed in this section. It is our observation that many mismatches could occur on the MPEG-2 encoding process by using current fixed N : M ratio encoders. These mismatches cause the decrease on the compression ratio and degradation in the decompressed video quality. In a higher level, the bit budget is not efficiently distributed based on scene complexity. For example, image quality is degraded at the high-motion shots while the encoder may spend unnecessary bit budge on the stationary shots. Ideally each shot should be assigned various N : M ratios depending on the shot complexity and degree of movement. For instance, if a shot has high motion activity, a small GOP size is needed and large GOP sizes should be assigned for stationary shots.

Figure 1.3 illustrates an example of using our proposed scheme for the same example given earlier in Figure 1.1. Note that the boundary of a

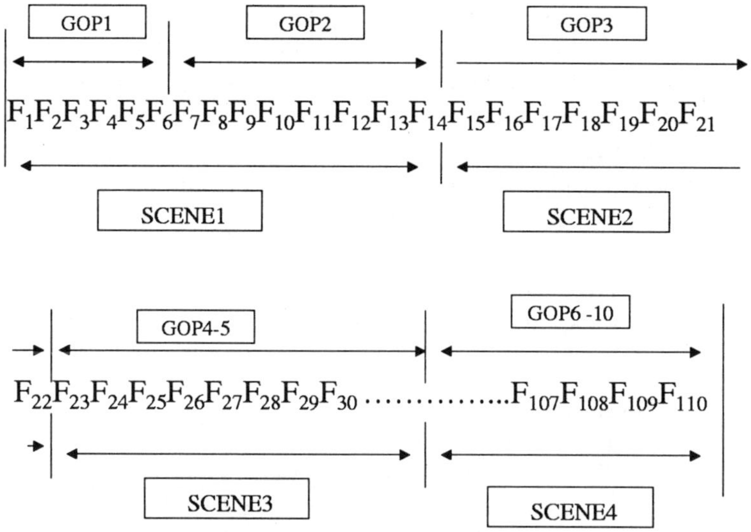

Fig. 1.3 An Example for Shot-Dependent GOP Allocation Scheme

GOP is now matched to the boundary of a shot. Therefore, the decrease of compression ratio and quality degradation caused by the mismatch can be avoided. For example, the first shot (labeled as 'SCENE 1' in the Figure 1.1) can have a high degree of motion during the first part, and then low degree of motion during the second part. Thus, the best GOP assignment is perhaps to have two GOPs line up in the first shot where the degree of motion starts to change. If the second shot contains mainly the stationary scene, perhaps the best GOP assignment is to have one with many B frames in order to achieve larger compression ratios. Shot 3 and 4 may require some repetitions on the medium sizes of GOPs.

Given this kind of flexibility, it becomes a widely open issue on how to determine the proper GOP selection and assignments. Given a video shot's characteristics on the image complexity and the motion activity after the preprocessing, should the system choose 2 GOPs for this shot? or should the system choose N=12, M=3? (why not N=20, M=4 or other combinations?) for a repetitive GOP? or should the system choose a single (and long) GOP for this shot? These questions are important since the answers benefit the end-users. In the current practice, these questions are usually left to the end users to determine. Therefore, a systematic study on answering these questions is very valuable. We will first analyze the impact on changing the N or/and M on the compression ratios.

There are many factors which affect the encoded MPEG-2 sizes. The variables that we apply in our analysis are listed in Table 1.1.

Notation	Meaning
L	Number of frames in a shot
N	Distance between two adjacent I frames
M	Distance between two adjacent reference frames
S_i	Average encoded size of all I-frames
S_p	Average encoded size of all P-frames
S_b	Average encoded size of all B-frames
S_L	Total size of the encoded frames
NUM_i	Number of I frames in a shot
NUM_p	Number of P frames in a shot
NUM_b	Number of B frames in a shot

Table 1.1 Notation and Meaning of Variables Used in the Analysis

Without loss of generality, we assume that $L = n * N$ where n=1,2,3, ... and the type of picture is not significantly changed because there are no scene changes in an individual shot. Since a MPEG sequence has three types of frames‡, the number of each frame type can be calculated by the following three equations.

$$NUM_i = \frac{L}{N} \tag{1.2}$$

$$NUM_p = (\frac{L}{N}) * (\frac{N}{M} - 1) \tag{1.3}$$

‡We are aware about the possible existence of D frames, but choose to ignore it in this paper to simplify the discussions.

$$NUM_b = L - NUM_i - NUM_p = L - \frac{L}{M} \tag{1.4}$$

The size of a compressed shot thus can be represented as follows:

$$S_L = NUM_i * S_i + NUM_p * S_p + NUM_b * S_b \tag{1.5}$$

By replacing the NUM_i, NUM_p and NUM_b from Equation (2)-(4), we can obtain the size of a compressed shot as follows:

$$S_L = (\frac{L}{N}) * S_i + ((\frac{L}{N}) * (\frac{L}{M} - 1)) * S_p + (L - \frac{L}{M}) * S_b \tag{1.6}$$

We assume that these compressed video frames all come from an independent shot. Therefore, it is reasonable to assume that the average sizes of the S_i, S_p and S_b will be constants. Since L is also fixed, we can analyze the impact on S_L by adjusting the values of N and M. Note that the interactions of S_L with the N and M can be complex.

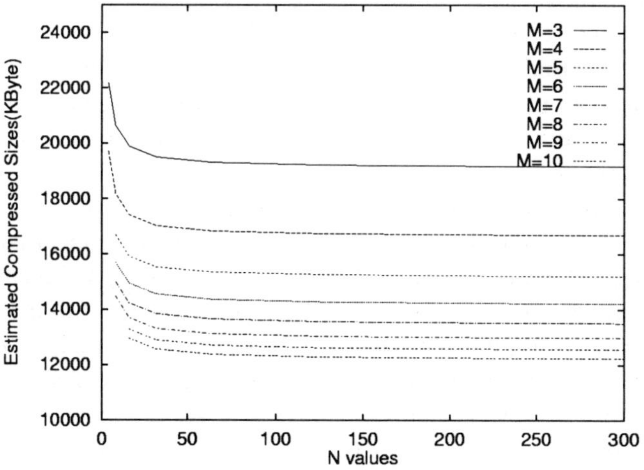

Fig. 1.4 The effect of changing values of N and M on the estimated compressed video sizes.

Figure 1.4 depicts the impact of increasing the values of N and M on the compressed sizes of a single shot. In order to illustrate the effects on using large values of N and M, the number of frames is set to be 1024. The average sizes of I,P and B frames are set according to our experimental traces. The purpose of this analysis is to identify the performance trend of the compressed sizes. Some of the trends can be identified as the following:

- If the values of M is fixed (e.g., $M = 3$), it can be expected that the compressed size can be reduced by increasing values of N. Since the distance of I frames is increased, the total number of frames contains less I frames but more P frames. The number of B frames remains close to the same number because of the fixed M values.
- The degree of reduction, however, indicates an interesting curve. When the values of N are relative small, the degree of reduction can be significant. For example, for $M = 3$, doubling the values of N from 4 to 8 will reduce the compressed size with a 7% reduction (i.e., from 22,186 KByte to 20,650 KByte). Similarly, a 3% reduction is achieved if the value of N is doubled to 16, while a 1% reduction is further achieved if the value of N is doubled from 16 to 32.
- For the values of N greater than 32, less than 1% reduction is expected, thus the compressed size remains to be only slightly reduced (i.e., close to flat curve in the figure). Nevertheless, if we increase the value of N from 4 directly to 32, a potential 15% reduction is expected.
- The effect on increasing the values of M also can be significant. While keeping the value of N fixed with a constraint that $M \leq N$ (e.g., $N = 64$), we will be able to analyze the impact of compressed sizes by increasing the values of M. Since the effect of increasing N becomes insignificant when the N is greater than 32, we choose to use $N = 64$ for the illustration. When the values of M is increased from 3 to 4, the compressed sizes are reduced from 19,306 KByte to 16,832 KByte (thus, a 14.6% reduction is expected).
- It is our belief that increasing the values of M reduces the number of P frames, and at the same time increases the number of B frames. Since the size of B frames is less than the size of P frames, reduction is feasible (i.e., reducing the size of $NUM_p * S_p + NUM_b * S_b$).
- A similar performance trend can be expected if the values of M is increased from 4 to 5 (e.g., 9.6% reduction), and from 5 to 6 (e.g.,

6.8% reduction). However, it is observed that the degrees of reduction are gradually lowered, and the gain becomes less significant. If we also consider to set the value of M equal to 6 instead of 3, we will expect to have about 33% to 34% reduction when N is 16, 32 or 64.

- Our observations indicate that changing the values of N will not affect the number of B frames, and therefore may cause less size reduction than changing the values of M. However, the reduction factors by changing M depends on the size of $NUM_p * S_p + NUM_b * S_b$. It does not guarantee that the total size reduction is always consistent. When the increasing size of $NUM_b * S_b$ (because of the increase of NUM_b) outperforms that decreasing size of $NUM_p * S_p$ (because of the reduction of the NUM_p), the total size of S_L can increase instead of continuing the trend of size reduction.

If we compare the combination of ($N = 4, M = 3$) with the ($N = 64, M = 6$), Figure 1.4 suggests that perhaps the reduction factor can be close to 55% (e.g., reducing the sizes from 22,186 KByte to 14,357 KByte) with joint considerations of N and M. Thus the analysis results are very promising in indicating that our proposed scheme should be able to take the advantage of the significant size reduction.

It seems that the optimal answers exist while using as large a M and N values as possible to obtain the maximal reduction. However, the compression gain is also dependent on the image complexity and motion activity (thus making the preprocessing on these two characteristics essential and valuable). Therefore, a fundamental research issue for an integrated compression system is to determine what kinds of (N, M) combinations should be adopted for different video content after the preprocessing. If this functionality can be achieved, end users will not be asked to input the (N, M) parameters and perform repeated time-consuming processes to generate the smallest file with acceptable quality. Therefore, our analysis and experimental results later presented in this paper can be classified as a pilot study of integrated compression systems. Note that our proposed method also can be further combined with the other schemes such as the quantilization tables for further reducing the total compressed file size.

1.5 Experimental Performance Results

Designing the experiments on the MPEG-2 compressions requires a careful examinations of the possible effects on the visual quality. While the subjective visual quality is always the final goal, we need some objective measurement in terms of objective descriptions. PSNR is thus used to measure image distortion and is given in dB in the following equation:

$$PSNR = 10\log_{10}(255 * 255/MSE) \tag{1.7}$$

Where

$$MSE = \frac{1}{W * H}\sum_{i=0}^{i=W-1}\sum_{j=0}^{j=H-1}[O(x+i, y+j) - R(x+i, y+j)]^2 \tag{1.8}$$

$O(x+i, y+j)$ is a pixel at the distance (i, j) with original macroblock at the position (x, y) and $R(x+i, y+j)$ is a pixel with the relative distance (i, j) to the reconstructed macroblock at the position (x, y).

We started our experiments from a common news content first. It is our intention that future efforts will be continued for other types of videos such as drama and sports videos. We chose a news video sequence with 8 shots with 903 video frames in total. Each video frame is captured from the S-VHS player with 352 by 240 pixel resolution. No compression is performed on the video frames while the frames are captured.

1.5.1 *Analysis on the Image Complexity and Motion Activity*

In order to understand the characteristics of each individual video shot, we have applied the pre-processing methods (introduced earlier in Section 3) on the test video.

Table 1.2 lists the motion activity and image complexity of every shot in the test video obtained from the pre-processing routine. The definitions that we used for *motion activity*, *image complexity* and *motion variance* were defined in Section 3. In general, the motion activity represents the percentage of moving macroblocks at each scene. Image complexity then indicated the variance of a residual image after forward ME/MC has been performed while the motion variance represents the motion fluctuation in

Table 1.2 Measurement of Motion Activity and Image Complexity

Shot	Frames	Numbers of Frames	Motion Activity (%)	Image Complexity	Motion Variance
1	0 - 183	184	11	261	70.47
2	184 - 432	249	28	67	128.85
3	433 - 466	34	10	61	29.5
4	467 - 521	55	5	68	6.7
5	522 - 563	42	24	81	20.6
6	564 - 702	139	15	67	36.22
7	703 - 740	38	18	80	97.4
8	741 - 903	163	5	49	0.9

the same scene.

To the best of our knowledge, there are no commonly agreed upon quantative ranges to determine the values of of high and low motion activity, image complexity and motion variance. Therefore, the values only represent some references to estimate the experimental results. For example, the 1st shot seems to have the largest image complexity (i.e., 261) when compared to the rest of the shots. Thus, we should expect that the compression improvement on the first shot will perhaps be moderate because of this unique characteristic of the first shot. The 2nd shot indicates the largest motion variance (e.g., 128.85) compared to the rest of the shots. On the other side, the 8th shot seems to have the lowest image complexity, motion activity and variance. Thus, we will probably get a better compression gain on the 8th shot.

1.5.2 *Detailed Investigations on the First Shot*

With these analyzed characteristics, we started the experimental investigations on the 1st shot. The goal is to explore different combinations of the (N, M) parameters as in the analysis, and to verify the same performance trend between the experimental and analytical results. The experiments were performed over a PC with a Pentium 166 MHz CPU. Our MPEG-2 software encoder was revised from [1].

The experimental results indicate that the analytical expectations on the effect of increasing the values of N and M are correct. The detailed observations are listed below:

- As predicted by the analysis, the compressed size was reduced by

Table 1.3 Size of encoded bit-streams using different combinations of (N, M) for the 1st shot

Case	N : M ratio Ratio	I : P : B ratio Ratio	SIZE (Bytes)	Average PSNR (dB)	% of Total Reduction
1	12 : 3	1 : 3 : 8	256,151 Bytes	**41.53**	NA
2	15 : 3	1 : 4 : 10	247,658 Bytes	41.50	3.3
3	30 : 3	1 : 9 : 20	220,871 Bytes	41.44	13.7
4	60 : 3	1 : 19 : 40	207,325 Bytes	41.41	19.1
5	120 : 3	1 : 39 : 80	199,244 Bytes	41.11	22.2
6	15 : 5	1 : 2 : 10	238,352 Bytes	41.22	6.9
7	20 : 5	1 : 3 : 16	226,066 Bytes	41.24	11.7
8	30 : 5	1 : 5 : 24	212,311 Bytes	41.17	17.1
9	60 : 5	1 : 11 : 48	199,082 Bytes	41.15	22.3
10	120 : 5	1 : 23 : 96	**190,673** Bytes	41.12	25.6

increasing values of N. We define the total reduction as the reduction ratio compared to the size in Case 1. With the fixed value of $M = 3$, we have observed that the compressed bit-stream has been reduced from 256,151 bytes to 247,658 bytes (i.e., 3.3% reduction) when the value of N is increased from 12 to 15. We also observed another 10% reduction when the sizes of N is doubled to 30.

- The degree of reduction, as predicted in the analysis curve, indicates a slower rate gradually. For example, for $M = 3$, doubling the values of N from 30 to 60 reduced the compressed size with a further 5.5% reduction (i.e., 19.1% for the total reduction). Similarly, only 3.2% of further reduction is achieved when the value of N is doubled to 120 (i.e., 22.1% for the total reduction). This trend is predicted by the analysis, and justified by the experimental results presented here.
- Since the length of the 1st shot is less than 240, frames, we were not able to generate the experimental results by doubling N to 240. However, it is expected that the compressed size will have only a slight reduction. (i.e., as indicated by the flat curve in the analysis). If we consider to increase the value of N from 4 directly to 120, a 22.2% reduction is achieved.
- The effect of increasing the values of M also generated further reductions. As indicated by the matching cases in the experimental results, we have observed a 3.3% to 3.4% reductions between Case

5 and Case 10, between Case 9 and Case 4, and between Case 8 and Case 3. Therefore, if we also consider to set the value of M to 5 instead of 3, we see that we achieved about 25.6% total reduction when N is 120.

- Since the 1st shot has large image complexity, the experimental results are a little different compared to our prediction. Since the image complexity is always high, the I frames require large bit budgets. Because of the already-high complexity, increasing the value of N (thus increasing the number of P frames) seems to be more effective than increasing the values of M (i.e., increasing the number of B frames).
- Note that the PSNR is not significantly affected by the size reductions. Although decreasing (which is expected), the loss on the PSNR was 0.41 for $N = 120, M = 5$. The rest of (N, M) combinations has even less loss on the PSNR. This promising result indicted that with proper sizes of N and M, we can achieve a higher compression ratio with reasonable quality.

1.5.3 *Extensions to Multiple Shots*

In general, the rest of shots in our test video follows the same performance trend as we introduced earlier for the 1st shot. However, the degrees are different. As we analyze later in this section, it seems to us that the potential gain is directly coupled with the degree of motion variances. For illustration purpose, we only discuss two shots, Shot 2 with the motion variance of 128.85 and Shot 8 with the motion variance of 0.9. These two shots actually represent two extreme cases in our test video since the 2nd shot has the largest degree of motion variance among the 8 shots, while the 8th shot has the smallest degree of motion variance. Figure 1.5 depicts the size reduction on the compressed video bit-streams with different combinations of the (N, M) for these two shots.

- The close-to-flat curve in the left figure indicates that the 2nd shot has a difficult content for the compression algorithm to work with. Therefore, the maximum gain on the reduction of the compressed sizes is only 10.8%.
- Another interesting behavior that we did not expect from the analysis was the surprising effects on increasing the values of M from 3

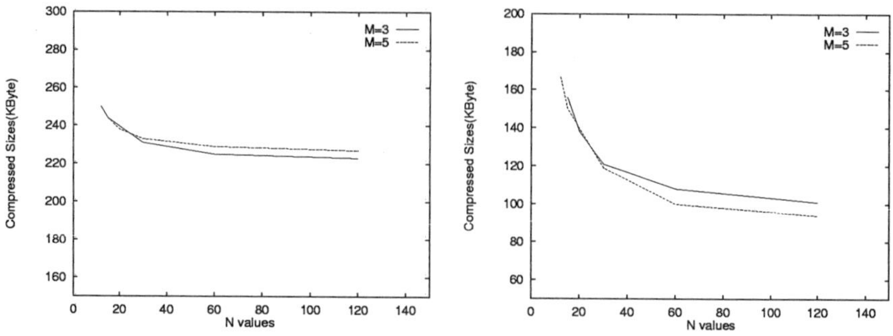

Fig. 1.5 The experimental results of the compressed video sizes for the 2nd shot (left figure) and the 8th shot (right figure).

to 5. Instead of further reducing the sizes, we have observed that the sizes of compressed video actually increased when the values of N are greater than 24. We further analyzed the contents of the second shot manually, and realized that there were fade-in/fade-out special effects within this shot. This special effect generates the large values of motion activity and variance. Therefore, the effect of changing the values of M seems to be significant on the selections of the P and B frames. Optimizing the proposed schemes for adapting the special effects is currently beyond the scope of this paper, but is certainly worthy to pursuit in the future.

- The 8th shot suggests that a very significant reduction can be made if the degree of motion variance is small. The deep curve in the right figure indicated quite a significant reduction. The deep the slope shows a large degree of reduction. The effect on the reduction is particularly significant when the values of N are less than 60. We observed a maximum 43.8% reduction on the compressed size with the combination of $(N = 120, M = 5)$ for this shot, and the loss of dB in PSNR was 0.004.

Table 1.4 lists the final recommendations on selecting the the proper combinations of (N,M) for every shot in the test video.

Table 1.4 Final recommendations on selecting the proper combinations of (N, M)

Shot	Frame	# of Frames	Suggested (N, M)	% of Total Reduction	# of dB lost using PSNR
1	0 - 183	184	120:5	25.6%	0.417
2	184 - 432	249	120:3	10.8%	0.247
3	433 - 466	34	30:5	26.8%	0.150
4	467 - 521	55	55:3	35.6%	0.140
5	522 - 563	42	42:5	21.1%	0.870
6	564 - 702	139	120:5	32.4%	0.514
7	703 - 740	38	20:5	16.6%	0.116
8	741 - 903	163	120:5	43.8%	0.004

Depending on the degrees of motion variances and image complexities, the reduction ratios compared to the conventional fixed (N,M) method are within a range between 10.8% and 43.8%. Our proposed scheme indicates promising results. The impact of choosing the right combinations of (N,M) was illustrated by the analysis and verified by the experimental implementation and evaluation. It turned out that increasing the values of N seems to have a reliable performance improvement on the reduction of the compressed sizes. The change of M can further reduce the compressed sizes. However, caution needs to be exercised on the possible counter-effect, which is the increase in the compressed sizes.

Many valuable lessons are gained from the preliminary results. For instance, the achieved reduction ratios on the compressed sizes seems to have a strong correlation with the degrees of motion variances. Figure 1.6 depicts the possible correlation between the reduction ratios and the degrees of motion variances for our test video.

The trend indicates that when the degree of motion variance is less than 40, a reasonably large reduction ratios between 25% to 45% can be expected. This potential benefit can save from 1.25 GByte to 2.4 GByte disk space given a typical 8-Mbps and 90-min MPEG-2 video with 5 Gbyte storage requirement. A 25% to 30% reduction ratio can be still expected when the degree of motion variance is between 40 and 80. When the motion variance is high (e.g., greater than 80), a reduction ratio between 10% to 15% can be expected. This guild-line can potentially benefit the multimedia system designers and architects on planning the distributed system design for storing the MPEG-2 compressed videos.

Certainly the gaining on one performance aspect sometimes leads to

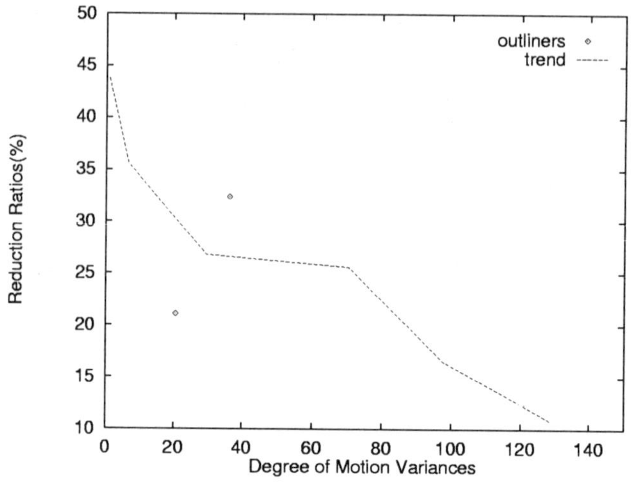

Fig. 1.6 The correlation between the degree of motion variances and the achieved reduction ratios.

paying the consequences on the potential loss on other performance aspects. For example, our proposed scheme has the potential loss (although minor) on the PSNR. Another affected performance factor is on the required time to compress the MPEG-2 videos. At the current stage, we are still focusing on off-line compression and hoping that our proposed scheme can efficiently compress the MPEG-2 videos with large reduction ratios and high PSNR. More guidelines will be recommended when we further investigate different kinds of contents (e.g., sports and music videos). It is a challenging task to apply all these considerations that requires a real-time MPEG-2 compression.

1.6 Concluding Remarks

By applying our proposed GOP allocation scheme, we were able to achieve a higher compression rate. Our augmented MPEG-2 system was able to reduce disk storage requirement up to 43.8% while maintaining the loss of the PSNR less than 0.8 dB when compared to current MPEG-2 scheme. The distance between two reference frames is a very important element in obtaining a high PSNR value or a high compression ratio. With a large size N, and often used P frames, a higher compression ratio can be achieved with reasonable quality. If the distance between two reference frames is too large, the temporal image correlation is reduced. The proper distance between two reference frames is found between 3 and 5 frames in most shots. We have observed a strong correlation between the reduction ratios and the degrees of motion variances. Many future directions are possible: (1) Generalization of the guidelines to different types of video content; (2) Incorporation of the bit-rate control mechanisms in the MPEG-2 scheme [8; 21]; and (3) Adaptation to the networking considerations [7; 14; 15; 18].

Acknowledgment

The author is grateful to Dr. Roberto Bamberger (now with Microsoft) and Dr. Tom Fischer at Washington State University for helpful comments on the early draft of this paper; Professor Kim Singhrs at Washington State University for helping us to capture the S-VHS video into the hard disks. The experiments were performed by Mr. Jeongbae Min within the School of EECS while he was a MSCS student at Washington State University.

Bibliography

MPEG Software Simulation Group (1997) "MPEG2 Video codec Version 1.2", *http://www.mpeg.org/~tristan/MPEG/MSSG.*

(1994) "Generic Coding of Moving Pictures and Associated Audio", *Draft International Standard ISO/IEC 13818-2.*

Akramullah, M. and Ahmad, I. and Liou, L. (1995) "A Data-Parallel Approach for Real-Time MPEG-2 Video Encoding", *Journal of Parallel and Distributed Computing,* 129–146.

Bhaskaran, V. and Konstantinides, K. (1995) "Image and Video Compression standards", *Kluwer Academic Publishers.*

Chan, E. and Rodriguez, A. and Gandhi, R. and Panchanathan, S. (1994) "Experiments on Block-Matching Techniques for Video Coding", *ACM Journal of Multimedia Systems,* **2**,228-241.

Chiu, Y. and Chen, L and Lee, Y. and Ku, C. (1996) "A 3-Step Search Motion Estimation Chip for MPEG-2 Applications", *SPIE Digital Compression Technology and Systems for Video Communications,* **2952**,608-616.

Kawashima, M. and Chen, C. and Jeng, F. and Singhai, S. (1993) "Adaptation of the MPEG Video-Coding Algorithm to Network Application", *IEEE Trans. Circuits and Systems for Video Technology,* 261–269.

Keesman, G. and Shah, I and Klein-Gunnewiek, R. (1995) "Bit-rate control for MPEG encoders", *Signal Processing: Image Communication,* **6**, 545–560.

Lauzon, D. and Vincent, A. and Wang, L. (1996) "Performance Evaluation of MPEG-2 Video Coding for HDTV", *IEEE Transactions on Broadcasting,* **42**, 88-94.

Lee, Y. and Lee, J. and Chang, H. and Nam, J. (1997) "A new Scene Change Control Scheme based on Pseudo-skipped Picture", *SPIE* **3024**, 159–166.

LeGall, D. (1991) "MPEG: A Video Compression Standard for Multimedia Applications", *Communication of ACM,* **34**,47-58.

Liu, H. and Zick, G. (1995) "Automatic Determination of Scene Changes in MPEG Compressed Video", *IEEE Int'l Sym Circuits and Systems.* Seattle.

Meng, J. and Juan, Y. and Chang, S. (1995) "Scene Change Detection in a MPEG Compressed Video Sequence", *SPIE*, **2419**, 14–25.

Pancha, P. and Zarki, M. (1993) "Bandwidth-Allocation Schemes for Variable-bit-rate MPEG Sources in ATM Networks", *IEEE Trans. Circuits and Systems for Video Technology*, 190–198.

Perkins, M. and Arnstein, D. (1995) "Statistical Multiplexing of Multiple MPEG-2 Video Programs in a Single Channel", *SMPTE Journal*, 596–599.

Puri, A. (1993) "Video Coding Using the MPEG-2 Compression Standard", *SPIE*, **2094**, 1701–1713.

Rao, K. and Hwang, J. (1996) "Techniques and Standards for image Video and Audio Coding", *Prentice Hall*.

Reininger, D. and Kwok, W. (1994) "Rate Control for VBR MPEG Video on Local Area Network", *SPIE*, **2188**, 153–161.

Tassel, J. (1996) "Advanced Television Systems", *Focal Press*.

Tiwari, P. and Viscito, E. (1996) "A Parallel MPEG-2 Video Encoder with Look-ahead Rate Control", *Proceeding of IEEE Intl. Conf. on Acoustics, Speech and Signal Processing*, 1994–1997.

Watanabe, H. and Ito, Y. (1994) "Extended MPEG2 rate control by analytical modeling of feedback system", *SPIE*, **2308**, 290–295.

Zabih, R. and Miller, J. and Mai, K. (1993) "A Feature-Based Algorithm for Detecting and Classifying Scene Breaks", *Proc. ACM Multimedia Conference 1995*, San Francisco, CA, 189–200.

Zhang, H. and Kankanhalli, A. and Smoliar, S. (1993) "Automatic Partitioning of Full-motion Video", *ACM Journal of Multimedia Systems*, **1**, 10–28.

Routing with Quality of Service Constraints

M'hamed Nour*, Abdelhakim Hafid+, J. William Atwood#

*Université de Montréal, IRO, Groupe de Téléinformatique, Montréal, H3C 3J7, Canada.

+Advanced Communication Engineering Centre, University of Western Ontario, London, Ontario, N6A 5B9, Canada.

#Concordia University, Department of Computer Science, Montréal, H3G 1M8, Canada.

Future networks, such as ATM, will support a wide range of multimedia services, such as voice and video, that exhibit diverse traffic characteristics but also require specific quality of service (QoS) guarantees. Most existing approaches that support QoS guarantees (1) assume the existence of a path between the communicating entities and (2) ask the nodes of the path to reserve enough resources to satisfy the requested QoS. The main drawback of these approaches is that they do not address the routing problem, which is closely related to QoS guarantees; if the routing is performed without QoS constraints, several retries may be necessary before the connection is established. Several routing procedures (with QoS constraints) are proposed in the literature; however, they consider only a subset of QoS requirements, e.g. bandwidth or delay, while routing the connection. In this paper, we present a routing procedure which considers different QoS classes; depending on the QoS class the connection belongs to, the procedure selects the "best" path that minimizes the parameters (of the class) while satisfying the whole requirements of the connection. For example, the path with the minimum end-to-end delay which satisfies the delay, the bandwidth and the loss rate requirements is selected in case the connection belongs to delay-sensitive class. The proposed routing procedure is essentially independent of network technologies, such as ATM or stop-and-go networks; however the network nodes should be capable of reserving resources when requested.

Keywords: routing, quality of service, multimedia applications, ATM

1. Introduction

Due to increasing demands of distributed multimedia (MM) applications, efficient and effective support of quality of service (QoS) has become increasingly important. To support QoS requirements, communication systems and end-systems must provide latency and bandwidth characteristics that allow timely transmission of information. Future systems must be able to support MM application requirements by providing suitable QoS management functions, such as QoS negotiation and QoS adaptation [8]. Several approaches have been proposed to support guaranteed performance at the communication system level [2,6, 10]. They all adopt a connection-oriented and reservation-oriented approach. The reservation protocols support QoS guarantees for each connection such as the maximum delay and loss rate. These parameters are negotiated during the establishment phase, and the request is rejected if the required resources, e.g., bandwidth, to guarantee the desired QoS cannot be allocated. Most of existing protocols that support the establishment of connections with QoS guarantees [2, 6, 10], perform the following steps:

(1) Send the reserve request to reserve the required resources to support the new connection, starting from the first node of the selected path between the source and the destination

(2) When an intermediate node receives the reserve request, it checks whether it has the necessary resources to support the requested QoS. If the answer is yes, then the reserve request is forwarded to the next node; otherwise a reject primitive is sent back towards the source node. Thus the previous nodes must free the resources that they reserved to support the requested service.

(3) When the destination node receives the reserve request, it must verify that the end-to-end QoS is satisfied by evaluating the levels of QoS supported by the different nodes of the selected path.

If the end-to-end QoS is not satisfied then a reject message is sent back towards the source node; each node de-allocates the reserved resources. Otherwise, a confirmation message with the remaining excess QoS "provided QoS-requested QoS" is sent back towards to the source node; for each component, the level of QoS is relaxed based on some established policies [12]. The differences among these approaches concern mainly the traffic model and the QoS parameters considered and the techniques used for resource reservation. The main drawback of those approaches is that they all assume that the path between the communication entities is initially known. While this may be reasonable when there is only one path between a source and a destination, it will increase the blocking probability (or decrease the probability of successful establishment of a new connection) when multiple paths exist: several retries (steps 1-2-3) are necessary before establishment. We believe that the issue of routing should be combined with QoS support since this will minimize the number of retries before establishment.

Several routing procedures (with QoS constraints) are proposed in the literature [1, 11, 15, 13, 7]; usually, they optimize a cost function while satisfying only a subset of QoS requirements. Ahmadi et al. [1] proposes a routing technique that minimizes call blocking (by minimizing the number of hops between the source and destination) while ensuring low end-to-end delay (no guarantees to satisfy the requested delay); only the requested bandwidth (throughput) is guaranteed to be satisfied. Another routing technique that routes connections while satisfying only bandwidth requirements is presented in [11]. A routing technique, which is described in [13], determines the path with the minimum cost; the cost of a path is the sum of costs of the nodes of the path, while the cost indicates a delay value (introduced by the node while accommodating the new connection).

In this paper, we propose a more general approach. We assume that connection requirements can be divided into four QoS classes: delay sensitive class, reliability sensitive class, delay and reliability sensitive class, or neither (classical routing). This gives us the following objective functions: (1) minimize the delay, (2) minimize the loss rate, (3) minimize both the delay and the loss rate, or (4) minimize the number of links (or hops). In response to a request to open a new connection, the proposed algorithm generates a sub-graph which contains only nodes and links which might support the connection requirements; for example a node/link with 3 Mbits/s as available bandwidth is rejected if the new connection requires 5 Mbits/s. Then, it uses a modified version of the Double-Sweep Algorithm [14] to find the "best" path minimizing certain QoS metrics depending on the QoS class of the new connection; obviously, this path should satisfy the connection QoS requirements. For example, the path with the minimum end-to-end delay which satisfies the delay, the bandwidth and the loss rate requirements is selected in case the new connection belongs to delay-sensitive class.

The proposed algorithm can be used to route (almost) any class of connections in opposition to existing routing algorithms which are restricted to particular classes. It is essentially independent of the mechanisms used within network nodes for providing QoS guarantees; more generally it is independent of network technologies, such as ATM or stop-and-go networks. We believe that the proposed routing algorithm will decrease notably the number of retries before the connection establishment and thus it will shorten the response time

The paper is organized as follows. Section 2 presents a formulation of the problem of routing with QoS constraints. Section 3 presents a Distributed Dynamic Routing Algorithm. Section 4 presents ideas how to use the proposed routing algorithm in ATM networks. Finally, Section 5 concludes the paper recalling our contribution and the future work.

2. A Framework to support Routing with QoS Constraints

The network can be represented by a finite undirected graph. Each node in the graph represents a network node and each edge represents a link to enable data transfer between the two nodes at both ends of the link. A link has a maximum capacity for transferring data; a node has a fixed maximum amount of resources, e.g., buffers and CPU slots. Thus, a node is capable of supporting only a finite number of concurrent connections. Consequently, a request to open a connection can be rejected by a node if there are not enough resources to support the request.

2.1. Node model

We associate a QoS agent [8] with a network node (Figure 1). The QoS agent of a node is an entity that provides the means to handle all the information about the performance of the component. When the QoS agent receives a request (ServiceInq), specifying the desired QoS, it runs some reservation mechanisms [6, 2, 4, 10] in order to compute the QoS that the component can support. Then, the component remains locked until the reception of a confirmation message (ServiceRes). At this time the QoS agent reserves (reserve_request) the required resources and unlocks the component. When the QoS agent receives a request to terminate the service it simply de-allocates (terminate_request) the reserved resources.
To support resource reservation activity (reserve_request), the QoS agent of a node can make use of analytical or experimental models: upon receipt of the service request, the QoS agent applies its model(s) to the requested level of QoS to check whether the resources available, at the component, can support the service requested [8]. The main QoS parameters we consider are: throughput, delay, and loss rate. Let us note that the jitter is derived from the delay parameter (jitter is defined as the difference between the maximum and minimum delay).

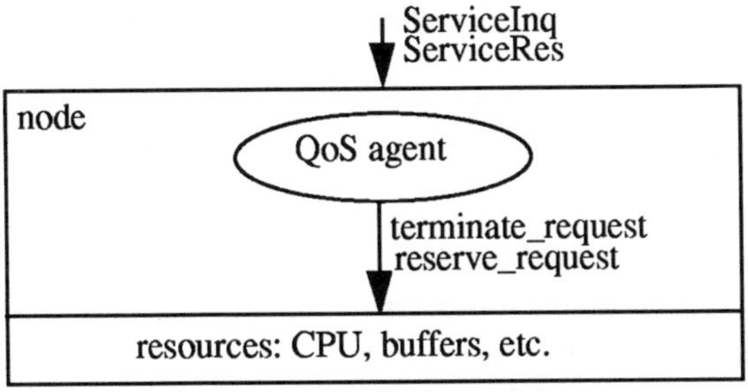

Figure 1. Node model

To compute the end-to-end QoS, ($throughput$, $delay$, $lossrate$), that might be supported for the new connection we have only to apply the following formulas:

$$throughput = \left(\underset{i}{minimum}\right)(throughput_i) \qquad \text{(I)},$$

$$delay = \sum delay_i \qquad \text{(II)},$$

and

$$\log(1 - lossrate) = \sum \log(1 - lossrate_i) \qquad \text{(III)}$$

where ($throughput_i$, $delay_i$, $lossrate_i$) indicates the level of QoS supported by the node C_i of the path (from source to destination)

Given the nature of end-to-end delay (Formula II) (respectively loss rate (Formula III)), the QoS agents are asked to compute the minimum delay (respectively loss rate) they can provide for the new request.

The operation ServiceInq() has four arguments: throughput th, delay d, loss rate lr, and flag $flag$. th is an input, while d, lr, and $flag$ are output. The QoS agent executes the following algorithm.

Algorithm

(1) input: th

(2) Upon receipt of ServiceInq (th, d, lr, $flag$) the following steps are executed:

(2.1) the QoS agent locks the component

(2.2) If the component has enough available resources to support th then

the QoS agent sets $flag$ to 1

else

the QoS agent sets $flag$ to 0

the QoS agent unlocks the component

the QoS agent returns the response to the entity that initiated ServiceInq()

endif

(2.3) the QoS agent computes the minimum delay d and loss rate lr that the component can actually support, given the throughput th

(2.4) the QoS agent returns the response to the entity that initiated ServiceInq()

(3) Upon receipt of ServiceRes (th, d, lr, $flag$) the following steps are executed:

(3.1) the QoS agent reserves the resources required to support (th, d, lr)

(3.2) the QoS agent unlocks the component

(3.3) the QoS agent returns the response to the entity that initiated ServiceRes()

The algorithm supports the processing of only one ServiceInq at a given time; that is, the component remains locked from the time it receives ServiceInq until the reception of the corresponding ServiceRes (during this period, the upcoming ServiceInq are ignored or queued). This is not an optimal approach in a context where several ServiceInq can be received during a small period of time. For this reason, we propose that in response to a ServiceInq, the QoS agent locks only a (maximum) fixed amount of the component resources. Then, the upcoming ServiceInq will be processed with respect to the component resources that are not locked.

2.2. Problem formulation

The problem of routing with QoS constraints can be mathematically represented as a set of objective functions to optimize given a set of constraints related to the current states of the network nodes and links and the requested QoS:

$$Optimize(Obj^j(\arg uments)) \quad \text{for } 1 \le j \le n$$

Given $Con^i(\arg uments^\dagger) \le 0$ for $1 \le i \le m$
where:

$obj^j(\arg uments)$ represents an objective function which may represent the cost to be paid by the user, the system reliability, etc. $\arg uments$ primarily concern the requested QoS, the static characteristics of the network in use, etc.

$Con^i(\arg uments^\dagger)$ represents the constraints to be satisfied while satisfying the objective functions. $\arg uments^\dagger$ concern primarily the current states of network and the requested QoS.

Definition 1: the *network* is defined by the tuple (C, L) where

- $C = \{C_1, C_2, \ldots, C_n\}$ represents the set of network nodes,

- L is an (n, n) matrix where $L(j, k) = 1$ if a link, $l_{j,k}$, exists between C_j and C_k, and $L(j, k) = 0$ otherwise.

Let us assume that (1) the processing rate of the connection S_i is ps_i; (2) the processing capacity of the system component C_k is pc_k; (3) the communication rate of the session S_i is cs_i; and (4) the capacity of a link $l_{j,k}$ is $cp_{j,k}$.

Definition 2: a path $S_{i,v}$ that might support the connection S_i is defined by the tuple $(SC_{i,v}, SL_{i,v})$ where: $SC_{i,v} \subseteq C$ represents the set of the nodes of the path $S_{i,v}$ and $SL_{i,v}$ represents the set of the links of the path $S_{i,v}$.

The mathematical program to solve in order to select an "optimal" path that supports the connection requirements in terms of QoS can be formalized as follows.

$$\min_{1 \le v \le V} \left(\sum_{C_m \in SC_{i,v}, l_{j,k} \in SL_{i,v}} (\cos tc(C_m, S_i) + \cos tp(l_{j,k}, S_i)) \right) \quad (1)$$

$$\forall C_j, C_k \in C \sum_{S_{i,x} \in S} cs_i \times gc(C_j, SC_{i,x}) \times gc(C_k, SC_{i,x}) \le cp_{j,k} \quad (2)$$

$$\forall C_k \in C$$

$$\sum_{S_{i,x} \in S} ps_i \times gc(C_k, SC_{i,x}) \le pc_k \quad (3)$$

$$\sum_{C_m \in SC_{i,v}, l_{j,k} \in SL_{i,v}} D(C_m, S_i) + D(l_{j,k}, S_i) \le D(S_i) \quad (4)$$

$$\sum_{C_m \in SC_{i,v}} \log(1 - LR(C_m, S_i)) \le \log(1 - LR(S_i)) \quad (5)$$

where S represents the set of all connections including the new one $S_{i,v}$; $gc(C_k, SC_{i,x}) = 1$ if $C_k \in SC_{i,x}$ $gc(C_k, SC_{i,x}) = 0$ otherwise; $min(f)$ represents the minimal value of f; $\mathrm{cos}tp(l_{i,k}, S_i)$ (respectively $\mathrm{cos}tc(C_m, S_i)$) represents the function that returns the cost of using a link $l_{j,k}$ (respectively node C_m) to support the connection S_i; $D(C_m, S_i)$ represents the delay required by C_m to queue and to process the data flow relative to S_i; $D(l_{j,k}, S_i)$ represents the delay required by the link $l_{j,k}$ to transport the data flow relative to S_i; $D(S_i)$ represents the requested end-to-end delay corresponding to S_i; $LR(C_m, S_i)$ represents the loss rate (due to buffer overflow) introduced by C_m while supporting S_i, and $LR(S_i)$ represents the requested end-to-end loss rate corresponding to S_i.

The cost may represent real money or another metric that enables measurement of a characteristic of interest such as QoS violation probability. The cost may depend not only on the requested QoS, but also on other factors such as the time of day, the day of the week, the identity of user, the security, etc. Expression (1) represents the objective function; expressions (2) and (3) represent the constraints the system must satisfy to ensure that the system (e.g., nodes) has enough capacity (e.g., processing power of the nodes) to accommodate the new connection without affecting the existing ones, while expressions (4) and (5) represent the constraints to satisfy by the system to meet the end-to-end delay and loss rate requirements of the new connection. Solving the mathematical program is a complex problem, however, calling for heuristics and knowledge-based techniques. QoS requirements (expressions 2, 3, 4, and 5) provide constraints on the function to solve. We can automatically derive a path satisfying the constraints, possibly going through some iterations. However, the solution should be an optimal one and the number of iterations must be bounded since there is no proof of the convergence of the mathematical program.

3. Distributed Dynamic Routing Algorithm

We assume that connection requirements can be divided into four QoS classes: delay sensitive class, reliability sensitive class, delay and reliability sensitive class, or neither (classical routing). This gives us the following objective functions (see expression 1 of the mathematical program): (a) minimize the delay, (b) minimize the loss rate, (c) minimize both the delay and the loss rate, or (d) minimize the number of links (or hops).

Routing connections with QoS constraints complicates the routing problem in two ways:

(1) Each link has to be described in terms of multiple metrics;

(2) Whether a link can participate in a path depends on the requirements for the connection being routed. Dijkstra's algorithm can minimize only one metric [5]; thus, minimizing the delay may imply an unacceptable bandwidth, or a high delay variance. Routing with multiple requirements can easily become an NP-complete problem in the number of links [9].

To compute feasible paths, taking into account the QoS requirements in terms of delay, loss rate and throughput, we propose an extension of k-shortest path algorithm that would proceed as follows:

(1) check the availability of the nodes and links of the network; the nodes and links that are at their maximum utilization are dropped; (2) using the result of the step 1, find three best paths verifying the end-to-end QoS requirements; (3) select the "best" path, if possible, from those that satisfy the entire set of QoS constraints.

3.1. Network Performance Parameter Measurement

We assume the existence of a procedure that calculates the values of QoS parameters available at each node; these values will be saved in a repository for instance. This is the role of QoS agents. It is worth noting that all nodes run exactly the same algorithm, in parallel.

3.2. Algorithm overview

Huang proves by simulation and comparison that his Loop-free path algorithm is better than Shortest-Feasible-path Routing (SFPR), Least Loaded Routing (LLR) and Two-level Shortest path Routing (TSPR) [9]. The idea behind the Loop-free path algorithm is a smart backtracking, which uses at each node a set of Preferred Neighbouring Nodes

(PNNs). Three metrics are used by Huang to evaluate the performance of the Loop-free algorithm: Call Blocking Rate (CBR), average path Distance (RD), and the average Call Setup Time (CST). Huang's algorithm does not present the calculation procedure of the PNNs, and does not consider any QoS constraints. We propose an extension of one of the k-shortest path algorithms (e.g, Double-Sweep Algorithm [14] which finds the k-shortest path lengths between a specified node and all other nodes in the graph) which uses backtracking on the PNNs taking into account the QoS parameters. Our algorithm uses Huang's simulation results; the execution order of this algorithm is about $k \times O(n^3)$, where n represents the number of nodes.

3.3. Description of a distributed Dynamic Routing Algorithm

The algorithm we propose consists of the following steps:

Step 1: Preparation and up-date of the subnet graph

The idea is to build a graph of the subnet, with each node of the graph representing a network node and each arc of the graph representing a communication line (link). Each arc will be labelled with the delay (the delay at the node connecting this link plus delay on the link: queuing delay+transmission delay+propagation delay), the bandwidth available, and the loss rate (the loss rate at the node connecting this link; we consider only losses due to the node's buffer overflow).

We assume that each node of the subnet will have the same graph with the values for each arc, so that distributed routing is possible. The values in the graph may change reflecting the real change in the subnet. The nodes communicate these values in a way to update of the graph's values at each node. The description of procedures used to exchange information among the nodes is beyond the scope of this paper.

Step 2. Generating a sub-graph

At each node we generate a sub-graph which contains only arcs with available bandwidth regarding the QoS class of the new connection to open. For example, if the new connection requires 3 Mbits/s and the available bandwidth at a certain arc is 2Mbits/s, then this arc will not be considered in the sub-graph.

Step 3. QoS-oriented PNNs creation [Class 1: delay sensitive or Class2: loss rate sensitive]

Before transmitting the connection traffic from one node to the other, the connection must be established, so the path must be computed. The source node will send a connection request to the intermediate node (the first intermediate node in the path). The connection request is a message that contains the specification of the traffic characteristics with the quality of service requirements in terms of bandwidth, delay, and loss rate.

Depending on QoS class of the new connection, the k-shortest path algorithm may be applied to the sub-graph to find best paths minimizing the sum of delay, with a variation to compute the values of the other metrics for these paths: such as the sum of log(1-loss rate) of the different arcs of the "optimal" path. During this operation, if one of the values of the metrics does not satisfy the requested values, the path will not be considered further. The requested values are the QoS parameter values specified in the connection request.

For each next hop, there may be several paths to the destination passing through this node. The proposed algorithm is able to find the "best" path to the destination passing through one of the next hops with the variation to compute the values of the other QoS parameters.

We propose to create the PNNs table with three choices. The PNNs Routing table for delay-sensitive class or loss rate-sensitive class is shown in Table 1.

The value field, e.g. valuei, will contain (delay value, bandwidth value, loss rate value, next node). Class 1 represents the delay sensitive applications, and Class 2 represents the reliability sensitive applications. The PNNs routing table will be updated at each major change in the Network Performance.

Table 1: PNNs routing table of sensitive -delay class (or loss rate-sensitive class)

Destinations	Best 1	Best 2	Best 3
Destination 1	Valuei	Valuej	Valuek
Destination 2	Valuei	Valuej	Valuek
...			
Destination n	Valuei	Valuej	Valuek

Step 3'. QoS-oriented PNNs creation [Class 3: delay and loss rate sensitive]

The idea is to compute k-shortest paths to different destinations, with the calculation of the values of the other metrics, and to keep in the PNNs table only the three best paths. This algorithm can be used to calculate the PNNs for Class 3 which represent delay and reliability sensitive applications. The PNNs routing table for Class 3 will have the same structure as the PNNs tables for Class 1 and Class 2.

To compute the PNNs table for Class 3, many techniques may be used. A technique example we used consists of the following steps:

(1) Use the double-sweep algorithm to compute $k1$ paths sensitive to delay, and $k2$ paths sensitive to loss rate (The values of k_1 and k_2 depend on the network size.);

(2) Sort the $k1+k2$ paths using delay as a sort metric, and drop the $\left\lceil \frac{(k1+k2-3)}{2} \right\rceil$ worst paths;

(3) Sort the $k1+k2-\left\lceil \frac{(k1+k2-3)}{2} \right\rceil$ paths using loss rate as a sort metric, and drop the $\left\lfloor \frac{(k1+k2-3)}{2} \right\rfloor$ worst paths;

(4) Fill the PNNs table with the three remaining values.

Step 3". QoS-oriented PNNs creation [Class 4: no sensitivity to delay and loss rate]

For QoS class 4, we propose to use Dijkstra's algorithm, which can quickly find the optimal path between two points that minimizes the sum of links metrics in the path.

Step 4. Backtracking using PNNs

When one node in the subnet will receive the connection request, it will use the PNNs table corresponding to the application class (the application which issues the request) and will send the connection request to the next node. This procedure will be repeated until the destination is reached. A formal description of this step may be found in [9].

At each node, for each connection request do:

- Send a connection request to the next node which corresponds to the node at the Best1 position of the PNNs table. The QoS parameter values contained in this request should reflect that the current node committed to support certain levels of QoS. This mainly consists of substracting the level of QoS the node committed to support from the QoS included in the request the node received.
  - If this connection request to the next node is accepted (which means that the actual node will receive an acceptance message from the next node) then the current node should send the acceptance message to the previous node.
    Else (which means that the connection request is rejected by the next hop)
    if the setup time expires then
      send the non acceptance message to the previous node,
      else

send a message to the next node using the PNNs table.
endif
endif

3.4. Illustrated example

In this example we assume that the user issue a request to open a new connection (delay-sensitive class) from node C to node D (Figure 2) with the following requirements: maximum delay: 7u; maximum loss rate: 10u; and minimum bandwidth: 100M. Because lack of space, we present only the PNN routing table generated at node C. We used a C program of the Double-Sweep Algorithm with our extensions looking for the ten best paths ($k = 10$).

Step 1: Preparation and up-date of the subnet graph

Each arc is labelled by the available bandwidth, the delay and the loss rate (Figure 2).

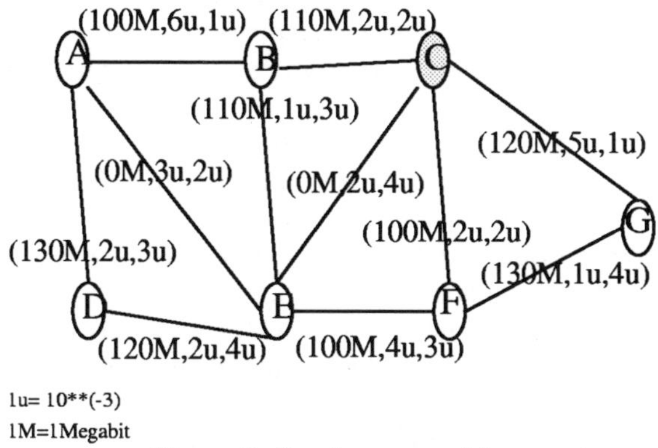

Figure 2. Graph generated by step 1

Step 2. Generating a sub-graph

This step will generate a sub-graph without arcs (A,E) and (E,C) since there is no bandwidth available at these arcs (see Figure 2).

Step 3. QoS-oriented PNNs creation

At this step, the double-sweep algorithm is applied to the sub-graph generated by step

2 with the calculation of the values of the loss rate for the three best paths.

Table 2: PNNs routing table (delay-sensitive class) at node C

Destinations	Best 1	Best 2	Best 3
B	2u, 110M, 2u, B	7u,100M, 8u,F	11u, 100M, 11u, G
F	2u, 100M, 2u, F	6u,120M, 5u,G	7u, 100M, 8u, B
G	3u, 100M, 6u, F	5u,120M, 1u,G	8u, 100M, 12u, B
E	3u, 110M, 5u, B	6u,100M, 5u,F	10u, 100M, 8u, G
D	5u, 110M, 9u, B	8u,100M, 9u,F	10u, 100M, 6u, B
A	7u, 110M, 12u, B	8u,100M, 3u, B	10u, 100M, 12u, F

Table 2 shows the three Best paths in terms of delay. Node C uses this table to select node B as the best next node; then, it sends a request to node B to find a path from B to D with the following requirements; maximum delay: 5u; maximum loss rate: 8u; and minimum bandwidth: 100M.

Upon receipt of this request, node B uses its PNNs routing table and selects node E as the best next node; then, it sends a request to node E to find the best path from node E to node D with the following requirements; maximum delay: 4u; maximum loss rate: 5u; and minimum bandwidth: 100M. Then, node E uses its PNNs routing table and selects node D as the best next node. Consequently, the path the algorithm produces is: C-B-E-D with the following characteristics: delay: 5u; loss rate: 9u; and bandwidth: 100M. Let us note that backtracking (step 4) was not necessary in this example.

4. Routing with QoS constraints in ATM networks

As stated before, the proposed routing algorithm is independent of network technologies in use. In this section, we describe the utilization of the proposed algorithm in Asynchronous Transfer Mode (ATM) networks.

4.1. ATM overview

ATM is a communications offering of the telephone companies, standardized by the ITU-T (formerly the CCITT), which is intended to provide a single interface for a wide variety of communications needs, varying from fixed rate isochronous services (voice, video), to variable rate isochronous services (compressed video), to variable rate asynchronous services (classical data communications, LAN interconnection). The variety and scope of the services proposed corresponds well with the requirements of MM traffic. ATM is structured as an ATM layer, which carries 53-byte *cells*, and an ATM Adaptation Layer (AAL), with the user applications as a third layer. Different AALs have been standardized to correspond to the various services described above. ATM provides connection-oriented services, with guaranteed QoS; the connection is identified by a Virtual Connection Identifier (VCI) and a Virtual Path Identifier (VPI). Setup of a particular service request is called *signalling* --major tasks that ATM signalling needs to perform include VPI and VCI assignment, resource assignment within the network to support the QoS, and setting of the switches at the ATM level, to permit rapid flow of the cells. Signalling information is transmitted over special virtual channels called Signalling Virtual Channels (SVCs).

4.2. Network Performance based Connection Admission Control Model

The Connection Admission Control (CAC) [3] determines if the connection can be accepted or not, traffic needed by Usage Parameter Control, routing and allocation of network resources. I.356 defines a list of ATM Performance Parameters; these Networks Performance (NP) parameters may be observed by the network at various points. [3] defines how to compute the NP parameters.
The proposed routing algorithm may be used by the CAC using the NP parameters to construct the PNNs table. This routing procedure provides alternate paths, to permit to the ATM networks to be able to achieve lower connection blocking probabilities and higher network throughput and satisfying QoS requirements [16].
This algorithm may be integrated into the Connection Admission Control in ATM Networks using different ATM Network Performance parameters. Simple Network Management Protocol (SNMP) and an Interim Local Management Interface-Management Information Base (ILMI-MIB) [3] will provide any ATM user with status and configuration information concerning the Virtual Path and Channel Connections available at its UNI. We are currently developing a CAC model which uses the ILMI-MIB and NP parameters in Virtual Path assignment and Virtual Circuit routing in ATM Networks.

5. Conclusion

We proposed a general formulation of routing with QoS constraints and a dynamic routing algorithm: we combine the issues of routing and QoS support. The proposed algorithm consists of two main activities:
(1) derive the set of paths that might satisfy the user requirements in terms of throughput, delay, and loss rate. The nodes that do not support the requested QoS are immediately rejected during the construction of possible paths.
(2) select the "best" path from the possible ones based on one or a combination of the

following: delay and loss rate. Such a path must satisfy end-to-end delay and end-to-end loss rate.

The proposed routing algorithm will decrease notably the number of retries before connection establishment, since the path is selected while taking into account QoS requirements.

A first attempt to use the proposed routing algorithm in ATM networks is presented. We are now working to evaluate the performance of the proposed algorithm by performing simulations and experiments in ATM networks. The results will be published in a future paper.

References.

[1] H. Ahmadi, J. Chen, and R.Guerin, Dynamic Routing and Call Control in High Speed Integrated Networks, IBM Technical Report, IBM Research Division, T.J. Watson Research Center. Yorktown Heights, NY, November 1991

[2] D.Anderson, G.Herrtwich and C.Shaefer, *SRP: A resource Reservation Protocol for Guaranteed-Performance Communication in the Internet*, Technical Report No. TR-90-006, ICSI, Berkeley, February 1990

[3] ATM Forum, *ATM User-Network Interface Specification V3.0*, The ATM Forum, 1993, PTR Prentice Hall

[4] C.Chou and K.Shin, *Statistical Real-time Video Channels over a Multicaccess Network*, Proc. High SPIE, 1994

[5] E.W. Dijkstra, *A Note on Two Problems in Connection with Graphs*, Numer. Math., 1, pp 269-271

[6] D.Ferrari and D.Verma, *A scheme for Real-Time Channel Establishment in Wide-Area Networks,* IEEE JSAC, April 1990

[7] R. Gawlick, A. Kamath, S. Plotkin and K. Ramakrishnan, Routing and Admission Control in General Topology Networks, Technical Report STAN-CS-TR-95-1548, Dpt. of CS, Stanford University, Stanford, California, 1995

[8] A.Hafid and G.v.Bochmann, *Quality of Service Adaptation in Distributed Multimedia Applications*, ACM MM Systems Journal (to appear)

[9] N. Huang, C. Wu, Y. Wu, *Some routing problems on Broadband ISDN*, Computer Networks and ISDN Systems, 1994.

[10] D.Kandlur, K.Shin and D.Ferrari, *Real-Time Communication in Multi-Hop Networks*, Pro. 11th International Conference on Distributed Computing Systems, 1991

[11] V. Compella, J. Pasquale and G. Polyzos, Two Techniques For Multicasting for Multimedia Applications, Proceedings of Third International Workshop on Network and Operating System Support for Digital Audio and Video, San Diego, California, November 1992

[12] R.Nagarajan, Quality of Service Issues in High Speed Networks, Ph.D. Thesis, University of Massachusetts, 1993

[13] C. Parris and D.Ferrari, A Dynamic Connection Management Scheme for Guaranteed Performance Services in Packet-Switching Integrated Services Networks, TR-011-93, ICSI, berkeley, California, 1993

[14] D.R. Shier, *Iterative Methods for Determining the k Shortest Paths in a Networks*, Networks, 6, pp 205-232

[15] R. Simha, B, Narahari, *Single path routing delay consideration*, Comput. Networks ISDN Systems 24 (1992) 405-419.

[16] E. M. Spiegel, T. Murase, *An Alternate Path Routing Scheme Supporting QoS and Fast Connection in ATM Networks*, Comput. Networks ISDN Systems (1994) 1224-1230.

Interactive Multimedia Systems

CONTENT-BASED VIDEO QUERY SYSTEM USING VISUALIZED SOUND INDEX

K. FUSHIKIDA, Y. HIWATARI, H. WAKI

Tokyo Waterfront Research Center
Telecommunications Advancement Organization of Japan
2-38, Aomi, Koutou-ku, Tokyo,
135-8070 Japan
E-mail: fusikida@be.mbn.or.jp

In this paper a content-based video query system using a multimodal index is described. As the multimodal index, representative frames (r-frames) of video scenes and corresponding visualized sound patterns are used. An image search engine is used not only for image retrieval but also for sound retrieval. Visualized spoken word retrieval experiments show that the image search engine can be effectively applied for visualized sound pattern retrieval. Collaborative parallel query experiments using the multimodal index for bird videos showed that parallel query using the multimodal indexes is effective in improving query accuracy compared with single query methods. Query experiments using the image-sound combined indexing method were also conducted. In the query process, candidate images and corresponding visualized sound patterns were simultaneously presented. The results of video index browsing experiments show the effectiveness of this method for efficient video understanding and retrieval.

1. Introduction

The recent rapid advances in high-speed networks, high-performance computers, high-capacity storage devices, high-quality video data compression techniques and the explosive growth of the Internet have resulted in a tremendous amount of interest in large-scale multimedia applications. Many future multimedia applications will require rapid and accurate search of the video data distributed on the global network. Moreover, a user-friendly query interface that helps users to understand the contents of video is also required.

Given these circumstances, the development of a powerful indexing, retrieving, and browsing scheme for large video databases has become essential. Efficient querying of a video scene requires that a multimodal index including text, images, sound, and any combination of these modes be interactively used.

We propose a multimodal retrieval scheme using a multimedia index, namely images and a corresponding visualized sound pattern that we call a "multimodal index" in this paper. Parallel querying using the multimodal index is discussed and compared with the conventional single index method. A video browsing experiment using the combined indexes of images and visualized sound images is also discussed.

This paper is organized as follows. Section 2 describes related works. Section 3 presents a multimodal retrieval scheme and sound visualization method. Section 4 describes the video retrieval system. Section 5 describes experiments and results. Section 6 concludes the paper and points to future research issues.

2. Related works

Much research is currently being done on the content-based image database query [1~7, 10, 15, 16]. However, automatic and sufficiently accurate video retrieval is not yet feasible and many difficult problems remain to be solved.

Indexing is one of the important problems in efficient image (including video) retrieval [7,15]. A text indexing is an effective way for video retrieval [9]. However, existing automatic text indexing techniques using meaning analysis of a video scene or speech recognition techniques such as word spotting [18] are not yet sufficiently refined for practical application. To improve retrieval efficiency, a symbolic method for image indexing has been discussed [19].

It is known that sound information can be an effective cue in retrieving a video scene [2, 3, 8, 21]. For example, in news or sports videos, a sound index plays an important role in retrieving a specific scene, such as a touchdown in American football, or a goal in soccer. For efficient understanding of video contents, each piece of index information should be presented in an effective manner to the user for rapid video browsing [15,16]. The effectiveness of sound information in video retrieval or video handling has been pointed out [17].

The sound visualization method of speech has been investigated as an aid for the auditory handicapped [12]. A speech sound visualization system using color representation of a formant parameter and pitch parameter has been discussed [11]. "Speech spectrogram reading" using sound spectrogram has also been discussed from a speech understanding point of view [13].

3. Multimodal retrieval for video query

3-1. Multimodal retrieval scheme

As typical video indexes, text indexes, image indexes, and sound indexes have been discussed for content-based retrieval. In general, an image index is effective in retrieving images from a visual database. An image index can be generated, for example, by using a representative frame (r-frame) selected from a video stream. As the attributes of the image, we can use color, shape, texture, structure, and so forth. However, in the following cases, for example, an image index is not always so effective.

- Goal scene retrieval for sports videos such as a soccer game on the green field.
- Animal image retrieval from a video scene including camouflage (mimicry, cryptic coloration).

For rapid video browsing, an image index can be used very effectively by displaying thumbnails simultaneously. A user can glance at multiple miniature images (thumbnails) simultaneously on the screen. Sound index is another dominant index for video. The entries in an image index can be viewed simultaneously on a screen. However, we can not listen to sound indexes of different scenes simultaneously.

Based on the characteristics of each index and the fact that the utility of each indexing mode depends on the kind of video, we propose a multimodal retrieval method using multi-viewer on the client machine. Figure 1 shows multimodal retrieval scheme. We focus on an image index and a corresponding sound index as the multimodal index in this paper. The effectiveness of the proposed method is evaluated in query experiments.

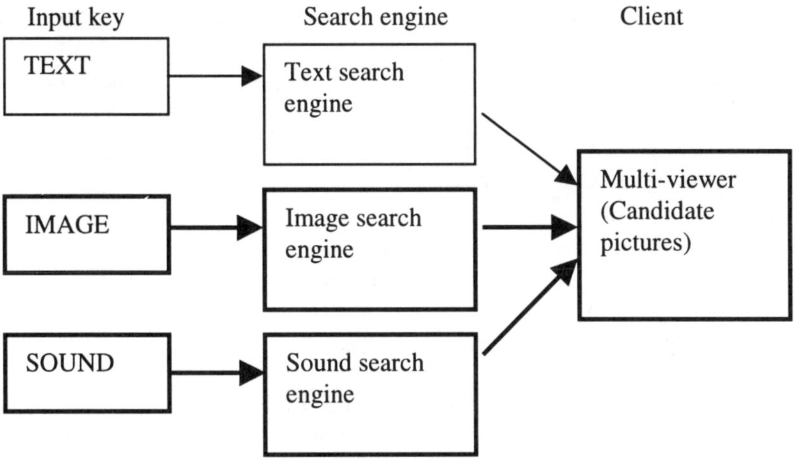

Figure 1. Multimodal retrieval scheme.

3-2 Sound visualization method

To get sound information corresponding to the image simultaneously, we propose using visualized sound information.

Sound power information is a primitive sound attribute for sound indexing. However, the information contained in the power value is quite limited. We adopted a time-frequency pattern of speech, the so-called sound spectrogram as the visualized sound pattern, because of its robustness and universality compared with the other parameter (e.g. formant or pitch) extraction methods. A Fourier transformation is calculated and the energy values of each frequency component are quantized into 8 levels. The energy levels are represented by a color from dark blue (low energy) to red (high energy). Figure 2 shows examples of sound spectrogram patterns.

Generally, visualized sound indexing has the following two advantages.

1. An image search engine can be used for sound retrieval.
2. We can "glance" at sounds of different scenes simultaneously.

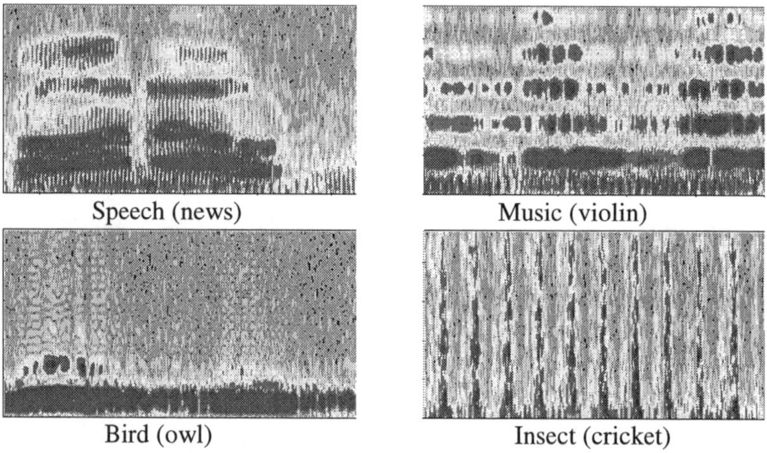

Frequency range: 0~5kHz, Duration: 1sec

Figure 2. Examples of visualized sounds (sound spectrograms).

3-3 Metrics of collaborativel retrieval method

To improve the search accuracy and reduce the search time, collaborative (parallel) retrieval scheme using distributed image search sites has been proposed and evaluated using search sites on an intranet [10]. In these papers, we discussed a parallel retrieval scheme using image attributes, namely shape and color. In this paper, we extended this scheme to the above multimodal retrieval using image and sound attributes.

As the evaluation measure, recall rank R_p is used for the collaborative retrieval. R_p is expressed by formula (1);

$$R_p = \mathrm{Min}\ \{ R_1, R_2, \ldots, R_M \}, \qquad (1)$$

where R_m (□=1,2,...,M) represents the rank of the target picture retrieved by the m-th site and M is the total number of image search sites.

This formula shows that Rp is smaller than any single-site query Rm.

$$R_p \ □\ R_m, \quad m=1,2,\ldots,M \qquad (2)$$

Here, we define the following metrics Q_m to evaluate the retrieval accuracy of the m-th search site as a percentage.

$$Q_m = (1 - R_m / T) \times 100 \qquad (3)$$

Where T represents the size of the database (i.e., total number of images).
The evaluation measure for collaborativel retrieval accuracy Q_p is defined by formula (4);

$$Q_p = \max \{Q_1, Q_2, \ldots, Q_M\} \qquad (4)$$

The details of the parallel query algorithms are described in other paper [10].

4. Video retrieval system

4-1. Indexing and retrieval system

Figure 3 shows the video query system for the distributed video database retrieval investigation. The video retrieval system consists of three servers, three clients and six video servers. This system has client-server architecture based on an intranet, and these systems are connected via an ATM network.

The image search engine installed on the server searches for similar pictures using the multimodal index database. The client provides a visual interface for retrieving images and video from the database. The user can browse the images and display the video through the viewer which is plugged in the Web browser. The VOD servers have a total capacity of 438 GB disk arrays, and store MPEG-2 video data stream. As a picture input to the image search engine, images, visualized sound, or a combination of these two can be selected.

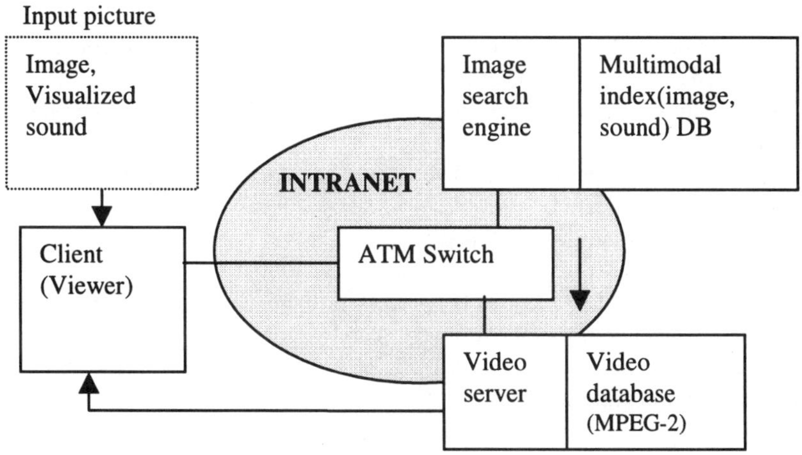

Figure 3. Video query system using multimodal indexes.

4-2. Image search engine

The content-based image search engine developed by Hirata et al. [4] is installed in the experimental system. It matches pictures input with images in the picture index file in the image search system, and retrieves candidate pictures. The algorithm of the image search engine is described below.

Image search engine algorithm:

1. Indexing (preprocessing)

A pictorial index is automatically created. Hirata et al. calls this pictorial index an abstracted image. The abstracted images are normalized to a standard size (24×24 pixels for a color index) in order to reduce memory requirements and the corresponding computational cost. Techniques for dividing and merging regions are also used to cope with deformed input pictures.

2. Retrieval processing

Step-1) Picture input.

Step-2) Normalization of input picture using affine transformation and median filter.

Step-3) Matching and selecting candidate pictures.

1) The correspondence between regions of the input key picture and those of the picture index is adjusted.
2) Similarity calculation. The similarity of images, G is

$$G = sSn + cCn \qquad (5)$$

where

Sn : the normalized score of shape similarity,

Cn : the normalized score of color similarity.

s and c are coefficients for determining the weight of the contribution.

We used (s,c) = (0.5,0.5) here.

3) Candidate pictures are selected by comparing the similarity measures of all picture indexes.

In this process, pictures that have a lower similarity value than a pre-determined threshold are rejected.

Step-4) Display candidate pictures.

Selected candidate pictures are presented to the user through the viewer.

Further details of the above image search algorithm are given in Hirata's paper [4]. We used the above image search engine not only for image retrieval but also for visualized sound pattern retrieval.

5. Experiments and results

Spoken word retrieval experiments, multimodal video frame retrieval experiments, and multimodal index browsing experiments were conducted using the visualized sound index described in section 3-2.

5-1. Spoken word retrieval

To investigate the ability of the image search engine to retrieve a visualized sound pattern, spoken word retrieval experiments were carried out. As the spoken word, 10 numbers and 10 Japanese nouns were pronounced by four male speakers and one female speaker. Corresponding target pictures of the same spoken words were retrieved by the image search engine.

As the sound database, 632 samples including 220 spoken word samples, 305 birdsong samples and 30 sound samples from soccer video were used. Word speech detection was conducted manually referring to sound spectrograms. Input spoken words and target words were pronounced separately. As the input-target pairs, 120 pairs [20 words × (4 males + 2 female)] were used.

Figure 4 shows an example of the spoken word retrieval viewer. Table 1 shows the results of the spoken word retrieval experiments. The average recall rank of the same speaker is 5.1 and retrieval accuracy is 99.2%. This method of speech sound retrieval is similar to speaker-dependent isolated word recognition.

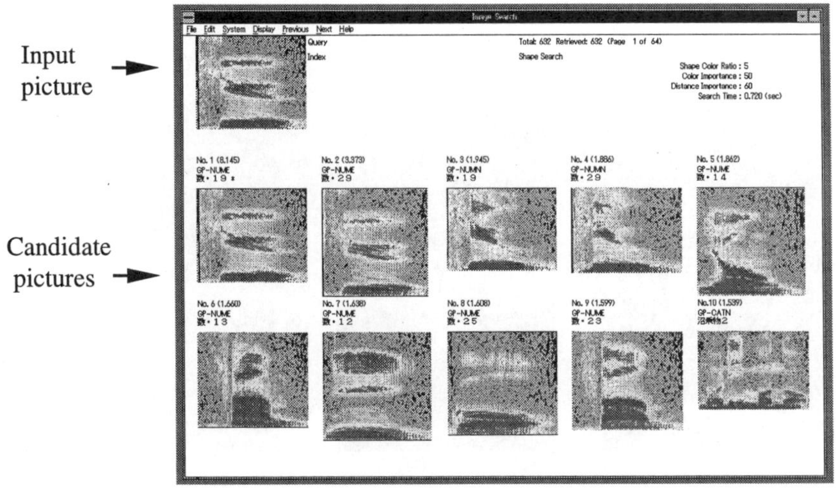

Figure. 4. An example of the spoken word retrieval viewer.

Table 1. Results of the 20-spoken-word retrieval experiment.

Target	Recall rank (R)	Retrieval accuracy (Q%)
The same speaker	5.1	99.2
Any other speaker	17.1	97.3

Database size = 632 samples, Input = 120 samples

The average of the recall rank of the same word by other speakers is 17.1 and retrieval accuracy is 97.3%. This method of speech sound retrieval is similar to speaker-independent isolated word recognition.

These results are comparable with conventional speech recognition systems and show that the image search engine can be effectively used for video retrieval by using visualized sound patterns [14].

5-2. *Multimodal retrieval experiment*

5-2-1. Retrieval using image indexes

Retrieval experiments using image indexes were conducted on a database of 769 frames extracted from colored video streams (including sports video from TV and the wild-bird video from the NHK Software) manually. The database included 391 bird pictures.

Figure 5 shows examples of the image index of a bird video. We selected 90 target pictures from 23 species of birds, and selected 23 input pictures. Target pictures were retrieved from the input picture of the same kind of bird.

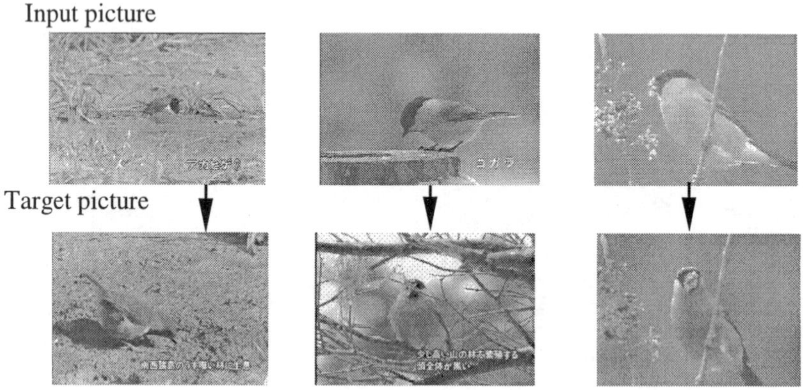

Figure 5. Examples of input images and target images.

Table 2 shows the average recall rank and the average retrieval accuracy (Q). The average recall rank is not so high (the number of rank is large). These results suggests that, in the case of bird video, the birds move and change their position frequently, it is difficult to search the target picture efficiently by using picture indexes.

Table 2. Comparison of average recall rank.□

Index	Recall rank (R)	Retrieval accuracy (Q%)
Image index	107	86
Sound index	32	95

Image database size = 769, Sound database size = 632

5-2-2. Retrieval using visualized sound indexes

Retrieval experiments using visualized sound indexes were conducted on a database of 632 sound patterns, including the songs of 305 birds. Sound data are obtained manually by viewing the sound spectrogram on the display. Frequency range of sound spectrogram is 0~5kHz and duration is about 0.5~1sec.

Figure 6 shows examples of visualized sound indexes of the birds song. The input pictures and target pictures correspond to the pictures used in the retrieval 5-2-1. In this experiment we selected 90 target sound indexes from 23 species of birds, and selected 23 input pictures.

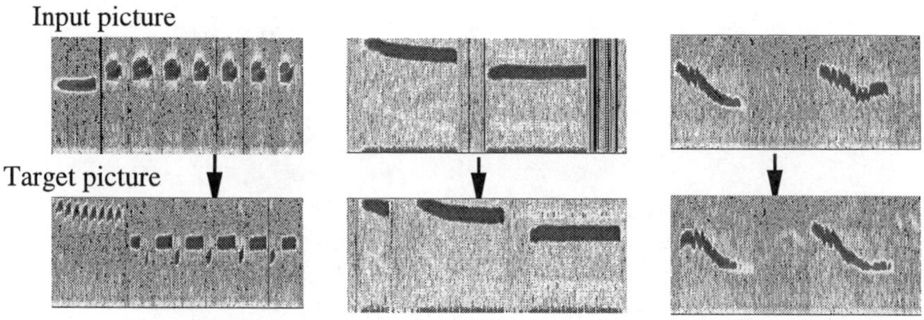

Figure 6. Visualized bird song sound pattern samples.

Table 2 lists the result of retrieval using the sound index to search the target sound indexes for the same bird species. The results show that retrieval using a visualized sound index is more effective than retrieval using an image index when searching the target scene for wild-bird video.

To improve retrieval accuracy, using plural birdsong patterns varying time position is considered to be effective in birdsong retrieval.

5-2-3. Collaborative retrieval using picture and sound indexes

To evaluate the collaborative parallel retrieval performance for the multimodal index, we practiced the retrieval using the image index and the sound index simultaneously. In this parallel retrieval, the user can search the target picture to be presented on both viewers at the same time.

The database is the same as that in 5-2-1 and 5-2-2. As the input pictures, 23 pictures and associated visualized sound (birdsong) are selected at random. □

We used the accuracy measure defined by formula (3) (for query by image index and sound index) and by formula (4) (for collaborative query). Figure 7 shows the multi-viewer example of the collaborative retrieval. The text index is also displayed to identify the candidate picture.

Sound Image

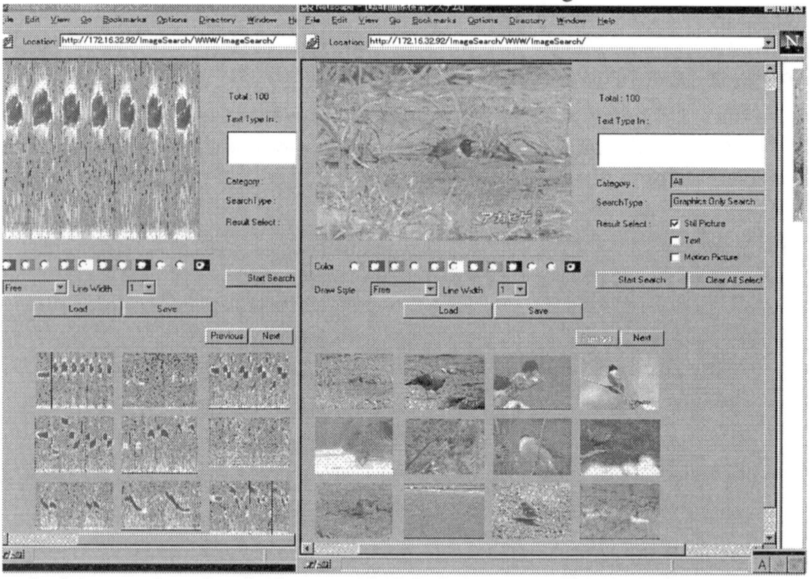

Left is sound retrieval viewer and right is image retrieval viewer

Figure 7. Viewer example of collaborative retrieval.

Table 3 shows the results of collaborative retrieval using image indexes and sound indexes. The results suggest that the image query and the sound query can compliment each other and the query accuracy can be improved compared with the single query method. However, it should be noted that the sound retrieval method can be effective only when the video scene contains meaningful sounds.

Table 3. Results of parallel retrieval using image indexes and sound indexes. (M=2)

Average retrieval accuracy (%)		
Image index (Q_1)	Sound index (Q_2)	Parallel(Q_p)
86	95	99

5-3. Video contents browsing using image-sound combined index

We have conducted visualized sound pattern categorization experiments using music sound, speech sound, and sound track of sports video and bird video [22]. This study showed that user can do at least rough categorization of sound spectrogram after short leaning time and visualized sound can be effectively used for video sound track browsing.

In this paper, retrieval and browsing experiments using a multimodal index were conducted for soccer and bird video.

Figure 8 and figure 9 shows examples of the simultaneous presentation of the multimodal indexes. The selected r-frames of video scenes are used as image indexes, and corresponding sound data are transformed into the colored sound spectrogram as visualized sound indexes. These indexes are combined and used as the image-sound index. The combined index can be understood easily by the user, to determine whether a scene is interesting or not. The user can also browse scenes with several sound images simultaneously. This helps the user to browse the contents of the video database efficiently.

Figure 8. Examples of multimodal index from soccer video.

Recall ranks were evaluated using the image-sound index, while changing the ratio of the area occupied by the sound index and the image index. The recall ranks of the image-sound combined index have the value between that of image and sound. The recall ranks of three different ratios (1:2, 1:3, 1:5) are almost the same in the preliminary experiment for highlight scene retrieval. We used a ratio of 1:5 because it made it easier to understand the scene condition.

Figure 9. Multimodal index examples of singing scenes.

In the soccer game, the spectators are shouting enthusiastically and the reporter is talking excitedly about the big event. Consequently, the sound spectrogram of the highlight indicates high intensity and most of the spectrogram is red. The combination of the sound index and the image index is useful for searching for the highlight scene from sports video or the singing scene from bird video.

The multimodal index browsing experiments show the effectiveness of the parallel sound index presentation. However, the experimenter needed a short period to understand the meaning of the sound index in order to use the sound spectrogram feature efficiently.

6. Conclusion and future issues

This paper describes a multimodal query system using not only images but also visualized sound indexes associated with the images or r-frames of video. Multimodal retrieval and browsing experiments for speech, bird videos, and soccer videos show the following results.

- The results of visualized spoken word retrieval experiments show that the image retrieval engine can be effectively used for visualized sound (colored sound spectrogram) retrieval.
- Collaborative parallel querying by the image and sound indexes can improve the accuracy of retrieval. This fact shows that the proposed multimodal indexing method can be effectively used for the interactive video query system.
- Browsing the multimodal indexes (image-visualized sound combined patterns) is effective for understanding the video contents and for picking up highlight scenes or bird singing scenes rapidly.

In the future, more work will be needed on an automatic multimodal index generation method including r-frame selection from a video stream.

References

1. Sakauchi M., Database vision and image retrieval. *IEEE Multimedia*, **1**(1):, (1995) pp. 79-81.
2. Brown M. G., Foote J. T., Jones G. J. F., Jones K. S., and Young S. J., Open-vocabulary speech indexing for voice and video mail retrieval, *Proc. ACM Multimedia 96 , Boston, ACM* (1996) pp. 307-316.
3. Hauptmann A.G., and Smith M., Text speech, and vision for video segmentation: The Informedia Project, *AAAI Fall 1995 Symposium on Computational Models for Integrating Language and Vision* (1995).
4. Hirata K., Hara Y., Shibata N., and Hirabayashi F., Media-based Navigation for Hypermedia system, *ACM Hypertext* (1993) pp. 157-173.
5. Del Bimbo A., Pala P., and Santini S., Image retrieval by elastic matching of shapes and image patterns. *IEEE Multimedia* (1996) pp. 215-218.
6. Flicker M., Query by image and video content : the qbic system. *IEEE computer* (1995) pp. 23-32.
7. Aigrain P., Zhang H., and Dragutin D., Content-based representation and retrieval of visual media: A state-of-the-art review, *Multimedia Tools and Applications* **3** (1996) pp.179-202.
8. Chen Y., Zeng W., Kamel I., and Alonso R., Integrated image and speech analysis for content based video indexing. *IEEE Multimedia* (1996) pp. 306-313.
9. Ono A., Amano M., Hakaridani M., Satou T., and Sakauchi M., A flexible content-based image retrieval system with combined scene description keyword. *IEEE Multimedia* (1996) pp. 201-208.
10. Fushikida K., Hiwatari Y., and Waki H., Content-based image query method using parallel retrieval scheme, *ICCIMA 98,*H. Selvaraj and B. Verma (Eds.), (World Scientific, 1998) pp. 830-835.
11. Watanabe A., Ueda Y., and Shigenaga A., Color display system for connected speech to be used for the hearing impaired, *IEEE Trans. ASSP-33* (1985) pp. 164-173.
12. Stewart L.C., Larkin W. D., and Houde R. A., A real time sound spectrograph with implementations for speech training for the deaf, *IEEE Int. Conf.. on ASSP* (1976) pp. 590-592.
13. Zue V. W., and Cole R. A., Experiments on Spectrogram Reading, *Proc. of ICASSP 79* (1979) pp. 116-119.
14. Rabiner L. R., and Wilpon J. G., Some performance benchmarks for isolated word speech recognition system, *Computer, Speech, and Language*, **2**, (1987) pp. 343-357.

15. Zhang H. J., Low C. Y., Smoliar S.W., and Wu J. H., Video parsing retrieval and browsing: An integrated and content-base solution, in *Proc. ACM Multimedia'95* (1995) pp. 15-24.
16. Arman F., Depommier R., Hsu A., and Chiu M. Y., Content-based browsing of video sequences, *Proc. ACM Multimedia '94* (1994) pp. 97-103.
17. Minami K., Akutsu A., Hamada H., and Tonomura Y., Enhanced video handling based on audio analysis, *IEEE Multimedia* (1997) pp. 219-226.
18. Gelin P., and Wellekens C. J., Keyword Spotting for Video Soundtrack *Indexing, IEEE International Conference on Acoustics Speech and Signal Processing,* **1**, (1995) pp. 9-46.
19. Chang S. K., and Liu S. H., Picture Indexing and abstraction techniques for pictorial databases, *IEEE Transactions on Pattern Analysis and Machine Intelligence*, **6** (1984) pp. 475-484.
20. Tao Y. and Grosky w. i., Image matching using the OBIR system with feature point histograms. *IFIP Visual Database Systems*, Y. Ioannidis and W. Klas (Eds.), (Chapman & Hall, 1998) pp. 208-213.
21. Fushikida K., Hiwatari Y., and Waki H., A content-based video retrieval method using a visualized sound pattern, *IFIP Visual Database Systems*, Y. Ioannidis and W. Klas (Eds.) (Chapman & Hall, 1998) pp. 208-213.
22. Fushikida K., Hiwatari Y., and Waki H., Visualized sound retrieval and categorization, *Advances in Computer Cybernetics, Vol.□ , ISAVIIA-98* (1998) pp. 68-73.

SCM - A MULTIMEDIA CONFERENCE SYSTEM

JOSÉ GONÇALVES P. FILHO
WANDRESON LUIZ BRANDINO
E-MAIL: ZEGONC,BRANDINO@INF.UFES.BR
Departamento de Informática, Universidade Federal do Espírito Santo

29060-970, Vitória, ES - Brazil

SON T. VUONG
E-MAIL: VUONG@CS.UBC.CA
Computer Science Department, University of British Columbia

Vancouver, B.C. V6T 1Z4 - Canada

In this paper, we discuss the development of a multimedia conferencing system, called SCM. The system implements ITU-T standards and supports most features found in existing multimedia conferencing systems, including video service, chatting area, cooperative document handling, multi point file transfer, voting support, and particularly a multicasting communication facility, which enjoys a great deal of reduction in bandwidth requirements.

1 Introduction

Multimedia conferencing systems constitute one of the most active areas in the distributed multimedia domain, driven by both scientific research interests and commercial viability. These applications allow their users to meet together via networks – the Internet - for the exchange of information and discussion of subjects of common interest, making use of several media formats and sharing their acoustic and visual spaces.

One of the main benefits of multimedia conferences is the overall reduction in travel time and costs to organize meetings. Surveys and researches have shown that a great part of the companies' staff time is spent on communication and that 60% of the business meetings could be substituted by electronic conferences [1].

In spite of the countless advantages, multimedia conferencing applications also impose severe restrictions on the host computer system as a whole. These include acquisition of analog data and real-time conversion into digital form, and algorithms for video and audio compression and multimedia synchronization. In addition, appropriate communication support is required, with multicasting facilities and guaranties of delay and jitter limits, as imposed by the continuous media.

Multimedia conferences have been investigated at several universities and research institutions around the world and they have been subjects of study by international standardization boards, e.g. ISO and ITU. In the last few years, several prototypes have been developed at academic institutions: *CU-SeeMee* [2] (Cornell University), *nv* [3] (Xerox), *IVS* [4] (INRIA), *vic* [5] (Lawrence Berkeley Laboratory and University of California at Berkeley and *TVS* [6] (PUC/Rio). Additionally, some systems are commercially available.

Besides the basic transmission of audio and video, multimedia conference systems offer a range of useful tools. These tools constitute a generic and flexible environment for conferencing and cooperative work, with functions adapted to support several kind of scenario, such as seminars, private meetings and distance learning.

ITU-T, in its series F.730 [7], T.120 [8], H.320 [9], and T.122 [10] recommends a group of functions for the development of multimedia conference applications, such as cooperative manipulation of documents, support for voting, files exchange, conference recording, cryptography, besides standards for audio and video compression. Additionally, at the *pre-conference* stage, it is usually possible to define various configuration parameters, e.g. type of conference, quality of audio and video, shared data base access privilege, security options, floor control policy and many others.

Our goal is to develop a conferencing system that implements functions suggested in international standards while taking advantage of the good properties of existing systems.

This paper presents a general description of a multimedia conferencing system, so-called SCM, developed jointly at the Network and Multimedia Research Laboratory of UFES/Brazil and the Distributed Systems Research Group at the University of British Columbia. In terms of functionality, SCM allows distributed video communication for a group of participants, with a mechanism for multicast communication, and offers a chatting area for interactive message exchanges. It also facilitates multi-point transfer of files during the conference, supports voting, allows private conferences inside the context of a global conference and also supports shared document handling. The audio processing is not implemented in this first version of the system owing to time limitation, but can be easily incorporated.

In contrast to most academic conference systems, that have been developed for Unix platforms, SCM was conceived for Windows 95/NT, which has increasingly gaining its popularity.

The remainder of this paper is organized as follows. Section 2 gives a brief survey of various existing conference systems. Section 3 introduces the SCM components. Section 4 shows an example of a SCM session and the Section 5 concludes the paper, with final remarks and suggestions for future directions.

2 Existing Conferencing Systems

This section present an overview of some academic conferencing systems, that have been developed in the last few years, and widely used experimentally over the Internet. The major features are presented as a basis for comparison and evaluation with the current version of SCM.

2.1 CU-SeeMe

CU-SeeMe [2] is one of the earliest and most popular multimedia conferencing systems developed for use over the Internet. Originally developed at Cornell University, a commercial version of CU-SeeMe is also available.

Although running under Windows/Machintosh, CU-SeeMe uses a UNIX machine to execute a special program called *reflector*, which is the server for the conference. CU-SeeMe adopts a centralized architecture, in which each machine sends its data to the server machine, that forwards them to other participant machines in the conference. This kind of centralized architecture is commonly used by the majority of existing systems for ease of implementation. However, it may be inefficient in certain communication configurations.

In CU-SeeMe, the concern to minimize data traffic in the net does not exist practically. The server machine running the program reflector must have good performance since it centralizes and manipulates all the participants' conference data. Furthermore, the server cannot act as a participant machine in the conference, because it is dedicated to provide services of conference data distribution for the participants. Figure 1 depicts a conference running under CU-SeeMe.

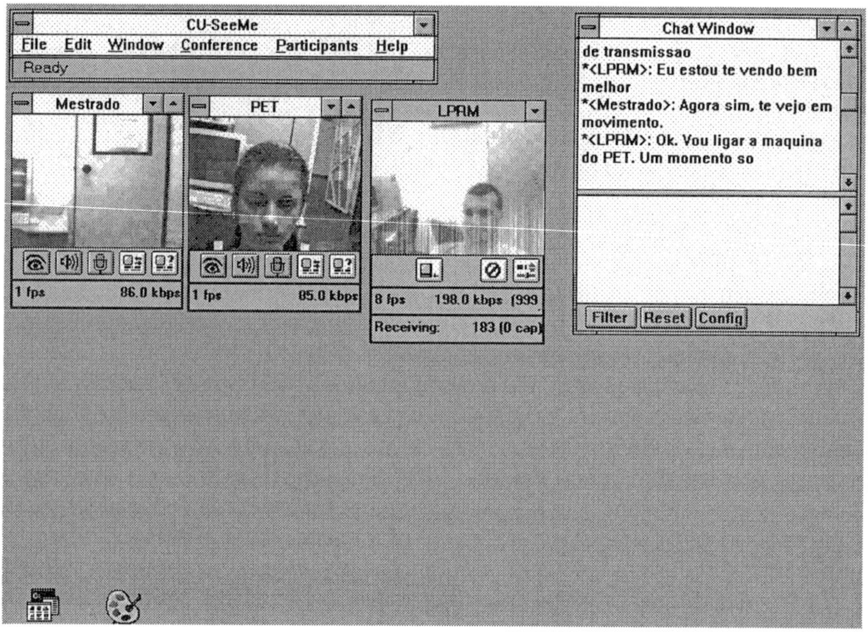

Fig. 1 – CU-SeeMe

2.2 *IVS*

IVS [4] is a conference system for Unix platforms developed at INRIA/France. IVS has a nice visual interface and adopts the ITU-T standards for audio and video coding.

IVS supports several interesting functions. In particular, among the discussed systems, it is the only one that allows the recording of parts of the conference, as suggested in the recommendation T.120 of ITU [8]. IVS uses the infrastructure of Mbone [11] for multicast communication.

The salient features of IVS are mainly related to audio and video transmission. Many configuration parameters of audio and video are user-definable. It is worth noting that the H.261 video codec and compression algorithms developed at INRIA and used in IVS have also been adopted in other systems, e.g., TVS [6]. Figures 2 and 3 show the IVS' audio and video control panels.

Some ITU recommendations are not supported in IVS, such as synchronization of audio and video streams, cooperative document handling, exchange of textual messages among the participants and support for voting.

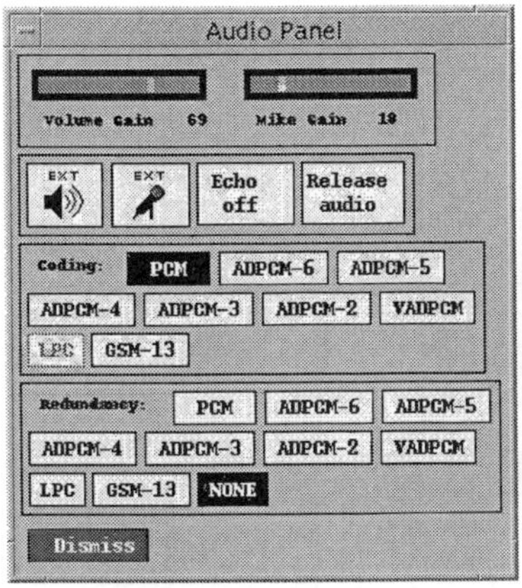

Fig. 2 – Audio Control

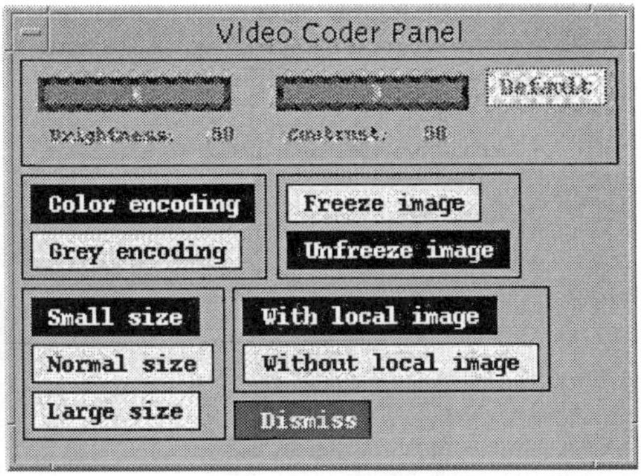

Fig. 3 – Video Control

2.3 *Nv–Network Vídeo*

Nv [3] is a conference system developed at Xerox PARC. It is one of the pioneers in the domain of continuous media transmission using Mbone and RTP (Real Time Protocol) for the transport of data through the Internet. This feature was later adopted in several other systems, e.g. IVS.

The system supports video transmission among its participants and offers a series of parameters for video configuration (Figure 4). Audio information handling and most other desirable features in a conference environment are not supported. The algorithms used for video compression are not standardized by ITU.

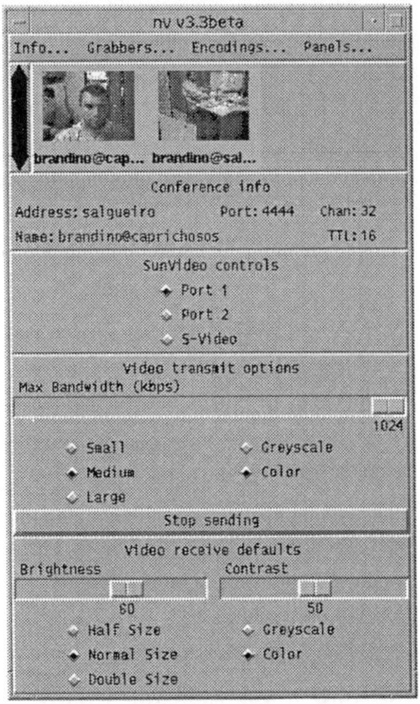

Fig. 4 - nv

2.4 *TVS*

TVS [6] is a multimedia conference system for Unix platforms developed at PUC, Rio de Janeiro. The system implements various features suggested by ITU-T, particularly manipulation of shared documents. The hypermedia model used in TVS, so-called Nested Contexts Model, conforms well to MHEG/ISO. The system also supports an elaborate voting feature.

The system adopts a centralized architecture, similar to CU-SeeMe. A new version of the system is under development and will run over ATM. Figure 5 shows a TVS conference.

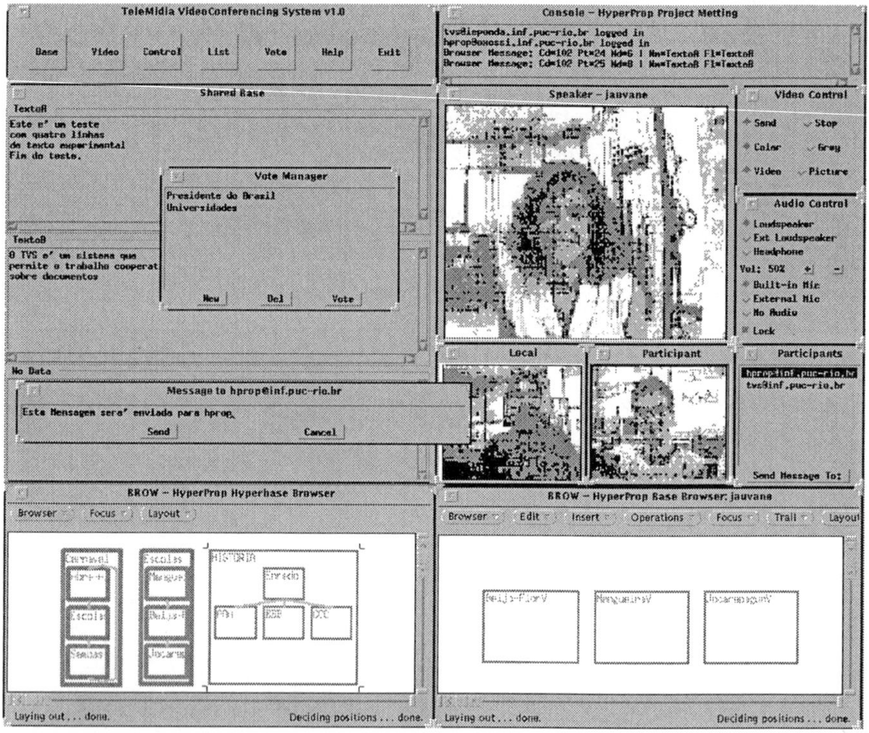

Fig. 5 – TVS

2.5 *Vic, vat, sd and wb*

These are a set of tools running on Unix platforms developed at the Lawrence Berkeley National Laboratory and the University of California at Berkeley. These tools allow users to transmit video (*vic*), audio (*vat*), schedule conferences (*sd*) and perform cooperative work via whiteboard (*wb*). Because these systems were developed separately, they do not support features such as synchronization among the audio, provided by *vat*, and the corresponding video, provided by *vic*.

Vic supports video transmission with several options of compression formats. Many configuration parameters are also user definable. The system uses Mbone for multicast communication.

Vat supports audio transmission. Similar to *vic*, the user can define several parameters of audio quality. Access control to a speech is made by registration in a list. Most experimental systems use this strategy, except for TVS that uses an algorithm of silence detection.

W*b* is a whiteboard tool for cooperative work, similar to the Paint Brush graphic editor. It offers to participants a work area, so they can express ideas through words or drawings, as commonly done in traditional meetings. The manipulation of the document is one participant at a time.

S*d* is a system that integrates *vic*, *vat* and *wb* in an unique interface. The schedules of conference are announced in the ambit of the global Internet. This way, any person can participate in any scheduled conferences.

3 The SCM System

As seen in previous sections, most of the systems examined were developed for Unix platforms. The current widespread usage of Windows 95/NT, however, suggests the shift of efforts in the construction of multimedia conference systems for this platform. We also note that most functions in existing conferencing systems are implemented in isolation, rather than being integrated into an effective tool. Most existing systems focus on the basic manipulation of the media audio and video.

Those factors motivated the development of SCM. The main goal is to develop a multimedia conference system for Windows 95/NT, composed of a group of integrated means that allows effective use of the system in several scenarios of electronic meetings.

A unique feature of SCM is on the multicast support mechanism. Its development was motivated by the lack of versions of the *mrouted* (the multicasting routing software used in Mbone) for Windows95/NT. An extended version multicast support that uses the ITU-T standard MCS – Multipoint Communication Service - is under development.

Another objective of the project is to investigate the viability of this system and technology. Performance measurements and evaluations will be conducted after the implementation of the definitive version of SCM, when all foreseen functions are incorporated. It is worth noting that the ITU-T recommendations served as the basis for the definition of the current version of SCM and as well as guiding the development of future versions of the system.

3.1 The SCM Model

A short description of the object model follows. SCM organizes the conference as a set of sessions. This organization provides users with the flexibility to start a private session while participating in a main one. Thus, a user can discuss and share information with other participants in a global presentation while discussing specific points with a particular participant in a private, point-to-point session.

A session is composed of a set of *services*, which can be used by participants subjected to access constraints. The major services offered include: *chat*, *voting*, *multi-point FTP*, *shared application* and *audio & video* services. All the services available in a main session are also accessible in a private session.

Each conference has a *conference chairman*, who is also a *conference participant*. The chairman has special tasks and privileges, including organize/schedule the conference, start and finish conferences, set up global and specific policies, rights and privileges that will affect the use of the facilities by the participants.

A session may also have a *session chairman*, who is the participant that starts a private session. This participant has extra privileges, such as canceling participation in private sessions and terminating sessions.

3.2 The SCM Components

The SCM system is organized as a set of inter-related modules, described as follows.

3.2.1 Control Module

This module implements mechanisms for the control of the overall conference and its private sessions. It is responsible for some specific, low-level tasks such as scheduling and floor control, and for the setting of high-level configurations options such as the number of video windows, frame rate and security options, among others. This module also coordinates the relationship between all other modules of the system.

3.2.2 Conference Server Module

It is a module attached to SCM to divulge in the Web the public conferences of SCM, by generating HTML pages of the conferences. Each conference server maintains a list of ongoing conferences and their participants.

3.2.3 Audio and Video Module

This module implements the basic services of audio and video communication. It uses ITU-T standards for dealing with audio and video compression and message coding. The audio and video synchronization scheme to be used will be based on time-stamps to simplify the implementation.

3.2.4 Chat Module

This feature adds a simple but important functionality to the system. It is particularly interesting when a station does not have audio resources but a user wants to join the conference from that station. In this kind of situation, the chat is a good option for exchange of information. Furthermore, it is a good communication option when the system lacks resources for presenting continuous media.

3.2.5 Multi Point File Transfer Module

This feature allows sending files in a multi point fashion, making use of the multicasting structure offered by the multicasting communication module. This facility is part of a major document transfer function, that aims at disseminating work results to selected users.

3.2.6 Cooperative Work Module

The cooperative work module provides a shared workspace that enables the execution of collaborative tasks. Using this feature, a group of users can create and manipulate documents of mutual interest, e.g. joint authoring of multimedia documents. The sharing of documents can be achieved in two approaches. One approach is based on cooperative development of specific applications, e.g. simultaneous edit of documents. The other approach is to create a software (communication) layer that allows the sharing of existing applications, e.g. a well-known text editor. These applications will be seen by all interested cooperative conference participants. The former approach is used in this first version of SCM.

The current available functions in this module include the cooperative edition of texts and drawings. These simple services allow basic cooperative work based on shared document handling. It is not our goal to implement in this first version all functionalities for effective cooperative work. Our goal is to set up a programming base to develop and group other functions together.

Since this module is important for making SCM effective in a large scale, further studies on cooperative work requirements and the implementation of a minimum group of functions that satisfy users' needs will be in order.

3.2.7 Voting Module

By maintaining basic accountancy and protection of votes, this module provides a mechanism for "voting" support in the course of a conference, thereby facilitating decision making on a specific theme. This feature is proposed in ITU-T conference standards, but implemented in very few systems (for example, in TVS). Although the implementation of this service still requires additional control functions and fine-tuning to be useful in a real conference environment, the basic functions supported by SCM constitute a base for any complex mechanism.

In SCM, the voting process is open to all participants. This means that any user can propose the creation and to participate in a voting. Besides, the vote is not secret, that is to say, each participant's vote is seen by all others. The accountancy of the votes is also seen at every moment by all users. The vote is obligatory, that is, all participants are required to vote. Furthermore, no new voting creation is allowed while a voting session is in progress and not yet closed, i.e. there is only one voting session at a time. The vote also does not carry weights.

3.2.8 Security Module

Only a basic security service is currently implemented in SCM. This is basically limited to the establishment and verification of access to the conference. Cryptography mechanisms, for example, area not provided. The provision of security mechanisms is an optional functionality as foreseen in SCM, that can be configured in the pre-conference stage.

3.2.9 Multicasting Module

Multicast addressing is an Internet standard, introduced in RFC 1112, that uses IP address class D. This kind of addressing permits to set up multi point connections, from one node to *n* selected destination nodes chosen from a maximum number of *m* nodes. Thus, it is a generalized form of unicast (n=1) and broadcast (n=m) addressing.

Multicasting is an important requirement in multimedia conference systems, where there is a need for addressing groups of users, and the use of point-to-point connections is simply too inefficient. The support of multicasting communication allows a large reduction in bandwidth requirements, that is particularly useful when conveying continuos media.

As mentioned before, support for multi-point communication has been employed in some multimedia conference systems, e.g. *vic*, *IVS* and *nv*. All of them utilize the framework provided by Mbone. The Mbone - Multicasting Backbone [11] is a virtual network that permits - by means of tunneling technique - the transmission of multicast packets using the current infrastructure provided by the Internet.

In its final version, SCM aims at incorporating the full concepts of *Multipoint Communication Services* (MCS), introduced by the recommendations T.120 and T.122 from ITU-T (October, 1996). Contrarily to Mbone, that addresses the multicast problem at the network level, the MCS approach supports multicasting at a higher layer. MCS provides a flexible and inexpensive way of implementing multicasting, without the need of any additional commercial multi-point routers and without the configuration problems found in *mrouted* software. The goal is to achieve a general multicasting mechanism that can be used in several kind of (sub) networks.

In the first version of SCM, the MCS multicast mechanism is not implemented. Currently, SCM software tries to supply a multicast data transport framework based on several point-to-point connections organized in such a way that allows a significant decrease in network traffic. In this scheme, each user informs the system where the received messages should be guided, such that messages originating from any user will reach all the other participants of the conference. Thus, in this version of the system, the choice of the route is not automated, but it rests on the user's responsibility. The current static solution tries to derive the maximum benefit from the knowledge of the topology of the network, that is, the more one knows about the topology, the better the configuration for multicasting.

4 Using SCM

4.1 *Start a Session*

At the start of a session, the system displays the screen as shown in Figure 6, which includes the IP address of the local machine and its corresponding status. At this time, the status is *disconnected*, meaning that the user is not connected to any conference. The user can take one of the two possible actions: creating a conference or getting connect to one already created.

The following menu items appear in this figure: *Conference*, *View*, *Options* and *Help*. Through these items, the user can create a conference, join a conference, start the chat service, close a conference, exit a conference, list the conference members, activate the local and remote video, start a cooperative work, transfer files, set up the multicast configuration routes and others.

Fig. 6 – Main menu

4.2 *Create a Conference*

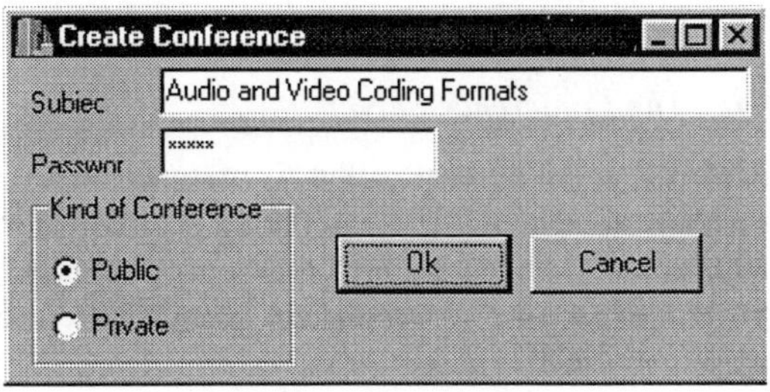

Fig. 7 – Creating a Conference

In case the user creates a conference, the system requires the subject and password (Figure 7). The system also asks the user to enter the nature of the conference (whether it is public or private). This information will be used by the Conference Server to control the access and to maintain the list of participants. As soon as the user creates a conference, its name, its e-mail and the IP address of its machine are added to the conference members list, which is maintained by the SCM control module. Additionally, in the case the conference is public, the subject of the conference and the creator's identification (denominated *chairman*) are sent to the Server of Conferences (CS) for cataloguing.

The SC address, as well as the user's name and electronic address are defined through the menu option *Personal Information*. As can be seen, SC takes charge of maintaining all the public conferences, and its participants, available for access through the Web and for consultation by its own SCM, when the user wants to know about the available public conferences.

With the conference created, the status of the system is changed to *listening*, meaning that the machine is awaiting other participants to join the conference. As soon as the user creates a conference, the system attributes some privileges. For example, the chairman's rights can be: to cancel a conference in a unilateral way and to cancel a voting or even to interrupt a file transfer in progress.

4.3 Connect to Conference

In the case the user wants to connect to an already created conference, the system asks him the IP address of the machine that hosts the conference (Figure 8). To find out about the available conferences it is sufficient to click *browse*. The system is then connected the Conferences Server (CS) and shows the names (subjects) and IP addresses of all the available public conferences (Figure 9). The user then selects one of them or it informs the address of a private conference, previously known, to which he/she wants to connect.

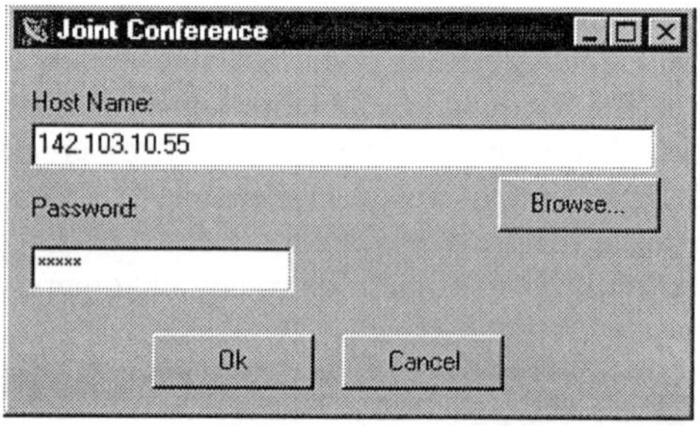

Fig. 8 – Joining a conference

4.4 The Conference Server

SCM has a sub-system called Conferences Server (CS), whose responsibility is to maintain all the public conferences visible for the users. The operation of SC is quite simple. When a public conference is created, a message notifying its name and the identification of its chairman is transmitted to SC, that includes it in the list of active conferences (Figure 9).

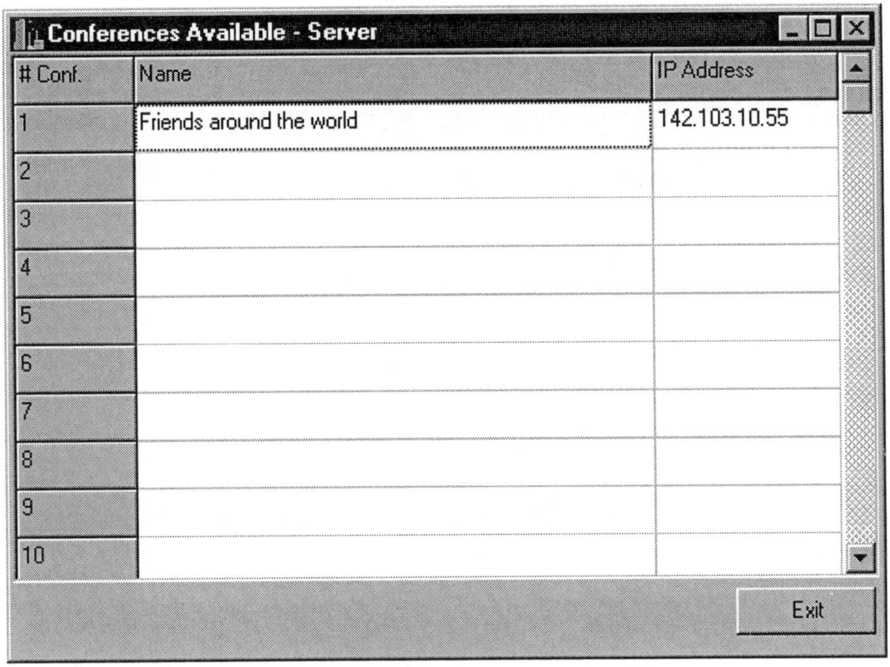

Fig. 9 – The conference server

Besides maintaining the list of conferences, SC creates a homepage containing the name of all the active conferences at the moment under SCM (Figure 10). Additionally, SC maintains a homepage containing the participants' names. At the time of creation, only the chairman is added to the list, but as people enter or leave the conference, messages are send to SC to update the list.

The feature of homepages creation is quite interesting since it makes known to users which conferences are running under SCM at any time. Thus, a user can selects which conference server he wants to connect to. Since the program SC can run simultaneously in several machines, this will allow the finding of public conferences under SCM in several sites.

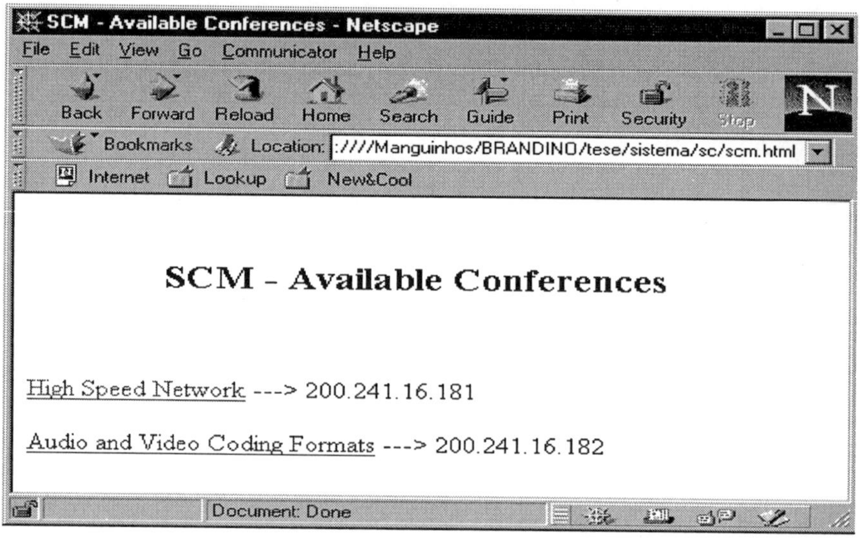

Fig. 10 – Available Conferences

4.5 *Setting up Multicast Configuration*

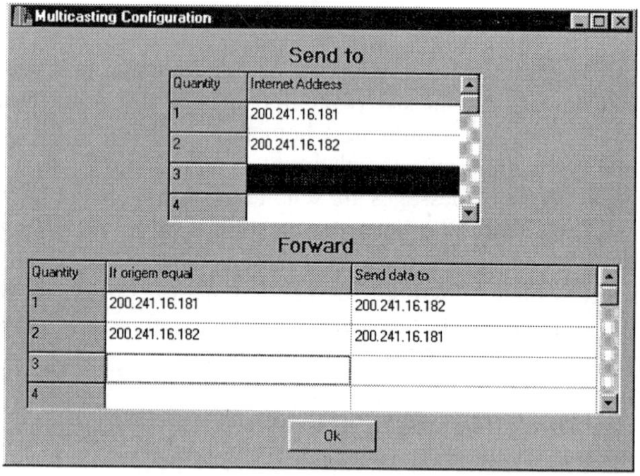

Fig. 11 – Multicasting Configuration at *piuma.lprm.inf.ufes.br*

One of the salient features of SCM rests in the ability to do conferencing without the need of additional software or equipment of multicasting routers. As we have seen, most current systems employ the architecture with a centralized server. This approach is popular due to its implementation simplicity. However, it has the disadvantage in inefficient use of communication resources because the same data are (re)transmitted several times, increasing the load in the backbones. Furthermore, the communication latency can be high and the central server is a potential bottle neck. The Figure 11 illustrates the multicasting configuration in the machine *piuma.lprm.inf.ufes.br* (200.241.16.180) during a conference between DI/UFES and UBC. The machines used in this experiment are shown below.

Machine	Country	User	E-mail
robson-win95.cs.ubc.ca (142.103.10.55)	Canada	Wandreson Brandino	brandino@cs.ubc.ca
Piuma.lprm.inf.ufes.br (200.241.16.180)	Brazil	José G. P. Filho	zegonc@inf.ufes.br
Manguinhos.lprm.inf.ufes.br (200.241.16.182)	Brazil	Verner Júnior	verner@inf.ufes.br

4.6 The Chat Service

To use the public chat service, the user only needs to type in the text in the area reserved for public chat in the screen. The system takes care of sending the message typed to all the participant machines, that are defined in the list "Send To" of the SCM multicast configuration (Figure 12). When the text arrives at a destination, it is displayed in a proper area of the screen and forwarded to all the machines defined in the list "Forward To". This process repeats until all the participant machines receive the textual information.

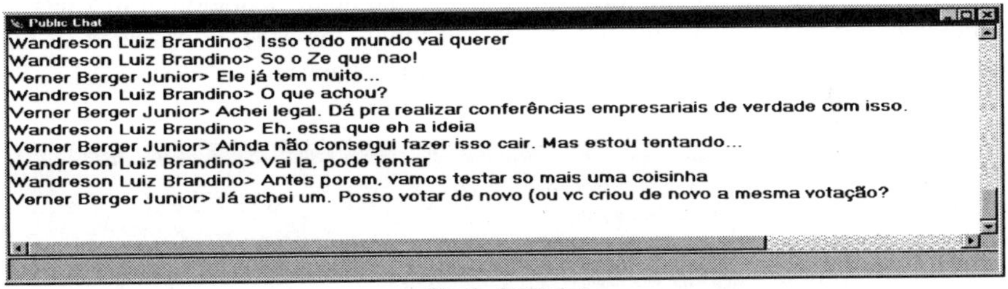

Fig. 12 – Public chat

The private chat service is a useful functionality uniquely introduced by SCM, because it allows a user, within a global conference, to maintain an exclusive chat with one of them. For example, engaging in discussion on some specific point of a project of an engineering application. Unlike the public chat, private chat makes use of point-to-point communication. To start a private chat all it takes for the user is to give the IP address or the hierarchical address of the receiving participant from the list of conference members. (Figure 13).

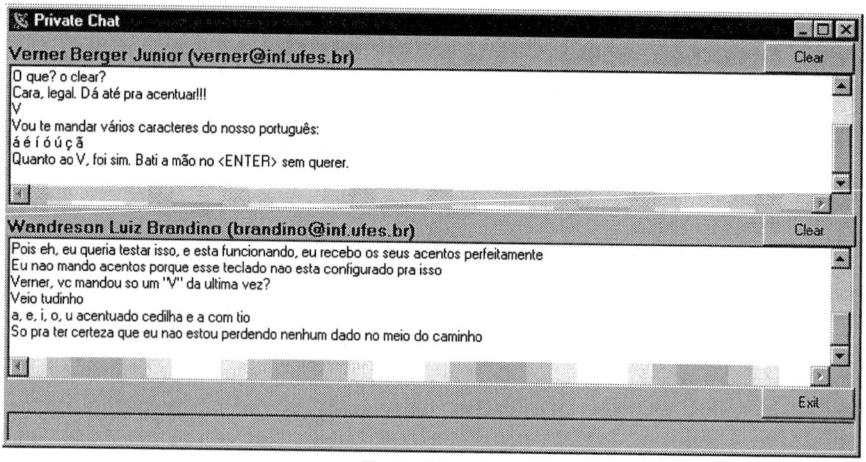

Fig. 13 – Private chat

4.7 *The Voting Service*

This service constitutes an important feature of the system, assisting users to make collective decisions on specific themes. Although the implementation of this service requires additional controls for use in real meetings, the scheme provided in this version of SCM forms the basis of more complex mechanisms.

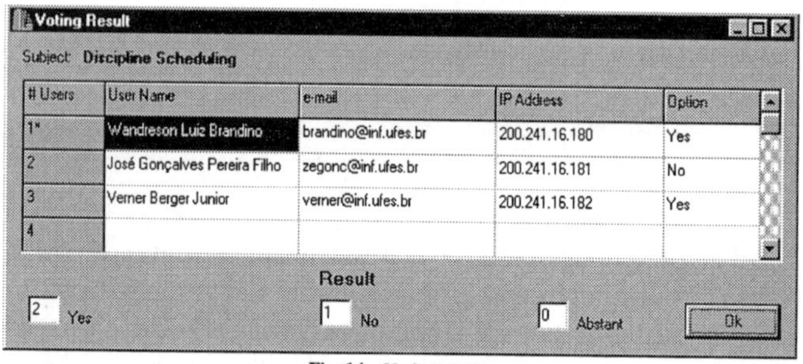

Fig. 14 – Voting results

In SCM, any user can propose a voting. When a voting is created, a message informing the subject of the conference is transmitted to the machine that created the conference. The control module check whether already there is a voting in progress. In that case, an error message is reported; otherwise, it is created and the other participants receive this information. At this time, the voting menu in the user's screen becomes inactive, indicating that no other participant of the conference can create a voting so long as there is one in progress and not yet terminated. Figure 14 shows the result of a voting in SCM.

4.8 Multi-Point Transfer of Files

This service is provided as an add-on function on top of the multicast facility. To transfer files to multiple destinations, the user simply types the name of the file (Figure 15) or selects the files using the associated *browse* button (Figure 16).

Besides keeping tract of the transmitted files, the system also maintains a list of the participants' received files.

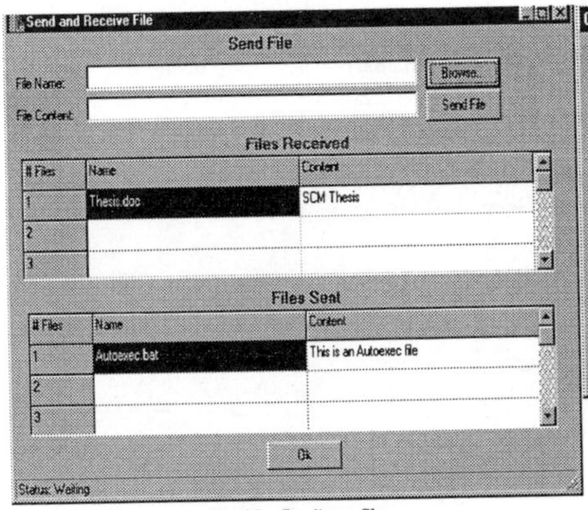

Fig. 15 – Sending a file

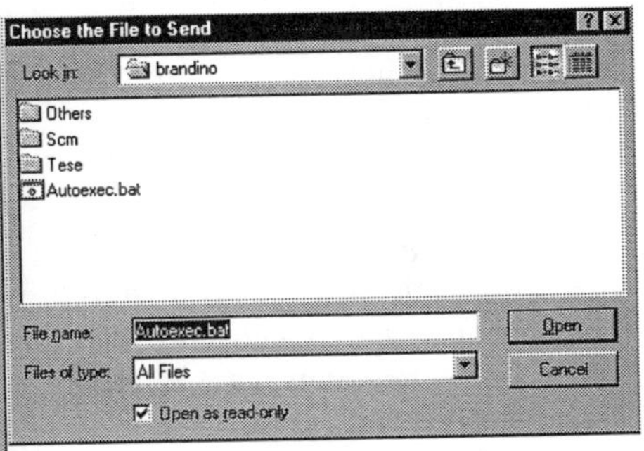

Fig. 16 – Selecting a file

4.9 Video Service

4.9.1 Local Video Capturing

At startup time, SCM checks whether there is any video camera installed in the system. In that case, it connects itself to the corresponding driver through an API function from VFW.H (Video for Windows). However, the image is only captured from the camera when the user activates the local video window (Figure 17).

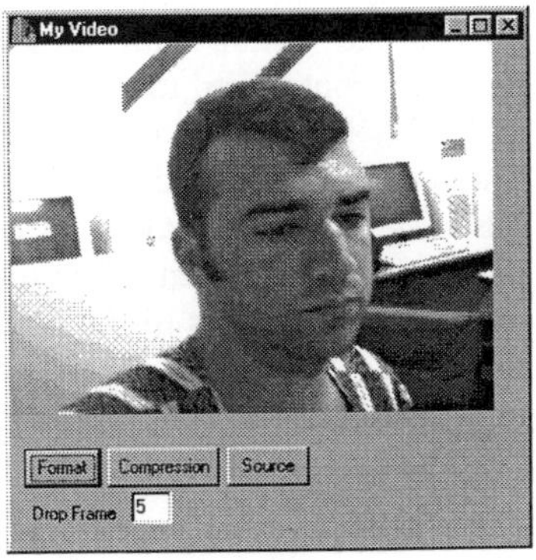

Fig. 17 – Local video

The Windows 95 operating system can manage several cameras simultaneously. In this version, the system starts using the first configured camera as default. From then on, the user can define various images parameters such as size, number of colors, options zoom and shine and contrast parameters (Figure 18). The *compression* button lists the video compression schemes that can be used in image capturing (Figure 19). The camera used in the experiment was the Connectix QuickCam.

Back to Figure 17, the *Drop Frame* option allows the setting of the transmitting video rate. By default, SCM uses a factor of 5:1, which means one transmitted frame to each five captured frames. This factor can be changed according to the desired quality. For real-time perception, this factor tends to zero, consequently the bandwidth and processing requirements become larger and heavier.

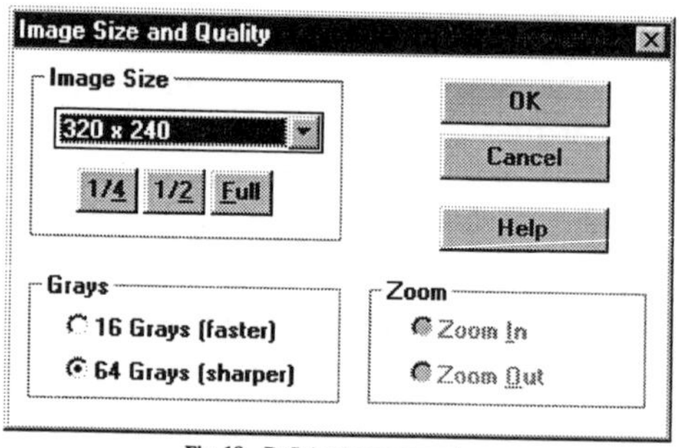

Fig. 18 – Defining image parameters

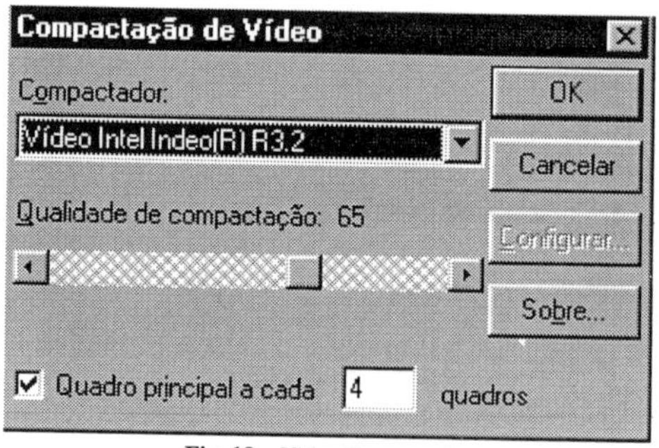

Fig. 19 – Video Compression

4.9.2 Remote Video

SCM asks the user to subscribe to a list when (s)he wants to be seen by other participants in the conference (Figure 20). When the user presses the button *Add to List* a control message containing the user's machine IP address is transmitted to the control module. The user is then added to a *List to Talk* and this list is a forwarded to all the other participants (Figure 21). The token of video transmission belongs to the first user in that list. The system transmits the video information to the other participants through the multicast structure previously configured.

Fig. 20 – Remote Video

4.10 Shared Workspace

The shared workspace is an area on user screen, visible to all users, where collaborative tasks can be carried out. As mentioned, using this feature, the users can cooperatively work on documents of common interest, e.g. joint authoring of a multimedia document. In this version, users can draw and write cooperatively. More complex functions can be incorporated in future versions.

Similar to the video service, the token control is based on registration in a list. When a participant has the token, the buttons that gives him the right of drawing and writing changes to active. Figure 22 shows an example of drawing in SCM.

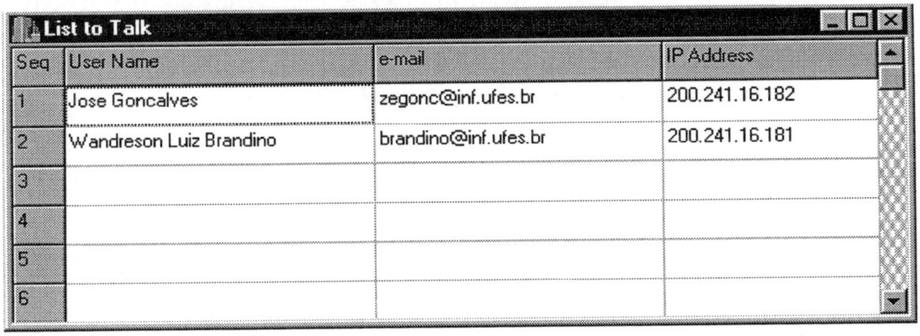

Fig. 21 - List to Talk

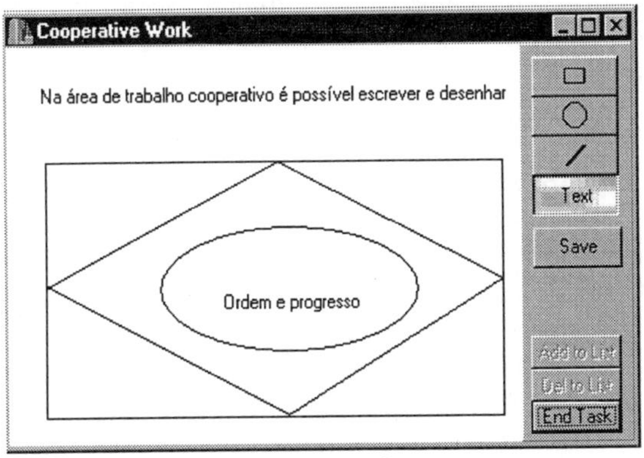

Fig. 22 – Shared WorkSpace

5 Conclusions

This chapter presents a general description of SCM, a multimedia conference system for Windows 95/NT platform developed at UFES/Brazil and UBC/Canada. SCM was designed with a group of integrated functions, selected with an aim to support diverse scenarios of virtual meetings. The system employs a static multicast mechanism, that minimizes the traffic in the network.

The SCM system is written in Borland C++ Builder and runs over TCP/IP. For video manipulation, the Microsoft interface of video programming VFW.H was used. In the sequence of this work, we intend to adapt SCM to run over Unix/ATM platforms.

We believe that making SCM operational on Windows 95/NT platform is a good appeal due to its increasing popularity. Furthermore, SCM is user-friendly and easy to install. Any user that has a computer with few resources can establish conferences using SCM.

Improvements can be made to SCM to make it a more flexible and effective tool. These include improvement in the cooperative work module, automation of multicast route selection and transmission of the continuous media through a specific multimedia transport protocol, now under development.

Bibliography

1. Tawbi M. W., La qualité de service dans systèms de communicattion multimédia: un cadre d'etude et spécification d'un protocole de négociation entre applications. Paris, France, 1993, Thèse de Doctorad, L'Université Pierre et Marie Curie.
2. Parker, T., "Cornell Welcome Page – http://CU-SeeMe.cornell.edu".
3. Frederick, R., "Experiences with real-time software video compression", Xerox PARC, July 1994.
4. Turletti T., The INRIA Videoconferencing System. ConneXions, v. VIII, n. 10, October 1994.- http://www.inria.fr/rodeo/personnel/Thierry.Turletti/me.html.
5. McCane, S.; Jacobson, V., "vic: A Flexible Framework for Packet Video" - ACM Multimedia 95, San Francisco, CA, November 1995.
6. Oliveira, J.C. de; Soares, L.F.G., "TVS - Um Sistema de Videoconferência com Documentos Compartilhados - Uma Visão Geral", WoSH'96 - II Workshop em Sistemas Hipermídia/XIV Simpósio Brasileiro de Redes de Computadores, May, 1996
7. International Telecommunication Union, Telecommunication Standardization Sector - "Telematic, Data Transmission, ISDN Broadband, Universal, Personal Communications and Teleconference Services: Operation and Quality of Service - Videoconference Service - General" - ITU-T Recommendation F.730, August 1992.
8. Data protocols for multimedia conferencing, ITU-T Recommendation T.120, July 1996
9. Narrow-band visual telephone system and terminal equipment, ITU-T Recommendation H.320, March 1996.
10. Multipoint communication service for audiographics and audiovisual conferencing service, ITU-T Recommendation T.122, March 1993.
11. Macedonia M., Brutzman D. "Mbone provides audio and video across the internet" IEEE Computer Magazine, April 1994.

INDEX